ORTHODOX CHRISTIANITY

Volume III:

The Architecture, Icons, and Music of the Orthodox Church

METROPOLITAN HILARION ALFEYEV

ORTHODOX CHRISTIANITY

Volume III:
The Architecture,
Icons, and
Music of the
Orthodox
Church

Translated from the Russian by Andrei Tepper

ST VLADIMIR'S SEMINARY PRESS
YONKERS, NEW YORK 10707
2014

Library of Congress Cataloging-in-Publication Data

Ilarion, Hieromonk.
  [Pravoslavie. English]
  Orthodox Christianity / Metropolitan Hilarion Alfeyev.
    p.   cm.
  Includes bibliographical references.
  ISBN 978-0-88141-878-1
  1. Russkaia pravoslavnaia tserkov'—History. 2. Orthodox Eastern Church—Russia (Federation)—History. 3. Russkaia pravoslavnaia tserkov'—Doctrines. 4. Orthodox Eastern Church—Russia (Federation)—Doctrines. 5. Russkaia pravoslavnaia tserkov'. 6. Orthodox Eastern Church—Russia (Federation). I. Title.
  BX485.I4313 2011
  281.9'47—dc22

                                          2011002385

Pravoslavie, Tom II.
originally published by Sretensky Monastery, 2008

Copyright © 2014 by Hilarion Alfeyev

ST VLADIMIR'S SEMINARY PRESS
575 Scarsdale Rd., Yonkers, NY 10707
1-800-204-2665
www.svspress.com

ISBN 978-0-88141-503-2

All Rights Reserved

PRINTED IN THE UNITED STATES OF AMERICA

Table of Contents

Preface   7

PART ONE
THE ORTHODOX TEMPLE

1   *Background. The Tabernacle and Solomon's Temple*   11

2   *Churches and Church-Building in the Byzantine Tradition*   21
Churches of the Post-Constantinian Era 21 • The Church as an Image of Man. "Divine Proportions" 34 • Cross-in-Square Churches in Byzantium 39 • National Traditions of Orthodox Church Architecture 42

3   *Russian Church Architecture*   49
Churches of Kievan Rus' 49 • Church Building Following the Mongol Invasion. Church Architecture in Muscovite Rus' 54 • Russian Church Architecture in the Post-Petrine Period 62 • Contemporary Church-Building in the Russian Church 71

4   *Arrangement of Churches and Church Objects*   75
Arrangement of Churches 75 • Objects of Liturgical Use 83

5   *Liturgical Vestments of the Clergy*   93

PART TWO
ICONS AND THEIR VENERATION

6   *Early Christian Painting. Frescoes of the Roman Catacombs*   109

7   *Iconographical Tradition in Byzantium*   115
Byzantine Mosaics and Frescoes of the Fourth Through Seventh Centuries 115 • Christian Icons of the Sixth and Seventh Centuries. Sinai's Encaustic Icons 122 • The Problem of the Origin of the "Canonical" Image of Christ. The Image Not-Made-By-Hands and the Shroud of Turin 127 • Iconoclasm and the Veneration of Icons 135 • Decorative Painting of Byzantine Churches. Basic Iconographical Types 148 • Byzantine Mosaics and Frescos of the Ninth Through Fourteenth Centuries 159 • Byzantine Icons of the Ninth through Fourteenth Centuries 173 • Book Miniatures 179

8   *Russian Icons*   185

Iconography in Rus'. Theophanes the Greek 185 • Saint Andrei Rublev and the Development of the Iconostasis. The Iconography of the Holy Trinity 191 • Dionysius and the Subsequent Development of Russian Iconography 195 • Post-Petrine Period. Academic Painting in Orthodox Churches 201 • Russian Icons in the Post-Revolutionary Period 205

9 *The Meaning of Icons*   211
The Theological Meaning of Icons 211 • The Anthropological Meaning of Icons 215 • The Cosmic Meaning of Icons 221 • The Liturgical Meaning of Icons 225 • The Mystical Meaning of Icons 234 • The Moral Meaning of Icons 238

PART THREE
CHURCH MUSIC

Section One: Liturgical Singing

10 *Background. Music in Ancient Israel and Ancient Greece*   245
Music and Song in the Old Testament 245 • Musical Arts of Antiquity 251

11 *Early Christian and Byzantine Church Singing*   263
Early Christian Music. The Teaching of the Holy Fathers Regarding Music and Singing 263 • Byzantine Church Music 274

12 *Russian Church Singing*   283
Church Singing in Kievan and Muscovite Rus'. Znamenny Chant 283 • *Partesny* Singing. Russian Liturgical Singing in the Post-Petrine Period 305 • Contemporary State of Liturgical Singing in the Russian Church 333

13 *Church Singing in Other Local Orthodox Churches*   337

Section Two: Bells and Bell Ringing

14 *Bells and Bell-Ringing*   345
Bells and "Bila" in Byzantium 345 • Bell-Ringing in Rus' 347

Select Bibliography   355

Preface

THIS IS THE THIRD VOLUME of a detailed and systematic exposition of the history, canonical structure, doctrine, moral and social teaching, liturgical services, and spiritual life of the Orthodox Church.

The basic idea of this work is to present Orthodox Christianity as an integrated theological and liturgical system—a world view. In this system all elements are interconnected: theology is based on liturgical experience, and the basic characteristics of church art—including icons, singing, and architecture—are shaped by theology and the liturgy. Theology and the services, in their turn, influence the ascetic practice and the personal piety of each Christian. They shape the moral and social teaching of the Church as well as its relation to other Christian confessions, non-Christian religions, and the secular world.

Orthodoxy is traditional and even conservative (we use this term in a positive sense, to emphasize Orthodoxy's reverence to church tradition). The contemporary life of the Orthodox Church is based on its historical experience. Orthodoxy is historic in its very essence: it is deeply rooted in history, which is why it is impossible to understand the uniqueness of the Orthodox Church—its dogmatic teaching and canonical structure, its liturgical system and social doctrine—outside of a historical context. Thus, the reference to history, to the sources, is one of the organizing principles of this book.

This series covers a wide range of themes relating to the history and contemporary life of the Orthodox Church. It contains many quotations from works of the church fathers, liturgical and historical sources, and works of contemporary theologians. Nevertheless, we do not claim to give an exhaustive account of the subjects discussed: this work is neither an encyclopedia, a dictionary, nor a reference work. It is rather an attempt to understand Orthodoxy in all its diversity, in its historical and contemporary existence—an understanding through the prism of the author's personal perception.

A special feature of these books is that they strive to provide a sufficiently detailed wealth of material. It is addressed to readers who are already acquainted with the basics of Orthodoxy and who desire to deepen their knowledge and, above all, to systematize it.

Volume One focused on the history and canonical structure of the Orthodox Church, Volume Two on the fundamental teachings of the Church, grounded in Scripture and Tradition. This third volume delves into the unique aspects of Orthodox art as expressed in its architecture, icons, and liturgical music.

We begin with a look at the biblical root of Orthodox church-building—the temple in Jerusalem. This allows us to gain a proper theological mindset for understanding the Orthodox temple as holy, consecrated space set aside for service to God. After tracing the development church architecture in both the Byzantine and Slavic churches, we arrive a systematic survey and anlysis of the icon in Orthodox Christianity.

Icons have become the most recognizable facet of Orthodoxy in the modern world. This second part helps us understand the role of the image in church life and worship by tracing its use, going back to the Church's earliest days in the catacombs of Rome. This includes an in-depth look at the evolving styles and materials used in creating icons.

The third part examines the role of music in Orthodox worship. Again, we begin with a look at the biblical underpinnings of song in worship, in particular the influence of King David and the psalms. This is followed by a study of liturgical music in Byzantine and Russian practice, as well as the foundational role of monophonic chant in both traditions. We follow the development of church music in Russia all the way through the end of the twentieth century and observe contemporary trends in Orthodox music all over the world.

And finally, we end with a short history of bells and bell-ringing in the Orthodox church, an ancient practice that has the distinction of being the only instrument traditionally used in all of Orthodox liturgy.

In future volumes, we will examine the services, sacraments, and rituals of the Orthodox Church, along with its ascetic and mystical teaching. The moral and social teaching of the Orthodox Church as well as its relations with other Christian confessions, other religions, and the secular world, will also be discussed.

PART ONE

The Orthodox Temple

Church of the Dormition of the Mother of God. Orchomenos, Greece. 9th c.

IN CONTEMPORARY ORTHODOX USAGE, the word *temple*, or *church*,[1] is used to denote a building used for performing church services, sacraments, and rites.

The period between the fourth and eighth centuries was a golden age of church building in both the Christian East and West. According to Church Fathers, especially Saint Dionysius the Areopagite and Saint Maximus the Confessor, churches gained theological meaning during that time as buildings intended for prayer and service to God. This was preceded, however, by a long period of history which began in Old Testament times and continued through the age of the early Christian Church (1st–3rd c.).

---

[1] In this case the word *church* is spelled with a lower case letter. It is capitalized to denote the society of believers universally or in a specific location.

I

Background.
The Tabernacle and Solomon's Temple

During the time of the patriarchs, the Hebrews had no special buildings for services to God. In this respect the ancient Hebrews differed from pagan nations, especially the Egyptians, who possessed a highly developed form of temple architecture. What the Hebrews did have were sacred places associated with God's appearances to man (Gen 32.30)[2]. Such places could be marked by pillars of stone on which oil was poured out (Gen 28.18–22). Altars were built in places of God's appearing (Gen 12.8, 26.25). These consisted of piles of rough-hewn stones on which bonfires were ignited under the open sky. Altars were also built on newly acquired plots of land (Gen 8.20, 33.20).

Following the exodus from Egyptian captivity, the Hebrews, under the leadership of Moses and according to the commandment of God, constructed a tabernacle—a transportable sanctuary (Ex 26.27). The tabernacle was a movable tent-temple of considerable size and was known to be a place of God's presence (Ex 25.8). This was where divine services took place and sacrifices to God were made. The tabernacle was situated inside a rectangular courtyard measuring one hundred by fifty cubits (Ex 27.18).[3] The courtyard of the tabernacle was surrounded by posts—twenty along each of the southern and northern sides and ten along each of the western and eastern sides (Ex 27.9–13).[4]

Aaron's Rod. Moses and Aaron in the Tent of the Meeting. Miniature, 13th c.

The exact size of the tabernacle is not indicated in the Bible. According to ancient commentators,[5] it was a tent measuring ten cubits high, thirty cubits long,

---

[2]Citations to Scripture generally accord with those in the King James Version; the language has been updated by the translator. Citations to the Psalms generally follow the Septuagint sequence.

[3]An ancient Hebrew cubit is equal to about fifty centimeters (twenty inches).

[4]Ten posts on the western side are mentioned only in the Septuagint; there is no mention of this in the Hebrew (Masoretic) Text of the Torah.

[5]In particular, Philo of Alexandria and Flavius Josephus.

Fixtures of the Tabernacle. Miniature, 12th c.

and ten cubits wide, and it was divided into two sections—the sanctuary measuring twenty by ten cubits and the holy of holies measuring ten by ten cubits. Religious objects were located inside the sanctuary including a golden lampstand with seven lamps (Ex 25.31–37), a table of showbread (Ex 25.23–30), an altar of incense (Ex 30.1–6), and a water basin (Ex 30.17–21). Inside the holy of holies was the ark of the covenant—a wooden chest with a golden cover (Ex 25.10–17) in which were kept the tablets of the covenant (1 Kg 8.9), Aaron's rod that budded, and an urn containing the manna (Heb 9.4). The holy of holies was separated from the sanctuary by a veil of blue and purple and scarlet fabric and fine woven linen, hung on four posts (Ex 26.31–32).

The tabernacle and all the objects therein were consecrated by the anointing of oil (Ex 40. 9–11), after which "the glory of the Lord filled the tabernacle. And Moses was not able to enter the tent of meeting, because the cloud abode upon it, and the glory of the Lord filled the tabernacle" (Ex 40.34–35). When the cloud rose from the tabernacle, the sons of Israel rolled it up, gathered their own tents, and continued on their way. At all other times, a cloud stood above the tabernacle by day and a pillar of fire by night.

Building a tabernacle conformed to the Hebrews' practice of worship, which entailed making many sacrificial offerings. Several varieties of sacrifice are described in the book of Leviticus (chapters 1–5). Foremost was the burnt offering—bringing a large or small horned animal (calf, sheep, goat) to sacrifice. The sacrificial animal was slaughtered using a sword, cut into pieces, and burned complete with all its entrails. Birds were also brought as burnt offerings. A cereal or meal offering consisted of bringing a handful of flour mixed with oil and frankincense, unleavened cakes, or grains of wheat. A peace offering consisted of bringing the entrails and fat of animals. Other sacrificial rituals existed for sin and guilt offerings.

This practice of blood sacrifice required an open space, and the outer courtyard of the tabernacle served this purpose. Blood sacrifices were not brought into the tabernacle, but incense was burned there daily (Ex 30.7–9). Each year, only once, the high priest entered into the tabernacle with sacrificial blood as a mark of atonement for the sins of the people of Israel (Ex 30.10; Heb 9.7).

Background. The Tabernacle and Solomon's Temple

The tabernacle was moved from place to place many times until, during the reign of King David, it was installed in Jerusalem, which had become the spiritual and political center of the Judaic state. Later, when their wanderings had ended and they had received the promised land as an inheritance, it became necessary for the Hebrews to build a temple of stone to replace the transportable sanctuary of poles and fabric. This idea came to King David, but God did not will for David to construct it (2 Sam 7.1–17). The temple was to be built during the reign of his son, King Solomon.

The construction of Solomon's temple was one of the most grandiose endeavors in the history of humanity. Thirty thousand men extracted lumber in Lebanon; eighty thousand were hewers of stone; there were seventy thousand burden-bearers and thirty-three hundred chief officers (1 Kg 5.12–18). The temple was built in seven years (1 Kg 6.38). By contemporary standards, especially when one considers the amount of labor and material used, the size of the temple may appear modest: its length was sixty cubits from west to east; its breadth was twenty cubits from north to south; its height was thirty cubits. It had a porch measuring twenty by ten cubits (1 Kg 6.2–3).[6] The walls of the temple were made of solid, polished stone and the inner walls and ceilings were overlaid with boards of cedar. Around its sides were added chambers measuring five cubits in height (1 Kg 6.10). Many details of the temple were made of solid gold.

As in the tabernacle, in the interior of the temple the sanctuary and holy of holies were to be found, and they contained the same objects as were in those places in the tabernacle. Adjoined to the temple was a large courtyard divided into two parts. The outer part was called the great court and the inner part was called the priests' court. Between these two parts were doors overlaid with bronze (2 Chr 4.9). An altar for sacrifices of burnt offerings stood in the inner court while the outer court was designated for the people participating in the worship service.

As in the tabernacle before it, blood sacrifices were offered daily in the temple. On special occasions and days of great feasts, thousands of cattle were sacrificed. To illustrate, on the day of the consecration of the temple by Solomon, a peace offering was made of twenty-two thousand bulls and one hundred and twenty thousand sheep. The altar could not contain all the animal and grain offerings (1 Kg 8.63–64). Priest Pavel Florensky described this:

---

[6]According to the Septuagint version. Concerning the proportions of Solomon's temple and their possible connection with musical harmony, see Margaret Barker, *The Great High Priest* (London and New York, 2003), 274–275.

An eternal fire burned on (the altar). It was not a hearth, but a conflagration into which flammable materials were incessantly added. Imagine the crack, whisper, and squeal of the fire on such an altar; imagine practically a cyclone forming above the temple. . . . Whole oxen were burned, not to mention an abundance of goats, rams, etc. Imagine the smell of burning flesh and fat . . . Sometimes priests walked up to their ankles in blood—the whole enormous court was covered in blood . . . .It flowed into the river Kidron—all of Palestine was fertilized by the residue of blood.[7]

Prophet and King Solomon. Icon of the Church of the Transfiguration. Savior-Kizhi Pogost. Beginning of 18th c.

The consecration of the temple by King Solomon and the transfer to the temple of the ark of the covenant, the preeminent holy object of the Hebrew people, became the most important event in the religious history of Israel. From that time on, the temple was Israel's major spiritual center and holy site. Jews prayed stretching forth their hands to the temple in which the glory of God was present (1 Kg 8.10–39). The temple became a great place of pilgrimage to which people journeyed from all over Palestine to offer a sacrifice to the Lord. At the same time the temple became the main symbol of state power in Israel. The prospering of the temple bore witness to the success of the state, whereas its fall and destruction corresponded with the loss of power by the Hebrew people.

Despite the exceptional importance given to the temple and its practice of sacrifice in ancient Israel, neither the temple nor its worship could in themselves cleanse and sanctify a person if that person did not reject evil deeds and idol worship and did not fulfill the commandments and laws of God. The prophets ceaselessly reminded the people of this fact:

> Thus says the Lord God of Israel: Correct your ways and your devices, and I will cause you to dwell in this place. Trust not in yourselves with lying words, for they shall not profit you at all, saying, it is the temple of the Lord, the temple of the Lord . . . But whereas you have trusted in lying words, whereby you shall

---

[7]Priest Pavel Florensky, "Theological Notes," *Bogoslovskie trudy* 17 (1977): 97–98.

Background. The Tabernacle and Solomon's Temple

not be profited; and you murder, and commit adultery, and steal, and swear falsely, and burn incense to Baal, and are gone after strange gods whom you know not, so that it is evil with you; yet have you come, and stood before me in the house, wherein my name is called, and you have said, we have refrained from doing all these abominations. Is my house, wherein my name is called, a den of robbers in your eyes? (Jer 7.3–4, 8–11).

Sacrifices and burnt offerings are an abomination to the Lord if they are offered by people sullied by idol worship and vices. The only worship pleasing to God is that which leads to a spiritual and moral rebirth:

"Of what value to me is the abundance of your sacrifices?" says the Lord. "I am full of whole-burnt-offerings of rams; and I delight not in the fat of lambs, and the blood of bulls and goats: neither shall you come with these to appear before me; for who has required these things at your hands? You shall no more tread my court. Though you bring fine flour, it is vain; incense is an abomination to me; I cannot bear your new moons, and your sabbaths, and the great day; your fasting, and rest from work, your new moons also, and your feasts my soul hates: you have become loathsome to me; I will no more pardon your sins. When you stretch forth your hands, I will turn away my eyes from you: and though you make many supplications, I will not hearken to you; for your hands are full of blood. Wash you, be clean; remove your iniquities from your souls before mine eyes; cease from your iniquities; learn to do good; diligently seek judgment, deliver him that is suffering wrong, plead for the orphan and obtain justice for the widow." (Is 1.11–17).

The history of the temple is inseparably linked to the history of the Hebrew people. The first temple in Jerusalem stood roughly from 950 BC until 586 BC when it was burned down by the Babylonian captain Nebuzaradan (2 Kg 25.9). During seventy years of exile in Babylon the Hebrews lived with the dream of restoring the temple. During this period the prophet Ezekiel had a vision of a man with a line of flax and a measuring reed in his hand—the length of the reed was six long cubits; that is, each cubit was a cubit and a handbreadth in length (Ez 40.3–5). The man, whose appearance was like bronze, went around the outer and inner courtyards of the temple, and also all of its buildings, taking measurements of the length and breadth of the walls, which the prophet wrote down.

Following the return of the Israelites from Babylonian exile in 538 BC, construction of a second temple began on the site of the first, but without the ark of the covenant. The second temple was built in 516 BC. According to the decree of the Persian king Cyrus, the temple was to have a height and breadth of sixty cubits (Ezra 6.3), but its actual size is not known. In 167 BC the temple was desecrated by troops of Antiochus Epiphanes; however, in 164 BC it was consecrated anew under Judas Maccabeus.

A great number of synagogues—buildings used for meetings—were constructed throughout all of Israel during the period of the second temple. In contrast to the temple, synagogues were not perceived as houses of worship; first and foremost they were houses of teaching in which pious Jews read and discussed the Torah. Even so, community prayers resembling divine services were made in the synagogues. But Israel's central place of worship remained the temple, to which people brought sacrifices prescribed by the Law.

The temple sank into desolation in the first century BC and around 20 BC the Judean king Herod the Great began a massive reconstruction and significantly expanded its dimensions. Elements of Greek classical architecture were used in building Herod's temple—columns, balustrades, galleries, and porticos. Herod's temple significantly surpassed Solomon's temple in terms of size. Construction and restoration works continued even after Herod's death. When Jesus Christ began his earthly service, the temple had already been under construction for forty-six years (Jn 2.20). The temple in Jerusalem was a gigantic complex of buildings which delighted people of the day with its beauty and magnificence. Flavius Josephus wrote:

> This temple . . . was built upon a strong hill. . . . The lowest part of this was erected to the height of three hundred cubits, and in some places more. . . . The works that were above were not unworthy of such foundations; for all the cloisters were double, and the pillars to them belonging were twenty-five cubits in height, and supported the cloisters. These pillars were of one entire stone each . . . and that stone was white marble; and the roofs were adorned with cedar. . . . The natural magnificence, and excellent polish, and the harmony of the joints in these cloisters, afforded a prospect that was very remarkable; nor was it on the outside adorned with any work of the painter or engraver. . . . Those entire courts that were exposed to the air were laid with stones of all sorts. . . . As to the holy house itself, which was placed in the midst (of the

inmost court), that most sacred part of the temple, it was ascended to by twelve steps; and in front its height and its breadth were equal, and each a hundred cubits, though it was behind forty cubits narrower; for on its front it had what may be styled shoulders on each side, that passed twenty cubits further. . . . This house, as it was divided into two parts, the inner part was lower than the appearance of the outer, and had golden doors of fifty-five cubits altitude, and sixteen in breadth; but before these doors there was a veil of equal largeness with the doors. It was a Babylonian curtain, embroidered with blue, and fine linen, and scarlet, and purple, and of a contexture that was truly wonderful. . . . This mixture of colors . . . was a kind of image of the universe; for by the scarlet there seemed to be enigmatically signified fire, by the fine flax the earth, by the blue the air, and by the purple the sea. . . . The outward face of the temple in its front wanted nothing that was likely to surprise either men's minds or their eyes; for it was covered all over with plates of gold of great weight, and, at the first rising of the sun, reflected back a very fiery splendor, and made those who forced themselves to look upon it to turn their eyes away, just as they would have done at the sun's own rays.[8]

Many of the events in Christ's life are connected with the temple. The Most Holy Virgin, in accordance with the statutes of the Mosaic law, brought the infant Jesus to the temple (Lk 2.22–39). Every year the parents of Jesus visited Jerusalem for the feast of Passover in order to worship in the temple (Lk 2.41). At one such visit, the twelve-year-old child Jesus stayed in the temple while his parents sought him, only later to find him sitting among the teachers questioning them. To the rebuke of his mother Jesus answered, "How is it that you sought me? Did you not know that I must be about my Father's business?" (Lk 2.42–49).

The Child Jesus in the Temple. Tablet. Novgorod. Turn of 16th c.

Christ kept the custom of visiting the temple every year at Passover throughout his entire earthly life. Moreover, according to the Gospel it was the custom of Jesus to visit the synagogue every Sabbath

---

[8]Josephus *The Jewish War* 5.5 <http://www.sacred-texts.com/jud/josephus/war-5.htm>, July 25, 2013.

Christ Driving the Money-changers from the Temple. Church of the Protaton. Karyes, Mt. Athos. 18th c.

day: "He went to the synagogue, as his custom was, on the Sabbath day" (Lk 4.16). Visiting the synagogue on the Sabbath and the temple on Passover comprised the basic prayer life of pious Jews when Christ lived and Jesus himself differed little in this from his countrymen.

Jesus called the temple the house of God (Mt 12.4) and his Father's house (Jn 2.16). He was zealous for the beauty of the temple. When he learned that sheep, oxen, and doves were being sold there and money-changers were trading, he drove out from the temple with a whip those who bought and sold, overturning their tables and pouring out their money. Further, he said, "It is written, 'My house shall be called a house of prayer,' but you have made it a den of thieves"(Mt 21.13).

Jesus said about himself, "in this place there is One greater than the temple" (Mt 12.6). Responding to a question from the Samaritans about where to give worship to God, in the temple in Jerusalem or on Mount Gerizim, Jesus said, ". . . the hour is coming when you will neither on this mountain, nor in Jerusalem, worship the Father . . . but the hour is coming, and now is, when the true worshippers will worship the Father in spirit and truth; for the Father seeks such to worship him" (Jn 4.21, 23). These words were both a prediction of the destruction of the temple in Jerusalem and a reminder that the worship of God cannot be limited to any one particular site.

The magnificence of the temple in Jerusalem, newly built by Herod the Great, delighted the disciples of the Savior. But in response to their delight Jesus predicted the temple's destruction (Mt 24.1–2). At the same time, answering questions from the Jews about what sign he would show to justify that he had authority to drive out the merchants from the temple, he said, "Destroy this temple, and in three days I will raise it up" (Jn 2.19). These words were used to reproach Jesus at his trial (Mt 26.61), and with these words the Jews disdained Jesus while he hung on the cross (Mt 27.40). But Jesus spoke not of the temple made by hands but of the temple of his body (Jn 2.21), which God raised three days after the Jews destroyed it.

Establishing the connection between the temple in Jerusalem and the temple of his body, Jesus foretold the creation of the Church as a worldwide temple, not

Background. The Tabernacle and Solomon's Temple

limited to one particular place, that would have its foundation in the Eucharist, where true worshippers would worship the Father in spirit and truth. The teaching that the Church is a temple whose cornerstone is Christ is found in the epistles of the apostles Peter and Paul (1 Pet 2.4–6; 1 Cor 3.11). Jesus Christ is the cornerstone "in whom the whole building, being fitted together, grows into a holy temple in the Lord" (Eph 2:20–21). Together all Christians comprise "the temple of the living God" (2 Cor 6.16) and "the body of Christ" (1 Cor 12.27). Each Christian individually is a member of the body of Christ (1 Cor 12.27) and the body of a Christian is the temple of the Holy Spirit (1 Cor 6.19).

For a certain time following Christ's death and resurrection, the custom of visiting the temple in Jerusalem was observed by the community of the Savior's disciples. In Acts we read that Christ's disciples continued "daily with one accord in the temple" (Acts 2.46). It also mentions that the apostles Paul and John went "to the temple at the hour of prayer, the ninth hour" (Acts 3.1). But Christians visited the temple not so much in order to participate in Jewish religious rites as to preach about Christ to the Jews (Acts 5.20). With this aim the apostles visited the synagogues (Acts 9.20; 13.14, 44; 14.1; 19.8) and houses of prayer (Acts 16.16).

Open Jewish resistance to Christian preaching probably made visiting the temple impossible for Christians. A divide between the temple and the Christian community grew very rapidly. An awareness took hold among Christians of not needing to visit the temple in order to worship God in spirit and truth (Jn 4.24). For this reason the first martyr Stephen, when addressing the Jews and recalling Solomon's construction of the temple, said, "The Most High does not dwell in temples made with hands," because heaven is his throne and the earth is his footstool (Acts 7.46–49).

The decisive break of the Christian community from the temple in Jerusalem was hastened, aside from persecution by the Jews, by the reception into the community of former pagans who had not undergone the rite of circumcision. Another reason was the fact that the Christian community left Judea quite promptly and dispersed throughout other parts of the Roman Empire. Finally, the temple itself was completely destroyed in AD 70 as a result of the short "Jewish War" when troops of the Roman commander Titus beseiged Jerusalem.

2

Churches and Church-Building in the Byzantine Tradition

CHURCHES OF THE POST-CONSTANTINIAN ERA

THE EARLY CHRISTIAN COMMUNITY DID NOT immediately have houses of worship. Christ celebrated the Last Supper in an ordinary house, in a large upper room furnished and ready (Mk 14.15; Lk 22.12). Upper rooms were places of Christian eucharistic gatherings after Christ's resurrection. These were rooms in private homes (Acts 1.13). Breaking bread in their own homes, Christians partook of food with glad and generous hearts (Acts 2.46). This domestic, private, and familial character of the first Christian eucharistic gatherings was far different from the ceremony of church services in the post-Constantinian period.

The Last Supper. Fresco. Studenica Monastery. Serbia. 13th c.

From the first through the third century, Christian services were often conducted in catacombs—large subterranean chambers, dug out of the earth at a depth of eight to twenty-five meters,[1] which served as burial sites. Catacombs existed in many towns of the Roman Empire, both in the West and East. They consisted of long corridors with walls of soft volcanic rock—tufa—in which places for tombs were carved out, one on top of the other. Rectangular-shaped churches were hewn out of the rock for divine services and commemorations of the dead. The most famous catacombs are situated in the suburbs of Rome. The total length of underground corridors in the Roman catacombs is several hundred kilometers. In total between six hundred thousand and eight hundred thousand bodies are buried in the catacombs.

Notwithstanding the common perception that underground churches served as places for Christians to hide during persecutions, the location of the catacombs was usually far too well known for this purpose. Catacomb churches were used for divine services and commemorations of the dead, especially the martyrs whose bodies were buried there. The tombs of the martyrs often became altars in catacomb churches. These churches, as well as individual tombs, were originally decorated with symbolic depictions, ornamentation, and subjects from ancient mythology. Later, images of Christ, the Mother of God, the saints, and events from biblical history appeared.

Visiting the catacombs every Sunday was the tradition of many pious Christians. Saint Jerome bore witness to this fact:

> While still a young lad, studying in Rome, I considered it my duty together with others of the same age to visit the places where the apostles and martyrs are buried and to go to the catacombs, dug into the earth at a considerable depth. Entering here, one sees walls, on both sides filled with the corpses of men. The place is so dark that it appears that the words of the prophet are fulfilled: "Let them go down to Sheol alive" (Ps 54.16). Here and there light penetrates from above, hardly enough to lessen for a moment the terror instilled by the darkness. Moving further and again becoming immersed in the darkness of night, one recalls involuntarily the words of the poet Virgil: "Everywhere the terror in my heart, and the silence itself, dismay me."[2]

---

[1]A.P. Golubtsov, from *Readings on Church Archeology and Liturgics* (St Petersburg, 2006), 95. [Works published in non-English languages are cited with their titles translated. One may assume that they are in the language of the place of publication, unless the contrary is indicated at the first ocurrence or in the bibliography.]

[2]Jerome *Commentary on Ezekiel* 12.11. PL 25.375. Quotation from Virgil *Aeneid* 2.755.

During the period from the first through the third century, in addition to the catacombs, the homes of wealthy Romans served as places for eucharistic gatherings, particularly in special rooms of these houses that were set aside for gatherings and business meetings; such rooms were called *basilicas*.

The term *basilica* is used to refer both to small rooms within palaces and private villas as well as to entire buildings of significant size, built in central squares of large cities, used for political meetings, court sessions, and business transactions. A basilica is a long rectangular-shaped building having a double-sloping roof. The entrance to the basilica is on one end of the building. The opposite end of the building has the form of an apse (Lat. *absis*, Gr. *apsis*, ἀψίς—vault, arch), a semi-circular projection. The basilica may be divided into several naves (Lat. *navis*—ship) having separate ceiling coverings. Generally the number of naves is odd (usually three, sometimes five). Naves are rectangular in shape and they are separated from one another by rows of columns connected by arches. The central nave is higher and usually wider than the side naves.

The most ancient of the well-known, large municipal basilicas are Basilica Porcia (184 BC) and the Aemilian Basilica (179 BC) in the Roman Forum. The most impressive basilica in the Roman Forum in terms of size was the Basilica of Maxentius and Constantine (AD 306–312), a gigantic triple-nave building having an area of six thousand square meters (about 19,700 square feet). Its central nave, culminating in a semi-circular apse, was covered by three vaults which leaned on

Basilica of Maxentius and Constantine, Rome.

eight pillars and was supported from the outside by buttresses. Tiers of arched openings were carved into the exterior walls.

The use of secular buildings for Christian services was widespread during the period of persecutions. Nevertheless, the first buildings constructed specifically for conducting Christian services appeared during that time. Churches of the first through the third century did not differ in their external appearance from secular structures. The architectural form of the Christian basilica derived from the form of the secular basilica. Only upon entering and seeing the painted walls and articles of liturgical use could one realize that he was standing in a Christian church. Rooms used for baptizing catechumens—baptisteries—were built separately.

The oldest of the above-ground Christian churches from this period to have survived to the present day is a church in the Syrian city of Dura-Europos. This Christian church, built in a border city on the banks of the Euphrates no later than the first half of the third century, coexisted with a Jewish synagogue and temples of Mithras, Zeus, Adonis, and other pagan deities. A small baptistery is attached to the church, and next to this are Roman baths. In 256 or 257, the city was seized by Persians, destroyed and later abandoned. The city was uncovered during excavations conducted between 1920 and 1930.

With the exception of the church in Dura-Europos, Christian churches of the pre-Constantinian period have not survived to the present day. This is due to the ruthless destruction of churches by pagans during the period of persecutions. Only the catacomb churches have been preserved, and thanks to them we have a rather complete understanding of Christian architecture and fine arts of the first through the third centuries.

Emperor Constantine's Edict of Milan (313) marked a major turning point for the Church and unlocked previously unforeseen possibilities for Christian church building. A multitude of churches were built on the territory of the Roman Empire during the fourth and fifth centuries. In 313 Emperor Constantine laid the foundation for the Lateran Basilica, which became the main church for services at which the Bishop of Rome presided. Other basilicas were founded in Rome in 324 on the sites of the tombs of the apostles Peter and Paul. In Bethlehem the Basilica of the Nativity of Christ was built between 326 and 333. In Jerusalem, on the site of the sepulcher of the Lord, construction of the Church of the Resurrection of Christ, having the form of a basilica, was completed in 336. During the first half of the fourth century other Christian basilicas were constructed in other cities in the eastern and western parts of the empire.

Churches and Church-Building in the Byzantine Tradition

The real "boom" in the art of Christian church building began not immediately following the Edict of Milan, but rather after the year 381, when the Arian heresy was decisively defeated. The construction of basilicas began on a massive scale during the reign of Emperor Theodosius at the end of the fourth century. "They were constructed in every city of every province, sometimes in groups of two or several in the case of an episcopal cathedral, a place of pilgrimage, a monastery, or most important city."[3] Basilicas were built in Italy, Gaul, Egypt, Syria, Palestine, Mesopotamia, Asia Minor, and on the shores of the Aegean Sea.

Constantine the Great presents the City of Constantinople to the Theotokos and Infant Christ. Mosaic. Hagia Sophia. Constantinople.

The shape of the basilica corresponds with the notion of the church as a ship—Noah's ark—in which Christians find salvation while advancing on the waves of the sea of life into the harbor of the kingdom of Heaven. This is spoken of in the *Apostolic Constitutions* (fourth century):

> When thou callest an assembly of the Church as one that is the commander of a great ship, appoint the assemblies to be made with all possible skill, charging the deacons as mariners to prepare places for the brethren as for passengers, with all due care and decency. And first, let the building be long, with its head to the east, with its vestries on both sides at the east end, and in this way it will be like a ship. In the middle let the bishop's throne be placed, and on each side of him let the presbytery sit down; and let the deacons stand near at hand, in close and small girt garments, for they are like the mariners and managers of the ship: with regard to these, let the laity sit on the other side, with all quietness and good order. And let the women sit by themselves, they also keeping silence.[4]

Like a ship, a church has its pointed front (the eastern apse) and its stern (the western portion). The imagery of a ship was further developed in later domed churches in which a spherical dome represented a sail filled with wind. But the proportions of the basilica coincided more with the image of a ship and the notion of forward motion. In domed churches the architectural configuration and especially

---

[3] André Grabar, *L'âge d'or de Justinien. De la mort de Théodose à l'Islam* (Paris, 1966), 5.
[4] *Apostolic Constitutions* 2.57. <http://www.ccel.org/ccel/schaff/anf07.ix.iii.vii.html>, July 25, 2013.

the arrangement of frescoes on the walls create the idea of circular motion. A viewer's gaze does not so much rush forward to the altar; rather, it moves in a circular motion from one sacred image to the next.[5]

The orientation of churches towards the East is mentioned in the *Apostolic Constitutions* and is an early Christian tradition.[6] According to Saint John of Damascus, "It is not without reason or by chance that we worship towards the East," but above all because God is spiritual light (1 Jn 1.5). Furthermore, in the Scriptures, Christ is called the sun of righteousness (Mal 4.2) and dayspring (Lk 1.78). Paradise was planted in the East (Gen 2.8), the veil and the mercy seat in the tabernacle of Moses were in the East, and the gate of the Lord was located in the East in Solomon's temple. "Christ, when He hung on the Cross, had His face turned towards the West, and so we worship, striving after Him." Ascending to heaven, he was taken up eastward and will appear from the East at his second coming (Mt 24.27). "So then," concludes Saint John of Damascus, "in expectation of his coming we worship towards the East. But this tradition of the apostles is unwritten. For much that has been handed down to us by tradition is unwritten."[7]

The eastward orientation imparts to the church and its services an eschatological meaning. According to Paul Evdokimov, "each faithfully directed prayer is an expectation and, in this way, it is eschatological in its very essence . . . The orientation of prayer towards the East, characteristic of Christians, differs from the Jewish orientation of prayer towards Jerusalem and the Muslim orientation towards Mecca. Entering the church, one moves in the direction of salvation, towards the dwelling of the saints and the land of the living, where the never-setting Sun shines."[8]

The basilica dominated as the architectural style of Christian churches for all of the fourth and fifth centuries. In western Christian architecture, the rectangular-shaped basilica remained as the principal church style throughout subsequent centuries. But in the East, beginning in the sixth century, designs which featured domes[9] developed, and a new style emerged: the domed basilica. This style was

---

[5] Viktor Lazarev, *Byzantine Painting* (Moscow, 1971), 100.

[6] See Hieromonk Gabriel (Bunge), *Earthen Vessels: The Practice of Personal Prayer According to the Patristic Tradition*, translated by Michael J. Miller (San Francisco: Ignatius Press, 2002), 57–71.

[7] John of Damascus *An Exact Exposition of the Orthodox Faith* 4.2. <http://www.bible.ca/archeology/bible-archeology-Jerusalem-temple-mount-east-orientation-jewish-temples-altars.htm>, July 25, 2013.

[8] Paul Evdokimov, *The Art of Icons: Theology of Beauty* (Klin, 2005), 166.

[9] Alexei Komech, "Architecture," in *The Culture of Byzantium: Fourth through First Half of the Seventh Centuries* (Moscow, 1984), 586–595; A. Jacobson, "Architecture," in *The Culture of Byzantium: Second Half of Seventh through Twelfth Centuries* (Moscow, 1989), 496–497.

Churches and Church-Building in the Byzantine Tradition 27

the predecessor to the cross-in-square church which predominated in the Christian East from the sixth through the ninth century. Compared to basilicas of the fourth century, the domed basilica of the sixth and later centuries represented a new step in the development of church architecture. The architectural configuration of the domed basilica emphasizes the sacredness of church space and is marked by a great variety of appearance, complexity, and harmony.

Byzantine churches of the fourth through eighth centuries were comprised of three parts: sanctuary, temple, and narthex. In triple-nave churches the sanctuary occupied the eastern part of the central nave; the table of oblation was situated in the northern nave while the southern nave served as vestry. Often the vestry was a room separate from the church or even a special annex.

The sanctuary was separated from the church by a screen. In early Byzantine churches this was a low parapet of carved panels or a portico of several columns on whose capitals rested a wide, rectangular beam called an *architrave*.[10] Depictions of Christ and the saints were situated on the architrave. In contrast to the iconostasis that emerged later, no icons were placed on the sanctuary screen itself and the space of the sanctuary remained completely open to the view of the faithful. The sanctuary screen often had a shape like the Greek letter *pi* (Π): in addition to the central façade it had two side fronts. The entrance to the sanctuary was situated in the middle of the central façade and was open and without doors.

An elevation for the reader called the *ambo* was installed in the middle of church buildings, especially large churches and cathedrals. The liturgy of the catechumens, including the reading of holy Scripture and the sermon, took place on the ambo.

The walls of many Byzantine churches were richly overlaid or decorated with holy pictures. A combination of marble facing and mosaics was typical. Mosaic depictions generally covered rounded surfaces in the upper parts of the interior, especially cupolas, the space under cupolas, vaults, and arches. Flat wall surfaces were overlaid with marble.[11] A combination of mosaics and frescoes—wall paintings executed on wet plaster—was characteristic of churches in later periods.

A classic and most spectacular example of the Byzantine domed basilica is the Church of Hagia Sophia in Constantinople, built by Emperor Justinian in 537 according to the design of the architects Anthemios of Tralles and Isidore of Miletus. Its height is 55.6 meters (182.4 feet). The main space of the church is a massive rectangle measuring 77 by 71.7 meters (253 by 235 feet) and divided into

---

[10]Lazarev, *Byzantine Painting*, 116.
[11]Ibid. 103–104.

Emperor Justinian Presents the Church of Hagia Sophia to the Mother of God and Infant Christ. Mosaic. Hagia Sophia in Constantinople.

three longitudinal naves. The central nave is crowned with a semi-spherical dome having a diameter of 31.5 meters (103.3 feet). The longitudinal naves are separated from one another by walls topped with an arched construction. Numerous colonnades support the church's vaulted areas. The flanking naves are significantly narrower than the central nave but include two floors, the upper floor intended for women. The galleries of the flanking naves and narthex are a suite of arched openings.

Hagia Sophia's arrangement of domes presents a work of true architectural genius. To build a structure of such size and then crown it with a gigantic dome lacking visible supports is a most complicated task. Rather than increasing the width of the walls in order to support the massive central dome, the architects devised a system of semi-domes. Two semi-domes join to the main dome from the east and west and to each semi-dome two smaller semi-domes are joined. The task of supporting the main dome was accomplished by numerous arches and vaults. As a result, the enormous force of pressure ("thrust") from the dome is dissipated and held in check. The resulting impression is that the dome hangs in the air. This impression is made stronger by the many closely placed arched windows situated along the base of the dome through which rays of light flow into the interior space of the church.

The Church of Hagia Sophia was an architectural wonder in its time and amazes us today with the scale of its design and structural originality. Procopius of Caesarea in the sixth century described it in this way:

> The church has become a spectacle of marvelous beauty, overwhelming to those who see it, but to those who know it by hearsay altogether incredible. For it soars to a height to match the sky, and as if surging up from amongst the other buildings it stands on high and looks down upon the remainder of the city, adorning it, because it is a part of it, but glorying in its own beauty,

because, though a part of the city and dominating it, it at the same time towers above it to such a height that the whole city is viewed from there as from a watchtower. Both its breadth and its length have been so carefully proportioned that it may not improperly be said to be exceedingly long and at the same time unusually broad. And it exults in an indescribable beauty . . . For it proudly reveals its mass and the harmony of its proportions, having neither excess nor deficiency, since it is both more pretentious than the buildings to which we are accustomed, and considerably more noble than those which are merely huge, and it abounds exceedingly in sunlight and in the reflection of the sun's rays from the marble. Indeed one might say that its interior is not illuminated from without by the sun, but that the radiance comes into being within it, such an abundance of light bathes this shrine. . . . And upon this circle rests the huge spherical dome which makes the structure exceptionally beautiful. Yet it seems not to rest upon solid masonry, but to cover the space with its golden dome suspended from heaven. All these details, fitted together with incredible skill in mid-air and floating off from each other and resting only on the parts next to them, produce a single and most extraordinary harmony in the work.[12]

Hagia Sophia's interior was no less inspiring than its architectural forms. Its columns were executed in marble and various shades of porphyry and the capitals of its columns were decorated with intricate engravings. All of its walls were richly encrusted with marble or overlaid with mosaics in which golden tones prevailed. Because iconoclasts destroyed many of the original mosaics, we can conjecture only very approximately concerning what subjects were found in the original mosaics. The majority of mosaics created anew in the post-iconoclastic period (9th–12th centuries) were destroyed by the Turks after they turned the church into a mosque in 1453. Only a few mosaic depictions hidden under a thick layer of plaster survived, and these were uncovered in the nineteenth century.

Hagia Sophia's sanctuary screen consisted of a colonnade with an architrave shaped like the Greek letter *pi* and supported by columns. The length of the architrave, which included the flanking façades, exceeded 30 meters (98 feet). Medallions with depictions of Christ, the Most Holy Theotokos, and saints were set on the architrave.[13]

---

[12]Procopius of Ceasarea *Buildings of Justinian I.* 1.27–47. <http://penelope.uchicago.edu/Thayer/E/Roman/Texts/Procopius/Buildings/1A*.html>, July 25, 2013.

[13]Lazarev, *Byzantine Painting*, 116.

Interior of Hagia Sophia.

From the altar a colonnade ran along the east-west axis to the ambo, which was situated in the middle of the church. The ambo stood several meters above the floor so that the voice of the reader or homilist could be heard at a significant distance. The ambo was a grandiose marble structure encrusted with precious stones. The sixth-century Byzantine poet Paul the Silentiary wrote, "As an island rises above the waves of the sea, adorned with ears of wheat, grape leaves, a floriated meadow and forested hills, so in the middle of the spacious church one beholds the tall ambo, crafted of marble, speckled with flower gardens of stones and other splendors of art."[14]

Over the altar table rose an extraordinary artwork called *ciborium* (Gr. *kivōrion*, κιβώριον—tent). Paul the Silentiary called this "a sacred tower" that rose into the

[14]Paul the Silentiary *Description of the Church of Hagia Sophia* 660–663; PG 86.2144B.

Churches and Church-Building in the Byzantine Tradition 31

air over the altar table and arched down from above—a four-edged canopy supported by silver columns. Over the canopy rose an eight-edged cone, sheathed with silver. Rising out of the apex was a chalice in the form of a lily, topped with a cross. Inside the chalice was a silver apple. Between the columns four richly decorated screens were hung over which candle-stands were placed.[15] The ciborium, crafted from silver, was richly adorned with gold and precious stones.[16]

Describing Hagia Sophia's interior, Procopius of Caesarea does not conceal his delight for its opulence and diversity:

> The whole ceiling is overlaid with pure gold, which adds glory to the beauty, yet the light reflected from the stones prevails, shining out in rivalry with the gold . . . Who could recount the beauty of the columns and the stones with which the church is adorned? One might imagine that he had come upon a meadow with its flowers in full bloom. For he would surely marvel at the purple of some, the green tint of others, and at those on which the crimson glows and those from which the white flashes, and again at those which nature, like some painter, varies with the most contrasting colors. And whenever anyone enters this church to pray, he understands at once that it is not by any human power or skill, but by the influence of God, that this work has been so finely turned.[17]

Hagia Sophia was conceived as a Christian version of three Old Testament structures for worship: the tabernacle, Solomon's temple, and the temple described in chapters forty through forty-seven of the book of the prophet Ezekiel.

The connection between Hagia Sophia and the tabernacle described in the Septuagint is quite evident. In particular, Hagia Sophia had twenty columns on both the northern and southern sides which corresponded exactly with the number of posts in the tabernacle. In the western wall of the church (the eastern wall of the narthex), there were nine entrances which corresponded with the number of openings between the ten posts of the eastern wall of the tabernacle. (Art historians compare this wall to the veil that separated the courtyard of the tabernacle from the outside world.[18]) The central space of Hagia Sophia—four gigantic pillars and a dome resting on them—could be perceived as an enlarged replica of the holy of

[15]Ibid. 720–744; PG 86, 2147AB.
[16]Izmail Sreznevsky, "The Ancient Byzantine Tabernacle," *Christian Antiquities and Archeology* (St Petersburg, 1863), 31–32 [Russian].
[17]Procopius *Buildings* I 1.54–61. <http://penelope.uchicago.edu/Thayer/E/Roman/Texts/Procopius/Buildings/1A*.html>, August 8, 2013.
[18]E.H. Swift, *Hagia Sophia* (New York, 1940), 34.

holies, with its veil on four posts.[19] A ciborium, rising above the altar and resting on four pillars, also represented the holy of holies.

No less evident is the connection between Hagia Sophia and Solomon's temple. According to legend, Emperor Justinian, upon entering the newly built church, uttered, "Solomon, I have outdone you!" For the Byzantine Greeks, this church had the same significance that Solomon's temple had for the Jews before its destruction. The connection with Solomon's temple was underscored by Hagia Sophia's overall architectural design. A spacious courtyard with a fountain was situated in front of its entrance—comparable to the outer courtyard of Solomon's temple. The interior space of the church was divided into the sanctuary, corresponding to the holy of holies, the body of the church, comparable to the temple's sanctuary, and the narthex, which can be compared to the court of the priests.[20]

Hagia Sophia contributed to the growing perception in the Christian East of the church as the "house of God"—a place of God's particular presence. The church was dedicated to Christ and its consecration took place on December 24, the eve of the nativity of Christ. Sophia—the Wisdom of God—spoken of in Proverbs and the Wisdom of Solomon, in the Christian tradition has been identified with Christ from times of old. The Byzantine Greeks gave special consideration to the words: "Wisdom built her house, and she supported it with seven pillars. She offered her sacrifices; she mixed her wine in a bowl and prepared her table. She sent her servants, inviting people to the bowl with a lofty proclamation, saying, 'He who is without discernment, let him turn aside to me'; and to those in need of discernment, she says, 'Come, eat my bread and drink the wine I mixed for you'" (Pr 9.1–5). These words were perceived as a symbolic description of the Eucharist itself as well as the church in which the eucharistic service is celebrated. Hagia Sophia was conceived as a house built by the incarnate Wisdom of God, where Christ himself invites those who believe in him to partake of his body and blood.

The construction of Hagia Sophia contributed to the growing notion of the church as an image of the universe, in which the dome represents the vault of the heavens and the space symbolizes the inhabited universe—the visible and invisible world. The connection between the church and the universe has its root in the perception of the universe as a united liturgical organism—a perception which

---

[19]Barker, *Hagia Sophia in Constantinople as the Temple* (to be published). The shape of this veil is not fully clear from the descriptions given in the Bible; however, the four posts on which it rested probably formed a square.

[20]Ibid.

can be traced back to the Old Testament.[21] In the psalms the universe is depicted as space filled with living and non-living beings. Each, in its own way, offers praise to the Creator:

> The heavens are telling the glory of God and the firmament proclaims his handiwork (Ps 19.1).

> Praise the Lord from the heavens, praise him in the heights! Praise him, all his angels, praise him, all his hosts! Praise him, sun and moon, praise him, all you shining stars! Praise him, you highest heavens, and you waters above the heavens! . . . Praise the Lord from the earth, you sea monsters and all deeps, fire and hail, snow and frost, stormy wind fulfilling his command! Mountains and all hills, fruit trees and all cedars! Beasts and all cattle, creeping things and flying birds . . . (Ps 148.1–4, 7–10).

The church is perceived as the meeting place of heaven and earth, angels and people, who participate together in the service to God, praising the Lord and Creator of heaven and earth. It is the place which unites all people who together stand before God in prayer—both those who are present at the service and those who are absent, both the living and the dead. The structure of the church, divided into several parts, symbolizes the hierarchical structure of creation and the unity of the spiritual and physical worlds. Saint Maximus the Confessor commented on this:

> The holy Church of God (is) a figure and image of the entire visible and invisible universe. . . . For a church, although put up as one building, is partitioned in conformity with a definite plan, with one place set aside for priests and servers, which we call the sanctuary, and another open to all the faithful, which we call the nave—and yet, the Church is essentially one, and not divided in kind by the differentiation of its parts. . . . The Church liberates the parts themselves from the differences in their vocation, and makes their sameness and unity evident to each, showing that each is made for the other, the nave having the virtue of a sanctuary, for it is sanctified by its dedication to the goal of the liturgy, while the sanctuary (for the clergy) is actually a nave (temple), for the worship in the sanctuary is joined to that in the nave as to its source. . . . The holy Church of God is an image of just the sensible world by itself; the sanctuary reminds one of the sky, the dignity of the nave reflects the earth.[22]

---

[21]See *Desk Manual for Clergy*, vol. 4, 9 [in Russian].
[22]Maximus the Confessor *The Mystagogia* 2–3, in Dom Julian Stead, O.S.B., trans., *The Church, the*

The very structure of the church, then, consisting of the temple and the sanctuary, is shown to be an indication of the hierarchical arrangement of the cosmos. (In reality, the church is comprised of three parts—sanctuary, nave, and narthex, although Saint Maximus treats the nave and narthex as a single unit.)

A more evident connection between the church and the cosmos is seen when observing how the interior wall icons are arranged. An entire subsequent chapter will be devoted to this subject. For now let it suffice to say that the interior space of Byzantine churches, by virtue of their mosaics, frescoes, and other sacred images, was arranged in such a way as to render all the diversity of the spiritual and material world. Sacred images allowed the space of the church to overflow spiritually and represented the ideal world, according to which the entire created cosmos is arranged.

The Church as an Image of Man. "Divine Proportions"

The church is at once both an image of the cosmos and an image of man. Saint Maximus the Confessor expressed this in the following way:

> God's holy Church is a symbol of man; its soul is the sanctuary; the sacred altar, the mind; and its body is the nave. A church is thus the image and likeness of God. The nave is used as the body should be used, for exemplifying practical moral philosophy; from the sanctuary the Church leads the way to natural contemplation spiritually as man does with his soul; and she embarks on mystical theology through the sacred altar.[23]

The notion of the church as an image of man and the temple as an image of the human body was not simply a speculative theological construction. Rather, it corresponded directly with the architectural features of the eastern Christian churches.

The connection between the church and the human body was primarily expressed in the fact that the system of measurements used for construction was based on the measurements of parts of the body. The basic unit of measurement was the cubit—the length of the arm from the elbow to the end of the middle finger. In

Liturgy and the Soul of Man: The Mystagogia of St Maximus the Confessor (Still River, MA: St. Bede's Publications, 1982), 68–69.

[23] Maximus the Confessor *The Mystagogia* 4, cited in Dom Julian Stead, O.S.B., trans., *The Church, the Liturgy and the Soul of Man: The Mystagogia of St Maximus the Confessor* (Still River, MA: St Bede's Publications, 1982), 71.

the Bible this measurement is called a cubit or a long cubit (Ez 40.3–5). The finger, the palm, and the foot were also used to measure length. The distance between various parts of the body was used as well, such as the distance between the end of the middle finger of the left hand and the end of the middle finger of the right hand (while holding one's hands outstretched and parallel to the ground)—called a *sazhen*. The distance between the tips of the fingers of the left hand (raised straight upwards) and the right heel was called an *oblique* sazhen. Measurements of length differed in various civilizations: ancient Hebrew, Egyptian, Roman, Greek, and Old Russian. But the systems of measurement always utilized the body parts of an adult man of average height (170–180 cm/ 5 ft 6 in to 5 ft 11 in). Byzantium, in particular, inherited the ancient Greek system of measurement which included the following units of measurement: *orgyia* or sazhen (179 cm/70.5 inches), double step (148 cm/58.3 inches), cubit (approx. 44.5 cm/17.5 inches), foot (approx. 30 cm/11.8 inches), width of palm (approx 7.5 cm/3 inches), and width of finger (1.85 cm/0.7 inches).[24]

The use of a system of measurement based on the parts of the human body facilitated integrity and harmony of architectural structures. At the foundation of the structure of the human body lies the principle of the harmonious correlation between the parts and the whole as well as the interrelation of parts between themselves. The principle of proportionality, signified by the Latin term *proportion* or the Greek term *analogy*, lies at the foundation of church architecture. Vitruvius, the Roman architect of the first century BC, indicated this principle in describing ancient (pagan) temples:

> The design of a temple depends on symmetry, the principles of which must be most carefully observed by the architect. They are due to proportion, which is called in Greek *analogia*. Proportion is a correspondence among the measures of the members of an entire work, and of the whole to a certain part selected as standard. From this result the principles of symmetry. Without symmetry and proportion there can be no principles in the design of any temple; that is, if there is no precise relation between its members, as in the case of those of a well-shaped man. For the human body is so designed by nature that the face, from the chin to the top of the forehead and the lowest roots of the hair, is a

---

[24]Concerning Byzantine measurements of length, see E. Schilbach, *Byzantinische Metrologie* (Munich, 1970). The author shows that the size of the measurement of departure, the Byzantine foot, was not the same in different churches. In Hagia Sophia it was equal to 31.23 cm (12.3 inches) but in other churches it could be a bit larger or smaller.

tenth part of the whole height.... The head with the neck and shoulder from the top of the breast to the lowest roots of the hair is a sixth.... The length of the foot is one sixth of the height of the body.²⁵

The head and neck together (from the shoulders) is proportionate to the whole body by the ratio of 1:6; the face to the body—1:10; the foot to the body—1:6. This proportionality, according to Vitruvius, was conveyed to the size of the Doric column: its creators measured a footprint in relation to the height of a man and, finding that the foot is proportionate to the body by the ratio of one to six, applied this relationship to the colonnade. The height of the Doric column together with its capital is greater than the column's width by six times. In this way, Vitruvius concludes, "the Doric column, as used in buildings, began to exhibit the proportions, strength, and beauty of the body of a man."²⁶

The principles of ancient architecture were not forgotten in the Byzantine period. On the contrary, in building Byzantine churches, during the period of Constantine, Justinian, and later, the same standards were used as in antiquity. Unlike metric measurements recognized in contemporary architecture, measurements of the human body possessed a hidden inner harmony. Applied in building, these measurements imparted just proportion and beauty. "When anthropometric measurements are used to measure buildings, they introduce to architecture the characteristic of interpenetration, that is—harmony. This is why we say that in architecture, man is the measure by which we judge a structure's harmony."²⁷

In Byzantine and Old Russian church architecture, the principle known as the *golden ratio* was widely applied. This principle received its name in the time of the Renaissance, but it was already well known by architects of ancient Egypt and Greece. Structures such as the Great Pyramids and the Parthenon in Athens were built in accordance with this principle. Its application in architecture combined with the principle of symmetry imparts harmony and just proportion to a building, brings order to its individual components, and transforms the sum of its parts into a united whole.

In geometry, when dividing a segment into two portions, a "golden ratio" or "divine proportion"²⁸ exists when the ratio of the larger portion to the smaller is

---

²⁵Vitruvius *The Ten Books on Architecture* 79. <http://www.gutenberg.org/files/20239/20239-h/29239-h.htm>, July 25, 2013.
²⁶Ibid.
²⁷I.S. Shevelev, *Concerning Shape Formation in Nature and Art: The Golden Ratio* (Moscow, 1990), 30.
²⁸The term "divine proportion" was coined by the fifteenth-century Italian mathematician Luca Pacioli. The term "golden ratio" (*sectio aurea*) was coined by his friend Leonardo da Vinci.

equal to the ratio of the sum of both parts of the segment to its larger section. Precisely such a relationship was considered by Plato to be the perfect proportion:

> ... Two things cannot be rightly put together without a third; there must be some bond of union between them. And the fairest bond is that which makes the most complete fusion of itself and the things which it combines; and proportion is best adapted to effect such a union. For whenever in any three numbers, whether cube or square, there is a mean, which is to the last term what the first term is to it; and again, when the mean is to the first term as the last term is to the mean—then the mean becoming first and last, and the first and last both becoming means, they will all of them of necessity come to be the same, and having become the same with one another will be all one.[29]

The given ratio is expressed arithmetically using the numbers 0.618 and 1.618. If a segment is divided into two parts, the relationship between its parts should be such that dividing the smaller part by the larger part will result in a constant irrational number equal to approximately 0.618. Dividing the larger part by the smaller will result in approximately 1.618. The golden ratio can be constructed using a double square—two squares united to form a single rectangle. In this case the long end of the double square will be proportionate to the short end with a ratio of 2:1.[30]

The principle of the golden ratio combined with the principle of symmetry is widespread in the organic world. It is seen particularly in the structure of the human body.[31] While in the human body no correlations occur at random, neither should there be any random and disproportionate correlations in the individual architectural components of the temple. In Byzantine craftsmanship, the effect of grandiosity was

---

[29] Plato *Timaeus* 31c–32a, translated by Benjamin Jowett. <http://www.doc.ic.ac.uk/~rac101/concord/texts/timaeus/>, July 25, 2013.

[30] The golden ratio is equal to the difference between the long diagonal of a double square and its short end to its long end. For example, if the sides of a double square are equal to 20 cm and 10 cm, the diagonal will equal 22.3 cm. The difference between the long diagonal and the short side of the rectangle equals 12.36 cm. The ratio of 12.36:20 will be equal to approximately 0.618 (and the ratio of 20:12.36 equal to approximately 1.618.)

[31] The body parts of an adult male are found to be proportionate according to axial symmetry or the "golden ratio." All paired body parts and corresponding segments are symmetrical (the right and left arms, right and left legs, shin of right leg and shin of left leg, etc.). In accordance with the golden ratio the following relationships are found: middle finger and palm; palm and hand; hand and elbow joint; forearm and elbow joint together and the hand; the distance from the navel to the crown of the head and the distance from the bottom of the foot to the navel; the distance from the end of the middle finger of lowered hand to the bottom of the foot and the distance from the crown of the head to the end of the middle finger.

achieved not only by virtue of the building's measurements, but also by virtue of proper use of the principle of proportionality. So, for example, in many domed basilicas, in particular the Church of Hagia Sophia, the width of the central nave relates to the width of the flanking nave with a ratio of approximately 0.62:0.38—which yields the golden ratio. The same, or nearly the same, ratio is found in Hagia Sophia in the following components: lower gallery of the flanking nave and its upper gallery; the height of the church from the floor to the base of the cross and the height from the upper gallery to the base of the cross; the diameter of the dome and the radius of the half-dome joined to it; the diameter of the dome and the height of both galleries; the radius of the half-dome and the radius of the altar's apse; the radius of the half-dome and the width of the four side chambers; the list could go on.

The laws of geometric proportions lay at the foundation of the correlation between the length, breadth, and height of the church and between the height of the columns and the height of the dome. Not a single measurement in the multifaceted structural design of the church was arbitrary. The measurement of every component of the interior and exterior is proportionate with the measurement of another component.

The art of proportionally uniting hybrid components can be seen as the major characteristic of Byzantine church building. The effect of which Procopius of Caesarea so eloquently wrote is achieved by virtue of proper proportions. He described how the length and breadth of Hagia Sophia are in such harmonious agreement that there can be nothing superflous in the church and nothing lacking. This shows forth the "united harmony of all creation."

Correct proportions of the church building were a guarantee not only of its beauty and longevity but also of good acoustics. It is well known that Byzantine churches possessed exceptional acoustic properties. This was especially needed in such large churches as Hagia Sophia where the voice of the priest or bishop had to be heard by all those present at the service. In the days when there were no electronic means of amplifying sound, other means were used. Primarily, the force of sound was amplified by arched openings and overhead coverings. Also, in order to improve the acoustic properties of churches, hollow clay vessels with their openings turned inward were installed in the walls and arches of the church.[32] In Rus' these vessels were called *golosniki*, and this term indicated their acoustic function (the Russian word *golos* means "voice"—Ed.). Golosniki fulfilled another important function: they lessened the weight of the arches.

---

[32] Auguste Choisy, *L'art de bâtir chez les byzantins* (Paris, 1968), 72.

CROSS-IN-SQUARE CHURCHES IN BYZANTIUM

The idea of proportionality in diverse parts of the church found its most perfect expression in the Byzantine cross-in-square churches of the ninth and subsequent centuries, as well as in the churches of Georgia, the Balkans, and Rus'. The floor plan of cross-in-square churches is either an equal-sided cross or a cross in which the lower end, corresponding with the western wing of the church, is longer than the other three ends. The upper end of the cross, corresponding with the eastern wing, is completed, as in a basilica, with a semi-circular or rectangular sanctuary apse. In those places where the longitudinal central nave crosses the transverse nave, four supporting pillars are installed, and the dome rests on these.

The floor plan of a cross-in-square church represents not only a cross but also a person with arms outstretched in the form of a cross. (This was the traditional attitude of prayer for ancient Christians.) The ratio of the western part of the central nave to its eastern part in many cases corresponded with the ratio of the lower part of the human body (up to the chest) to its upper part (from the chest to the top of the head). The arms of the transept are equal in length and this proportion corresponds with the equality of length of a person's arms. The ratio of the transept's arm to the western arm of the central nave corresponds to the ratio of an outstretched arm to the lower part of the body (from the chest to the feet).[33]

Ruins of the Basilica of Saint John in Ephesus.

The shape of a cross was already used in church architecture in the fifth century. The church of the Apostle John in Ephesus (fifth century) was a grandiose structure consisting of four basilicas united in crosswise form. The same construction lay at the foundation of one no less grandiose structure of the fifth century, the church of the Monastery of Saint Simeon the Stylite near Aleppo in present-day Syria. In both cases, however, the cruciform shape was achieved by adding three additional basilicas to the main basilica.

---

[33]In the Chronicle of the Abbey of Saint Tron (eleventh century) concerning the newly built cross-in-square church it is written: "A new church is built, as the teachers say, according to the size of a human body. The sanctuary portion together with the areas surrounding the sanctuary corresponds to the head and neck, the choir to the chest cavity, both branches, outstretched to the sides, to the arms, the nave to the stomach, and the second transept in the west to the legs." Citation: *General History of Architecture* IV, 640.

The genesis of the cross-in-square church was different. This church is a domed basilica, shortened along the east-west axis and intersected with a nave running cross-wise (transept), imparting the shape of a cross to the basilica. Some Byzantine domed basilicas of the sixth century, in essence, were similar to the cross-in-square churches, especially the Church of the Holy Apostles, built in Constantinople in the years 536–550 by Anthemius of Tralles. Procopius of Ceasarea commented on the beginning of the construction of this church:

> Two straight lines were drawn, intersecting each other at the middle in the form of a cross, one extending east and west, and the other which crossed this running north and south. On the outside these lines were defined by walls on all of the sides, while on the inside they were traced by rows of columns standing above one another. . . . The two arms (*pleurai*) of this enclosure which lie along the transverse line are equal to each other, but the arm which extends toward the west, along the upright line, is enough longer than the other to make the form of the cross.[34]

In the second half of the ninth century the cross-in-square church became the predominant form of church architecture in Byzantium. Compared to the grandiose domed basilica, the greater technological simplicity of this type of church contributed to its broad proliferation.

The Church of the Holy Theotokos in Skripou (Boeotia), built in the years 873–874, is a fine example of the cross-in-square church of this period. The church forms a cross and is capped by a dome. At the root of its design is a triple-nave basilica intersected in the center by a nave running cross-wise. The church is richly embellished on both the outside and inside. Its main apse is decorated with bas-reliefs and medallions having depictions of animals as well as rich ornamental designs of vegetation.

The design of cross-in-square churches is often a square divided into nine cells (compartments) by four supports bearing a dome: the four ends of a cross fit into the square. The five-nave church of the Monastery of Christ Akataleptos (The Incomprehensible Christ) in Constantinople, dating to the end of the ninth century, was built according to this plan.

An essential change in proportions towards "verticalization" is observed when comparing Byzantine cross-in-square churches at the turn of the second millenium with domed basilicas of the sixth century. Over the entire period of the second

---

[34]Procopius *Buildings I* 4, 11–13.

half of the first millenium, Byzantine churches gradually "stretched" in height. This "stretch" was achieved both by shortening the length of the western part of the central nave and by increasing the height of the church's walls in relation to their length. Furthermore, the shape of the church's dome was changed: it became smaller in diameter but larger in height, because of its being placed on tall drums.

Church of the Monastery at Nea Moni.

At the beginning of the second millenium magnificent cross-in-square churches were built in the monasteries of the holy mountain Athos: The Great Lavra, Iveron, Vatopedi. Outstanding examples of cross-in-square architecture are the *katholika* (principal churches) of the monasteries of Nea Moni on the island of Chios (1042–1056), Hosios Loukas (1011 or 1022), and Daphni (around 1080). Active church building continued in the late Byzantine period and included, in particular, the Cathedral of Hagia Sophia in Trebizond (between 1238 and 1263), Church of the Paregoretissa in Arta (1282–1289), and the Church of the Holy Savior of the Monastery of Chora in Constantinople (beginning of the fourteenth century). Bell towers began to appear in some Byzantine churches at the turn of the ninth century. Scholars observe an Italian influence[35] in their appearance.

After the fall of the Byzantine Empire the traditions of Byzantine church architecture were preserved to some extent in the Ottoman Empire. Turkish Muslim architecture was strongly influenced by Byzantine architecture. (To be convinced, one need only compare the Church of Hagia Sophia in Istanbul with the Blue Mosque situated next to it.) The construction of Christian churches in the post-Byzantine era continued in territories occupied by Turks, but cross-in-square architecture in this period ceased to predominate. In the eighteenth and nineteenth centuries, basilica-type structures with three naves and crowned with short domes became widespread.

After the liberation of Greece from the Ottoman yoke in the nineteenth century, the construction of churches on territories previously belonging to the Ottoman Empire significantly intensified. By this time, western trends had penetrated into Greek church architecture and several churches were built in neo-classical style. Towards the end of the nineteenth century the eclectic style became dominant; in this style, separate elements of neoclassicism were combined with traditional

---

[35] A. Kazarian, "The Byzantine Empire/Architecture" *in Orthodox Encyclopedia*, vol. 8, (Moscow, 2007), 302.

Byzantine motifs, and in some cases with elements of the baroque and gothic styles. The triple-nave basilica remained the dominant architectural form for Greek Orthodox churches of this period.

A rebirth of interest in cross-in-square architecture based on the Byzantine model was seen throughout the twentieth century. The eminent Greek architect G. Nomikos built more than two hundred churches in the neo-Byzantine style, including many cross-in-square churches and domed basilicas. One of this architect's most famous creations is the Cathedral of Saint Nectarios of Aegina on the island of Aegina (1973–1994), conceived as a smaller copy of Constantinople's Hagia Sophia.

National Traditions of Orthodox Church Architecture

In the border regions of the Byzantine Empire, and also beyond its limits, where eastern Orthodox Christianity was spreading, Byzantine architectural traditions developed and acquired an expressive national character. A connection with Byzantine origins was especially preserved in the architecture of Georgia and the Balkans.

In Georgia, the construction of churches began immediately after the nation's baptism in the year 326. The first Georgian churches were built by masters invited from Greece. The earliest of the extant Georgian churches are the chapel of the Nekresi Monastery (last half of the fourth century), Bolnisi Sioni (478–493), Anchiskhati in Tbilisi (sixth century); these all have the form of basilicas. From the second half of the sixth century, churches with a central dome became the standard style. An example of this type of church is the Church of Jvari in Mtskheta (586/7–604). Church building did not cease in the period of fragmentation, civil strife, and Arab invasions (from the second half of the seventh through the tenth century). But the acme of Georgian church architecture was reached after the political unification at the turn of the eleventh century. Between 1010 and 1029 the grandiose Svetitskhoveli Cathedral was built in Mtskheta; here Georgian kings were crowned from the twelfth century on. Cathedrals appeared in other cities of Georgia, including Oshki, Kutaisi, Kartli, and Kakheti.[36]

Church of the Monastery of Jvari.

[36] I. Elizbarashvili, "Georgian Orthodox Church: Church Arts/Architecture," in *Orthodox Encyclopedia*, vol.13 (Moscow, 2003), 283–289.

Magnificent cathedrals and small rural and monastery churches continued to be built in Georgia from the twelfth century through the fourteenth. Extraordinary examples of Georgian architecture are the Church of the Gelati Monstery (twelfth century), the churches in Betania, Kintsvisi, and Timotesubani (turn of the thirteenth century), and Zarzma Monastery (beginning of the fourteenth century). The second half of the fourteenth century and all of the fifteenth were a time of decline in church architecture. Church building resumed only in the sixteenth century. In the architecture of the sixteenth through the eighteenth centuries traditional Georgian standards were prevalent. Influence from abroad (especially Iran) was minimal and affected only individual architectural and decorative elements.

The characteristic and most striking feature of Georgian churches is the cone-shaped dome (similar domes are found only in Armenian architecture). The development of this shape for the dome was a gradual process. As in Byzantium, over time the dome, together with its foundation, increased in height. In churches of the sixth and seventh centuries, such as Jvari, short and rather flattened domes stand on short foundations. By the twelfth century the height of the drum and dome had increased by several times over what it had been in earlier times. In the structures of the sixteenth century, such as Akhali-Shuamta, the foundation became disproportionately tall. The church acquired a vertical and emphatically "upwardly outstretched" characteristic.

Many Georgian churches are decorated with bas-reliefs. In the period from the seventh through the middle of the eleventh century, depictions of people and angels held an important place in the sculptural decor of churches. Beginning in the middle of the eleventh century ornamental decor was common. After the thirteenth century a decline in interest in sculptural decoration occurred, although some churches continued to be decorated with bas-reliefs. One of the most common compositions was the "Exaltation of the Cross," in which two angels uphold the cross in a circle (this composition was already seen in Jvari). A constant figure in sculptural decoration was Saint George the Greatmartyr, the heavenly protector of Georgia.

In the nineteenth century, when the Georgian Church lost its autocephaly and became part of the Russian Church, some Georgian churches were built in the Russian style with onion domes, but the majority of churches preserved traditional Georgian forms. Church building in Georgia was interrupted following the Russian Revolution of 1917 and resumed only at the turn of the twenty-first century. Contemporary church architects look to traditional Georgian forms, although

Holy Trinity Cathedral (Sameba) in Tbilisi.

the rules of proportion inherited from Byzantium are usually not observed. The finest example of contemporary Georgian architecture is Holy Trinity Cathedral (Sameba) in Tbilisi (2002–2006). Many elements of traditional Georgian architecture are reproduced in this magnificent cathedral, but a proportionate correlation between the building's individual parts is not retained. The contemporary architect incorporated only external forms of traditional Georgian architecture; he failed to grasp the inner logic of the architects of old and could not (or did not wish to) reproduce that architectural rule according to which Georgian churches were built over the span of many centuries.

Balkan church architecture of the end of the first and first half of the second millennium is essentially a variety of Byzantine church architecture with the addition of several characteristic national features.

The earliest Christian structures on the territory of modern day Bulgaria belong to the fourth through seventh centuries. In this period in Bulgarian church architecture the triple-nave basilica with semi-circular apse to the east was most prevalent. In later centuries the cross-in-square church became predominant. Characteristic Bulgarian features before the tenth century were: the use of *pastoforia*,[37] side coverings, annexes from the east and west, towers on the western façade, a courtyard on the south side, and the unification of several naves under a single roof.[38]

The cross-in-square church remained dominant in Bulgarian church architecture in the period of Byzantine rule (beginning in 1018) and in the age of the second Bulgarian kingdom (about 1185–1396). The famous Boyana Church of Saint Nicholas was built in the period between the tenth and twelfth centuries. It is in the form of a cross fit into a square (in 1259 a new narthex was added). Active church building took place in the thirteenth century in Tarnovo, the capital of the Bulgarian kingdom, and its suburbs. The Church of Peter and Paul in Tarnovo—an excellent example of cross-in-square architecture—dates to the beginning of the thirteenth century. Cross-in-square churches continued to predominate in municipal church architecture in Bulgaria right up to the middle of the eighteenth century when the

---

[37] Pastoforium (Gr. *pastoforia*, παστοφόρια)—additional extensions to the central apse.

[38] M. Vaklinova, "Early Christian and Early Byzantine Art on the Territory of Bulgaria" in *Orthodox Encyclopedia*, vol. 5 (Moscow, 2002), 595.

basilica became widespread. The domed basilica became prevalent beginning in the middle of the nineteenth century.

After the liberation of Bulgaria from the Turkish yoke in 1878, a new golden age of church architecture was observed. Masters from Russia, Austria, and other countries worked together with Bulgarian architects. Russian architects, in particular, helped to create Alexander Nevsky Cathedral in Sofia (1904–1912). The cathedral is a cross-in-square structure of impressive dimensions (the height of its dome is forty-five meters (147.6 feet), while its area is seventy by fifty-two meters (229.7 x 170.6 feet) and its capacity nearly five thousand people). Since 1951 Alexander Nevsky Cathedral has been the patriarchal cathedral.

A number of examples of Byzantine architecture are located on the territory of modern day Serbia, including Kosovo and Metohija. One of the earliest examples of the Rascian style of church architecture[39] is the Church of the Theotokos Euergetes at Studenica Monastery (1183), established by Prince Stefan Nemanja and designed in the form of a single-nave domed basilica. An excellent example of Serbian church architecture is the church of the Gračanica Monastery (*c.* 1315). It is rectangular in shape with a cross fit into it. A rectangular outer narthex with its own dome is joined to the church.

A final example of the Rascian style is the main church of the Dečani Monastery (1334/1335), built according to the design of architect Vitus of Trifun. It is a cross-in-square structure that combines Serbian, Byzantine, and Romano-gothic motifs in its architecture and decor. The drum of the dome is set on a cubic foundation built into a double-sloping roof. The church is richly adorned with sculptural and bas-relief depictions of people, angels, animals, and vegetation.

An overall decline in Serb culture resulting from the collapse of the Serbian kingdom after the death of King Stefan Dušan (1331–1355) and the defeat of the Serbs in the battle of Kosovo (1389) figured ill for the state of church architecture. After many Serb lands were integrated into the Ottoman Empire (1459), the pace of development for church building in Serbia significantly slowed and many ancient churches fell into desolation. The construction of churches resumed in those Serbian territories which at the turn of the eighteenth century

King Stefan Uroš IV Dušan. Fresco. Lesnovo Monastery. Circa 1350.

---
[39]Named after the state of Rascia in the Morava Valley.

were part of the Austro-Hungarian Empire. But the western style was predominant in the Orthodox church architecture of Austro-Hungary. Externally, these churches did not differ from Catholic churches. The possibility of returning to Byzantine models in church architecture did not occur again until the turn of the twentieth century, after the realization of Serbian independence.

Cathedral of Saint Sava in Belgrade.

Contemporary Serbian church building is characterized by a striving to restore its connection with Byzantine sources. The largest construction project of the Serbian Orthodox Church was the Cathedral of Saint Sava in Belgrade. Its construction began in 1935 but, due to World War II and the subsequent establishment of a communist regime in Yugoslavia, the project was halted and resumed only in 1985.

The church was consecrated in 2004 but decoration work continues to the present day. The Church of Hagia Sophia was used as a model during the planning phase, although its proportions were changed. The Belgrade cathedral surpasses Constantinople's model in terms of height (sixty-five meters), area (eighty-one by ninety-one meters), and the diameter of its dome (thirty-five meters), making it Europe's largest Orthodox church.

The fate of Orthodox churches in the Balkans was always directly related to political events occurring in Balkan countries. Foreign invasions proved disastrous to the state of church building. Many outstanding examples of architecture were completely wiped off the face of the earth as a result of foreign intervention or occupation. In our day, at the turn of the twenty-first century, Orthodox churches of Kosovo and Metohija have already fallen victim to vandalism by ethnic Albanians. Since 1999, when United Nations international forces were brought into Kosovo and Metohija, nearly two hundred churches were destroyed on the territory of these Serbian provinces, and many of these churches were architectural monuments of the tenth through thirteenth centuries. The remaining, intact churches and monasteries, which include Dečani and the famous Patriarchate of Peć, are now kept under the continuous protection of peacekeepers.

The particularities of the geopolitical situation of Romania and its historical development have had a significant influence on the architecture of Orthodox churches in that country. Located at the junction of eastern and western civilizations, Romania was for centuries a meeting place of various cultures. Byzantine and western influences coexist in the architecture and decoration of Romanian churches. Cross-in-square and basilica constructions coexist harmoniously and spherical domes coincide with sharp-pointed, spired peaks.

The golden age of Romanian church architecture occurred between the fifteenth and seventeenth centuries. The famous "painted" churches in the monasteries of Bucovina—namely Voroneț (1488), Humor (1530), Sucevița (1582–1584), and others—belong to that period. They are called "painted" because their outer walls are covered with frescoes depicting the saints. These paintings give the churches a unique and distinctive appearance. In design these churches are rectangular, stretched-out along the east-west axis, and have three altar conchs or semi-domes. The building is crowned with a double-sloped roof and a sharp-topped dome in the shape of a spire on top of a high drum.

A unique example of Romanian church architecture is the Church of the Descent of the Holy Spirit at Dragomirna Monastery (1606–1609). Like many other Romanian and Moldavian churches, it has the form of a triconch but it is distinguished by its unusual proportions. The height of the church is forty-two meters (137.7 feet) and its length is equal to its height while its breadth is a mere 9.6 meters (31.5 feet). Elongated in both length and height, this church is crowned with a tall drum on which rests a hat-shaped dome.

In later periods, one finds elements of many different styles in the architecture of Romanian Orthodox churches. These include classical, baroque, and gothic influences. At the turn of the twentieth century there was a heightened interest in Byzantine models. The cathedral in Sibiu (1902–1904) was built according to the model of Constantinople's Hagia Sophia, although two towers, attached to the western façade, are executed according to traditional Transylvanian baroque architecture. Byzantine influence is evident also in the structure of the cathedral in Sighișoara (1934–1937), which is crowned with a spherical dome on top of a massive drum.

3

Russian Church Architecture

Churches of Kievan Rus'

THE FIRST RUSSIAN CHURCHES WERE DESIGNED by Byzantine architects or in accordance with Byzantine models. The first cross-in-square churches appeared during the reign of the Great Prince Vladimir in Kiev. These included the famous Church of the Theotokos which received the name "Church of the Tithes" (989–996) for the reason that Vladimir gave one tenth of his treasury to its construction.

A golden age of church building, however, occurred during the reign of Yaroslav the Wise, when magnificent cross-in-square churches appeared in the large cities of Kievan Rus': Saint Sophia Cathedral in Kiev (1037–1044), the Saint Sophia Cathedrals of Novgorod

Holy Transfiguration Cathedral in Chernigov.

(1045–1052) and Polotsk (middle of the eleventh century), and Holy Transfiguration Cathedral in Chernigov (around 1036).

Kiev's Saint Sophia Cathedral is a masterpiece of Byzantine and Old Russian architecture. Designed by architects from Constantinople with the participation of Kievan masters, it has no direct counterpart in Byzantine architecture. The cathedral is a cross-in-square church with thirty cupolas. The interior space of the church is divided into five naves with five apses. The church is bordered with double-tiered galleries on its northern, western, and southern sides. The length of the cathedral excluding its galleries comprises 29.5 meters (96.8 feet) while its breadth measures 29.3 meters (96.1 feet). Including its galleries, its length and breadth are 41.7 meters (136.8 feet) and 54 meters (177.2 feet). Its height to the summit of the main cupola is 28.6 meters (93.8 feet) and each side of the square under the cupola measures 7.6 meters (24.9 feet). The interior walls of the church are decorated

49

with mosaics crafted from cubes of multi-colored smalt and covered with frescoes executed with water-based paints. The overall area covered by mosaics comprises 260 square meters (853 square feet) while the area covered by frescoes is nearly three thousand square meters (ten thousand square feet).

Saint Sophia Cathedral in Novgorod.

Novgorod's Saint Sophia Cathedral is a five-nave cross-in-square church with three main apses. Like Kiev's cathedral, it is bordered by double-tiered galleries on the northern, western, and southern sides. The central part of the cathedral is intersected by cylindrical vaults which form a cross, over which five cupolas rise. Yet another cupola crowns a tower with a staircase, situated in the south-western part of the cathedral. The basic measurements of the cathedral without its galleries are: 27 meters in length (88.6 feet) and 24.8 meters in breadth (81.4 feet). Together with the galleries, its length is 34.5 meters (113.2 feet) and its breadth is 39.3 meters (128.9 feet). The nearly square-shaped area under the cupola has sides of 6.19 and 6.28 meters (20.3 and 20.6 feet). The width of the cathedral's walls is 1.2 meters (3.9 feet). The height from the level of the ancient floor to the dove on top of the cross of the central cupola is thirty-eight meters (124.7 feet).

Intensive church construction continued during the reign of the successors of Yaroslav the Wise in Kiev and also in Novgorod, in Vladimir in Volhynia, in Vladimir-on-Klyazma, and in other cities of Rus'. During the second half of the eleventh and twelfth centuries new massive churches appeared: the Dormition Cathedral of the Kiev Caves Lavra (1073–1078), the cathedral of Saint Michael's Golden-Domed Monastery in Kiev (1108–1113), Saint Nicholas Cathedral in Novgorod (1113), Saint George Cathedral of Saint George (Yuriev) Monastery (1119), Dormition Cathedral in Vladimir-in-Volynia (1160), Dormition Cathedral (1153–1160) and Saint Dimitri Cathedral (1195–1196) in Vladimir-on-Klyazma. Other smaller churches are masterpieces of Russian architecture, such as Holy Transfiguration Cathedral in Pereslavl-Zalessky (1152), the Cathedral of the Holy Savior of Saint Euphrosyne Monastery in Polotsk (middle of twelfth century), and the Church of the Protection of the Mother of God on the Nerl (1165).

At the turn of the thirteenth century, church architecture developed with much activity in the territory of Smolensk. Architects from that region were invited to work in other cities of Rus' including Ryazan, Novgorod, Pskov, and Kiev. The architectural style of Smolensk of this period was marked by a striving to create a tower-like shape by observing the principle of successively increasing the building's height from its periphery to its center. Churches, stretched-out in height, expressed the common architectural ideal of the period. Some scholars perceive the influence of the western European gothic style in this "verticalization" of Russian churches. It is well known that during this period Polish and Hungarian masters worked in western Rus', especially in the Galician lands. In Kholm in the 1230s, a certain "artful Avdiy"[1] decorated the church with sculptural motifs and encrustation on stone and installed "Roman glass" (stained-glass panels)[2] in its windows. As we have already seen, the process of the gradual "verticalization" of churches began in Byzantium. This process continued in Rus' where it was possibly influenced by western European architecture.

Cathedral of Saint Dimitry in Vladimir.

As in Byzantium, churches in Rus' were built with the altars facing towards the East. East was understood to be the place on the horizon at which the sun rose on the day of laying the foundation stone of the church.[3]

The most common building material was brick. Various types of stone were also widely used. Stone boulders were commonly used to build foundations. Walls were generally built using a combination of brick and stone. Stone was also used in the process of facing walls. The most common binding materials were various types of lime mortar, finely ground ceramic called *tsemianka*, and sand.[4]

In designing church buildings, Russian architects used a system of proportions inherited from Byzantium. The diameter of the main dome was normally used as the basic measure or, in the later period, one side of the square under the dome was used.[5] The dimensions of the other elements of the building were interconnnected by a system of multiple or irrational ratios. These ratios were formed on the basis of the system of measurement inherited from Byzantium

---

[1] Avdii=Obadiah. The Slavic "artful" connotes "master" or "skilled artisan."
[2] Irina Buseva-Davydova, "Russian Church Art: 10th–20th Centuries" in *Orthodox Encyclopedia* (Moscow, 1997), 522.
[3] P. Rappoport, *Construction Industry of Ancient Rus' (10th–13th Centuries)* (St Petersburg, 1994), 106.
[4] Ibid., 5–8, 37–46, 74.
[5] K.N. Afanas'ev, *Construction of Architectural Forms by Old Russian Architects* (Moscow, 1961), 195, 200, 209.

(and before that, ancient Greece and ancient Egypt) which was based on the articulations of the human body.[6] Various types of sazhens were used for measurements. For example, in Novgorod in the twelfth century, the *measured* sazhen (175.6 cm/5.7 feet), *small* sazhen (142.2 cm/4.7 feet), *large* sazhen (216 cm/7.1 feet), *whole* sazhen, and others were used. Each sazhen consisted of four cubits. Therefore, one cubit of a measured sazhen (44 cm/17.3 inches) differed in length from one cubit of a small sazhen (35.5 cm/14 inches) or one cubit of a large sazhen (54 cm/21.3 inches).

This system appears complicated and confusing to us who are accustomed to using meters and centimeters, or other contemporary measurement systems. Nevertheless, Old Russian architects used this system with virtuosity in creating unsurpassed architectural masterpieces.

Architects were able to use two different types of sazhen when designing an architectural monument. In science this method became known as the method of paired measurement. A property of interpenetrating likenesses was imparted to the building when the method of paired measurement was applied. The paired measurement defines the order between the principal and co-subordinate elements. The principal element is measured using the larger measurement, while that which is secondary in importance is measured using the smaller measurement. The result is that "the space of the church is defined as a unified sequence of mean-proportional relationships. The breadth of the church is linked to its entire depth and the height of the space under the dome, while the breadth of the ring under the dome is linked to the breadth of the church and the height of the dome."[7]

In using the method of paired measurement, a relationship equal to the "golden ratio" was achieved. Novgorod's Savior Church on Nereditsa (1198) serves as an example of this. It is a cube-shaped building with a nearly square floor plan, with four pillars on which rests a dome. Two different sazhens were used in building the church, the measured sazhen and the small sazhen. The former relates to the double of the latter by the proportion of the golden ratio (0.618). Accordingly, the latter relates to the former in the proportion of a "double golden ratio" (0.809).[8]

[6]For more on this, see B.A. Rybakov, "Mathematics of Old Russian Architects," in *From the History of the Culture of Ancient Rus'* (Moscow, 1984), 82–103.

[7]Shevelev, *Shape Formation*, 34, 45–46.

[8]The double golden ratio (0.809) of a segment, divided according to the principle of the golden ratio (0.618) is equal to the correlation of the whole to the doubled larger portion of the segment (this correlation is equal to 1.618 divided by 2). If the length of the entire segment is 80.1 mm, in dividing it at the point of golden ratio the larger portion of the segment is equal to 49.5 mm, which doubled is equal to 99. The relationship of 80.1:99 is equal to 0.809.

Russian Church Architecture

In designing the church, "the application of a large-scale, universal system of calculation using sazhens was used by which doubling and dividing measures in half resulted in sequences based on the 'golden ratio'."[9] The distance from the square under the dome to the eastern wall is equal to ten small sazhens while the distance to the western wall is ten *measured* sazhens. The nucleus of the church is set inside a circle of ten cubits of a measured sazhen. The diameter of the drum and the breadth of the square under the dome are found to be in accordance with the golden ratio, while the diameter and height of the drum are in accordance with the double golden ratio.[10] By virtue of the strong interrelationship of the measurements of its main architectural elements, the church has an appearance of harmony and completion.

A characteristic of the exterior design of several Old Russian churches was the abundance of bas-reliefs on wall surfaces. Distinct from the painting of the church's interior walls, which consisted of especially religious subject matter, bas-reliefs on the façades of churches generally consisted of floral ornamentation. Images of birds and animals were common. Pinnacles of Old Russian architectural plastic arts are the cathedrals of Vladimir and Suzdal in Rus', especially the façades of the Church of the Protection of the Mother of God on the Nerl, Saint George Church in Yuryev-Polsky, and the Cathedral of Saint Dimitry in Vladimir. Bas-reliefs of the church of the Protection of the Mother of God on the Nerl depict King David, seated on a throne with the "psaltery" (harp) in his left hand while animals and birds listen to his playing. Christian subjects including feasts and depictions of the saints dominate the images of the façade of Saint George Church in Yuryev-Polsky (1230–1234) but one subject from antiquity is also found—"The Ascension of Alexander the Great."

King David. Bas-relief of the Church of the Protection of the Mother of God on the Nerl. 1165.

The walls of Vladimir's Cathedral of Saint Dimitry are adorned with images of people, animals, emblems, masks, and plants. Figures of prophets, Old Testament patriarchs, and martyrs are found in the small arcades of the lower register. A composition depicting all of creation offering a hymn of praise to God is presented on the western wall, in all three arcades. A prophet holding

[9] I.S. Shevelev, *The Principle of Proportions* (Moscow, 1986), 160.
[10] Idem, *Shape Formation*, 49; Idem, *Proportions*, 160–163.

a scroll in his hand is found in the center of the composition. He is surrounded by angels, prophets, winged horses, lions, and other animals, birds, and plants. Similar compositions are found on the southern and northern walls. Overall there are nearly three hundred figures on each wall. This rich symbolism emphasizes the significance of the church as an image of the cosmos, a liturgical organism in which every member, including plants and animals, is called to praise God:

> . . . rows of wild beasts, fanciful animals, birds and plants . . . recurring many times and clearly intended as ornamentation—the unifying theme is the glory of the great world of God, ineffable in its "wonders" and unknown in its mysteries. Decorations are compatible with the overall religious mood. Birds from the heavens are in fast flight, streaming together with angels who fly towards the Wisdom of God, seated in glory on the King's throne. Lions and fearsome griffins approach with trepidation the footstool of the throne, while beneath them, plants are in luxuriant bloom. In a word, the decorative aspect defers to the overall religious theme. . . . The world presented here is not the simple, real world known to all, but rather the world of the Wisdom of God which reveals itself by divine enlightenment . . .[11]

Church-Building Following the Mongol Invasion. Church Architecture in Muscovite Rus'

The energetic advancement of church architecture in Rus' was interrupted by the invasion of the armies of Batu Khan in 1238 and the submission of the Russian lands to the Golden Horde. In subsequent decades many churches were burned down or demolished and former centers of church building fell into decline. In the few churches built during this period, a tendency prevailed toward modest dimensions and scant decoration. This was primarily the result of the strained material conditions in which clients, architects, and builders found themselves.

By the end of the thirteenth century, however, a resurgence of church building was already observed in regions where political and civil consolidation was taking place. The fortification of new principalities made the construction of new cathedrals necessary. Among these was the Holy Transfiguration Cathedral in Tver (1285–1290).

In the second quarter of the fourteenth century active construction began in Moscow, where the Dormition Cathedral (1326–1327), the Cathedral of the Savior

[11] *Russian Antiquities*, 6, 29–30.

on the Bor (1330), and the Belfry of Saint John Climacus (1329) were built. In 1367, when the first Moscow Kremlin was built, all of these structures were located within the Kremlin. Not one of them has survived to the present, and consequently new churches having the same names were built on the sites of the original churches.

Cathedral of the Savior on the Bor. Photo beginning of 20th c.

Among the most significant churches of the period of the last quarter of the fourteenth and first half of the fifteenth centuries are the Dormition cathedrals in Kolomna (1380) and Zvenigorod (around 1400), the Cathedral of the Nativity of Savvino-Storozhevsky Monastery (1405), the Cathedral of the Savior of the Andronikov Monastery in Moscow (around 1420), and Holy Trinity Cathedral of Holy Trinity-St Sergius Lavra (1422–1423).

The last quarter of the fifteenth century and the beginning of the sixteenth were marked by the construction of five extraordinary examples of church architecture on the territory of the Moscow Kremlin. These are the new Dormition Cathedral (1475–1479), the Annunciation Cathedral (1489), and the Archan-

Cathedral of the Nativity. Savvino-Storozhevsky Monastery.

gel Cathedral (1505–1508), as well as the churches of the Deposition of the Robe (1484–1486) and the belfry-church of Saint John of the Ladder known as the *Bell Tower of Ivan the Great*. Together they form a united ensemble of churches designed to highlight the role of Moscow as the new church center of Rus'.

The chief architects of the three Kremlin cathedrals were Italians. Aristotle Fioravanti of Bologna built Dormition Cathedral, the Venetian Aloisio the New built Archangel Cathedral, and Bon Fryazin (in Italian, Marco Bono—Ed.) was commissioned for the project of the Bell Tower of Ivan the Great. Vladimir's Dormition Cathedral was used as a model for Moscow's Dormition Cathedral, but its architect did not blindly copy his model. Rather, he favored the tradition of Russo-Byzantine architecture while applying techniques of western European building arts. The outcome was a cathedral of proper shape with strictly geometric proportions built on the Kremlin's Cathedral Square. The vaults of the cathedral rest on six pillars, two of which are square (they separate the altar from the remaining space of the church) and four are rounded, column-shaped pillars.

By the time of the construction of the Kremlin cathedrals in Rus', the tradition was firmly rooted of separating the sanctuary from the rest of the church with a tall wall of icons that was known as the iconostasis. This phenomenon was not known in Byzantine church architecture of the first millennium; there the sanctuary was separated from the rest of the church by a transparent screen. Small sacred images (in medallions) were placed on the architrave. At the end of the first and beginning of the second millennium (it is difficult to establish the exact time), icons of Christ and the Most Holy Theotokos began to be placed in the space between the columns of the sanctuary screen. They were either hung on the architrave or placed vertically on the partitions between the columns. In this way, the sanctuary screen was gradually reconceived and transformed into an iconostasis while still in Byzantium. Over the centuries the number of icons increased. But in the Greek tradition the iconostasis never grew to such dimensions as are characteristic of post-Mongol Rus'. To this day, iconostases in the Greek East are comprised of a single tier. Royal doors are not tall and sometimes they are altogether absent.

In Rus' the iconostasis came to stand as the main element of the church's interior adornment. In the post-Mongol period multiple-tiered iconostases became widespread. The number of tiers increased over the centuries so that by the fifteenth century triple-tiered iconostases appeared; by the sixteenth century four-tiered iconostases, and by the seventeenth century five, six, and seven tiers appeared.

Another visible difference between Russian and Byzantine churches was the shape of the dome, which in Rus' gradually acquired the shape of an onion bulb. As noted earlier, there already existed in Byzantium the tendency of gradually increasing the height of the drum under the dome while simultaneously making the diameter of the dome smaller. In Rus' this tradition continued, but the very shape of the dome acquired a different, more "verticalized" outline as well. The origin of onion domes as well as the time of their appearance is the subject of discussion among scholars. Some scholars identify their appearance in the thirteenth century[12] while others believe that they emerged much later, for instance, at the turn of the seventeenth century.[13] It is even suggested that onion domes were inspired by the helmets of Russian warriors. Whatever the case may be, onion domes became

---

[12]Boris Rybakov, *"The Tale of Igor's Campaign" and its Contemporaries* (Moscow, 1971), 12; Nikolai Voronin, "Architectural Monument as a Historical Source (Notes to Statement of a Question)," *Soviet Architecture* 19 (Moscow, 1954), 73.

[13]Alexei Lidov, "The Canopy over the Holy Sepulchre: On the Origins of Onion-Shaped Domes," in *The Iconography of Architecture* (Moscow, 1990), 58.

firmly established in Russian church architecture, although they never completely replaced the traditional late-Byzantine semi-spherical form.

The famous art historian Prince Eugene Trubetskoi wrote about the spiritual meaning of onion domes at the turn of the twentieth century. He saw in the bulbous shape of onion domes the image of a flame:

> In the ancient church not only the main domes but also the subsidiary ones above the outer walls, and the climbing exterior ornaments, often have the flame-like, pointed form of a bulb. Sometimes all these parts combine into a pyramidal bulbous shape. In the general elan toward the cross everything seeks the flame, imitates its form, narrows to a peak in its gradual ascent. But only when it reaches the real point of contact of the two worlds—that is, at the foot of the cross—does this ardent aspiration burst into a bright flame and unite with the celestial gold.[14]

As in Byzantium, it was customary in Rus' to erect a cross on top of the dome. Whereas the cross in Byzantium had four ends, in Russia a cross having two extra cross bars and a total of eight ends became ubiquitous. The eight-ended cross in Rus' came to be perceived as "Orthodox" as opposed to the "Catholic" four-ended cross.

Sometimes a crescent moon is found on the bottom part of crosses on domes. According to the information available to us, this type of cross adorned the domes of several churches of the twelfth century, in particular the Church of the Intercession of the Holy Virgin on the Nerl, the Cathedral of Saint Dimitry in Vladimir, and Assumption Cathedral in Staraya Ladoga. Here, the crescent moon in no way represents a Muslim symbol and does not indicate, as it is sometimes suggested, the superiority of Christianity over Islam. The crescent moon was one of the state symbols of Byzantium (it symbolized royal power) and only after the conquest of Constantinople by the Turks did it become a symbol of the Ottoman Empire. The depiction of the crescent moon is found on Old Russian icons, vestments, and book miniatures. Moreover, the cross with the crescent moon brings to mind an anchor (the symbol of salvation, concordant with the symbolism of the Church as a ship), a blossomed cross, a chalice, or a trampled-upon snake.

Side chambers, built to the right and left of the main sanctuary, were yet another essential way in which Russian churches differed from Byzantine churches. We

---

[14]Eugene Trubetskoi, "Two Worlds in Old Russian Icon Paintings" in Gertrude Vakar, tr., *Icons: Theology in Color* (Crestwood, NY: St Vladimir's Seminary Press, 1973), 65; hereafter *Icons*. Italics are the author's.

Cathedral of the Protection of the Most Holy Theotokos on the Moat. Moscow.

recall that in Byzantine triple-nave churches the sanctuary was located in the center of the central nave, whereas side naves were occupied by the table of oblation and vestry. In Russian churches the table of oblation was gradually transferred to the central sanctuary while side naves were used as additional rooms having their own altars and tables of oblation. Churches with three sanctuaries, one at the center and two at the side, became quite widespread, but there could be even more side-sanctuaries. Moscow's Church of the Protection of the Most Holy Theotokos on the Moat, which is famous as the Church of Saint Basil the Blessed, contains nine side-sanctuaries. A record twenty-nine side-sanctuaries are contained in the Resurrection Cathedral of the New Jerusalem Monastery.

An architectural style featuring churches with a "tent-like" roof became widespread in the sixteenth century. The tent-roof church is a structure in which a tower that is tall and narrow at its top expresses the central motif. Tent-roof churches, built of stone, emerged in the sixteenth century as an independent and totally original architectural style having no direct counterpart in Byzantine or any other tradition of church architecture. However, these churches did appear during a period of direct involvement of Italian masters.

Church of the Ascension in Kolomenskoe. Moscow.

The first famous tent-roof church is the Church of the Ascension in Kolomenskoe (1532–1533). The tent-shaped roof of the church is mounted on a tall octagonal superstructure which rises from the basic quadrilateral structure (*chetverik*) of the church, and the church is not crowned with an onion-shaped dome. Clearly, the octagonal superstructure serves as the drum for a dome and the tent-roof itself serves as the dome. In the majority of other famous tent-roof churches, a small cupola is placed on the top of the tented roof. In multiple-domed tent-roof churches (in particular, the Church of Saint Basil the Blessed), the dome, located at the top of the tent-roof, was significantly smaller than the other domes.

Russian Church Architecture

The floor plan of the Church of the Ascension in Kolomensk is an equal-sided cross; however, the height of the church exceeds the length of its *chetverik* by virtue of the elongated tent-roof. This church amazed and delighted its contemporaries, both Russian and foreign, with its architectural form. In the middle of the nineteenth century, in his letter to Prince V.F. Odoevsky, the French composer Hector Berlioz described his impression of the church:

> There was nothing more striking to me than the monument of Old Russian architecture in the village of Kolomensk. Much have I seen and admired and many things have astonished me, but that era, the medieval period in Russia, which left its mark in this village, was a wonder of wonders to me. I have seen Strasbourg Cathedral, which was built over centuries; I have stood next to the Milan Cathedral, yet aside from mortared embellishments, I found nothing there. But here before my gaze stood the beauty of perfection and I gasped in awe. Here in the mysterious silence, amid the harmonious beauty of the finished form, I beheld architecture of a new kind. I beheld man soaring on high. And I stood amazed.[15]

The secret of such a strong effect of the church on its viewer is explained not only by the originality of its architectural form but also by the harmony of its proportion, drawn up with maximum care and precision. The Kolomensk church's system of proportions was analyzed in detail by Joseph Shevelev. It was built on the principle of the same paired measurement which more than four centuries earlier had been used in building the Church of the Savior on the Nereditsa: *measured* sazhens and *small* sazhens. Movement from one size to another is made according to the relationship between these two measures and the golden ratio. By the masterful use of this system of proportional interconnections, the effect achieved is one of the church stretching upwards.[16]

---

[15] Lev Lyubimov, *The Art of Ancient Rus'* (Moscow, 1981), 270. <http://bridgetomoscow.com/kolomenskoye-museum-estate_2>, July 25, 2013.

[16] The starting point of the proportional sequence is the lowest point of the church, the *chetverik*, placed on the *podklet* (ground floor); the end of the sequence is the highest point of the cross. Proportions develop in the following way (M—*measuring* sazhen, T—*small* sazhen): "The height of the *chetverik*, including the *podklet* (57T), relates to the height of the tent, including the height of the *ordernoi* part of the eight-sided form, bearing the tent (57M), as the height of the drum, including the crown (15.2T), to the height of the order of the eight-sided form (15.2M), as the height of the cross (12.2T) relates to the height of the drum with the crown (12.2M), as the width of the cross—its horizontal span (10T)—relates to the height of the cross (10M), as the lower bar of the cross (5.5T) to the highest bar of the cross (5.5M)"; see Shevelev, *Principle of Proportions*, 167.

Another excellent example of tent-roof architecture is a church mentioned earlier—the Church of Saint Basil the Blessed on Red Square in Moscow (1555–1561). This church was built on the order of Ivan the Terrible as a memorial to the capture of Kazan. In structural terms, the church presents an ensemble which includes a tent-roof church surrounded by eight more churches which are positioned symmetrically and interconnected by a system of passages. Each of the eight churches is adorned with windows, corbel arches (*kokoshniki*), bays, and cornices and is crowned with a drum and dome, each of which is unique. Essentially this is a unique type of "church-city" whose interior space is divided into numerous sections. Each section has a finished look while remaining a part of the intended overall architectural ensemble.

The exterior design of the Church of Saint Basil the Blessed demonstrates a trend that began in the sixteenth century and was further developed in the seventeenth century: enhancing the church's decor with kokoshniki, cornices, platbands, tiles, and other elements involving the use of patterns. Some see in this trend signs of secular influence on church architecture and a striving to make the church appear more like royal or boyar palaces. In reality, however, "rich decoration first became widespread in churches, not in secular buildings, and is clearly explained by the desire to decorate the house of God 'more than all others' and in accordance with tastes which had changed with the times."[17]

*Resurrection Cathedral.
New Jerusalem Monastery.*

In this respect the grandiose Resurrection Cathedral of New Jerusalem Monastery is unique. Its construction began under Patriarch Nikon and was completed only after his death (1658–1664, 1678–1685). The cathedral is a cross-in-square church with four pillars, surrounded on three sides with double-tiered galleries. Its design corresponds to a prototype—the Church of the Sepulcher of the Lord in Jerusalem; however, the decoration of the church's exterior and interior, which uses tiles of polychrome ceramics and white-stone fretwork, has little in common with its model in Jerusalem. At the east side a crypt—an underground church—is built into the church. At the east side a rotunda adjoins the church and contains the chapel of the Sepulcher of the Lord. The rotunda is crowned with a tent-roof measuring eighteen meters (fifty-nine feet) in height. The tent-roof of Resurrection Cathedral differs noticeably from

---

[17] Buseva-Davydova, *Church Arts*, 528.

traditional tent-roofs of the sixteenth and seventeenth centuries by its proportions, which are significantly wider at the bottom than traditional tent-roofs, and also by the presence of three rows of windows projecting outwards.

An important element of Old Russian Church architecture is the bell tower and belfry. The bell tower is a tower-like structure commonly crowned with a dome. It could be built into the church itself or it could stand separate from it. The tower is divided into several tiers. The upper tiers are smaller in area than the lower ones. The bells are usually situated in the upper tier, as this is conducive to the dispersion of sound to a great distance. Sometimes the bells are placed in different tiers. Sound from the bells flows out through wide, arch-shaped windows.

The Bell Tower of Ivan the Great, mentioned earlier, is a most brilliant example of a Russian bell tower. Situated on the territory of the Moscow Kremlin, it was originally a triple-tiered pillar nearly sixty meters (about two hundred feet) in height. Two lower tiers of the bell tower were designed as an eight-sided form while the upper tier consisted of a single short gallery crowned with a small dome. Bells of various sizes were situated on all three tiers. In the year 1600 the bell tower was expanded so that its height increased to eighty-one meters (265.7 feet). Eighteen bells are contained in the Bell Tower of Ivan the Great, the largest of which, called "Dormition," weighs four thousand *poods*.[18]

Bell Tower of Ivan the Great. Moscow. 16th–17th c.

In contrast to the bell tower, the belfry was not a tower-like structure. Its design could be an elongated rectangular form—either a tall wall crowned with several arched openings, in which bells are situated, or an oblong addition to the western wall of a church. A classic example is the belfry of the Rostov Kremlin (built between 1682 and 1687). It is a wall with an upper gallery, covered with a double-pitched roof on which four domes rest on tall, narrow drums. The largest bell, which is called *Sysoy* and weighs two thousand poods (thirty-six tons), was placed under the largest dome; the remaining bells were placed under three smaller domes. Belfries were often preferred to bell towers for practical

Belfry of the Rostov Kremlin. 1682–1687.

---

[18] A pood is approximately equal to 16 kg (roughly 36 lbs).

considerations: more bells could be placed in an oblong gallery than in a narrow bell tower. The bells of a belfry were operated directly from the ground.

During the entire history of church building in Rus', starting in the pre-Mongol period, the building of wooden churches developed simultaneously alongside the building of stone churches. It is evident that in terms of sheer numbers, wooden churches significantly surpassed more expensive stone churches. Wooden churches were widespread in rural areas but they were built in cities as well. For example, right up to the seventeenth century, church building in Kostroma primarily involved wood. Wooden churches were built from common lumber consisting of logs fastened together to form a quadrangular structure. Each row of logs was called a *crown*. The lowest crown was usually placed on a stone foundation. The quadrangular framework was crowned with a small dome. Sometimes several frameworks were joined together to form a cross-in-square construction.

Wooden churches are not as long-lived as stone churches and for this reason many have not survived to our day. The earliest wooden churches preserved today date back to the sixteenth century. A unique collection of wooden churches is found on the island of Kizhi, by the waters of Lake Onega. A pearl of the architectural ensemble at Kizhi—the Church of the Transfiguration (1714)—is a cross-in-square church crowned with twenty-two bells installed on four tiers and closely stuck together. The bells stand on tall kokoshniki. The domes and kokoshniki are covered with small, wooden shingles called *lemekh*, commonly used when building with wood in northern Rus'. The central part of the church is surrounded by spacious galleries and a tent-shaped bell tower stands adjacent to the church.

Russian Church Architecture in the Post-Petrine Period

At the beginning of the eighteenth century, Peter the Great carved a "window to Europe." Through this window foreign tastes and standards came gushing profusely into Rus'. Petrine reform touched all aspects of church life including church building. Traditional cross-in-square churches came to be replaced with new architectural structures which had no intrinsic connection with the church architecture that had developed over many years in Byzantium and Rus'. The most significant churches of this period reproduce western models of the baroque period. The interior of churches is also oriented on baroque models foreign to the Orthodox tradition. Italian architects or Russians who had studied in the West were appointed to manage the construction of churches. While in the sixteenth century Italian architects appointed to build the cathedrals of the Moscow Kremlin tended to observe the traditions of Russian models, the opposite now came to be: Russian architects began to reproduce western models.

Western standards began to penetrate into Russian church architecture even before the beginning of Peter's reforms. At the end of the seventeenth century the style known as "Naryshkin baroque" (named after the boyar L.K. Naryshkin, the uncle of Peter) became widespread in church architecture. This style was characterized by a complication of architectural construction, symmetry of composition, application of semi-circular forms in the design of side sanctuaries, an abundance of decoration, and a rejection of a great many elements of traditional Russian architecture in order to conform to western baroque standards. The Church of the Intercession (1690–1694) in Moscow's Fili district was built in this style. The foundation of the church is a chetverik with semi-circular projections adjoined to it. A wide octagonal structure is placed on top of the chetverik, and another structure (a bell tower) is placed on top of that structure. Yet another structure stands on this one and serves as the foundation for a faceted dome (whose shape is reminiscent of the domes of Austrian and Bavarian churches). Richly decorated with white-stone platbands and delicate tracery ornamentation, the church resembles a cake prepared by a skillful pastry cook.

Church of the Protection of the Most Holy Theotokos in Fili District. Moscow.

The Church of the Sign in Dubrovtsi (1690–1694) was built according to the same design. It is the most fanciful example of the Naryshkin baroque style. The upper octagonal superstructure is crowned not by a dome but by a depiction of a royal crown. The portal of the church is decorated with statues of saints, made by Italian masters in the manner characteristic of the period of the Renaissance.

At the beginning of the eighteenth century, churches were still measured using *arshins* and sazhens, but Peter changed the meaning of traditional Russian measurements by coordinating them with the English foot. A great sazhen was reduced by approximately one percent and became equal to seven English feet (213.36 cm). Other elements of measurement were correspondingly changed. The reduced great sazhen came to be called simply *sazhen* and all the diversity of other Old Russian sazhens was abolished. The possibility of using the method of double measurement disappeared together with the measures. Consequently, the traditional means of constructing proper proportions in Rus' receded into the past.

Saints Peter and Paul Cathedral. Saint Petersburg.

Peter did not see the connection between faith and the shape of church buildings. In 1699, after the capture of Azov, he ordered that three mosques be converted into Orthodox churches. In the construction of the northern capital of the empire, scores of Orthodox churches were built; however, all of the major churches of Saint Petersburg were built in accordance to models of western Catholic cathedrals. In designing and constructing the Cathedral of Saints Peter and Paul (1712–1733), the architect Domenico Trezzini used the shape of an elongated rectangular basilica. On the western side a heavy triple-tier bell tower was added, capped by a tall, narrow spire on which a gilded sculpture of an angel holding a cross was placed. The total height of the bell tower, together with the spire and sculpture, comprises 122.5 meters (about 402 feet). (And at that height, it stands one and a half times higher than the Bell Tower of Ivan the Great.)

During the reign of Empress Elizabeth Petrovna (1741–1761) the dominance of western standards in church building lessened to some extent. Elizabeth felt that the "Roman manner" did not befit Orthodox churches and she sponsored the building of churches in the "Greek style," by which she primarily had in mind five-dome cruciform-style churches.[19] The Italian architect Bartolomeo F. Rastrelli built the Resurrection Cathedral of Smolensk Monastery (1748–1764) in this style. The cathedral has no direct link to traditional Russian architecture either in its proportions, its external appearance, or its interior. The church is a typical example of the baroque style with its characteristic luxuriant decoration. A similar architectural conception lay at the foundation of the five-dome church in Moscow dedicated to Saint Clement of Rome (1742–1774).

During the reign of Catherine the Great (*1762–1796), the baroque style was replaced with classicism, the architectural style of all of Europe in the eighteenth century. This style was characterized by austerity and logic of form, with a penchant

---

[19] Buseva–Davydova, *Church Arts*, 530.

for the square, circle, and cross, and by the use of antique elements of decoration, especially columns with capitals. Holy Trinity Cathedral of Saint Alexander Nevsky Lavra (1776–1790), built according to the design of Ivan Starov, is an example of early classicism. The design of this church is similar to that of Saint Peter's Basilica in Rome. The cruciform interior space of the church is divided into three naves. Vaults rest upon massive pylons. The church is capped by a wide-domed rotunda. The façade of the church is decorated with a monumental portico with six Doric columns. Two bell towers, also decorated with columns, rise on the west side over the porch.

Moscow's Church of the Transfiguration of the Lord (1834–1836) on Bolshaya Ordynka Street was built in the style of classicism according to the design of the architect Osip Bovet. The church's floor plan is two circles, placed on the sides of a square with curved edges. The main space of the church is located in the center of a rounded construction which is crowned with a dome that stands on a short drum with rectangular windows. The dome is supported by twelve marble columns. The circular space of the central space runs into a square-shaped space in which two flanking side sanctuaries are situated. On the western side, the church is connected to a circular bell tower.

Another example of late classicism is Saint Isaac's Cathedral (1818–1858) in Saint Petersburg, built according to the design of the French architect Auguste de Montferrand. The height of this grandiose structure is 101.5 meters (about 333 feet) while its length and breadth are nearly one hundred meters (328.1 feet). The outer diameter of the dome is 25.8 meters (84.6 feet). Portals with colonnades are built along four sides. (The form of the portal, as in many buildings, is in the classical style reminiscent of the Parthenon in Athens.) The drum of the dome is also decorated with colonnades. The total

Saint Isaac's Cathedral. Saint Petersburg. 1818–1858.

number of columns is one hundred and twelve, all made up entirely of granite. On the corners and top of the pediments are statues of the twelve apostles.

A general characteristic of churches from the post-Petrine period, built in the baroque or classical style, is often the absence of a correlation between the form of the structure and its liturgical purpose. Often a huge church would have a disproportionately small sanctuary, resulting in discomfort during divine services. In some very large churches the sanctuary was so distant from the main part of the church that it was difficult for worshippers to see and hear the service. The rejection of arched constructions, as well as other traditional elements of Byzantine and Russian architecture that allowed for the amplification of sound, negatively affected the acoustics of churches.

Whether it was luxuriant baroque decoration or colonnades in the spirit of antiquity, the interior adornment of churches of this period was hardly compatible with the form and content of Orthodox worship. The impression of foreignness between the architectural forms of churches and the liturgical service taking place within them was made greater by the substitution of traditional Orthodox iconography with pictorial images executed in the sentimental manner characteristic of works by Renaissance artists.

Alongside churches constructed in the baroque and classical style, churches were built in the Russian Empire in the cross-in-square style throughout all of the eighteenth and nineteenth centuries. Saint Petersburg belonged mainly to the "avant-garde," where the tastes of the emperors and empresses became the main criterion for architectural styles. Country estates of the nobility and landed gentry imitated the tastes of the imperial capital. Together with these new architectural forms, traditional forms of church architecture recalling the era of Muscovite Rus' were preserved and developed in provincial cities, towns, and villages.

Holy Trinity-Saint Sergius Lavra.

It is important to note that, throughout the history of Russian church architecture, disparate architectural styles could be found side-by-side within a single time period and within a single complex of churches. The architectural ensemble of the Holy Trinity-Saint Sergius Lavra serves as an example of this. The lavra was created between the fifteenth and nineteenth centuries and stands as a unique "collection" of churches and buildings which represent all the major stylistic trends occurring during this time span. The white stone Trinity Cathedral (1422–1423) was built in the traditional Muscovite architectural style of the fifteenth century. The Church of the Holy Spirit (1476) reproduces traditional Pskov architecture. The main cathedral of the lavra, Dormition Cathedral (1559–1585), was built according to the model of the Kremlin's Dormition Cathedral. The Church of Venerable Zosima and Savvatiy of the Solovetsky Islands (1635–1638) is an example of the tent-roof architecture. The richly decorated trapeza of the Church of Venerable Sergius of Radonezh (1686–1692) is similar to the architecture of palaces and boyar mansions of the end of the seventeenth century. The architecture of the Gate Church of Saint John the Baptist (1693–1699) has vividly expressed baroque elements (the so-called *Stroganov style*) and the Chapel-over-the-Well (end of the seventeenth century) is a typical example of Naryshkin baroque. The small eight-sided Church of Saint Micah (1734) is covered with a so-called *Dutch* roof and capped by a small dome. The Church of the Virgin of Smolensk (1746–1748) and its eighty-eight meter high (289 feet) bell tower (1741–1770, by architects Dmitry Ukhtomsky and Ivan Michurin) are typical structures of the Elizabethan baroque. The obelisk (1792), which stands in the lavra's central square, belongs to the period of classicism. The architectural ensemble is completed by structures created in the Russian style of the seventeenth century and executed according to the design of architect A. A. Latkov at the end of the nineteenth century.

A renewed interest in traditional forms of church architecture occurred in the second quarter of the nineteenth century. This happened in parallel with the growth of national self-consciousness and the increase in anti-western sentiment in Russian society. This break is reflected in the history of the design and construction of Moscow's Christ the Savior Cathedral (1839–1883). The original plan for the church, devised by Aleksandr Vitberg in 1817, was conceived as a memorial to the victory in the War of 1812. According to his plan, the church was intended to be a massive construction in the style of classicism with a domed rotunda of gigantic breadth. Porticos with colonnades were to be situated along four sides of the church (similar to Saint Isaac's Cathedral in Saint Petersburg). The cathedral's courtyard was to be decorated by a prolonged, ellipse-shaped colonnade (similar to the colonnade of Saint Petersburg's Kazan Cathedral) and obelisks.

During the reign of Nicholas I, the decision was made to reject this ambitious project in favor of a different plan prepared by the architect Konstantin Thon. The new project was consistent with the new influences. The cathedral was conceived as a synthesis of Byzantine and Russian architectural styles; however, overall it was founded on classicism. A leaning towards ancient Russian models was expressed through the church's five domes and four pillars. The overall corpus of the church was girded by a covered gallery. Keel-shaped gables called *zakomari* were incorporated in the design of the church and its domes were onion-shaped. The sanctuary's canopy was designed in the form of an eight-sided tent-roof church, and this imparted originality and novelty to the project while at the same time connecting it stylistically with the traditions of Old Russian architecture. The cathedral's location on a high hill on the shores of the Moscow River, in direct proximity to the Kremlin

Original Design for Cathedral of Christ the Savior. Architect: A. Vitburg. Watercolor. 1825.

Cathedral of Christ the Savior. Moscow. 1837–1883.

while at the same time remaining at some distance from it, in such a way that the church did not flow into the ensemble of the Kremlin cathedrals, made it one of the most recognized architectural structures in Moscow.

The grandeur of the Cathedral of Christ the Savior delighted many people of its day. Still, praise for the cathedral and its architect was by no means universal. According to critics, Thon incorporated the exterior forms of the Old Russian style without sufficient penetration into its inner essence. Specifically, as far as it is known, Thon did not use Old Russian measurements in designing the Cathedral of Christ the Savior. As we have seen, these were the key to building structures with proper proportions. Mathematical measurements, which lay at the foundation of Old Russian church building, were of little interest to Thon. He merely incorporated a few external elements from the Old Russian architectural style. As a result, the church appears to be similar to Old Russian churches but it is devoid of harmony and proportionality. One of its critics, Prince Eugene Trubetskoi, saw in the architecture of the Cathedral of Christ the Savior the expression of an overall spiritual decline, expressed in the loss of the image according to which Old Russian churches were built:

> Present-day Russia is divided from this image by the abyss of her spiritual decline. We can measure it by simply taking a walk in Moscow, outside the Kremlin, and studying the architecture of the "forty times forty" churches that used to be Moscow's glory. We shall see some classical monuments to mindlessness, that is meaninglessness. . . . There are belfries capped by a gilt Empire column that would make a fairly handsome stand for a livingroom clock. . . . Every inhabitant of Moscow knows the church capped by a crown instead of a bulb—because the Empress Elizabeth was crowned in it.[20] One of the largest monuments to costly senselessness is the church of the Savior. It resembles a huge samovar around which patriarchal Moscow has cozily foregathered. Essentially, these monuments to modernity express the mood that has caused

---

[20] The church referenced here is the Church of the Renewal of the Temple of the Resurrection in Barashi, where, according to tradition, Empress Elizabeth Petrovna was married to Count Razumovsky. At the present time the church, considerably reconstructed during the Soviet period, is not used for divine services.

the ruin of a great religious art. What we have here is not merely poor taste but something much bigger: deep spiritual deterioration.[21]

This harsh assessment of Russian church architecture of the post-Petrine period is completely subjective, and in relation to the Cathedral of the Savior, it is greatly unfair. Despite its flaws, indicated above, the architecture of this church shows an obvious penchant for traditional forms. Compared with the examples of the Elizabethan Empire style mentioned by Trubetskoi, the Cathedral of Christ the Savior represents an important step on the path to liberation from "western captivity" in church architecture.

At the turn of the twentieth century, certain trends referred to as "Russian" or "Neo-Russian" are seen. The most vivid example of the "Russian" style is Saint Petersburg's Church of the Resurrection of Christ, the Church of the Savior on Spilled Blood (1883–1907). The majority of details of the exterior and interior are copied from churches of the seventeenth century. The exterior of the church is consciously modeled after the Yaroslavl churches and somewhat after Moscow's Cathedral of the Protection of the Most Holy Theotokos on the Moat, commonly known as Saint Basil's Cathedral. Specifically this is seen in the decorative richness, the abundance of tile and mosaic decoration, and architectural details such as corbel arches (kokoshniki), gables, engaged columns, and protruding cornices. At the foundation of the composition of the church lies a *chetverik* on which an eighty-one meter high (265.7 feet) tent rests. On the west end a bell tower is attached to the *chetverik* and crowned with a dome. The nine domes of the cathedral are coated with gold-leaf and enamel. Inside, the church is completely overlaid with mosaics with an overall area of more than 7,000 square meters (about an acre and three quarters).

The creators of Saint Petersburg's Savior on the Waters Church were greatly inspired by an effort to emulate Old Russian architectural models, especially the Cathedral of Saint Dimitry in Vladimir. This church-memorial, which was consecrated in 1911, was dedicated to the memory of sailors who perished in the Russo-Japanese War. Plaques bearing the names of the deceased were hung on the interior of the church. The church survived a mere twenty years and functioned for only seven. In 1918 it was nationalized by the Bolsheviks. Divine services ceased and in 1931 it was demolished.

Many churches were built in Russia and beyond her borders in the same style, in particular Saint Nicholas Cathedral in Vienna (1893–1899), the Church of the

---

[21] Trubetskoi, *Icons*, 65–66. Edited by the author.

Cathedral of Saint Nicholas. Vienna.

Church of the Resurrection of Christ in Sokolniki District. Moscow. 1909–1913.

Nativity of Christ in Florence (1899–1903), and Saint Nicholas Cathedral in Nice (1903–1912).

The most magnificent of these churches is Vienna's Cathedral of Saint Nicholas. It is the largest church of the Moscow Patriarchate outside of its canonical territory. Built according to the design of the Saint Petersburg architect G.I. Kotov, the cathedral is a tent-roof church having five cupolas and a bell tower capped by a sixth cupola. The height of the church together with its cross is nearly sixty meters (197 feet). The tent rests upon four columns of red granite with carved capitals reminiscent of the architectural elements of Byzantine churches. The cathedral is divided into upper and lower churches. The interior space of the upper church has the form of a cross fit into a the square of the walls. The building is bordered by a gallery reminiscent of similar galleries in Old Russian churches.

"Neo-Russian" is the name given to the style of church architecture which arose in the last quarter of the nineteenth century and survived right up to the Russian Revolution of 1917. This style is characterized by a rejection of direct copying of individual decorative elements and a striving to a more general reproduction of stylistic details of Russian architecture. At the same time it seeks to incorporate individual elements of the modern style. A vivid example of this combination of styles is Moscow's Church of the Resurrection in Sokolniki (1910–1913). It is a cross-in-square church with four columns; however, its sanctuary apse is directed towards the south, not the east, which violates a centuries-old tradition. Wide gables (*zakomari*) are found at all the cross-ends of the church's floor plan. The church is crowned with a tent-roof with a vertically elongated cupola. Four narrow drums, on which four cupolas rest, adjoin the tent-roof. Another four cupolas are positioned on the outer corners of the church's roof. The interior space of the church contains three naves. A disproportionately small sanctuary stands at a significant elevation and is situated in the southern portion of the central nave. Two more side sanctuaries are located in the flanking naves. The church reveals the intentional stylization of secondary elements of both its exterior and interior in the "Russian Style" and, as a whole, represents a considerable departure from the traditional proportions of Old Russian churches.

Contemporary Russian Church-Building

Followinng the Russian Revolution of 1917, the tradition of church building in Russia was interrupted. The 1920s and especially 1930s were marked by the mass shutdown and destruction of churches. Churches were systematically destroyed right up to the 1970s. Only individual churches that the state declared to be architectural monuments were preserved. Churches constructed through the fifteenth century, as well as some later structures, were included in this category. The principles used in selection were not always and everywhere the same. In some places, remarkable churches of the sixteenth century were destroyed. These include Saint Nicholas Church in Moscow's Myasniki district and the cathedral of the Pavlo-Obnorsky Monastery in the diocese of Vologda. In other places, nineteenth-century churches which did not possess particular artistic value were preserved. The destruction of churches sometimes had a utilitarian goal, such as constructing a highway or another building, but most often, ideological necessity was hidden behind formal motivations. Churches were destroyed arbitrarily. For example, in some parts of Moscow, such as Zamoskvorechye District, many churches were preserved, whereas other regions were almost completely "purged" of church buildings. Of the churches that were not destroyed, many were defaced or refashioned as secular structures and suffered a complete loss of interior decoration.

Restoration of church life at the turn of the 1990s was the reason for a massive rebirth of church building on all the territories of the former Soviet Union. This rebirth is taking place in three ways.

First, restoration work is being done to return an original appearance to churches that were not destroyed, but were rebuilt or refashioned during the Soviet period. Today churches of this type number in the thousands.

Second, churches resembling lost original churches, including exact replicas, are being constructed on the sites of destroyed churches. The Kazan Cathedral on Red Square is an exact replica of the church previously destroyed. The Cathedral of Christ the Savior, rebuilt in 2000, does not completely reproduce the demolished

Kazan Cathedral on Red Square. Moscow.

church, although its outer appearance is extremely close to the original. The previous church stood on a tall hill which was destroyed following the demolition of the church. Rather than restoring the hill, the decision was made to create a lower church, bordered by a wide gallery containing numerous buildings including a hall for ecclesiastical assemblies with a capacity of fourteen hundred people. The marble bas-reliefs that adorned the cathedral in the nineteenth century were not restored, but new bronze ones were created in their place. In 2007 a viewing platform was installed on the roof of the cathedral. This changed the appearance of the cathedral when compared to the original structure.

Finally, new works of church architecture are continually being created. Many are modeled after traditional churches, both Russian and Byzantine. In some cases they are modeled after churches from the era of baroque and classical styles. It is characteristic for many newly built churches to have a combination of different styles in relation to both architectural and decorative aspects. An example is the cathedral of Saint Theodore Ushakov in Saransk (2006), which is built in the style of classicism and calls to mind one of the churches of Saint Petersburg, but its towers are decorated with Old Russian onion domes.

The combination of various architectural styles does not always appear convincing from an aesthetic perspective. An example is the architectural design of the church complex of the Cathedral of the Holy Trinity at Borisov Ponds in Moscow (2004). The official description of this church states that it is built in the "Byzantine style," but this manner of describing the church is clearly used here very broadly. Only certain elements of the layout and external decoration are reminiscent of Byzantium. Four apses connected in the form of a cross lay at the basis of the design. A drum for a dome rests in the center of the cross. The dome's shape remotely calls to mind a dome from Byzantine churches. But the height of the church slightly surpasses its length and breadth and the diameter of the dome is considerably larger than necessary for a church of its size. As a result, a partial resemblance to a Byzantine church is achieved, but it appears flattened out on four sides and elongated in height. To make a comparison using the human body (and such a comparison is necessary when discussing the Byzantine style), the church resembles a person whose body size surpasses the size of his head only by a mere two or three times.

Besides the disproportion just mentioned, the church complex is marked by a vivid stylistic eclecticism. Four corners of the church are decorated with gigantic gilded statues of double-headed eagles with outstretched wings reminiscent of a chimera of medieval cathedrals in the gothic style. A wide-paved road leading to the church has street lamps, as if moved from old Saint Petersburg boulevards. In no way do these fit harmoniously with the proclaimed Byzantine style. Finally, the massive dome of the church and the wings of the apses are adorned in a screaming light blue color having golden "streaks." Taken together, all of this suggests pretensions of innovation rather than a striving to imitate the "Byzantine style," no matter how loosely that notion may be understood.

It is possible that just such an aesthetic corresponds with the tastes of a new time, but this is not the dominant trend in contemporary church-building today. Most common is a trend towards a more authentic reproduction of stylistic details of Old Russian and Byzantine styles, and sometimes direct copying of ancient models or of individual elements. Without a doubt, this trend warrants a positive assessment. Even so, the results of the creative process would probably be far more impressive if contemporary architects, when resurrecting architectural forms of ancient churches, paid more attention to studying Russian church art, especially the laws of proportionality which the architects of Byzantium and Russia mastered with perfection.

Building in proper canonical proportions is impossible without using the ancient system of measurement based on the articulations of the human body and without using irrational relationships that are based on the relationships of a diagonal of a double square and its sides. The metric system, which was introduced by figures of the French Revolution at the end of the eighteenth century and legalized by Bolshevik authorities after the Russian Revolution of 1917, is perfectly suited to building secular buildings, but it is difficult to use it to create a space of a sacramental character. It is impossible to try to build a church in the Byzantine or Russian style without using the measurements and proportions that lie at the root of these styles. In the same way, it is impossible to properly understand this style in its historical perspective: "To discuss the history of architecture outside of metrology . . . is impossible. It would mean depriving architecture of its language, by which, from ancient times, art journeys together with the building process in one conglomerate. It would mean rendering architecture's integral essence powerless.

It would mean denying architecture its 'tuning fork' used for harmonic tuning. In part this was done by the canonization of the meter in opposition to the ancient measurements."[22]

At the turn of the twenty-first century a rebirth is occurring, a rebirth of wooden craftsmanship that was characteristic of Rus' throughout its Christian past. Wooden churches are being built again not only in towns and villages but also in cities. In Moscow the practice of building small wooden model churches in the suburbs of large cities near metro stations is becoming widespread. The construction of such churches, which does not require much money, is being realized by numerous companies that, besides houses of worship, build housing complexes, bath houses, and other housing structures. Without a doubt, the serial production of churches is a phenomenon which was not known in Byzantium or Rus', but it is a sign of the times that reveals the acute need for church buildings after seven decades of their mass destruction.

---

[22]Shevelev, *Shape Formation*, 28.

4

Arrangement of Churches and Church Objects

Arrangement of Churches

Notwithstanding the great diversity of shapes and architectural styles used in building churches, the interior arrangement of Orthodox churches always follows certain guidelines. These guidelines, or "canons," emerged in Byzantium at about the beginning of the second millennium and have not undergone significant change since then.

Traditional Orthodox churches are divided into three parts: the sanctuary, the nave (the church itself), and the narthex.

In ancient churches, the *narthex* was the room in which catechumens and penitents prayed during the divine services. These were people who did not partake of communion at the celebration of the Eucharist. According to the Typikon, certain parts of divine services are to be conducted in the narthex; in particular, the *litiya* during the all-night vigil should be served there. The *panikhida* (a short memorial service for the departed) is also to be served in the narthex, although in practice it is normally served in one of the flanking areas of the church.

In many contemporary churches the narthex is either altogether absent or completely blends in with the central section of the church. This is due to the fact that the functional significance of the narthex was lost long ago. In the contemporary Church catechumens and penitents do not constitute a separate category of the faithful and, therefore, the functional need for the narthex as a separate room no longer exists.

The *nave* of the church is the place where the laity congregates during divine services. In ancient times, the liturgy of the catechumens was conducted in the center of the church. Sermons were spoken there and the bishop read prayers over the catechumens and faithful as well as the infirm and demon-possessed. The

Central Section of the Cathedral of Sretensky Monastery in Moscow.

deacon read the litanies there. Essentially, the central portion of the church is where the divine services were conducted, while only the Eucharist was celebrated in the sanctuary. Later, the majority of church services were transferred to the sanctuary, but today some parts of the services are still conducted in the center of the church. The *polyeleos* is served in the center of the church during both matins and the all-night vigil on Sundays and feast days. This is also where the faithful are anointed with holy oil. Furthermore, the Gospel is proclaimed by the deacon in the center of the church. At hierarchical services, the bishop is greeted and vested in the center of the church. At such services, the entire beginning of the liturgy up to the small entrance takes place there as well.

In ancient churches, the cathedra (which then was called the *ambo*) was situated in the center of church. This is where the holy Scriptures were read and the homily was spoken. At the present time, this type of cathedra is found only in cathedrals. When the divine service takes place in the center of the church, the hierarch stands upon the cathedra. During the Divine Liturgy, the deacon proclaims the Gospel from it.

As a rule, an *analogion* (stand) is found in the center of every church. The icon of the patron saint of the church or the icon of a saint being commemorated on a particular day rests upon the analogion. A candlestand is placed in front of it. (Others stand before icons throughout the church as well.) The use of candles in the church is one of the most ancient customs and has passed down to us from the days of the first Christians. In our day, the use of candles not only has symbolic meaning but also signifies making an offering to the Church. Candles that are placed by the faithful before icons in churches are not purchased in a store or brought from home. Rather, they are bought in the church itself and the money from the proceeds is used to support the church.

Electric lighting is used in contemporary churches, but some parts of the services should be conducted in partial or even complete darkness. Full lighting is customary during the most celebratory moments of the services, such as during the polyeleos at the all-night vigil, or throughout the Divine Liturgy. The church lights are completely extinguished during the reading of the six psalms during matins. Partial darkness is customary at the services during Great Lent.

The chandelier is the main light source of the church (Gk. *polykandelion*, πολυκανδήλιον—literally, "having many lamps"). In large churches, the chandelier is of great size with many (from twenty to one hundred or even more) candles or light bulbs. It is attached to a long steel cable which hangs from the central dome. There may be smaller chandeliers in other parts of the church as well.

The ancient custom of lighting candles and lampadas during certain parts of the services is kept in the monasteries of holy Mount Athos, where electric lighting is not used. For this purpose, at the beginning of each service a monk designated as the *ecclesiarch* lights the lampadas which hang before the icons. Some candles are lit only at certain moments of the service—for example, candles placed before icons and candles which serve to provide light to the church interior. A chandelier having the form of a hoop hangs under the dome of the church. Candles are placed on it and lit during the most celebratory moments of the service using a special splinter attached to the end of a long pole. At some moments the chandelier with candles is swung from side to side in such a manner that patches of light from the candles move about the church. Together with the peal of bells and particularly celebratory and melismatic singing, this motion creates a festal mood.

Some people think that a characteristic difference between Orthodox churches and their Catholic and Protestant counterparts is the absence of seats. Actually, all ancient directives for serving in the church presupposed that seats were to be present in the church because it is in fact proper to sit during certain parts of the services. In particular, the psalms and also the readings of the Old Testament and epistle were heard while sitting. So were readings from the writings of the Church Fathers and also certain Christian hymns, such as *kathisma hymns*, whose name itself indicates that they were listened to while sitting. Standing was considered necessary only at the most important moments of the divine service, such as during the reading of the Gospel and during the eucharistic canon. Certain liturgical exclamations passed down to the present day, such as "Wisdom, aright!"[1] and "Let us stand aright, let us stand with fear!" were originally the deacon's call to the faithful, inviting them to stand up for certain prayers, as they were sitting during the previous prayers.

The absence of seats in the church is a custom of the Russian Church but by no means is it characteristic of Greek churches where, as a rule, benches are provided for all who participate in the divine services. The absence of seats in Russian churches surprised Greeks who visited Russia even in the seventeenth century. Paul of Aleppo was a deacon and one of the pilgrims who accompanied the Antiochian patriarch Macarius in his travels in Russia. After attending a very long Russian service, he shared his impressions:

Patriarch Macarius of Antioch. Miniature. Royal Book of Titled Heads. 1672.

On Saturday we listened to their liturgy, from which we departed no sooner than our legs were useless from standing so long, since in the churches there are no seats.... You could imagine then, reader, standing in church without moving, like stones. We suffered much from tiredness, as the soul was torn apart by exhaustion and longing.... Being among them, we were in amazement. We left the church, hardly feeling our legs from tiredness and ceaseless standing.... Knowledgeable people told us that if someone wishes to shorten his life by fifteen years, let him go to the land of the Muscovites and live among them as an ascetic.[2]

The author's feelings are likewise familiar to people today who often complain about the absence of benches. But some Russian Orthodox churches have places around the periphery of the church designated for sitting. These places are intended for elderly and infirm

---

[1] "Wisdom, aright!" is a most ancient liturgical exclamation meaning, "Wisdom, stand aright!" (that is, stand upright, for that which will be read is wisdom).

[2] Paul of Aleppo, *Travels of Patriarch Macarius to Moscow in the Middle of the 17th Century* (St Petersburg, 1898), 13–14, 57–58.

parishioners. The custom of sitting during readings and standing only for the most important moments of the service, however, is not characteristic of most Russian Orthodox churches. It is preserved only in the monasteries where *stasidii*—high wooden chairs with collapsible seats and high elbow-rests—are installed for monks around the walls of the church. It is possible to either sit or stand in the *stasidii* by leaning one's hands on the elbow-rests and having one's back lean against the wall. There would be nothing dishonorable if *stasidii* or another type of chair were to be installed in parish churches. It would make the Orthodox services not only more "humane" in relation to the faithful, but it would also give rebirth to one of the elements of ancient ceremony.

The walls of the nave of the church are usually decorated with frescoes or mosaics. The *iconostasis* separates the nave from the sanctuary and is found in the eastern part of the church. In front of the iconostasis is the *solea*— an elevation for the clergy. The central part of the solea generally has the shape of a semi-circular projection and is called the *ambo*. The homily is pronounced from here and some actions take place, such as the small and great entrances during the liturgy. Also, the dismissal—the final blessing at the end of every service—is said from the ambo.

The left and right sides of the solea form the *kliros*, where the choir is usually located. In many Orthodox churches two choirs—one located on the right side and the other on the left—take turns singing. In some instances an additional kliros is formed on the second floor in the western part of the church. This situation creates a unique stereo effect because the choir is located behind the faithful while the clergy is located in front of them.

Located in the center of the lower arch of the iconostasis are doors which are called in the Russian tradition *royal gates* and in the Greek tradition *holy doors*. The origin of the term "royal gates" is not completely known. Some suppose that this name reflects the symbolism of the great entrance which depicts the Savior, the "King of kings" and "Lord of lords," who "comes to be slain, to give himself as food to the faithful," carrying his cross. Others think that the central gates of the sanctuary received the name "royal" because tsars and emperors passed through them. It is true that, in Russian practice, emperors entered into the sanctuary through the royal

Royal Gates. Yaroslavl. Middle of 17th c.

gates during coronation ceremonies. They communed in the sanctuary together with the clergy and received the Body of Christ in the hand and communed of the Blood of Christ from the chalice (empresses did likewise).[3] In Byzantium the gates which were called "royal" were those leading from the narthex to the nave of the church, or the doors through which the emperor entered the church.

At the northern and southern sides of the iconostasis there are two side doors. The liturgical procession always exits from the sanctuary through the northern door and enters again through the royal gates. The deacon also exits to the solea for litanies through the northern door and re-enters the sanctuary through the southern door.

The *sanctuary* is the most holy place of the Orthodox church and is similar to the Holy of holies of the ancient temple of Solomon. Often the sanctuary is perceived as a type of closed space, "behind the scenes," where clergy and servers can hide from the eyes of the faithful. This perception fundamentally contradicts the meaning of the sanctuary as a place of God's special presence. The divine glory which once filled the holy of holies in Solomon's temple dwells within the sanctuary. Each person in the sanctuary should keep a pious silence, interrupted only for the reading of prayers or necessary instructions given during the services. In the sanctuary, conversations concerning other subjects are not allowed.

Only those members of the clergy who participate directly in the divine service should be in the sanctuary. The custom, now common, of inviting "honored guests," be they members of the government or sponsors of the church, to be present in the sanctuary during the divine services should not be encouraged. All honored guests should be present in specially designated places in the nave or in one of the kliroses. The priest should not commune individuals in the sanctuary who are not vested in the order of priest or deacon. This means subdeacons and readers. Only those who have received ordination in the sanctuary may be communed in the sanctuary. Those who received orders outside the sanctuary (readers and subdeacons) should commune outside the sanctuary.

The *altar table* is situated in the center of the sanctuary, across from the royal gates. It is used for celebrating the Eucharist. The altar table is the most holy place of the sanctuary—equivalent to the altar or ark of the covenant in the ancient

---

[3]Empress Anna Ioannovna, during her wedding ceremony (1730) was taken into the sanctuary through the royal gates and communed with the clergy. Empresses Catherine (1742) and Catherine II (1762) communed in the same manner at their coronations. See M. Zheltov, Archpriest Sergei Pravdoliubov, "Divine Service of the Russian Church: 10th–20th Centuries," in *Orthodox Encyclopedia*, vol. 9 (Moscow, 2005), 512.

temple of Solomon. In the practice of the Russian Church, only members of the clergy may touch the altar table; members of the laity are forbidden to do so. A member of the laity also may not stand before the altar table or pass through the royal gates. Even candles on the altar table may be lit only by the clergy. In contemporary Greek practice, however, members of the laity are not forbidden to touch the altar table.

The altar table has the shape of a cube, and is made of stone or wood. In Greek churches rectangular altar tables are common. These look like long tables placed parallel to the iconostasis. The upper stone slab of the altar table rests on four columns, and the inner space of the altar table is open to view. In the Russian practice, the horizontal surface of the altar table has, as a rule, a square shape, and the altar table is fully wrapped by an *inditia*—a covering which fits the shape of the altar table. The traditional height of the altar table is one *arshin* and six *vershoks* (98 cm/38.6 inches). Underneath the upper slab of the altar table, in the center, the bishop places a particle of the relics of a martyr or saint during the consecration of the church. This tradition comes from the ancient Christian custom of celebrating the liturgy on the tombs of the martyrs.

In some churches a ciborium is installed over the altar table similar to what was found in the Church of Hagia Sophia in Constantinople. A ciborium usually consists of four columns or pillars, situated at the four corners of the altar table. A roof, which may have the shape of four slopes, is installed above the capitals of the columns. According to the ancient tradition, a dove, symbolizing the Holy Spirit, is hung under the roof of the ciborium. (Another style has an image of a dove in the center of the lower part of the roof.)

The space behind the altar table, in the eastern part of the sanctuary, is called the *high place*. The throne of the hierarch is found here, around which benches are situated for the priests to sit on. According to the Typikon, the bishop's throne should be situated at the high place not only of cathedrals but of all churches. The presence of this throne witnesses to the connection between the church and the bishop. Without the blessing of the bishop, a priest does not have the right to conduct services in a church.

Patriarch's Throne at the High Place of Christ the Savior Cathedral. Moscow.

Royal Gates and Catapeteasma. Saint Theodora of Thessalonica Monastery. Thessalonica. Greece.

The *table of oblation* is found along the left side of the altar table, in the northern part of the sanctuary. It has the appearance of an altar table but is often smaller. The table of oblation is intended for conducting the preparation for the liturgy—the *proskomedia*. The holy gifts are placed on the table of oblation at the end of the liturgy, after the communion of the laity.[4]

In the tradition of the Russian Church, a lampstand having seven lampadas and the appearance of a Jewish menorah is placed in the sanctuary on the eastern side of the altar table. In Greek churches this lampstand is not present, and it is not mentioned in the rubrics for consecrating a church. It was not originally an article of the Christian church; rather, it appeared in Russia in the Synodal period as a reminder of the seven-branched candelabra in Solomon's temple (see Ex 25.31–37).[5] The lampstand is the only object in the sanctuary that does not directly serve a liturgical function.

At times when services are not being conducted and also at certain moments of the divine services, the central entrance to the sanctuary (royal gates) is closed with a curtain called *catapeteasma* (Gr. *katapetasma*, καταπέτασμα—veil). In contemporary Russian practice the catapeteasma is a rectangular cloth hung from the upper edge of the royal gates to the floor. Usually the curtain is of a dark-red color and a four- or eight-ended cross is embroidered on it. Richly adorned catapeteasmas were used in former times.[6]

---

[4] It should be noted that the contemporary usage of the terms *altar table*, *table of oblation*, and *high place* differ from the usage found in service books. In these books, the term "table of oblation" is used to refer to what we now call the altar table. What is now referred to as the table of oblation is called the "offering." The word "throne" (Slavonic *prestol*/Gr. *thronos*, θρόνος) is reserved for the "high place," where the bishop's throne is situated. For this reason, during the singing of the Thrice Holy, when the bishop or priest moves from his normal place of serving in front of the altar table to the high place, the deacon exclaims, "Bless, Master, the high throne."

[5] There is a symbolic depiction of the Old Testament tabernacle in one of the chronicles of the Vatopedi Monastery on Mount Athos, dating to the thirteenth century. Among the items depicted is an image of a lampstand with seven lamps in the form of a menorah with the inscription λυχνία (*lychnia*—lamps). See illustration in V. Prokhorov, "Tetramorph or Gospel Symbols Depicted on the Walls of the Church of the Entry of the Most Holy Theotokos into the Temple in Hilandar Monastery on Mount Athos," in *Christian Antiquities and Archeology*, vol. 4 (St Petersburg, 1863), 5–9.

[6] A vivid example is the catapeteasma of 1556, gifted to the Hilandar Monastery on Mount Athos by Tsar Ivan the Terrible, on which Christ is depicted wearing a hierarch's vestments (sakkos, omophorion, and

Objects of Liturgical Use

During church services, various objects are used, and these have both practical functions and symbolic meaning. Some of these are: the antimension, Gospel book, chalice, diskos, star, spear, spoon, covers and aer, and incense, as well as other items used during hierarchical services.

The *antimension* (literally "in the place of an altar table," from the Greek *anti*, ἀντί— "in place of" and the Latin *mensa*—table) is a rectangular cloth which lies on the altar table during the divine services. Originally the term *antimension* signified a small movable table used for conducting divine services outside of a church. In the fourth century the practice became widespread in Byzantium of using a consecrated plate or cloth for celebrating the Eucharist where there was no consecrated altar table or where the altar table had been desecrated by heretics (iconoclasts). This practice was described in particular by Saint Theodore the Studite.[7]

Research suggests that the antimension first appeared as a piece of cloth as a result of the impossibility, due to great distances, for Byzantine hierarchs to personally consecrate all churches in the diocese under their jurisdiction. "For this reason it was considered sufficient, when consecrating a church, to lay down on the altar table a piece of cloth which had been spread on an altar table already consecrated by a bishop. This was the origin of the antimension."[8] In the thirteenth century antimensia were consecrated by bishops during the consecration of churches and distributed to those churches at which the altar tables remained unconsecrated. If an altar table was properly consecrated, it could be served at without an antemension. Patriarch Manuel II of Constantinople (1244–1254) wrote about this:

> We know that antimensia are prepared when a bishop himself performs the consecration of a church, right from the cloth which has been spread and wrapped on the altar tables, which is cut into pieces, signed and distributed to the priests. Without the antimension it is not permissible to serve. . . . It is not necessary to lay the antimension on all altar tables, but only on those for which

---

miter) and blessing with both hands. The Mother of God dressed in a queen's raiment and Saint John the Baptist are next to the Savior. The composition is framed with thirty medallions showing images of saints. The rich embroidery of the catapeteasma is adorned with pearls and precious stones. See V. Prokhorov, "The Catapeteasma of Ivan the Terrible, Gifted to Hilandar Monastery on Mount Athos" in *Christian Antiquities and Archeology*, vol. 6 (St Petersburg, 1863), 1–2.

[7] Theodore the Studite, *Epistle 40 to Naukratius* PG 99, 1056 B.

[8] I. Karabinov, "The Holy Chalice in the Liturgy of the Presanctified Gifts," *Christian Reading* 6 (St Petersburg, 1915), 751.

it is unknown whether they have been consecrated or not, since the antimension takes the place of a consecrated holy altar table. Where the altar table has been consecrated, there is no need for an antimension.[9]

Antimension. Stavronikita Monastery. Mount Athos. 1717.

Beginning in the thirteenth century, however, the practice arose of placing the antimension even on consecrated altars.[10] This custom is now maintained in all local Orthodox Churches even though the order for consecrating an antimension, printed in the hierarchical service book, is titled "Order for a Bishop to Consecrate Antimensia on which a Priest May Serve when the Holy Table does not Contain Relics."[11]

In accordance with the practice of the Russian Orthodox Church, a particle of a relic of a saint or martyr is sewn into the antimension. This is a reminder of the ancient tradition of celebrating the liturgy on the tombs of the martyrs. The practice of sewing relics into the antimension is unknown in the Greek Church,[12] where the presence of a particle of a relic in the sanctuary of the church is considered sufficient. Relics of saints were not sewn into Old Russian antimensia either. There are no traces of the presence of relics in a Russian antimension from the year 1149, described by I.I. Sreznevsky.[13] The absence of relics in Old Russian and Greek antimensia is understood by the fact that the antimension was perceived first and foremost as a certificate which granted the right to conduct services in a given church. It was the signature of the bishop that gave meaning to the antimension, not the relics of a saint, since there were relics of a saint located underneath the altar table. At the present time, however, the relics of a martyr or saint are sewn into all antimensia, in Russian practice.

The shape of the aforementioned antimension of 1149 is nearly square (36 cm/14.2 inches in length and 35 cm/13.8 inches in width). An image of an eight-ended cross is found in the center and the following inscription is contained around

---

[9] Ibid.
[10] M. Zheltov, I. Popov, "Antimension" in *Orthodox Encyclopedia*, vol. 2 (Moscow, 2001), 489–490.
[11] See *Bishop's Service Book*, vol. 2, 28.
[12] Here and henceforth we mean by "Greek Church" all the local Orthodox Churches in which services are conducted in the Greek language (especially the Patriarchates of Constantinople and Alexandria as well as the Greek and Cypriot Churches).
[13] Izmail Sreznevsky, "Antimension of 1149," in *Christian Antiquities and Archeology* 4 (St Petersburg, 1863), 1–4.

its edges: "Altar of the Holy Martyr George. Consecrated by the Archbishop of Novgorod Nifont by the order of Bishop of Rostov Nesto(r) during the pious rule of Prince George, the son of Monomakh, in the month of September the first, in the year 6657, in the indiction the twelfth."[14] The most common antimensia today are rectangular, with dimensions of approximately 40 cm x 60 cm (15.7 x 23.6 inches), and with an image of the burial of the Savior.

The inscription on the antimension indicates the title and name of the consecrating bishop, the date of consecration and the church for which it is intended. For example, "Consecrated by His Holiness Patriarch of Moscow and All-Russia Alexei II in the year 7507 from the creation of the world and 1999 from the birth of Christ in the month of August on the 8th day. Granted for serving in the Church of Saint Nicholas in Vienna." In the Synodal period the inscription on the antimension also contained the name of the tsar ruling at the time: "During the rule of the Most Pious, Most Autocratic, Great Sovereign Emperor Alexander Nicholaevich of All-Russia with the blessing of the Most Holy Governing Synod, consecrated by the Most Reverend (name, title, etc.)." On contemporary Greek antimensia the inscription reads: "Divine and sacred oblation, consecrated for performing divine mysteries on any place in the dominion of our Lord Jesus Christ. Consecrated in the sacred church (name of church, name and title of bishop, date)."

The antimension is signed by the bishop for a specific church. Only in certain situations may it be given by hand to an individual priest. An example would be if a priest performs missionary service where no churches are found. In the period of persecutions of the Church, the antimension could be signed without indicating a specific church. The author of this book has at his disposal an antimension dated 13/26 September, 1935, on which the inscription, written by Archbishop Pavlin of Mogilev, reads: "Blessed to celebrate the Divine Liturgy 'wherever it will take place'."

According to Saint Simeon of Thessalonica (fifteenth century), the material used for preparing the antimension should be linen "since linen comes from the ground as the Lord's grave was in the ground."[15] Contemporary Greek antimensia are usually made from linen or silk while Russian antimensia are made from silk. The antimension is kept folded on the altar inside a cloth called the *iliton*. A flat *sponge*, used for wiping particles of the body of Christ or crumbs from prosphora, is

---

[14] The peculiarity of this *antimension* is, as the inscription states, that it was consecrated by one bishop for a church located within the diocese of another bishop's jurisdiction.

[15] Simeon of Thessalonica *Concerning the Holy Church* 127. PG 155, 333 A.

placed inside the folded antimension. During the Divine Liturgy, at the time of the litany of fervent supplication and the litany of the catechumens, the antimension is unfolded and the Eucharist is celebrated on the unfolded antimension.

The holy Gospel also lies on the altar table. It is brought out of the sanctuary at several moments of the service to be read or venerated. The Gospel is usually a large book with a richly adorned cover. In days of old both the Gospel and the liturgical vessels were kept in a special room in the church called the *skevophylakion* ("vessel depository"). Later, however, the Gospel came to be left on the altar table both during and between services.

The *tabernacle* is a vessel used for guarding the reserved holy gifts and stands on the eastern side of the altar table. It is normally made of silver or another metal in the form of a small, openwork church crowned with a cross. The holy gifts are kept in the church in case it becomes necessary to commune the sick in a time of emergency. These gifts are prepared for the entire upcoming year at the Divine Liturgy on Holy Thursday. In ancient churches, the reserved gifts could be kept in a special vessel which had the form of a dove and hung over the altar table, under the arch of the ciborium.[16]

Two lit candles are placed on the altar table during the divine services as a reminder of the true Light who enlightens every man who comes into the world (Jn 1.9).

Chalice with a Depiction of the Twelve Apostles. First Half of 8th c.

A *chalice* is used (Gr. *poterion*, ποτήριον—a vessel used for drinking) when celebrating the liturgy. The chalice is round and has a high stand with a circular base. Normally the chalice is silver or silver-plated. Chalices made of pure gold and adorned with precious stones were used in some old churches. In poorer churches, chalices made of glass, tin, copper, iron, and even wood were used.[17] Wine is poured into the chalice during the liturgy and, after the invocation of the Holy Spirit, it becomes the blood of Christ. The eucharistic chalice symbolizes the very cup from which Christ communed his disciples at the Mystical Supper. For this reason the chalice is treated with particular reverence. Following

---

[16]Srezenvsky, *Tabernacle*, 32–33. The tabernacle was hung by chains attached to the roof of the ciborium or to the ceiling so that rodents could not reach it.

[17]Wooden liturgical vessels from the time of Saint Sergius of Radonezh are kept in the Ecclesiastical Archeology Classroom of the Moscow Theological Academy.

Arrangement of Churches and Church Objects

the liturgy it is washed several times with warm water and then kept in a special place. Only members of the clergy may touch the chalice.[18]

The same reverence is shown to the *diskos* (Gr. δίσκος—a round dish, a circle). The diskos is a round dish on a stand with a round base on which, during the liturgy, bread which is intended for celebrating the Eucharist and called the Holy Lamb is placed. The diskos is usually made together with the chalice (as a pair) from the same material and is adorned in a similar fashion. The diskos is a reminder of the dish from which Christ took bread at the Mystical Supper to distribute to his disciples.

Diskos. Russia. Kon. 17th c.

A *spear* is used to cut the eucharistic bread. It is a flat knife with a sharpened tip (like the end of a spear) and is set in a wooden handle. This liturgical object symbolizes the spear with which the side of the crucified Savior was pierced (Jn 19.34). It was probably used in the liturgy as early as the fifth or sixth century and possibly earlier.[19] We find references to the spear in the writings of Saint Germanus of Constantinople,[20] Saint Theodore the Studite,[21] and in Byzantine liturgical chronicles.

A *spoon* is used to commune the laity in the Orthodox Church. It is a small spoon with a cross on the end of its handle. It is made of gold, silver, tin, or another type of metal which does not oxidize over time.[22]

Yet another object used during the Divine Liturgy is the *star*. This item is made from two metal arches which are connected with a screw and bolt to form a cross. The star is placed on the diskos over the eucharistic bread during the proskomedia. As a liturgical symbol, the star is associated with the star of Bethlehem (Mt 2.9).

Covers are used to cover the chalice and diskos during the liturgy. They are crosses made of cloth which have a square in the center of the cross. This center square usually has a hard lining and covers the top of the vessel while the four ends of the cross hang down and cover the vessel's four sides. Covers were used in the

---

[18] Canon 21 of the Council of Laodicea (around 343) forbids subdeacons from touching the holy vessels. This prohibition extends to the lower orders of the clergy (readers and singers) as well as members of the laity.

[19] Robert F. Taft, SJ, *The Great Entrance. A History of the Transfer of Gifts and other Pre-anaphoral Rites (A History of the Liturgy of St John Chrysostom, vol. 2)* in Orientalia Christiana Analecta 200 (Rome, 1978), 349.

[20] Germanus of Constantinople *Church History*. PG 98, 397 C.

[21] Theodore the Studite *Against the Iconoclasts* 2. PG 99, 489 B.

[22] We will discuss the origin of this liturgical object in a later volume.

Chalice Cover. Russia. 18th c.

Aer. 14th c.

ancient Church to protect the holy gifts (the eucharistic bread and wine) from dust, flies, and other flying insects.

The *aer*, a rectangular cloth, is also used as a covering. The aer (Gr. *aer*, ἀέρ) is one of the earliest objects of the Church's inventory. It is mentioned in the fifth century by Theodore of Mopsuestia, in the eighth century by Saint Germanus of Constantinople, and after the tenth century in numerous liturgical manuscripts.[23] In the Byzantine and Old Russian traditions, aers of great size (up to 2 meters/6.6 feet in length) were common; these contained images of the crucifixion of Christ, of his burial, and of the Savior Not-Made-by-Hands surrounded by angels and saints. In contemporary Russian practice, the aer is a rectangular cloth with approximate dimensions of 60 cm by 80 cm (23.6 inches by 31.5 inches); it has an image of a four-ended cross in the middle. At the time of the great entrance, the deacon places the aer over his left shoulder. In Greek practice, the aer is also a four-sided cloth, but it has long ribbons tied to its two upper corners and the deacon hangs the aer on his back and ties the ribbons in the front.

At certain moments of the service, when liturgical processions take place (especially at the time of the small and great entrances of the Divine Liturgy), a candle bearer carries a candle placed in a long candle holder. There may be two candle bearers, in which case they normally carry a candle holder which has the form of a long pole. Sometimes the deacon carries this candle during the service (especially during the censing performed by a priest at the beginning of the all-night vigil or at the polyeleos). During services performed by the ruling hierarch of a diocese, a candle bearer stands to the left side of the royal gates, in front of the icon of the Holy Theotokos, and holds a candle placed in a long candle holder called *primikirion* (Gr. *primikerion*, πριμικήριον).[24]

A *censer* is used during the services of the Orthodox Church. It is a vessel consisting of a cup and a cover hanging on chains and connected to a handle held

---

[23] Taft, *The Great Entrance*, 35, 216–217.

[24] The *primikerion* is not used when a vicar bishop or the bishop of another diocese performs the divine service.

by a sacred server. Bells are attached to its chains and make a sound while censing. The censer is used for the burning of incense, for which a piece of pressed charcoal is placed in the cup and incense (sweet-scented wood resin) is placed on top of the charcoal.

Censing—burning of fragrant incense in a special cup used for this purpose—is one of the most ancient elements of the service. The custom of censing during the service was inherited by the Christian Church from ancient Jewish worship. Censing is mentioned many times in the Bible. According to the Book of Exodus, God commanded Aaron through Moses to perform a censing before the ark of the covenant (Ex 30.7–8). Moses "put the golden altar in the tent of the congregation before the veil and he burnt fragrant incense upon it; as the Lord had commanded Moses" (Ex 40.26–27). The Book of Revelation mentions censing: "Then

Censer. Moscow Kremlin. 1598.

another angel, having a golden censer, came and stood at the altar. He was given much incense, that he should offer it with the prayers of all the saints upon the golden altar which was before the throne. And the smoke of the incense, with the prayers of the saints, ascended before God from the angel's hand" (Rev 8.3–4). Since scholars suppose that the visions of the Apocalypse to some degree reflect the liturgical practice of the early Church, we may assume that censing was conducted during divine services in Christian communities as early as in the time of Saint John the Theologian.

Censing is one of the means of bestowing honor and reverent veneration on holy things, whether icons, crosses, or other sacred objects. In the teaching of the Church, the honor paid to an image is transferred to its prototype. Censing before an icon of Christ is an act of rendering honor to Christ, as censing before the image of the Theotokos or a saint is a way of bestowing honor to them. It is symbolic, however, that the sacred server censes not only the images of the saints but also all the people who are present in the church, thereby bestowing honor to every person created in the image and likeness of God. Man, present in the church, is as if equal to an icon and the censing reminds him that he is called to spiritual perfection, holiness, and deification.

Dikerion and Trikerion. Mount Athos. 18th c.

Fan. Mount Athos. 1661.

Special items of the hierarchical service are the *dikerion* (Gr. *dikerion*, δικήριον) and *trikerion* (*trikerion*, τρικήριον). These are two hand-held, ornamental candlesticks in which two (dikerion) or three (trikerion) candles are placed. The use of the dikerion and trikerion at the patriarchal liturgy began in the twelfth century.[25] Originally these candlesticks were ascribed only to kings and patriarchs (and not to all bishops) as they were perceived as attributes reflecting the dignity of teaching. This is mentioned in the twelfth century by Theodore Balsamon, the patriarch of Antioch, who insisted that the right to bless the faithful with candlesticks belonged to kings, patriarchs, autocephalous archbishops of Bulgaria and Cyprus, and also a few metropolitans to whom the kings had given this right.[26]

Later the dikerion and trikerion came to be used by all hierarchs at church services. The trikerion is interpreted symbolically as an indication of the three Persons of the Holy Trinity, while the dikerion indicates the two natures of Jesus Christ.[27] Candles placed in the trikerion and dikerion may be connected at the top in such a way that a single flame is formed. A more common style has crossing candles whose top ends are directed in different directions.[28]

Fans (Slavonic *ripida*, from the Greek *rhipidion*, ῥιπίδιον—large fan) are other articles of the hierarchical service. In the fourth century they consisted of large fans placed on long poles and were meant for brushing flying insects away from the holy gifts. The beginning of the liturgy of the faithful is described in the *Apostolic Constitutions* in this way: "Two deacons from both sides of the altar hold large fans made from thin leather or peacock's feathers or from canvas and gently chase away flying insects so that they do not fly into the chalice."[29] Besides the aforementioned

---

[25] Jacob, "Le chandelier à trois branches de l'évêque Pantoléon: A propos de l'inscription de Georges de Gallipoli," *Bolletino della Badia greca di Grottaferata* 53 (1999), 187–199.
[26] Theodore Balsamon *Reflections*, PG 138, 1016D–1017C.
[27] Simeon of Thessalonica *Concerning the Holy Temple* 59, 61. PG 155, 721BC.
[28] Deacon Mikhail Zheltov, "*Dikirion*" in *Orthodox Encyclopedia*, vol. 14, 693.
[29] *Apostolic Constitutions* 8, 12.

materials, fans could be made of parchment and painted with varied colors. Later, after losing their utilitarian significance, fans were made of wood or metal, covered with gold, and decorated with precious stones. Fans could be made in the form of a circle, oval, square, rhombus, or eight-pointed star.[30] An inscription was sometimes found on fans which read, "Holy, Holy, Holy."

The Heavenly Liturgy. Angel-Deacons with a Fan and Censer. Fresco. Gračanica. 14th c.

Eagle rugs (Slavonic *orletsi*) are round rugs bearing the image of an eagle flying over a city. Eagle rugs are placed under the feet of the bishop during services in such a way that the head of the eagle points in the direction in which the bishop is facing. The image of an eagle flying over a city symbolizes the main function of the bishop which is defined in Greek by the word *episkopi* (ἐπισκοπή—oversight). Eagle rugs came into use in Byzantium in the thirteenth century; there they were awards given to the patriarchs in Constantinople by the emperor. A double-headed eagle—the emblem of the empire—is depicted on Byzantine eagle rugs. Russian eagle rugs, which contain an image of a single-headed eagle, became widespread. The eagle rug is mentioned in the Russian order for installing a bishop, dating to 1456, which states that the metropolitan should stand on an eagle rug while serving before the altar table. The same order indicates that there ought to be a depiction of a single-headed eagle on the dais installed for the consecration of a bishop.[31]

A processional cross hoisted on a long pole is used during services at which the primate of a local Church presides (for instance, the patriarch of Moscow and All-Russia). A subdeacon stands to the right of the royal gates, opposite the candle-bearer, and bears the cross. A subdeacon walks before the primate of the Church and bears the processional cross whenever the primate enters the church or departs from it, and also during all liturgical processions.

---

[30] V. Prokhorov, "Fans in Novgorod's Saint Sophia Cathedral," in *Christian Antiquities and Archeology* 3 (St Petersburg, 1863), 13–14.

[31] *Desk Manuel for Clergy*, IV, 107.

5
Liturgical Vestments of the Clergy

During Orthodox services all the sacred servers are vested in sacred clothing according to their rank. Deacons, subdeacons, and readers wear a *sticharion*—a long garment having wide sleeves, which hangs to about 10–15 cm (4–6 inches) above the ground. A deacon wears *cuffs*, each bearing an image of the cross, on his left and right forearms. The *orarion,* a long ribbon with inwoven crosses which hangs to the ground in the back and front, is worn on the deacon's left shoulder. The sticharion, orarion, and cuffs are made from brocade of various colors. Subdeacons wear the orarion by girding themselves with it in the form of a cross.

In celebrating the Divine Liturgy, the priest is vested in a sticharion (called a *podriznik* in Slavonic), which has a shape different from the deacon's sticharion. It runs down to the heels, has narrow sleeves, and is made of a light white material (silk or cotton). The priest wears an *epitrachilion* (or stole) over the sticharion. It is a wide double band with inwoven crosses. The epitrachilion is donned over the head and hangs almost to the floor. A *belt* having a cross in the middle is worn over the epitrachilion. Like deacons, priests wear cuffs during the services. Some priests are awarded the right to wear the *nabedrennik* and *epigonation*. The nabedrennik is a rectangular cloth attached to a long ribbon which hangs on the shoulder. The epigonation is the same type of cloth but in the form of a rhombus.[1] The outer garment of the priest is called a *phelonion*.[2] It is a cloak with openings which is donned over the head, covers the shoulders and chest, and hangs in the back nearly to the floor. Some priests are awarded the right to wear the *kamilavka*—a purple cylindrical hat. As a mark of special distinction, a priest may be awarded the right to wear a *mitre*—a richly adorned semi-spherical headdress resembling a crown. Priests of the Russian Orthodox Church wear a cross on their chests both during and between services.

[1] In the Greek Church the *nabedrennik* is not used. Only the *epigonation* (Gk. ἐπιγονάτιον) is used.
[2] The Greek word *phelonion* (φελόνιον) is of the neuter gender while in Slavonic the word *phelon* is masculine. In the contemporary practice of the Russian Church, though, the word *phelon* firmly takes the feminine gender. In English, however, the term is considered neuter since the object is inanimate.

Sticharion. 1635, 1646.

Cuffs. Mount Athos. 1727.

During services, a hierarch wears a sticharion different in shape from that of a priest (Sl. *podsakkosnik*), because it has slits in the side and is fastened together by buttons. The hierarch wears the belt, epigonation, and cuffs over his sticharion. The *sakkos* is then donned—a shortened stikharion with shortened sleeves. It is buttoned up on the sides and adorned with bells. On his chest, the hierarch wears a cross and *panagia*—an oval-shaped medallion which usually bears the image of the Most Holy Theotokos. The *great omophorion* is placed on the shoulders of the hierarch. It is a wide band which covers the hierarch's shoulders. It hangs down on the front from the left shoulder while the other end hangs from the same shoulder but onto the hierarch's back. In some cases, the *small omophorion* is donned in the place of the great omophorion. It is a band of the same width, but shorter, with both ends hanging in the front. The hierarch's *mitre* has a cross on its top. At some moments, the hierarch takes into his hands a long staff with cross on top. In some cases, the hierarch performs the service wearing the *mantia*—a cape with a long train.

We shall briefly examine the history of the origin of the clergy's serving vestments and their symbolic meaning.

The apostolic Church did not have special vestments for sacred serving. Christ celebrated the Mystical Supper in regular clothing and the apostles wore their everyday clothes during the celebration of the Eucharist. As a result, however, of the Eucharist being transformed from a meal into a ceremonial service, everyday clothing came to be treated as sacred. When that clothing ceased to be commonly used, it was preserved in the usage of the Church. Different clothing, having special liturgical purposes, appeared as well.

One of the most ancient elements of liturgical clothing is the *sticharion* (Gr. *sticharion*, στιχάριον). It is a type of tunic which deacons wear as outer garments and priests and bishops wear under the phelonion. In the words of Saint Simeon of Thessalonica, the stikharion symbolizes the purity and perfection of the priestly rank.³ Saint Nicholas Cabasilas (1332–1371) noted that the deacon's sticharion has sleeves, which signifies the deacon's readiness to take action. The priest's phelonion, on the other hand, does not have sleeves, which signifies that the priest is deprived of human energy insofar as during the liturgy God acts through him.⁴

The *orarion* has been an essential component of the deacon's vestments from ancient times. It is mentioned in the twenty-second and twenty-fifth canons of the Council of Laodocea (364). In Byzantine frescoes, the archdeacon Stephen and other holy deacons are depicted wearing the sticharion with the orarion hanging over the left shoulder. In many icons and frescoes they are depicted also with a censer in the right hand. Saint Simeon of Thessalonica interprets the orarion as symbolizing an angel's wings.⁵

Phelonion. 1652.

The most ancient component of the liturgical vestments of bishops and priests, besides the sticharion, is the *phelonion* (Gr. *phelonion*, φελόνιον). Saint Simeon of Thessalonica refers to this garment as φαινόλιον (*fainolion*) and writes that it "reveals (*fainei*, φαίνει) the highest strength and enlightenment bestowed from on high."⁶ In apostolic times the phelonion was a sleeveless wool coat used as an outer garment. The phelonion is mentioned by the Apostle Paul (2 Tim 4.13) as an article of everyday clothing. There were various styles of phelonions and they could be worn on one shoulder or on both so that the front ends were pulled forward. The phelonion could be four-sided with tassels on the sides and fringes. However, in the Christian tradition, the most widespread type of phelonion had the shape of a bell, with a circular opening for the head. It was donned over the head and covered the entire body of the man wearing it. It could have the same length in the front as in the back or it could run higher in the front than in the back. In some cases, the phelonion was shorter on the side of the right arm and longer on the side of the left arm.

At a later time, when hierarchs began to wear the sakkos instead of the phelonion, the phelonion was preserved as a basic liturgical vestment for priests. The

---

³Simeon of Thessalonica *Concerning the Holy Temple* 33. PG 155, 712A.
⁴Nicholas Cabasilas *Concerning the Sacred Vestments* 1. SC 4–bis, p. 364.
⁵Simeon of Thessalonica *Concerning the Holy Temple* 35. PG 155, 712B.
⁶Ibid., PG 155, 713D.

Epigonation. Mount Athos. 1727.

Epitrachilions. Mount Athos.

phelonion which is used in the Greek Church up to the present day is similar to those depicted in Byzantine frescoes. In the Russian Church in the Synodal period, the phelonion acquired a slightly different shape. In the front it was cut from the bottom in such a way that the priest's arms remained uncovered and in the back its top end was raised. This type of phelonion is worn today in the majority of the churches of the Russian Orthodox Church.

During the time of Saint Simeon of Thessalonica, a priest wore an *epitrachelion* (Gk. *epitrachelion*, ἐπιτραχήλιον), belt (Gk. *zoni*, ζώνη), and epigonation (Gk. *epigonation*, ἐπιγονάτιον). Cuffs (Gk. *epimanikia*, ἐπιμανίκια) were a component of both the priest's and deacon's vestments. Saint Simeon interprets the epitrachilion as a symbol of the grace of the Spirit descending from on high while the belt is a symbol of chastity. The epigonation is a symbol of the victory over sin and cuffs are a symbol showing that God acts in the divine service through the hands of the priest.[7]

In the ancient Church, the bishop was distinguished by the omophorion (Gr. *omophorion*, ὠμοφόριον)—a white band with black crosses; it covers the shoulders of the bishop and descends from the left shoulder with one end in front and the other end in the back. Made from sheep's wool, the omophorion symbolizes the lost sheep that the bishop, as the good shepherd, carries on his shoulders.[8] Saint Simeon of Thessalonica wrote:

> The omophorion signifies . . . the incarnation of God the Word—that he, having found us, the lost sheep, took us onto his shoulders, taking on the entire human essence, united it with himself and made it divine, bringing that received (essence) to the Father by death and the cross and resurrected and raised us. For this reason crosses are depicted (on the omophorion) and it is

[7] Ibid., PG 155, 712D–713D.
[8] The white color of the omophorion with black crosses corresponds with the color of a white sheep having black hooves.

made from wool and is donned by the bishop on his neck, sometimes around the shoulders from the front and back.[9]

During the first millennium there was no essential difference between styles of vestments in the West and the East. Both in Rome and Constantinople bishops were vested in the phelonion and omophorion, but it is true that over time the omophorion grew wider in the East than in the West. In western mosaics of the sixth century, saints are depicted wearing the phelonion and a thin omophorion. Pope Felix is depicted in this way in the Church of Saints Cosmas and Damian in Rome as is Saint Apollinaris in the Church of Sant' Apollinare in Classe near Ravenna and saints in the Basilica of San Vitale in Ravenna. Saints are depicted wearing phelonions and wide omophorions in the collection of manuscripts of the writings of Saint Gregory the Theologian (ninth and tenth centuries), in the *Menologion* of Basil II (around 985), and on numerous Byzantine frescoes and mosaics including the mosaics of Hagia Sophia in Constantinople and Saint Sophia Cathedral in Kiev.

In the period from the sixth through the twelfth centuries the style of phelonions and omophorions in the Orthodox East practically did not change. Byzantine mosaics, frescoes, and miniatures, as well as frescoes of the Saint Sophia Cathedral in Kiev, witness to this fact.[10] The "phelonion with crosses" came into use as an article of the hierarch's vestments no later than the twelfth century. It is made from material ornamented with equal-sided crosses. In Greek this material is called πολυσταύριον (*polystavrion*—having many crosses).[11]

Saints are depicted in the frescoes of Hagia Sophia wearing vestments which include, besides the phelonion and omophorion, the epitrachilion, cuffs, and epigonation. The epitrachilion looks like a long band which descends to the heels while the epigonation is a cloth of sewn fabric worn on the right thigh. The origin of the epitrachilion is connected with the orarion. The ephtrachilion is essentially an orarion which is not worn on the left shoulder but on the neck in such a way that both sides hang down in the front. These two sides are fastened together with buttons.

---

[9]Simeon of Thessalonica *Concerning Holy Ordinations* 208. PG 155, 421BC. Cf. also his *Concerning the Holy Temple* 44, PG 155, 716BC. The interpretation is traced back to Saint Germanus of Constantinople's *Church History*, PG 98, 396A.

[10]V. Prokhorov, "Materials Related to the History of Clergy Clothing: Phelonion," in *Christian Antiquities and Archeology* 3 (St Petersburg, 1863), 21.

[11]Ibid., Book 12, 105.

Sakkos. Mount Athos.

Sakkos of Saint Peter, Metropolitan of Moscow.

The *sakkos* (Gr. *sakkos*, σάκκος), from the Hebrew *sakk* meaning "sackcloth" was a part of the emperor's wardrobe in Byzantium. This garment had no sleeves and was donned over the head and buttoned on the sides. In the eleventh and twelfth centuries, emperors began to give the sakkos as a gift to patriarchs in Constantinople. Patriarchs wore the sakkos only on Christmas, Pascha, and Pentecost. Several bishops began to wear the sakkos in the fourteenth and fifteenth centuries, but the phelonion continued to be the traditional hierarchical vestment.[12] By this time the sakkos had acquired short sleeves. Saint Gregory Palamas, the archbishop of Thessalonica, is depicted on icons wearing the omophorion and a sakkos with short sleeves. Many Greek bishops began to wear the sakkos in the sixteenth century. By that time the sleeves of the sakkos had become longer, yet shorter than the sleeves of a sticharion.

It is difficult to determine exactly when bells first appeared on the sakkos. It is evident, however, that they serve as a reminder of the bells worn by Aaron on his robe, that their sound "will be heard when Aaron is serving as a priest, entering and leaving the holy place before the Lord" (Ex 28.30). Bells produce a ringing sound whenever the bishop moves around the church.

The sakkos first appeared in Russia no later than the fourteenth century as a liturgical vestment of Moscow's metropolitans. The sakkos of Metropolitan Peter (1308–1326) is preserved to this day. It was sewn in 1322 from light-blue satin material on which crosses in circles are woven with gold. Both a "large" and "small" sakkos survives from Metropolitan Photius (1409–1431). They are distinguished by their unusual richness of surface embroidery. After the establishment of the patriarchate in 1589, the sakkos became a vestment of Moscow's patriarchs. The sakkos was worn in the seventeenth century by metropolitans and some archbishops. In 1705 it was established that all hierarchs of the Russian Church must wear the sakkos.

---

[12] Nicholas Cabasilas mentions the phelonion and omophorion as the basic elements of the hierarch's vestments in the fourteenth century and does not mention the sakkos at all. See Nicholas Cabasilas, "Concerning the Sacred Vestments" 3, SC 4–bis, 366.

The mitre was not an attribute of the hierarch's vestments during the earliest days. The scholar Aleksei Dmitrievsky believes "this adornment for the bishop's head was made an article of their rank fairly recently." He wrote that "nothing but a complete silence is maintained regarding the mitre in all the ancient and later services for consecrating not only a bishop, but also a metropolitan and even a patriarch, which includes Greek, south-Slavic, and also our Slavonic-Russian service books, hand-written as well as printed and even those used in the practice of serving in the East and in Russia."[13]

Mitre. Mount Athos.

Although it is a relatively new phenomenon that the mitre is attributed to every bishop, the use of the mitre by individual hierarchs reaches back to deep antiquity. The origin of the mitre is found in the turban, the liturgical headdress of the Old Testament high priests. Saint John Chrysostom refers to the mitre in this very context.[14] There are numerous testimonies of the mitre as an attribute of the Alexandrian patriarchs. Saints Athanasius and Cyril of Alexandria are often depicted in ancient frescoes wearing white hats having black crosses. It was the custom of the Alexandrian patriarchs to wear such mitres. During the time of Saint Simeon of Thessalonica (fifteenth century), many other bishops in the East wore mitres, but traditionally it was still considered an attribute primarily of the Alexandrian patriarch. To the question, "Why do bishops and priests, with the exception of the Alexandrian patriarch, serve with uncovered heads and why is it better to serve with an uncovered head," Saint Simeon of Thessalonica answered:

> All eastern hierarchs and priests, with the exception of the Alexandrian (patriarch), conduct the sacred serving with uncovered heads. . . . But, perhaps, somebody will ask whether it is not irreverent that the Alexandrian patriarch covers his head with the sacred covering (Gr. *hieron epikalymma*, ἱερὸν ἐπικάλυμμα) as do countless others in accordance with ancient tradition? I do not ask this, for those who act in this way (and it serves as a justification) act according to the most ancient, or more accurately—"most lawful"[15]—tradition. Actually, the

---

[13] Aleksei Dmitrievsky, "Mitre, Historical-Archaeological Essay," *Handbook for Rural Pastors,* No. 11 (Kiev, 1903) (Reprinted in *Moscow Diocesan News*, No. 4–5, 2003); References the following editions: *Relations of Russia with the East*, 88, 101; *Proskynitarion of Arsenius Sukhanov*, 82.

[14] St John Chrysostom *Concerning the Holy Priesthood* 3, 4.

[15] That is to say, "of the Old Testament."

"lawful"[16] high priest wore on his head a turban (Gr. *kidarin*, κιδάριν), which is called a *mitre* (Gr. *mitran*, μίτραν), as bishops who wear it like to call it. Perhaps they have it as the likeness of the image of the crown of thorns of the Master and King—which was on his head.[17]

In the sixteenth century, when the patriarchs of Constantinople, Alexandria, and Jerusalem celebrated the divine services together, only the Alexandrian patriarch wore a mitre. A Russian envoy present at the service in Constantinople in 1585 bore witness to this fact.[18] Performing the service alone, the patriarch of Constantinople donned a mitre shaped like a king's crown. The mitre may have been a gift from one of the Byzantine emperors to the Constantinopolitan patriarch. Another possibility is that the patriarch of Constantinople began to wear the mitre after the fall of the Byzantine Empire. "For Greek national self-love it was completely natural, after the fall of Constantinople in 1453, to place the crown of the emperors, who already no longer existed, on the head of its ecumenical patriarch, the chief and single guardian of the interests of Orthodoxy and the nationality itself in the entire Muslim East."[19] Gradually the patriarch of Constantinople passed the crown-shaped mitre down to other Greek bishops.

In the middle of the seventeenth century, only the patriarch wore a mitre during a cathedral service in the Patriarchate of Jerusalem. The Russian traveler Arseny Sukhanov was present at the service on Holy Friday and was a witness to this fact:

> Every metropolitan wore a sakkos, and all were without caps.[20] Furthermore, nobody wore a cap anywhere, except for the patriarch. They have no caps and never had any. The metropolitan of Nazareth, having a worn-out hat, humbly asked the sovereign if he might deign to order a new one made, and the bishop of Nazareth, when he had arrived, gave this sovereign's cap to the patriarch as well as a sakkos. And from the beginning there were no caps in Nazareth and at the present time they will not wear them. And it is said that the patriarch, receiving it, pawned it. And while he was with us the metropolitan of Nazareth did not wear a cap when serving both with and without the patriarch.[21]

---

[16] Again, this means "of the Old Testament."
[17] Simeon of Thessalonica *Concerning the Holy Temple* 45. PG 155, 716D–717A.
[18] A.N. Muraviev, *Relations of Russia with the East*, Part 2 (St Petersburg, 1860), 149.
[19] Dmitrievsky, *Mitre*.
[20] In the Slavic Bishop's Service Book (*Chinovnik*) the mitre is called a "cap"(*shapka*).
[21] "Proskynitarion of Arsenius Sukhanov," *Orthodox Palestinian Collection*, Edition No. 21 (vol. 7, ed. 3) (St Petersburg, 1889), 82.

Liturgical Vestments of the Clergy

In 1642 the sovereign Tsar Mikhail Fedorovich presented a mitre to the monastery of Saint Catherine on Mount Sinai which is preserved to this day in the monastery's *skevofilakia* (room where the holy vessels are kept). It measures 20.5 cm (8.1 inches) in height, has a cross on top, and is adorned with eight icons, pearls, and precious stones. Another mitre, prepared in 1636 and presented to the monastery by Christians from the town of Yannin, has a height of 25.5 cm (10 inches). It is a magnificent work made of bronze and finished with precious stones, pearls, numerous icons, and depictions of cherubim. A third mitre, given to the monastery by "Protosyngellos" Nicephorus of Crete in 1678, has a height of 20.5 cm (8.1 inches) and besides precious stones and pearls, it is adorned with polychrome enamel.

Mitre of Saint Job, Patriarch of Moscow. 1595.

Originally the liturgical headdress of Russian hierarchs was the *kukol* (a rounded *klobuk*). Beginning in the fifteenth century, the mitre emerged in the service of Russian hierarchs, when it had the appearance of a prince's hat. They were decorated with embroidery and precious stones and were sometimes lined with fur on the bottom. The Russian mitre-cap differed in shape from crown-shaped Byzantine mitres. For this reason, the latter caused bewilderment for connoisseurs of local church rituals. One such connoisseur who was present during the service of the patriarch of Jerusalem Theophan in Moscow in 1619 observed, "The cap he was wearing was without a border on black velvet . . . like a gilded crown with stones planted and with no depictions of saints, but on the top is placed a cross and on the sides four cherubim and seraphim."[22] In the sixteenth and seventeenth centuries, Greek hierarchs were pleased to receive Russian mitre-caps from Russian tsars, metropolitans, and patriarchs, but they did not use them but rather pawned them or refashioned them. Russian mitre-caps with sable linings did not conform to the eastern climate.[23]

The crown-shaped mitre appeared in Russia in the seventeenth century when it was adopted from Greek hierarchs by Patriarch Nikon in 1653.[24] All hierarchs in Russia began wearing mitres of that style. Mitres were also given to some archimandrites. This was made permissible by the decree of Peter the Great in 1705. In

---

[22] *Readings in the Society of History and Russian Antiquities.* Book 2, Part 2, 166.

[23] Dmitrievsky, *Mitre.* With a reference to the next publication: *Relations of Russia with the East.* Ch. 1, S. 88, 101. *Proskynitarion of Arsenius Sukhanov,* 82.

[24] *Antiquities of the Russian State,* Part 1, 124–132

1786 Catherine the Great awarded a mitre to her spiritual father, Archpriest John Pamphilov, and beginning in 1797, by the decree of Tsar Pavel I, the mitre came to be awarded to deserving archpriests as a mark of special distinction.

In contrast to the Greek Church in which all mitres are topped with a cross, two types are used in the Russian Church—with and without a cross. Originally the mitre with a cross appertained to the patriarchs of Moscow. In 1686 the right to wear a mitre with a cross was extended to the metropolitan of Kiev. Later, all metropolitans received this right while all archbishops, bishops, and archpriests as well as archimandrites and mitred archpriests wore the mitre without a cross. At the end of the 1980s, during the patriarchate of Patriarch Pimen, the Holy Synod established, in accordance with the Greek custom, that all hierarchs of the Russian Church are to wear mitres with a cross. The mitre without a cross now is worn by archimandrites and mitred archpriests.[25]

The hierarch's *staff* (Slavonic *zhezl*) is a symbol of the Church's power while, at the same time, it is a symbol of the wanderer's way of life. The right to carry a staff during services is given to all hierarchs and also to some archimandrites and the abbots of monasteries. It is a variation of a shorter staff, which was used by bishops of the ancient Church during times of travels. In contemporary practice hierarchs carry a shorter staff outside of church services and the staff with a cross on top during services. The short staff is a wooden stick which stands from the ground to the chest and has a rounded handle. The staff is usually taller, reaching to the shoulders of the hierarch, and is topped with a cross in the form of a bow or a two-headed snake with heads turned towards a cross in the middle. The two-headed snake is a symbol of the wisdom and teaching authority of the hierarch.

In the Russian tradition the staff is wrapped in a cloth made of brocade (Sl. *sulok*), which covers the hand of the hierarch while he holds the staff. The sulok is a purely Russian invention. Originally it was intended to protect the hierarch's hand from cold weather when liturgical processions around the church took place during the winter months (for example, the processional walk "to the Jordan" on the feast of the Theophany). Later the sulok became a fixture on the hierarch's staff during services inside the church as well.[26]

---

[25] In the West the mitre acquired the shape of a pointed crown, widening from the base and becoming narrow on the top. Such pointed mitres can be seen in paintings from the Middle Ages. The mitre was worn by western bishops including Roman popes. Beginning in the fourteenth century, popes wore the tiara—an egg-shaped hat made from three crowns, symbolizing the secular and spiritual power of the pope on earth and also his power over the next life. The tiara in the Roman Church was eliminated by Pope John XXIII (1958–1963) and subsequent popes have worn mitres identical to those worn by other Latin bishops.

[26] However, a *sulok* is not placed on the patriarch's staff.

Liturgical Vestments of the Clergy

The hierarch's *mantia* is a vestment buttoned at the neck and at the level of the hem, having a long train with long red and white stripes sewn on the fabric. According to the interpretation of Saint Simeon of Thessalonica, these stripes (Gr. *potamoi*, ποταμοί) symbolize the teaching worthiness of the hierarch as well as various gifts given to him from above.[27] In the Russian Church the patriarch wears a green mantia while metropolitans wear a blue one and archbishops and bishops wear a mantia of purple. In the Greek Church all hierarchs wear a wine-colored (maroon) mantia. Two velvet rectangular patches called *tablets* (Slavonic *skrizhali*) bearing a depiction of crosses or seraphim are sewn into both sides of the mantia at the level of the chest. Similar rectangular patches, often bearing the two first letters of the rank and name of the hierarch,[28] are sewn into the bottom of the mantia at knee-level. The hierarch's mantia did not appear in this form until the eighteenth century.[29]

In the Russian Church the term *panagia* (from the Greek παναγία—All-Holy) is used to describe an object which the Greeks call ἐγκόλπιον (*enkolpion*), which literally means "on the breast" (Slavonic *nanedrennik*). In Byzantium this word was used to describe tabernacles in which either a particle of the relics of saints was carried on the breast or the reserve holy gifts were transported. In Byzantium the enkolpion was considered an indispensable attribute of the bishop right up to the fifteenth century. The enkolpion is first mentioned in this way by Saint Simeon of Thessalonica. The Byzantine enkolpion had various forms (ovul, round, rectangular, cross-shaped). The Mother of God or one of the saints was depicted on its face and it was sometimes adorned with precious stones. The enkolpion ceased to be used as a tabernacle in the post-Byzantine period and acquired the significance of marking the distinction of the bishop on his breast. Having this meaning, *enkolpion* was passed on to Russia with the name *panagia*.

Beginning in the middle of the eighteenth century bishops began to be given two enkolpions at the time of their consecration—one having the shape of a cross and the other bearing the image of the Mother of God. The Moscow Council of 1674 permitted metropolitans to wear the enkolpion and cross over the sakkos, but only on the territory of their diocese. The Novgorodian metropolitan could wear the enkolpion and cross in the presence of the patriarch. From the middle

---

[27]Simeon of Thessalonica *Concerning the Holy Temple* 37. PG 155, 712. In the given case, Simeon of Thessalonica speaks of *istochniki* (vertical stripes) on the hierarch's sticharion.

[28]For example, the letters "M" and "S" stand for "Metropolitan Seraphim," while "A" and "K" stand for "Archbishop Kirill" and "B" and "D" for "Bishop Dmitri."

[29]*Desk Manual for Clergy*, vol. 4, 148.

of the seventeenth century, Moscow patriarchs and Kievan metropolitans wore two enkolpions and one cross. At the present time, the right to wear two panagias and one cross is given to all the heads of local autonomous Orthodox Churches.[30] Other bishops wear the panagia and cross during church services while outside of services they wear only the panagia.

In the ancient Church priests did not wear crosses on the breast. The four-ended, gold breast cross was introduced in the Russian Orthodox Church as an award for deserving priests by the decree of Emperor Paul I on December 18, 1797. On February 24, 1820, by the decree of the Holy Synod, priests who had served abroad received the right to wear a cross "from his Majesty's Cabinet"—these crosses were known as "Cabinet crosses." Beginning in the nineteenth century, deserving priests were awarded jeweled crosses and some archimandrites even received the right to wear the panagia.[31] Finally, by the decree of Emperor Nicholas II on May 14, 1896, the silver cross came to be awarded as a mark of distinction to every priest. At the present time, the silver cross is given to every priest at his ordination while the gold cross (the cross described above as dating from the year 1797) and the jeweled cross may be awarded as a mark of special distinction or many years of service.[32]

Several rules exist concerning the wearing of crosses by priests in the local autonomous Orthodox Churches. In the Greek tradition only archimandrites and distinguished archpriests (Gr. *protosygkelos*, πρωτοσύγκελος) have the right to wear a cross, while the majority of priests do not wear a cross. In the churches of Slavic tradition the practice was adopted from the Russian Church of the Synodal period to allow all priests to wear crosses. In the Romanian Church, not only all priests but archdeacons wear crosses as well. They wear the cross over their sticharion during the divine services.

It is worth saying a few words about the colors of vestments. In the Russian Church seven colors are used: gold, white, blue, red, wine-colored (purple), green, and black. It is customary to serve in gold vestments on Sundays throughout the entire year with the exception of Sundays during the Great Fast. Gold is also worn

---

[30]As a rule, if the hierarch wears two panagias, one depicts the Mother of God and the other depicts Jesus Christ. In accordance with "The Situation Concerning Awards in the Russian Orthodox Church," confirmed by the Episcopal Assembly of 2004, in addition to the patriarch of Moscow and All Russia, the right to wear two panagias is given to the metropolitan of Kiev and All Ukraine.

[31]In particular, the future Metropolitan of Moscow Philaret received this right while he was an archimandrite. Also, the famous church composer and theologian of the nineteenth century Archimandrite Theophan (Alexandrov) received this right.

[32]Until the year 2004 some clergymen in the Russian Orthodox Church received the right to wear two or three crosses, but that custom has since been eliminated.

on Christmas and several other feast days. White vestments are worn on Theophany, Holy Saturday, and Pascha and also on the feast of the Ascension and days commemorating the bodiless heavenly hosts. Blue is worn on all feast days of the Theotokos. Green vestments are used on the Entry of the Lord into Jerusalem, Pentecost, and days commemorating venerable saints. According to the Russian tradition, red vestments are worn throughout the entire paschal period as well as on days commemorating martyrs. It is customary to serve wearing purple (wine-colored) vestments on Sundays of the Great Fast and days commemorating the Cross of Christ. Finally, black vestments are usually worn on weekdays of the Great Fast.[33] Twice a year it is customary to re-vest during the church service. On Great Saturday servers re-vest from black into white vestments. During the midnight service of Pascha, servers re-vest from white into red vestments.

It should be noted that the symbolism of colors is a rather recent phenomenon in the Russian Church and not completely rigid. For example, in some churches it is customary to wear gold vestments on Christmas while in others white. In the Russian Church Abroad, which inherited the liturgical traditions of the Synodal period, the sacred servers wear white vestments[34] during the entire paschal period, while in the Moscow Patriarchate in the post-Revolutionary period the tradition of serving in red vestments emerged.[35]

In local autonomous Orthodox Churches, there are various traditions regarding the use of vestments of different colors during services. In the Greek Church it is not at all customary to attribute the color of vestments to a particular feast, while in the Georgian Church the color of vestments can vary depending on the rank of servers. For example, the patriarch may wear white vestments while the bishops serving with him may wear red, while deacons may wear green, and subdeacons and readers may wear gold.

---

[33]Black vestments were first introduced in 1730 on the occasion of the funeral of Emperor Peter II.

[34]Cf. Protopresbyter Valery Lukyanov, *Service Notes, Attempt at Understanding the Practical Aspects of the Divine Services of the Orthodox Church* (Jordanville, 2001), 25.

[35]Perhaps this tradition was due to the improper understanding of the Slavic expression from the paschal verses "Pascha krasnaya" (its literal meaning is "wonderful Pascha," not "red Pascha"), or from the tradition of dying eggs red.

PART TWO

ICONS AND THEIR VENERATION

Savior Not-Made-by-Hands. Icon. Novgorod School. c. 1100.

I cons occupy an exceptional place in the Orthodox Church. They are the side of the Orthodox tradition which, during the last several decades, has considerably extended beyond the borders of "canonical Orthodoxy." Reproductions of icons are seen today in Orthodox as well as Catholic and Protestant churches and even in non-Christian places. Icons are silent and eloquent preachers of Orthodoxy not only within the confines of the Church, but also in a world which is alien to—and even hostile to—the Orthodox Church. In the words of Leonid Ouspensky, "While during the years of iconoclasm the Church fought for icons, in our own time icons fight for the Church."[1] Icons fight for Orthodoxy, truth,

[1] Leonid Ouspensky, *Theology of the Icon* (Paris, 1989), 467.

and beauty. Ultimately, icons fight for human souls, because the salvation of souls is the objective and meaning of the Church's existence.

In this chapter we will explore the main landmarks of icon painting as it developed in the Christian Church. We will then examine Orthodox icons in their theological, anthropological, cosmic, liturgical, mystical, and moral aspects.

6

Early Christian Painting. Frescoes of the Roman Catacombs

THE DEVELOPMENT OF CHRISTIAN PAINTING took place while early Christianity was retreating from its Jewish roots.

It is well known that it was strictly forbidden in the Jewish tradition to make images of God, people, and animals. Ornamentation depicting vegetation was permitted as were certain symbolic images. The interior decorative arrangement of Solomon's temple contained a pictorial element. Inside the temple, cedars were carved with the likeness of gourds and blossoming flowers. There were also statues of cherubim standing ten cubits high and on the temple's walls were carved figures of cherubim and palm trees and blossoming flowers (1 Kg 6.18–29). Ornamentation of vegetation and symbolic images, such as signs of the zodiac, were typical decorations found in synagogues.

The prohibition against depicting people in the Jewish tradition, however, was not always strictly observed; exceptions to the rule did exist. The walls of the Jewish synagogue in Dura-Europos (first half of the third century AD), for example, were adorned with frescoes depicting subjects from the Old Testament. These included: the birth of Moses, the visions of Prophet Ezekiel, the Israelites crossing the Red Sea, Prophet Elijah standing up to the false prophets of Baal, Elijah raising the widow's son from the dead, and others. The existence of an entire complex of frescoes depicting biblical subjects in the synagogue in Dura-Europos is explained both by the influence of the art of antiquity and the proximity of the synagogue to the Christian church.

Sources of Christian painting must be sought not in Jewish but in Greco-Roman traditions, in which the fine and sculptural arts were widespread and advanced. Christian icons were the successors to antiquity's funerary pictures both in form and function.[2] This is confirmed by a comparative analysis of early Christian icons and

---

[2]Hans Belting, *Likeness and Presence: The History of the Image Before the the Era of Art* (Moscow, 2002), 117.

Moses. The Israelites Crossing the Red Sea. Fresco. Jewish Synagogue in Dura-Europos. First half of the 3rd c.

the so-called Fayum mummy portraits—Egyptian funeral images found by archeologists in Fayum and other Egyptian towns (more than seven hundred images are known to scholars).[3] Men and women wearing Roman clothing are depicted in these portraits, which were generally executed on cypress or cedar panels measuring about forty by twenty centimeters (15.7 x 7.9 inches). The oldest Fayum portraits (first and second centuries BC) were executed in the technique of encaustic painting. Paint is prepared from pigments and beeswax and is heated before being placed on the board. Egg tempera was more commonly used in the latest portraits (third to fourth centuries AD). From an artistic perspective, the Fayum portraits were completely realistic images of the deceased. At the same time there is an aspect of idealization and heroization in the depictions. Facial features are consciously made to look more noble than they were and the appearance of the deceased is given an exalted character.

Sources of Christian images painted on walls can also be discovered in the frescoes of antiquity such as those preserved in Pompeii. Thematically, Christian art gradually departed from antique models between the second century and the end of the fifth. But with regard to painting technique, Christian artists continued to rely upon the traditions of antiquity.

The making of early Christian painting can be seen in the example of the wall paintings of the Roman catacombs. These pictures, dating from the second through the fifth century, can be placed into three categories: symbols and symbolic images; images influenced by antique models but reconceived in the Christian spirit; pictures of Christian subjects and icons. All of these images possess a moral-didactic character and are called to reflect basic truths of Christian teachings. The majority of the images were executed as frescoes, but mosaics are encountered as well (especially in the Catacombs of Saint Domitilla).

Fish and Loaves. Fresco. Catacombs of Saint Callistus. Rome.

Symbols used in early Christian art include: a fish, anchor, ship, grapevine, lamb, basket with loaves, phoenix, and many more. The fish is one of the earliest and most widespread Christian symbols and is interpreted

---

[3]Susan Walker and Morris Bierbrier, *Fayum: Misteriosi volti dall'Egitto* (Milan: Leonardo Arte, 1997), 29.

Early Christian Painting

in different ways. The Greek word ΙΧΘΥΣ (*ICHTHYS*) served as an abbreviation of the words Ἰησοῦς Χριστὸς Θεοῦ Υἱὸς Σωτήρ (*Iesous Christos Theou Yios Soter*—Jesus Christ, Son of God, Savior). Moreover, a fish was perceived as a symbol of baptism. One of the most ancient symbols of the Eucharist, found in the Catacombs of St Callistus, is the depiction of a fish with a basket containing loaves and wine on its back. Other eucharistic symbols used were a grapevine, a cluster of grapes, and two peacocks drinking from a cup. A ship, ship's wheel, sailboat, and anchor were symbols of the Church as Noah's saving ark. A phoenix served as a symbol of the resurrection and immortality. The image of the Good Shepherd—a youth in shepherd's clothing carrying a lamb or young goat on his shoulders—was a symbol of Christ. Another of the most important Christological symbols was a lamb, often depicted inside a circle or having a halo around its head. All of the symbols mentioned here had pagan origins, but by being included in the everyday practice of Christians, they were transformed into a visual expression of the sacraments—which helped Christians to recount the fundamental truths of the faith to one another.

The Good Shepherd. Fresco. Catacomb of Priscilla. Rome.

Orpheus—a Type of Christ. Fresco. Catacombs of Marcellinus and Peter. Rome.

Paintings having themes of antiquity that were reconceived in the Christian spirit included depictions of Gorgon Medusa, scenes from the poems of Homer, and depictions of Orpheus with his lyre. In early Christian literature (especially that of Clement of Alexandria), Orpheus often emerged as a type of Christ. As Orpheus tamed beasts by his playing of the lyre, Christ subdues people by the word of the Gospel. Orpheus was also perceived as a Greek counterpart to David, the biblical singer of psalms.[4] In frescoes of the Catacombs of Saint Domitilla, Orpheus is depicted sitting on a rock and holding his lyre while surrounded by birds and animals (doves, a peacock, snake, horse, lion, sheep, turtle, and hare) who listen to his singing. The figure of Orpheus is set inside an octagon around which decorative scenes and scenes from biblical history are found: Daniel in the lions' den, Moses extracting water from the rock, and the raising of Lazarus.[5] In

---

[4] See V.F. Nicolai, F. Bisconti, D. Mazzoleni, *Roms christliche Katakomben: Geschichte–Bilderwelt–Inschriften* (Regensburg, 2000), 103.

[5] N.V. Pokrovsky, *Essays on Monuments of Christian Art and Iconography* (St Petersburg, 1910), 25.

Jesus Christ. Fresco. Catacombs of Commodilla. Rome.

this way, in the consciousness of the painter, the image of Orpheus is inseparable from the history of salvation. In this fresco the ancient painter embodied in paint the early Christian conception of ancient philosophy and mythology as a "tutor leading to Christ."[6]

Finally, Old Testament and Christian subjects occupy a notable place in catacomb paintings. The most common subjects from the Old Testament are Noah in his ark, the sacrifice of Abraham, Jonah in the belly of the whale, Jonah cast out onto the shore by the whale, Daniel surrounded by lions, Moses extracting water from the rock, and Moses removing his sandals before the burning bush. Subjects from the New Testament include: the worship of the Magi, the conversation of Christ with the Samaritan woman, the raising of Lazarus, and the feeding of the multitudes with bread and fish. Some of Christ's parables, especially the Parable of the Sower and the Parable of the Ten Virgins, were also reflected in catacomb paintings.

If one examines the catacombs as an integrated ensemble and sees in such an ensemble a unified program of paintings, the central figure in this program is Christ. Images of Christ in the catacombs may be placed into three categories: *symbolic* (having the form of a dove, the Good Shepherd, etc.); in the form of a young, beardless, Greco-Roman man with short hair (for the sake of discussion we shall call the type of this image of Christ *antique*); and in the form of a middle-aged man with a beard and long hair (we shall call this type *iconographic*). The "antique" type of Christ is found in frescoes of the second through fourth centuries, particularly in the scene from the Catacombs of Via Dino Compagni of Christ conversing with the Samaritan woman, the mosaic scene in the Catacombs of Saint Domitilla showing Christ raising Lazarus from the dead, and a depiction from the same catacombs of Christ with the apostles. The "iconographic" type is encountered in a series of frescoes beginning in the fourth century. The earliest known to scholars are found in the Catacombs of Commodilla. In these works Christ is presented with a long beard and long, wavy hair. His gaze is not fixed on the viewer but rather off to the side. This type of depiction emerged later than the "antique" type and became common in the post-Constantinian period.

---

[6]This understanding is found in Saint Clement of Alexandria and Origen and also in the Cappadocian Fathers of the fourth century.

Early Christian Painting 113

In the fresco of the Catacombs of Marcellinus and Peter (between the fourth and sixth centuries), Christ is presented as a middle-aged man having a long, cone-shaped beard, large eyes, and long hair, parted in the middle. The Savior is seated on a backless throne. His right hand is raised in a blessing gesture while he holds an opened scroll in his left hand. His head is surrounded by a halo next to which the Greek letters Α and Ω (*alpha* and *omega*) are seen. He is dressed in a brown *himation* (Gr. *himation*, ἱμάτιον—cloak) and wears light sandals on his feet. Under his feet is a rectangular pedestal painted in accordance with the rules of "reverse perspective." The apostles Peter and Paul, dressed in bright Roman clothing, stand on the two sides of Christ. Peter is depicted as an old man having a short gray beard and short hair. Paul is shown to be balding with a long, dark, cone-shaped beard. The right hand of Peter indicates the Savior while the right hand of Paul is pressed against his own heart. In the bottom row are images of the martyrs Gorgonius, Peter, Marcellinus, and Tiburtius, all dressed in Roman togas, their faces looking upwards at Christ. Between them, in the middle and under the Savior's throne, is the image of a lamb with a halo around its head. Over its head is the monogram of Christ, and the letters Α and Ω are written inside the halo. This composition attests to the fully developed iconographical canon whose fundamental characteristics were to be preserved in the post-Constantinian period.

Christ Surrounded by Apostles and Saints. Fresco. Catacombs of Marcellinus and Peter. Rome.

Prophet Jonah Cast Overboard. Fresco. Catacombs of Marcellinus and Peter. Rome.

An important place in the iconographical program of the catacombs is held by the image of the Mother of God with the Infant Christ. The most ancient depictions of the Mother of God (dating from the second century) are found in the Catacomb of Priscilla. She is presented seated and with covered head, wearing the clothing of a Roman woman. In her arms is the Infant Christ. Before her stands a young man in the clothing of a prophet or philosopher (presumably the Prophet Isaiah or Joseph the Betrothed).[7] In the scene of the Adoration of the Magi in the Catacombs of Marcellinus and Peter, the Virgin Mary is depicted in three-quarter

---

[7] Pokrovsky, *Essays*, 49–50.

Mother of God with Infant Jesus. Catacomb of Priscilla. Rome. 3rd c.

view and without a head covering. She is seated on a throne, holding the Infant Christ in her arms. The Magi approach her with gifts. In the fresco of the Catacombs of Saint Agnes, the Mother of God is presented in full face view in the *orans* posture (hands raised upward). Her hair is luxuriant and her head is only slightly covered. The Infant Jesus is depicted in the foreground, at the level of her chest; he is also shown in full face view.

The image which most closely resembles the canonical type of the icon of the Mother of God is found in a fresco at the Catacombs of Commodilla (fifth or sixth century). She is presented wearing a dark garment which completely covers her head and body. Only her face, neck, and hands remain uncovered. The Infant Christ has a scroll in his hand and is seated on her knees. The martyrs Felix and Adauctus are depicted on either side of her, while to her left and in the foreground is the widow Commodilla—the wealthy Roman woman in whose memory the catacomb church was built.

Adam and Eve. Fresco. Catacombs of Marcellinus and Peter. Rome.

Besides images of Christ and the Mother of God, we encounter in the painting of the catacombs images of apostles, martyrs, prophets, and hierarchs (Roman popes). Compositions containing multiple figures have their place among scenes showing one or two figures and even individual portraits. Images of a symbolic character appear together with completely realistic painting; Christian and antique subjects coexist in harmony.

Catacomb paintings reveal the world of the early Christian Church in all its diversity. It is the Church whose iconographic tradition is in the process of being shaped, the Church that is engaged in a tense dialogue with the pagan world and active missionary work among pagans. It is the persecuted Church whose richest internal resources are only partly reflected in its fine arts. It is the Church transfixed by eschatological expectation of the coming kingdom of God. It is the Church in which the boundaries between the world of the living and the dead, between the past, present, and future, have been wiped away.

7
Iconographical Tradition in Byzantium

Byzantine Mosaics and Frescoes of the Fourth Through Seventh Centuries

THE FLOURISHING OF CHURCH BUILDING that took place in the fourth through seventh centuries resulted in a powerful surge of Christian fine arts. The walls of magnificent churches created throughout the entire empire were adorned with frescoes and mosaics. Moreover, individual icons, painted on panels, began to appear in churches.

The iconographic canon was by no means established immediately. This is testified in part by the epistle of Saint Nilus of Sinai, the disciple of Saint John Chrysostom, to the eparch Olympiodorus in about AD 400. Olympiodorus intended to "place icons and depict various hunting and fishing scenes" in the martyr's church he was building. But Saint Nilus called this "juvenile" and advised him to "make the image of a single cross in the sanctuary on the eastern side of the church, because by one saving cross the human race is saved." Concerning the western and eastern walls, Saint Nilus instructed, "Allow the hand of the most artful painter to fill the church from both sides with images from the Old and New Testaments so that those who are uneducated and cannot read the divine Scriptures may examine the painted images and recall the courageous feats of those sincerely serving God."[1] Judging from this, we may assume that the walls of churches were painted both with decorations having no particular religious meaning as well as with images of the holy cross and biblical scenes.

The mosaics of Ravenna give the most complete picture of Christian monumental fine arts of the fifth and sixth centuries. This city, by virtue of its unique geopolitical location, became an exceptional center of Christian fine arts. From 402 until 476 Ravenna was the capital city of the western empire. From 493 until 540 it was occupied by the Ostrogoths and in 540 it was captured by the Byzantines.

---

[1] Nilus the Ascetic *To Olympiodorus the Eparch* Letter No. 4, 59. PG 79, 577CD.

Latins as well as Greeks, Syrians, Armenians, and members of other nationalities lived in Ravenna. Byzantine emperors as well as Roman popes and Gothic chieftains participated in the building and adornment of churches in Ravenna.

The mosaics of Ravenna are distinguished by their rich colors. Bright, vibrant tones are prevalent in them—green, dark blue, light blue, gold, brown, red, and white. The mosaics of the mausoleum of Galla Placidia, the daughter of Emperor Theodosius I, date to the first quarter of the fifth century and are considered to be the oldest of the Ravenna mosaics. The mausoleum is a building of modest size with a cruciform floor plan and four lunettes. The lower level of the walls is revetted with marble while the upper level of walls and arches is covered with mosaics. The space under the dome is adorned with a mosaic depicting a starry sky. In the center of the dome is a cross inside a circle. In the southern lunette, the martyr Saint Lawrence is shown holding a cross in his right hand and the open Gospel in his left hand. A burning fire underneath an iron grate is found in the center of the composition (according to tradition, the martyr was burnt to death). Across from the fire and opposite the figure of the martyr is depicted a small book cabinet with four Gospels—according to Matthew, Mark, Luke, and John. A depiction of the Good Shepherd is found in the northern lunette. He is a young, beardless man with long wavy hair, sitting in a graceful antique pose and leaning on a large four-ended cross held in his left hand. With his right hand the Good Shepherd feeds the sheep that surround him. The sheep are presented in various positions but their heads are all turned towards the Pastor. Apostles wearing white tunics are placed in the other lunettes. The walls of the mausoleum are richly adorned with ornaments and details such as stars, plants, and various geometrical shapes.

Chronologically, the next structures and decorations to appear were those of the baptistery attached to the cathedral.[2] The baptistery's mosaics date back to the third quarter of the fifth century and are a fine collection devoted to the theme of baptism. A scene of the baptism of Christ is found in the dome but the original mosaic of this composition has been lost, so it is impossible to judge its original appearance. A mosaic in the space under the dome, composed of two registers, is in far better condition. The first register, adjacent to the scene of the baptism of Christ, consists of images of the twelve apostles bearing martyrs' crowns in their hands, wearing Roman clothing, against a dark blue background. The second register, directly under the first, is ornamental and appears to contain symbolic depictions

---

[2] Some sources call this the Baptistery of Neon from the name of Bishop Neon under whom it is presumed the mosaics were created (451–473).

Iconographical Tradition in Byzantium

of episcopal thrones (armchairs and pillows, tables with opened Gospel, thrones topped with crosses).

A similar composition is contained in the Arian Baptistery and dates to the first quarter of the sixth century. Christ is depicted in the dome as a young man, beardless and with long wavy hair. He is completely unclothed and submerged up to the waist in the waters of the Jordan. Saint John the Baptist is on the shore of the Jordan. He has a beard and long hair that reaches lower than his waist. John is dressed in a hair shirt with uncovered arms and legs. A pastor's staff is in the left hand of the Baptist while his right hand is placed on Christ's head. On the other end of the river is an old man with gray hair who embodies the Jordan. As in the Orthodox Baptistery, the space under the dome of the Arian Baptistery contains depictions of the apostles and beneath them, episcopal thrones.

The Basilica of Sant' Apollinare Nuovo was built by the Ostrogoth king Theodoric in the beginning of the sixth century. Three registers of images are situated at the sides of the central nave. The upper row consists of twenty-six compositions illustrating various scenes from the Gospel. Here Christ is depicted with a beard and long hair. But Christ appears without a beard in the scene of the last judgment. Next to him stand two angels and various peoples are presented in the form of six lambs. Windows alternate with monumental figures of prophets and apostles in the second register. The third register depicts processions of women martyrs (on the northern wall) and men martyrs (on the southern wall), moving from west to east in the direction of the sanctuary apse. The procession of female martyrs begins from the Port of Ravenna, depicted on the western part of the southern wall, and concludes with the scene of the Adoration of the Magi and a depiction of the Mother of God on a throne surrounded by archangels. The procession

Baptism of the Lord. Mosaic. The Arian Baptistery. Ravenna.

Last Judgment. Mosaic. Sant' Apollinare Nuovo. Ravenna.

Martyrs. Mosaic. Sant' Apollinare Nuovo. Ravenna.

Christ surrounded by Angels, the Martyr Vitale, and Bishop Ecclesius. Mosaic. San Vitale. Ravenna.

of the male martyrs begins at the palace of King Theodoric, depicted on the southern wall across from the Port of Ravenna, and concludes at the sanctuary apse with an image of Christ sitting on a throne. In this way, the interior space of the basilica is arranged as one grandiose liturgical scene. The effect is to unite saints and worshippers in common adoration of Christ and veneration of the Mother of God. The scene unites prophets, apostles, men and women martyrs, earthly leaders, and also the parishioners of the church who, by their presence during the services, themselves become a part of the composition—comprising the lowest register.

A most impressive mosaic ensemble is located in the Basilica of San Vitale, built in 540, following the conquest of Ravenna by the Byzantines. Surviving mosaics in the sanctuary apse witness to an iconographic program that had been worked out in great detail and that reflected basic dogmas of Christianity and the distinctiveness of the period in which the church was built. In the sanctuary apse Christ is depicted as a beardless youth with wide open eyes. He is seated on a light blue celestial sphere. In his left hand he holds a scroll with seven seals while his right hand holds out a martyr's crown to Saint Vitalis. An archangel and Saint Vitalis stand by Christ's right side while a second archangel and Bishop Ecclesius stand at his left side. A cross-in-halo encircles Christ's head and the sky and clouds are depicted above his head. At the bottom of the composition is ornamentation depicting the earth, grass, and flowers. To the sides of the central composition, on the right and left sides, are images of the church's benefactors—on the left side is Emperor Justinian with his retinue and Bishop Maximian while on the right side is the Empress Theodora surrounded by her retinue. In the center of the dome's space is a figure of a lamb with a halo around its head. The lamb is surrounded by four archangels standing on light blue spheres. Most of the space under the dome is covered with ornamentation depicting animals, birds, fruits, and plants.

Empress Theodora accompanied by her Retinue. Mosaic. San Vitale. Ravenna.

The walls of the sanctuary apse are adorned with scenes from biblical history. The main composition of the northern wall of the apse is the hospitality of Abraham. In the center of the composition are three men in white garments seated at a table under a tree. On the table are three loaves of bread. To the left of the men is Abraham who wears a short brown garment and offers the men a dish with a calf in it. Behind Abraham is Sarah, laughing under the roof of a house. Abraham is also depicted on the right side of the composition wearing a long white garment, bearing a sword in his hand. Before him stands an altar on which the young Isaac sits with hands tied behind his back. In this way, the hospitality of Abraham and the sacrifice of Isaac by Abraham are united in a single composition. On the opposite, southern wall of the apse is an image of a throne with a covering. A cup is on the throne and over it is a blessing hand. To the left of the throne is Abel, bringing a lamb to sacrifice. On the right side is Melchizedek with bread in his hands. Other personages in the composition found in the sanctuary apse are Moses, Isaiah, and Jeremiah. Thematically, all the mosaics of the sanctuary apse are united by a common Christological theme and submit to the central figure of Christ seated in the celestial sphere.

Of special interest is the mosaic of the sanctuary apse of the Church of Sant' Apollinare in Classe which dates to the sixth century. The center of the composition shows a medallion in which is a richly ornamented cross is positioned. The Greek word ΙΧΘΥΣ is written above the cross. The letters A and Ω (*alpha* and *omega*) are found beside the cross and the Latin inscription *Salus mundi* (Salvation of the world) is seen under the cross. The cross is encircled by six-pointed gold stars on a light blue ground. On the sides of the medallion, soaring on the clouds, are the half-figures of Moses and Elijah as well as three lambs symbolizing the apostles Peter, James, and John. Indeed this is nothing other than a depiction of the Transfiguration of the Lord, but the

Saint Apollinaris. Mosaic. Basilica of Sant' Apollinare in Classe. Ravenna.

central figure of Christ is replaced with a cross with the face of Christ where the two beams meet. Another composition is positioned beneath this scene. In the center of the composition is Saint Apollinaris, the heavenly patron of the church. His hands are raised and he is wearing the garb of a bishop (*phelonion* and *omophorion*). On each side of the saint are six lambs turned towards him. The bright green background of the composition presents grass on which elements of a landscape, trees, and flowers are depicted in orderly fashion. Viewed together these two compositions present a monumental picture of the cosmos, including the heavenly world and the earthly. In the center of the celestial world is the transfigured Christ symbolized by the cross. In the center of the earthly world is a deified man abiding in harmonious union with nature.

For their richness of content, brightness of color, and variety of composition, the mosaics of the Ravenna churches and baptistery constitute an unsurpassed collection. The mosaics of Ravenna reveal to us a Church no longer persecuted and taking shelter in the catacombs, but rather a Church prospering and benefiting from the protection of secular power—a Church at the pinnacle of glory and power.

Ravenna is not the only city in which monuments of mosaic art from the pre-iconoclastic period have survived. Other monuments are found in Rome (Church of Santa Maria Maggiore), in Milan (Church of San Lorenzo, Church of Sant'Ambrogio), on Mount Sinai (Monastery of Saint Catherine), in Thessalonica (Basilica of Saint Demetrius), and in a number of other cities in the East and West.

Thessalonica's oldest mosaics date to the end of the fourth and beginning of the fifth centuries and are found in the Rotunda of Saint George. Martyrs are depicted with faces executed in proper antique proportions and large, wide open eyes. The mosaics of the Monastery of Saint David (second half of the fifth century) present the vision of the Prophet Ezekiel. Christ, depicted as a beardless youth with long hair, is in the center of the composition. He is seated on a rainbow, and rays of various colors of the rainbow proceed from him. His head is encircled by a halo. The figure of Christ fits completely within a circle supported by four animals symbolizing the four evangelists. Extremely interesting are the mosaics of the Church of Saint Demetrius (seventh century) in which the Thessalonian martyr is depicted in various compositions in the company of bishops, deacons, and benefactors of the church.

Transfiguration. Church of the Monastery of Saint Catherine. Sinai.

The mosaics of the sanctuary apse of the main church of the Monastery of Saint Catherine on Mount Sinai date to the middle of the sixth century. In terms of both theme and style they have much in common with the mosaics of Ravenna which were created at the same time. The Transfiguration is the main theme of the composition, but in contrast to the composition in the Church of Sant'Apollinare in Classe, this composition is conceived using historical, rather than symbolic, elements. Christ is depicted in the center of the composition with long straight hair and a cone-shaped beard, dressed in white clothing with a golden border. The figure of Christ, standing at full height, fits within the contours of a rich, almost lapis or

Iconographical Tradition in Byzantium

royal blue oval. Rays proceeding from Christ are directed to other persons active in the composition—Moses and Elijah, who stand at full height on the right and left sides of Christ, and three apostles who are plunged down in dramatic poses at his feet. A mosaic frame completes the composition. Above are medallions with depictions of the twelve apostles and below are medallions with depictions of prophets.[3] Two of the monastery's igumens are depicted in the corners. Over the sanctuary apse on two sides are medallions with images of Saint John the Baptist and the Mother of God. Above them are two flying angels with multi-colored wings (the colors of the wings recall the feathers of a peacock). Each angel holds in one hand an orb with the depiction of a cross and in the other, a cross attached to a long pole. The angels face a medallion in which a lamb is portrayed against the background of a golden four-ended cross. On the left side, above the angels, Moses is depicted removing his sandals before the Burning Bush, while on the right side, Moses is shown receiving the tablets of the Law from the hand of God.

While the collections of mosaics which survive from the early Byzantine period give a very detailed view of the level of mosaic art of that period, one cannot say the same of frescoes. Only isolated examples and fragments of frescoes have survived from the sixth through eighth centuries in places such as the Church of Saint Demetrius in Thessalonica (most frescoes were lost in a fire in 1917), the Monastery of the Mother of God Drosiani on the island of Naxos (in Greece) and in the Roman Church of Santa Maria Antiqua.

In this sense special value is presented by the frescoes of the Church of Saint Maria in Castelseprio (Northern Italy), which underwent conservation in 1944. Scholars do not agree on the dating of the frescoes. Some deem them to be works of the pre-iconoclastic period (sixth through eighth centuries) while others attribute them to the ninth century, or even the tenth. The opinion is widespread that these frescoes appeared around the seventh century; consequently, these would be among the earliest collections of wall paintings to have come down to us, aside from the Roman catacombs. Among the subjects of these frescoes are: the Annunciation, the Meeting of Mary and Elizabeth, Mary's trial by water (a rather rare subject based on Numbers 5.11–28, which is encountered in the mosaics of Kiev's Saint Sophia, Ateni Sioni Church in Georgia, and several other churches), the Journey to Bethlehem,

---

[3]One of the medallions contains an image of King David that outwardly resembles the image of Emperor Justinian seen in Ravenna's Church of San Vitale. Some scholars suppose that the author of the Sinai mosaics, which were created during the reign of Justinian, decided to portray the emperor as the biblical David. See Kurt Weitzmann, *Studies in Classical and Byzantine Manuscript Illumination* (London, 1971), 20.

Journey to Bethlehem. Fresco. Church of Santa Maria in Castelseprio. Italy.

the Nativity of Christ, the Adoration of the Magi, and the Meeting of the Lord. Christ is depicted in one of the medallions with a cruciform halo. Two other medallions with images of the Mother of God and Saint John the Baptist have not survived. The Empty Throne (Gr. *Hetoimasia*) is depicted over a triumphal arch with flying angels turned towards it, holding standards (long wands) and orbs in their hands. In the opinion of Viktor Lazarev, "the most interesting aspect of Castelseprio's frescoes is the style, which astonishes us by its liberty and . . . realism, brimming with living echoes of the art of antiquity. Slender, ethereal figures are shown in diverse and unusual positions. . . . The manner of execution is exceptional in its characteristic confidence and vast artistry, which unwittingly compels us to recall the wall paintings of Pompeii."[4]

Christian Icons of the Sixth and Seventh Centuries. Sinai's Encaustic Icons

Mosaics and frescoes represent all of the surviving monuments of Christian fine arts up to the sixth century. Not a single icon painted on a board has survived from this period. Moreover, the number of icons dating from the sixth and seventh centuries is extremely small. It is certain that many ancient icons were lost over time. Many icons were destroyed in the period of Iconoclasm. So we can assert with a fair degree of certainty that the creation of icons on wooded panels was not widespread up to the sixth century. At any rate, there were no special places for such icons in churches. It has already been stated that the sanctuary was separated from the rest of the church by a screen at a significantly later time. The walls of the church were adorned with mosaics and frescoes or revetted with marble. Wooden icons were not hung on the walls.

The earliest icons existing today that were painted on wooden panels are from the Monastery of Saint Catherine on Mount Sinai. (For this reason they are referred to as "Sinai" icons, although they originated in various places.) All were executed in the technique of encaustic painting and painted in a bright, realistic manner. They have much more in common with the models of antiquity, especially the Fayum mummy portraits, than with icons of the post-iconoclastic period.

[4]Lazarev, *Byzantine Painting*, 71.

One of the most famous of the Sinai icons is the image of Christ Pantocrator, dating to the first half of the sixth century. Christ is depicted as a middle-aged man with a long beard and long hair parted in the middle. Folds of skin are seen on his forehead and under his eyes. His ear lobes and neck are uncovered. The right hand of Christ is raised in a gesture of blessing. His index and middle fingers are raised while the fourth finger and little finger are bent towards the thumb. Christ is dressed in a dark blue himation, under which a dark *chiton* (χιτών—undergarment) with gold *laticlave* (galloon, lace) is visible. A closed book with a richly adorned binding bearing the image of a cross is in Christ's left hand. A golden halo with an inscribed cross is over his head. In the background is the back of a throne on which the Pantocrator solemnly sits. The iconographic style used in this icon was to be preserved for many centuries, right up to the present day.

Christ Pantocrator. Icon. Mount Sinai. First half of 6th c.

The Sinai image of the Pantocrator is painted in a realistic style with bright and thick brushstrokes. The holy face of Christ in the described image is asymmetrical. If one were to divide the image with a vertical line down the middle, the left side of the icon (or the right side of the depicted Christ) will present a fully harmonious image executed in the tradition of antiquity, while disharmony is found in the right side of the image. Some art historians perceive in this asymmetry a conscious effort to make an image of the two natures of Christ, divine and human. But one cannot dismiss the possibility of a later reworking of the original image—the interference of a later artist. The color of the hand of the Savior, which differs considerably from the color of his face (which would be impossible if the face and hands were created by one and the same artist at the same time), speak in support of such a hypothesis.

The Sinai icon of the Most Holy Theotokos with the holy great martyrs George the Victory-bearer and Theodore Stratelates dates to the second half of the sixth or first half of the seventh century. In its composition the icon recalls the already mentioned fresco from the catacomb of Commodilla, in which the Theotokos is depicted together with the martyrs Felix and Adauctus. As in the catacomb fresco, the Sinai icon presents the Theotokos seated on a throne with the Infant Christ on her knees. She is dressed in a dark-blue robe (Gr. *maphorion*, μαφόριον—veil,

The Mother of God with the Great Martyrs George the Victory-Bearer and Theodore Stratelates. Icon. Sinai. Turn of 7th c.

The Apostle Peter. Icon. Sinai. Turn of 7th c.

or robe) which completely covers her body and leaves visible only her face, neck, and hands. The gaze of the large dark eyes of the Virgin is fixed to the side. Her mouth is of a bright red color. Her face is abundantly covered with white paint and a bright rose color is on her cheeks and chin. The saints are presented wearing various garments of Roman warriors and in their right hands they bear crosses. Behind the Sinai Theotokos and saints are two angels with heralds' wands in their hands. The faces of the angels are turned to the hand of God from which a ray of light descends upon the head of the Theotokoks. The turn of the head of the angels and their dynamic postures contrast with the static positions of the Theotokos and two martyrs.

The encaustic icon of the Apostle Peter dates to this same period (second half of the sixth and first half of the seventh century), making it one of the earliest depictions of the preeminent apostle. We see a man of mature age (forty-five to fifty years old) with short-cut gray hair, a slightly curly gray beard, a wide nose, full lips, powerful, open neck, and the imposing torso of a Roman warrior. The apostle is dressed in a white Roman toga. In his left hand is a staff with a cross on top and in his right hand is a bunch of keys. The head of the apostle is surrounded by a golden halo above which are medallions with images of Christ, the Theotokos, and a young saint—presumably John the Theologian.[5]

One of the early Sinai encaustic icons is called "Rejoice" (Χαίρετε, *chairete*). It depicts the appearance of the risen Lord to two women. Christ is dressed in a dark red himation over a light blue tunic. His face is turned to the women and his hand is raised in a gesture of blessing. One of the women stands with hands reaching out to him and the other is plunged down at his feet. Over the standing woman

---

[5] Constantinos Manaphes, Σινά. Οἱ θυσαυροί τῆς Ι. Μονῆς Ἁγίας Αἰκατερίνης [Sinai: The treasures of the holy monastery of St Catherine] (Athens: 1990), 94.

Iconographical Tradition in Byzantium

is the abbreviation ΑΓ ΜΡ which stands for *Hagia Maria* (Ἁγία Μαρία—Holy Mary). On early icons this inscription was used to denote the Mother of God. The designation ΜΡ ΘΥ (*Meter Theou,* Μήτηρ Θεοῦ—Mother of God) did not appear until the post-iconoclastic period.[6] Consequently, "the other Mary" from Matthew 28.1; 9–10 is associated with the Mother of God. This corresponds with the eastern Christian tradition by which the Mother of God was first to see Christ following his resurrection.[7]

Three Sinai icons of the sixth century were removed in the middle of the nineteenth century by Archimandrite (later Bishop) Porfirii (Uspensky) and at the present time are kept in the Kiev Museum of Western and Eastern Art.[8] The Mother of God is depicted in one of these icons in a dynamic pose that recalls more the portraits of antiquity than a Christian icon. The gaze of her large eyes with dark pupils is turned neither to the viewer nor to the Infant Christ, but to the side—beyond the bounds of the icon. The Infant Christ sits on the left arm of his Mother and with her right arm she embraces him as if protecting him. The gaze of the Infant is fixed in the same direction in which the Theotokos looks.

Another icon presents Saint John the Baptist in full height. In the upper left-hand corner of the icon is a medallion with an image of Christ and in the right-hand corner, a medallion with an image of the Theotokos. The gaze of the Baptist is fixed on the face of Christ, and his right hand points to him, while in his left hand John holds an open scroll with the inscription "Behold! The Lamb of God who takes away the sin of the world!" (Jn 1.29). His long curly hair is tousled and falls at his neck while his beard is disheveled. Before us is a fully realistic image of an anchorite. His figure is dynamic and his face and gestures are extremely expressive.

The third of the fourth-century icons removed by Porfirii (Uspensky) from Mount Sinai presents the martyr saints Sergius and Bacchus. Two youths in the dress of Roman warriors with crosses in their right hands are depicted. The faces of the youths are almost identical and their gazes are fixed on the viewer. Curly hair covers their foreheads and ears and their heads are encircled by halos. On the necks of the martyrs are iron hoops with which, according to tradition, they were led through the city before their execution. The head of Christ is shown in a medallion

---

[6]Weitzmann, *Studies,* 106.

[7]In the fourteenth century this tradition was reflected by St Gregory Palamas in Homily XVIII "The Sunday of the Myrrh-bearing Women. In it is spoken also about how the Mother of God first saw the Lord risen from the dead."

[8]Museum of Art named after B. and V. Khanenko.

above the martyrs' heads. In contrast to the icons of the Mother of God and John the Baptist, which were described earlier, the martyrs are depicted in static poses and their faces are marked with a countenance of passionlessness.

The last of the encaustic icons of Sinai, chronologically, is the depiction of the three children in the Babylonian furnace; this icon dates to the seventh century. In the eighth century encaustic painting gave way to painting in egg tempera. A new style which tended to use more schematic and graphic elements came to replace the realistic style of antiquity.

Crucifixion. Icon. Sinai. 8th c.

This change was already seen in the Sinai icon of the crucifixion, dating to the eighth century. This icon is the first known image of the dead Christ and the first example of an image of Christ wearing a crown of thorns.[9] The eyes of the Savior are closed and his arms are outstretched at a right angle to his body. His feet stand on a pedestal nailed to the cross, which distinguish the icon from later Byzantine depictions of the crucifixion. The Savior is dressed in a long dark red vestment that covers his body nearly to the feet but leaves the arms fully revealed. By the cross stand the Mother of God (over her is the inscription ΑΓ ΜΡ) and Saint John the Theologian. Their gazes are fixed on Christ. On either side of Christ's cross are the significantly smaller figures of the two thieves. One of the thieves is depicted as still alive with opened eyes and a loincloth wrapped around his waist. His hands are tied behind his back and his gaze is fixed on Christ. The figure of the other thief has not survived. Above the thieves are written their names—Dismas and Gestas—known from tradition. Beneath the Savior's cross three warriors are depicted and these figures are even smaller than thieves. Above the cross are four half-figures of angels turned towards Christ as well as the inscription "King of the Jews." The sun is depicted in the upper left-hand corner of the icon and in the right-hand corner, which has been lost, it is evident that the moon was depicted.

---

[9]Manaphes, *Sinai*, 94.

Iconographical Tradition in Byzantium

The Problem of the Origin of the "Canonical" Image of Christ. The Image Not-Made-By-Hands and the Shroud of Turin

Christ's image depicted on the Sinai icon of the Pantocrator constitutes a fully-formed canonical type. We know, however, that in early Christian painting Christ was depicted in a totally different way—as a young, beardless man. Insofar as we can tell, this canonical type of Christ appeared no earlier than the fourth or fifth century. But by the sixth century, the new type had almost completely replaced the "antique" type. (The antique type was preserved only in transformed images, such as that of the Savior Emmanuel.)

What is the genesis of the canonical image of Christ? Where did this characteristic face with a beard and long hair parted in the middle come from, after several centuries in which a completely different image dominated? A simple answer to this question is hardly possible, but one hypothesis demands serious attention—the one that connects the canonical appearance of Christ with the tradition of the Image Not-Made-By-Hands, located first in Edessa and later in Constantinople. This tradition is carefully preserved by the Orthodox Church and the day of the transfer of the image from Edessa to Constantinople is commemorated as a feast day in the Church up to the present time.

The first mention of the Image Not-Made-By-Hands is found in the *Teaching of Addai*—a Syrian literary text conventionally ascribed to the turn of the fifth century. In this work the story is told of King Abgar of Edessa, who suffered from "some kind of disease." The king sent his archivist Khannan to Christ after hearing of him. Jesus refused to come to visit Abgar but promised that after his ascension he would send his disciple to him to heal his disease. "When the archivist Khannan saw that Christ said that, as far as he was the king's painter, he set to drawing the image of Jesus using the best paints and brought the image back with him to Abgar the king, his lord. When King Abgar saw the image, he took it with great joy and placed it with extreme reverence in one of the rooms of his palace."[10]

Abgar Receives the Image Not-Made-By-Hands. Icon. Sinai.

---

[10] Acts of Addai the Apostle. Cited in M. Mescherskaya, *The Legend of Abgar: An Early Syrian Literary Monument* (Moscow, 1984), 187.

Another version of the same story is contained in the Greek *Acts of Thaddeus* (seventh century). The story tells of Ananiah (Khannan) who was sent by King Abgar to the Savior in order to make his portrait. Although he looked intently at the face of Christ, Ananiah was unable to make his portrait. The Savior then, taking a cloth, washed his face and wiped it with the cloth. Immediately his face left an image on the cloth. After receiving the cloth from the hands of Ananiah and venerating the holy object, King Abgar was immediately healed of his disease.[11]

In this way a Syrian literary text speaks of a portrait made from life, called in Greek the *Image Not-Made-By-Hands* (*acheiropoieta*, ἀχειροποίητα). In both cases, we are talking about a portrait made during Christ's lifetime, a portrait that faithfully reflects his true image.

But the second version of the history of King Abgar became well known in Byzantium. The Image Not-Made-By-Hands is mentioned at the turn of the seventh century by Evgarius Scholasticus, in the eighth century by Saint John of Damascus,[12] and at the beginning of the ninth century by Saint Theodore the Studite and George Syncellus.[13] The Edessa Image is mentioned in the ninth century in the works of Saint Nicephorus, patriarch of Constantinople. In one of his tracts in defense of the veneration of icons he wrote, "Since by the request of one of the faithful Christ left an image of his face on a canvas and sent it to him, why should anyone make vain accusations of others who make an image of him?"[14] In another place the saint retells the story of King Abgar according to the version found in the Greek *Acts of Thaddeus*.[15]

Early Christian sources say nothing of the location of the Image Not-Made-By-Hands. Its appearance is connected with the capture of Edessa by the Persian king Khosrau I in AD 545. According to the Church historian Evagrius, when Khosrau was preparing to storm the city, the despairing inhabitants of the city brought the "God-created Image-Not-Made-by-Hands which Christ God sent to Abgar when he wanted to see him." The inhabitants sprinkled the image with holy water and then with the same water they sprinkled the embankment built by Khosrau. Later they managed to burn the embankment and in three days Khosrau was infamously defeated.[16] A later version of the same story recounts that the Image Not-Made-by-

---

[11]Evgarius Scholasticus *Ecclesiastical History* 4, 27.
[12]See John of Damascus *An Exact Exposition of the Orthodox Faith* 4, 16.
[13]See Theodore Studite, Letter 409 (*Epistulae* pp. 44–45); Geogrius Synkellus (*Ecloga chronographica*, pp. 399–400).
[14]Nicephorus of Constantinople *Refutation against Constantine Copronymus* 1; PG 100, 260A.
[15]Ibid., 3, 42; PG 100, 461AB.
[16]Evagrius Scholasticus *Ecclesiastical History* 4, 27.

Hands was miraculously discovered by Bishop Eulabios of Edessa in a walled-up niche, where it had been preserved for several centuries. After the faithful processed with the cross and the newly discovered image, the Persian hordes departed from the city.

For four centuries (545 through 944) the Image Not-Made-By-Hands was preserved in Edessa and was the city's most sacred object. Many pilgrims streamed to the city to venerate it. Word of the image spread far beyond the limits of Edessa and many copies proliferated in the East and West. A characteristic feature of these copies is the fact that only the face of Christ is depicted on a cloth, while his neck, shoulders, and hands are not shown. A very old copy of the Image-Not-Made-By-Hands, well known by its Greek name *Mandylion* (Μανδύλιον) dates presumably to the sixth century and is located in the Vatican. A similar copy of later origin (near the middle of the tenth century) is kept in Genoa. Moreover, the image of Christ's face on ordinary icons, in which he is depicted to the chest, waist, or in full height, acquired features similar to those of the Image Not-Made-By-Hands. The most vivid example is the Sinai icon of the Pantocrator which has already been described.

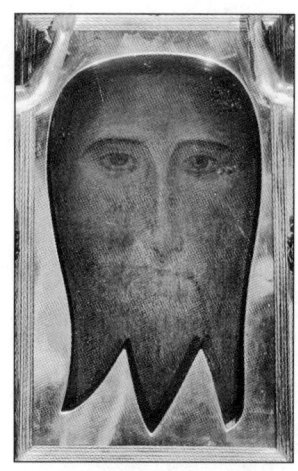

"Mandylion." Image of Christ Not-Made-By-Hands. Icon. Vatican. 6th c.

In 944 the Image Not-Made-By-Hands was ceremoniously transferred from Edessa to Constantinople. The image arrived in the Byzantine capital on August 15 on the feast of the Dormition of the Most Holy Mother of God and was first placed in the Blacharnae Church. The next day the image was ceremoniously transferred to the Church of Hagia Sophia and from there to the palace's Church of the Virgin of the Pharos. This became the image's permanent home for the next two hundred and seventy years.

Traces of the Image Not-Made-by-Hands were lost following the sack of Constantinople by crusaders in 1204. As is the case with many other sacred objects of the Eastern Church, it may have ended up in the hands of crusaders and been taken out of the Byzantine capital to the West. It would seem that the history of the Image Not-Made-by-Hands would come to an end on this note.

One hundred and fifty years later, however, a new history began. In 1357 an object appeared in the possession of the French knight Geoffroi de Charny, well known today by the name *Shroud of Turin*. It is a long canvas, measuring

Holy Face of the Shroud of Turin. Negative Image.

approximately 4.4 meters by 1.1 meters (14.4 feet by 3.6 feet), on which an unclothed man having long hair and a beard is depicted. His hands are folded in the form of a cross over his waist. One part of the shroud contains a frontal depiction of a man while the other part reveals his image from the back. The images are situated along the canvas in such a way that the head of the man in both cases is in the middle of the canvas and his feet are at the ends. In other words, the images are turned in directions opposite one another. If one considers that the shroud is a burial winding sheet and that the image on it is the imprint of the body of a deceased man, then it is evident that the body was laid on one half of the canvas and then covered with the other half of the canvas—that is, the canvas was laid over the head of the deceased.

Since the year 1578 the shroud has been kept in the Turin Cathedral. Although by no means immediately, the Catholic Church acclaimed the shroud to be the canvas in which Christ was wrapped after being taken down from the cross and the image on the shroud to be the authentic image of Christ Not-Made-By-Hands. During the twentieth century scientists attempted many times to call this opinion into question by bringing forth various hypotheses regarding the possible origin of the shroud and its dating. The supposition has been made that it is a work of art dating to the Middle Ages and a masterful fake, although attempts to prove it to be a fake have been unsuccessful.

The main argument opposing the supposition that the shroud is from the Middle Ages and of handmade origin is the fact that after many years of researching the chemical composition of the shroud's image, scientists have come to a single positive conclusion: "The shroud is not a painted depiction."[17] This is known because researchers were unable to find any traces of paint on it, and no methods of creating visual images—other than those using pigments—were known in the Middle Ages. Moreover, at the time of the Middle Ages it was believed that during the crucifixion nails were driven into the palms of hands. If an artist were making a forgery of the shroud, he would have depicted wounds in the palms. Besides that, traces of blood are found on the shroud in the area of the wrist of each arm. Only

---

[17] Alan Adler, "The Shroud Fabric and the Body Image: Chemical and Physical Characteristics," in S. Scanneini and P. Savarino, eds., *The Turin Shroud. Past, Present and Future: International Scientific Symposium, Torino, 2–5 March 2000* (Turin, 2000), 67.

Iconographical Tradition in Byzantium   131

very recently did it become known to scientists that, at the time of Christ, nails were driven into the wrists, not the palms of the hands, during crucifixions.

Scholars have not arrived at a unanimous opinion regarding the image found on the shroud. According to some theories, it could have appeared because of the evaporation of moisture from the surface of the body of the deceased man. According to others, the image could have been formed by a radioactive emanation. In both cases the image would be the result of some kind of chemical process, the nature of which remains unknown. In this case, the source of the image would not be the brush of an artist but the very body of the dead man wrapped in the shroud. This hypothesis is supported especially by the fact that, according to the research that has been conducted, the image on the shroud is brighter in those places where the canvas had close contact with the body and fainter in those places where there was some distance between the canvas and the body.

Is there a connection between the Shroud of Turin and Edessa's Image Not-Made-By-Hands? For a long time such a connection was denied, primarily on the basis that the entire body of the Savior is imprinted on the shroud whereas the Image Not-Made-By-Hands, as far as one can judge from its numerous copies, contained only the print of Christ's face. But in the last quarter of the twentieth century, a number of scholars came to the conclusion that the Shroud of Turin and the Edessa image are one and the same object.

First of all, the conclusion was made on the basis of crosswise folds contained on the shroud. The folds witness to the fact that the shroud was folded eight times and kept for a prolonged period of time in a folded state. The Edessa Image Not-Made-By-Hands may well be identical to the portion of the shroud on which the face of Christ is imprinted, and this portion of the folded shroud could have been shown to pilgrims who came to venerate the image, first in Edessa and later in Constantinople.

Second, a number of literary sources witness to the fact that until the year 1204 the burial shroud of Christ was located in Constantinople. Robert de Clari, the author of *The Conquest of Constantinople*, written in the beginning of the thirteenth century, wrote, "And among others was a church called the Church of the Mother of God of Blachernae where a shroud is kept in which the Lord was wrapped and which is exhibited every Friday so that the image of our Lord may be clearly seen. And nobody, neither Greek nor Frank, knows what happened to this shroud after the conquest of the city."[18] In 1205 Theodore Angelos wrote in a letter to Pope

---

[18] Robert de Clari, *The Conquest of Constantinople*, 92, in Hopf, *Chroniques greco-romaines inédites ou peu connues* (Paris, 1873), 71.

Innocent III, "The Venetians partitioned the treasures of gold, silver, and ivory while the French did the same with the relics of the saints and the most sacred object of all, the shroud in which our Lord Jesus Christ was wrapped after his death and before the resurrection. We know that the sacred objects are kept by those who plundered them in Venice, in France, and in other places, but the holy shroud is preserved in Athens."[19]

Third, according to several sources, the Edessa Image included an image not only of the face of Christ, but also of his entire body. In particular, one of the Latin manuscripts of the tenth century[20] includes an account dating to the eighth century. Making reference to a man named Smera from Constantinople, the account states that in Edessa is kept a linen cloth having an image of the entire body of Christ and not only his face: "King Abgar received a cloth on which one can see not only the face but the whole body (non tantum faciei figuram sed totius corporis figuram cernere poteris)."[21]

Fourth and last, a series of sources witnesses to the traces of blood on the Image Not-Made-By-Hands. The most vivid witness of this kind is a homily spoken by Archdeacon Gregory of the Church of Hagia Sophia in 944 on the occasion of the transfer of the Image of Christ Not-Made-By-Hands from Edessa to Constantinople.[22] In this homily Gregory first recounts the legend of King Abgar in the version known in Byzantium. But when the discussion concerned the question of the Image Not-Made-By-Hands itself, Saint Gregory wrote:

> He will do this straight away for us if we so desire, if we look upon the reflection and the immense beauty it is depicted with.[23] For this is not the art of painting, which provides a door[24] for the mind to consider the original and depicts images. This reflection was imprinted from a living original. Painting establishes a complete form with various beautiful colours,[25] representing the

---

[19] The text of the letter was preserved in the manuscript Codex Charularium Culisanense, fol. CXXVI (copia), kept in the National Library of Palermo. The text was published in P. Rinaldi, "Un documento probante sulla localizzazione in Atene della Santa Sindone dopo il sacheggio de Constantinopoli," in L. Coppini and F. Cavazzuti, *La Sindone, scienza e fede* (Bologna, 1983), 109–113.

[20] Codex Vossianus Latinus Q 69. The manuscript is kept in the Library of Leiden University. An analogous text is found in the Vatican manuscript Vatican Codex 5696.

[21] Text is published in P. Savio, *Ricerche storiche sulla Santa Sindone* (Turin, 1957).

[22] An eleventh-century manuscript containing the full text of the homily was discovered at the end of the twentieth century by Italian scholars J. Zaninotto in the Vatican archives. The Greek original of the homily together with the French translation was published in 1997. (See André-Marie Dubarle, "L'homélie de Grégoire le Référendaire pour la reception de l'image d'Edesse," *Revue des Études Byzantines* 55 (1997), 14–29.)

[23] Literally, "with what beauties it is written."

[24] "Door" is indeed the word used here in the original.

[25] Literally, "with many-colored coloring paints."

cheeks with a blooming red, the encircling of the lips with red, it paints the beard with flowery gold, the eyebrow with shining black, the whole eye in beautiful colours, the ears and nose in a different way, overshadowing the flanks of the imprint with a compound of qualities and showing the chin with hair. This reflection . . . however, has been imprinted only by the sweat from the face of the originator of life, falling like drops of blood, and by the finger of God. For these are the beauties that have made up the true imprint of Christ, since after the drops fell, it was embellished by drops from his own side. Both are highly instructive—blood and water there, here sweat and image. Oh equality of happenings, since both have their origin in the same person. The source of living water can be seen and it gives us water, showing us that the origin of the image made by sweat is in fact of the same nature as the origin of that which makes the liquid flow from the side. This is just like a spring pouring out fresh water as it were from two vessels, which water the tree of life.[26]

In this way, Archdeacon Gregory's sermon clearly speaks not only of traces of blood on the face of Christ but also of traces of blood from the wound in his side (Jn 19.34), and this mention testifies to the fact that the image on the shroud is the image of the body of Christ. It appears that the archdeacon is in no way troubled by the circumstance that the image he is describing in no way corresponds with the legend of Abgar which he references.

The discrepancy between the legend and the image that the residents of Constantinople witnessed in 944 is also reflected in *The Legend of the Edessa Image*, written soon after the transfer of the image from Edessa. The account states that when Jesus prayed on the eve of his death on the cross, drops of sweat from his brow were like drops of blood (Lk 22.44), and at the end of his prayer he wiped his face with a cloth and drops of blood were imprinted on it.[27] This *Legend* is attributed to Emperor Constantine VII Porphyrogenitus, who saw the Edessa Image with his own eyes after it was transferred to Constantinople. Thematically this legend has much in common with the western legend of Veronica who gave a cloth to Jesus when he was going up to Golgotha: Jesus wiped his face with the cloth and his face with drops of blood was imprinted upon it.[28]

---

[26]Dubarle, "L'homélie," 14–29; Mark Guscin, trans., *The Sermon of Gregory Referendarius*, < http://www.shroud.com/pdfs/guscin3.pdf>, September 9, 2013.

[27]Greek text in E. von Dobschütz, *Christusbilder: Untersuchungen zur christlichen Legende* (Leipzig, 1899), vol. 3, p. 53.

[28]The legend of Veronica emerged by the eleventh century. The first reference to it is found in Petrus Mallius' essay "History of St Peter's Basilica" (c. 1160). This tells of a "chapel of the Holy Mother of God

Considered together, these testimonies give sufficient basis to the assertion that the Edessa Image Not-Made-By-Hands is the very object well known today by the name "Shroud of Turin"—only folded eight times. Still, one cannot rule out the possibility that the Image Not-Made-By-Hands and the Shroud of Turin are two separate objects. The Gospel makes mention of the burial cloths of Christ and "a handkerchief that had been around his head, not lying with the linen cloths, but folded together in a place by itself" (Jn 20.7).[29] It is possible that a handkerchief was placed on the face of Christ under the upper part of the shroud during his burial, and that the face of the Savior was imprinted on this cloth while also being imprinted on the shroud. In this case, it is necessary to suppose that the image on the handkerchief was identical with the image on the shroud. Of course, if one accepts the legend of King Abgar as a historical fact (either in the Byzantine or Syriac version), then one can speak of yet another image of Christ—his portrait made during his lifetime. But in any of the three mentioned cases, one and the same face of Christ would be depicted on the cloth—that of a man with a beard and long hair.

It was this Holy Face Not-Made-By-Hands—whose proportions completely correspond to the Sinai icon of the Savior—that received fame in the sixth century and was proliferated in numerous copies. And it was the proliferation of these very copies that caused the earlier, antique type of the face of Christ, which we see in the frescoes of the Roman catacombs and in some mosaics of Ravenna, practically to fall out of use altogether. In a paradoxical way, Christians of the second through fifth century did not know what Christ looked like in reality, and therefore they could imagine him as a beardless youth. Christians of the sixth and later centuries, thanks to the discovery of the Image Not-Made-By-Hands, came to know the true face of the Savior. The discovery of this face served as a powerful stimulus to the development of iconography in the entire Orthodox East.

---

named Veronica which maintains . . . a positively authentic cloth of Christ, which he pressed to his holy face before his passions . . . when his sweat with drops of blood fell to the ground." Belting, *Likeness and Presence*, 601.

[29]Concerning the link between the Shroud of Turin and the gospel accounts of Christ's funeral cloth see Ghiberti, *The Gospels and the Shroud: The Turin Shroud, Past, Present and Future*; International Scientific Symposium, Torino, 2–5 March, 2000 (Turin, 2000), 275–280.

Iconographical Tradition in Byzantium 135

Iconoclasm and the Veneration of Icons

The Image of the Savior Not-Made-By-Hands became an important argument in the defense of the veneration of icons during the period in which such an argument was especially needed by the Church.

In the short history of the Christian Church given in a previous volume, it was mentioned that the roots of Iconoclasm possibly lay in the growing strength of Islam.[30] Several scholars agree with this point of view. At any rate, the first official prohibition of images appeared not in Byzantium but on the territory of the Arabic caliphate. In 721 Caliph Yazid II issued a prohibition against using icons in Christian churches.[31] The Byzantine Emperor Leo III the Isaurian, who issued an iconoclastic edict in Byzantium several years later, came from Syria and was acquainted with the Arab mentality.[32]

Other scholars attribute the rise of Iconoclasm to the influence of Judaism, Monophysitism, and Paulicianism, but they have been unable to provide substantial proofs of such influence.

Finally, a number of scholars suppose that Iconoclasm was originally a characteristic of the Church and that only in the post-Constantinian period, under the influence of the veneration of images of the emperor, did holy images emerge in the Christian Church. Hans Belting, for example, asserts that the proliferation of the image of Christ in the sixth century was a novelty that required legalization. In the words of this scholar, the Church resisted images in worship for a prolonged period of time but eventually submitted. "The teaching concerning images emerged immediately after their acceptance, and this teaching later justified the use of icons in worship by the theological argument concerning the nature of Christ."[33] Many Protestant scholars adhere to this point of view, seeing in Iconoclasm the first attempt at a religious reformation with its objective the freeing of Christianity from the influence of Hellenism and paganism.

To prove their case, these scholars cite several texts belonging to two authors of the fourth century, Eusebius of Caesarea (*c.* 264–340) and Epiphanius of Cyprus (*c.* 315–403), which allegedly lend witness to the iconoclastic character of the early Christian Church. In one of their letters (which is preserved, however, only in

---

[30]See *Orthodox Christianity*, vol. 1, pp. 54ff.
[31]A. Vasiliev, "The Iconoclastic Edict of Caliph Yasid II. Ad 721," *Dumbarton Oaks Papers* 9/10 (1955), 23ff.
[32]Belting, *Likeness and Presence*, 163.
[33]Ibid., 159, 169–170.

the refutation of Nicephorus of Constantinople), Eusebius addresses a Christian woman who asked him to send her an icon of Christ:

> You have written to me regarding a certain icon of Christ wishing that I send it to you. What icon are you referring to and what type should it be that you call it the icon of Christ? . . . What icon of Christ are you seeking? The authentic, unchanging image, which bears the characteristics of Christ in essence, or, on the contrary, that form which he took upon himself for our sake, being clothed in the image of a servant (Phil 2.7)? . . . I can imagine that you are requesting the icon of his divine form. After all, Christ himself instructed you that nobody knows the Son, as only his Father who begot him (Mt 11.27). Probably, you wanted to receive his depiction in the image of a servant, that is, in the form of poor flesh, which he put on for our sake. But we are instructed regarding flesh as well, that it was penetrated with the glory of the Godhead, that in it that which is dead was swallowed up by life (1 Cor 15.52–54; 2 Cor 5.4). . . . But if you say that you would like from me not the depiction of a man who became God, but an icon of his mortal flesh, as it appeared before his transfiguration, then I will reply: Do you really not recall from the Scriptures that God forbids the creation of the likeness of anything from above in the heavens or here below on the earth (Ex 20.4)?[34]

To what degree does this text—assuming, of course, that it is authentic[35]—reflect the perspective of the early Christian Church on holy images? First of all, as Cardinal Christophe Shönborn notes, "one cannot read into this text an *overall* rejection of Christian art. Symbolic and allegorical depictions of Christ, known in abundance from the time of Eusebius, are not rejected by him. What is being discussed is only the icon, on which Christ must be depicted *exactly*—that is, as he really was—and Eusebius only rejects a representation which is *similar*."[36]

Moreover, Eusebius had Arian inclinations and considered Christ to be the creation of God. The material body of Christ was, according to Eusebius, merely an instrument in the hands of God, similar to a harp in the hands of a musician.

---

[34]Eusebius of Caesarea *Letter to Empress Constantia*, PG 20, 1545AB–1550A.

[35]The authenticity of the letter of Eusebius is disputed in C. Murray, "Art and the Early Church," *Journal of Theological Studies* 28 (1977), 326–336. Other scholars, on the other hand, insist on its authenticity (See St. Gero, "The True Image of Christ: Eusebius' Letter to Constantia Reconsidered," *Journal of Theological Studies* 32 (1981), 460–470. Some ascribe it to Eusebius of Nicomedia (K. Schäferdiek, "Zur Verfassenfrage und Situation der Epistula ad Constantiam ad imagine Christi," *Zeitschrift für Kirchengeschichte* 91 [1980], 177–186.)

[36]C. Shönborn, *The Icon of Christ: Theological Foundations* (Milan–Moscow, 1999), 61–62. Italics are the author's.

When Christ suffered on the cross, his divinity remained passionless, as likewise a musician does not suffer if his harp breaks into pieces and its strings are sundered.[37] In the history of the incarnation, the body of Christ ends up being something of a casual detail whose necessity vanishes after the resurrection of Christ. It is characteristic of Eusebius that he perceives the eucharistic gifts—the Body and Blood of Christ—merely as "symbols of the divine economy"[38] and "symbols of the inexpressible words of the New Testament."[39] The meaning of the Eucharist for Eusebius primarily consists of the symbolic remembrance of the sufferings of the Word of God, not in the communion of his divine Body and Blood.

Such a theological arrangement existed, of course, in the ancient Church, but it was far from prevalent. Moreover, it was rejected by the Church together with other aspects of Arian Christology. For Eusebius the divine Logos is the image of God the Father and the body of Christ is an image of this image. Accordingly, the depiction of the body of Christ becomes an image of that corruptible and mortal image that is not worthy of veneration. We encounter a fundamentally different approach, for example, in Saint Cyril of Alexandria, for whom the image of God the Father is the incarnate Word, that is, the divine Logos together with his human nature. The body of Christ is inseparably tied to his divinity and filled with the life-creating energy of the Spirit.[40] The human nature of Christ and his body cannot be perceived merely as an instrument:

> When someone acknowledges in Christ just the role of an instrument, does he not then unwittingly take away from him his active sonship? . . . Consider one whose son sings wonderfully and plays the lyre. Can he then place the lyre and musical instrument in the same category as his son? . . . The lyre is used in order to demonstrate one's art, but a son remains a son even without an instrument. In the same way, when some say that a man born of a woman was received (through the Logos) as an instrument for the sake of working miracles and preaching the Gospel, they are obliged to consider also each of the holy prophets to be instruments of the Divinity . . . and in this case Christ would in no wise surpass them. He would in no wise be superior to those who came before him if, like the prophets, he was employed as an instrument.[41]

[37] Eusebius of Caesarea *The Proof of the Gospel* IV 13,7 (*Demonstratio Evangelica*, GCS 23, p. 172).
[38] Eusebius of Caesarea *The Proof of the Gospel* VIII 1, 79–80 (*Demonstratio Evangelica*, GCS 23, p. 366.)
[39] Ibid., VIII, 2, 119 (*Demonstratio Evangelica*, GCS 23, p. 389.)
[40] Cyril of Alexandria *Commentary on John* 4, 3, PG 73, 604BD.
[41] Ibid., *Epistle 1, to the Monks of Egypt*, PG 77, 32D—33B.

Saint Ephiphanius of Cyprus. Fresco. Gračanica Monastery. Kosovo. 14th c.

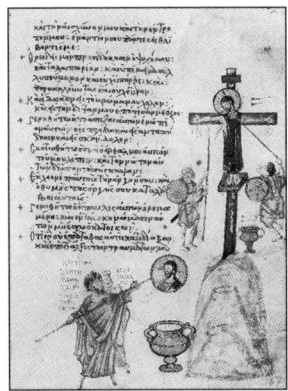

Iconoclasts John the Grammarian and Antony I Kassymates Paint Over an Icon. The iconoclasts are identified here with those who crucified Christ. Miniature from the Chludov Psalter. 9th c.

... This is why we reject the idea that the temple[42] received from the Virgin was employed as an instrument. On the contrary, we adhere to the faith of the divine Scriptures and Holy Fathers and state that the Word became flesh.[43]

The text cited from the letter of Eusebius of Caesarea together with the well known "iconoclastic" fragments from the essays of Epiphanius of Cyprus (whose authenticity is also questioned[44]) cannot be perceived as a reflection of the faith of the Church in the fourth century. The use of icons in worship had not yet become widespread, and the theology of icons had not yet been formulated. Disagreements could therefore arise concerning the veneration of icons. But it is not truthful to conclude, as some Protestant scholars do, that the Christian tradition was at first iconoclastic. Examples of early Christian representational arts that have survived to our day witness against such conclusions. These artworks are not many in number, but had such works not undergone systematic destruction first by iconoclasts and later by Arabs and Turks, many more of them would exist today.

The theological foundation of the veneration of icons was worked out during the Christological debates of the fifth through the seventh centuries. During that period the fundamental artistic characteristics of Christian representational arts were set forth. What is customarily called the iconographic canon took shape—a particular collection of iconographic subjects and the means of artistic expressiveness. Of course, the canon continued to be perfected and became more complex in the post-iconoclastic period, but in the Sinai icon of

---

[42]i.e., "flesh"
[43]Ibid., PG 77, 36B.
[44]The Orthodox tradition in the person of St John of Damascus, St Nicephorus of Constantinople, and the Fathers of the Seventh Ecumenical Council refute the authenticity of these excerpts. The opinions of scholars on this question vary. For more detail, see Leonid Ouspensky, Anthony Gythiel, trans., *Theology of the Icon*, vol. 1 (Crestwood, NY: St Vladimir's Seminary Press), 131–132.

the sixth century and other images of that period we already recognize the canonical subjects, which were to remain fundamentally unchanged for centuries.

The iconoclastic crisis lasted more than one hundred years. During that time, power in the empire shifted from iconodules to iconoclasts and back again to iconodules. Iconoclasm was "a regressive movement turning Christian art back to conventional symbols and allegories."[45] Moreover, Iconoclasm became the first attempt of religious reformation in the history of Christianity:

> Iconoclasm is principally a religious phenomenon. We face disputes concerning the "true religion," the purity of the Church, the "worship in spirit and truth." This in no way excludes the fact that Iconoclasm "as all teachings of the early Church, held political and social implications as well."[46] Sources suggest that Emperor Leo III considered himself to be a religious reformer. He felt himself to be called to restore in the empire the authentic faith which seemed to be censuring itself and leaning towards idolatry. The veneration of icons, in his opinion, was idolatry and idolatry needed to be uprooted.... Leo III considered himself to be a king and high priest, called by God to cleanse the house of God of all idolatry. He saw himself as a new Moses, a pastor given by God for the God-chosen people—that is, the Roman Empire.[47]

Iconoclasm was not a movement opposed to the fine arts in general. It was a movement opposed to holy images. As witnessed by Saint Theophanes the Confessor in 726, the first icon to be destroyed was an image of Christ over the Bronze Gate of the emperor's Great Palace in Constantinople.[48] This image was replaced with a cross. Icons of the Savior, the Mother of God, saints, and scenes from the Old and New Testaments were destroyed throughout the entire empire. In the church in Blachernae, images depicting subjects from the Gospel were pulled down and replaced with "trees, flowers, various birds, and other animals amidst shoots of plants and swarming cranes, ravens,

Venerable Theophanes the Confessor. Fresco. Dionisiou Monastery. Mt Athos. 16th c.

---

[45]G. Kolpakova, *Art of Byzantium: Early and Middle Periods* (St Petersburg, 2007), 262.

[46]Protopresbyter Georges Florovsky, "Origen, Eusebius and the Iconoclastic Controversy," *Church History* 19 (1950), 79.

[47]Shenborn, *Icon of Christ*, 141.

[48]Theophanes the Confessor, *Chronography* 1 405, 5–11. Translated with commentaries in Russian in I. Chichurov, *Byzantine Historical Essays* (Moscow, 1980).

and pelicans."⁴⁹ The mosaics of the Dome of the Rock in Jerusalem (691–692) and Umayyad Mosque in Damascus (705–711) give an idea of the artistic standards of the iconoclasts. The basic principles of the iconoclasts' aniconic art (from the Greek ἀν- *an-*, "without" and εἰκών, *eikon*, "image"), which allowed images of plants, animals, and architectural structures, were embodied in these mosaics. Symbols such as a cross, a lamb, and the "prepared throne" (a depiction of a throne with the Gospel resting on it) were widely used in mosaics and murals of churches during the iconoclastic period.

Whatever the external reasons for Iconoclasm, it is evident that there existed a marginal iconoclastic trend within the Christian Church at the time leading up to the eighth century. This trend would have probably died out on its own had the emperors not breathed new life into it. Otherwise it is difficult to explain the fact that an enormous number of the clergy, including bishops, began to support iconoclasts (three hundred and thirty-eight bishops participated in the iconoclastic council of 754). But another thing is equally evident: the Christian Church confronted Iconoclasm with all her guns, so to speak. The Church's best theological powers came to wage battle with heresy. First and foremost, it was the monastic ranks, but also thousands of the pious laity—for whom the use of icons was an inalienable component of their personal spiritual and liturgical experience—who came to the defense of icon veneration.

The main ideological basis for Iconoclasm was the Old Testament prohibition against images. The first commandment of the Decalogue of Moses reads: "You shall not make for yourself an idol or a likeness of anything in heaven above, or in the earth beneath, or in the waters under the earth. You shall not bow down to them or serve them, for I, the Lord your God, am a jealous God . . . " (Ex 20.4–5). It is evident, though, that the Old Testament prohibition against images was directed not against the representational art *per se*, but against the worship of idols with which these arts in ancient times were inextricably linked. The author of Deuteronomy explains why one cannot make idols and likenesses:

> Lest you transgress and make to yourselves a carved image, any kind of figure, the likeness of male or female, the likeness of any beast of those that are on the earth, the likeness of any winged bird which flies under heaven, the likeness of any reptile which creeps on the earth, the likeness of any fish of those which are in the waters under the earth; and lest having looked up to the sky, and

---

⁴⁹Stephen the Deacon, *The Life of Stephen the New: Vita sancti Stephani Junioris*, PG 100, 1120C.

having seen the sun and the moon and the stars, and all the heavenly bodies, you should go astray and worship them, and serve them, which the Lord God has distributed to all the nations under heaven (Deut 4.16–19).

The danger of idol worship consists in the attempt to depict the invisible God with the aid of painting or sculpture. The author of the biblical book emphasizes that the true God is invisible and undepictable, and when Moses conversed with God on Mount Sinai, people did not see God but only heard his voice:

And you drew nigh and stood under the mountain; and the mountain burned with fire up to heaven: there was darkness, blackness, and tempest. And the Lord spoke to you out of the midst of the fire a voice of words, which you heard: and you saw no likeness, you heard only a voice. . . . You saw no similitude in the day in which the Lord spoke to you . . . out of the midst of the fire (Deut 4.11–12, 13).[50]

The image of the invisible God would be tantamount to the worship of idols because no one statue or one portrait could be adequate to depict the One whom it is impossible to depict or represent.

This point was not rejected by the iconodules. But they insisted that the depiction of God became possible thanks to God's incarnation. Not the depiction of the invisible God the Father but the depiction of the Word of God as he revealed himself to men—in human form. In contrast to Eusebius of Caesarea, iconodules considered the body of Christ worthy of veneration because it is united with the Godhead. In rendering worship to Christ, depicted in his bodily aspect, we worship the invisible God who became visible for the sake of our salvation:

I do not venerate the creation instead of the Creator, but I venerate the Creator, created for my sake, who came down to his creation without being lowered or weakened, that he might glorify my nature and bring about communion with the divine nature. I venerate together with the King and God the purple robe of his body, not as a garment, nor as a fourth person (God forbid!), but as called to be and to have become unchangeably equal to God, and the source of anointing. For the nature of the flesh did not become divinity, but as the Word became flesh immutably, remaining what it was, so also the flesh became the Word without losing what it was, being rather made equal to the Word hypostatically. Therefore I am emboldened to depict the invisible God, not as

---

[50] Abridged by the author.

invisible, but as he became visible for our sake, by participation in flesh and blood. I do not depict the invisible divinity, but I depict God made visible in the flesh. For if it is impossible to depict the soul, how much more God, who gives the soul its immateriality?"[51]

Any depiction of the invisible God would be the fruit of human imagination and a lie against God. The veneration of such a depiction would be the veneration of the creation, not the Creator. However, the New Testament is a revelation of God who became Man; that is, he became visible for people. With the same insistence as that with which Moses says that people on Mount Sinai did not see God, the apostles say that they saw him: ". . . and we beheld his glory, the glory as of the only begotten of the Father" (Jn 1.14). "That which was from the beginning, which we have heard, which we have seen with our eyes, which we have looked upon . . . concerning the Word of life" (1 Jn 1.1). And if Moses emphasizes that the people of Israel did not see "any likeness" but only heard the voice of God, the apostle Paul calls Christ the "image of the invisible God" (Col 1.15) and Christ himself says of himself: "He who has seen Me has seen the Father" (Jn 14.9). The invisible Father reveals himself to the world through his image and icon— through Jesus Christ the invisible God became a visible Man.

That which is invisible is undepictable while that which is visible can be depicted, since it is then reality and no longer the fruit of imagination. The Old Testament prohibition against depictions of the invisible God, according to the thought of Saint John of Damascus, is a precursor of the possibility of depicting him once he becomes visible:

> For it is now clear that you cannot depict the invisible God.[52] When you see the bodiless become human for your sake, then you may accomplish the figure of a human form; when the invisible becomes visible in the flesh, then you may depict the likeness of something seen. . . . Depict all these in words and in colors, in books and on tablets.[53]

The Jews were prohibited from making depictions because of their inclination to worship idols. But we, Christians, "have received the habit of discrimination from God and know what can be depicted and what cannot be delineated in an

---

[51] John of Damascus, *Three Treatises on the Divine Images*, Andrew Louth, tr. (Crestwood, NY: St Vladimir's Seminary Press, 2003), 22.
[52] In the Old Testament.
[53] John of Damascus, *Three Treatises*, 88–89.

image."⁵⁴ Venerating an icon, a person offers reverence to the material flesh of Christ which is none other than the "visible side of God." In contrast to his invisible side, his visible side may be depicted.⁵⁵

In the words of Saint John of Damascus, one may depict only that which was revealed to men during the earthly life of Christ. "His ineffable descent, his birth from the Virgin, his being baptized in the Jordan, his transfiguration on Tabor, what he endured to secure our freedom from passion, the miracles, symbols of his divine nature, performed by the divine activity through the activity of the flesh, the saving cross, the tomb, the resurrection, the ascent into heaven."⁵⁶ Saint John considers that it is possible to depict saints on icons as well. Saints are Christ's warriors, his army. Let the earthly emperor divest himself of his own army before he deprives Christ of his army. Let him put aside his own diadem and then let him put aside that of the saints.⁵⁷

Saint John of Damascus differentiates between several types of veneration. The first type of veneration is worship and belongs only to God. The second type is offered to his friends—the saints. Veneration may be offered also to holy places and sacred objects. There is also veneration which people offer to one another out of respect.⁵⁸ In order to give more weight to his argument, Saint John cites the distinction between *worship* (λατρεία, *latreia*) and *veneration* (προσκύνησις, *proskynesis*). The first is offered to God while the second is offered to the Mother of God and the saints.

As Saint Basil the Great wrote before him,⁵⁹ Saint John of Damascus states that the honor offered to an image is passed to its prototype. The honor offered to the icon of Christ passes to Christ himself. Bowing down before the depiction of Christ's passions, we render reverence not to a board and paint but to the Savior himself depicted on the board. The honor offered to the Mother of God "passes to the One made flesh by her," and the honor offered to the saints "proves one's love for the Master of all things."⁶⁰ And so, concerning icons which are not icons of Christ: the true prototype is not even the one depicted on the icon but Christ himself—the source of all holiness and sanctity.

⁵⁴Ibid., 88.
⁵⁵Ibid., 29.
⁵⁶Ibid., 24.
⁵⁷Ibid., 71.
⁵⁸Ibid., 27–28.
⁵⁹Basil the Great *On the Holy Spirit* 18 (Yonkers, New York: St Vladimir's Seminary Press, 2011), 81.
⁶⁰John of Damascus *Exact Exposition*, 4, 16.

Saint John of Damascus. Icon. Mount Athos. 14th c.

Saint John of Damascus defines an image as "a likeness depicting an archetype, but having some difference from it."⁶¹ An image is "a likeness and pattern and impression of something, showing in itself what is depicted," but an image is "not like the archetype … in every respect."⁶² The connection between the image and the archetype, according to Saint John of Damascus, is guaranteed by the fact that the image bears the name of the archetype: "Divine grace is communicated to material objects through the name borne by what is depicted."⁶³ The name of the prototype sanctifies the image and transforms it into an icon: "Submit to the tradition of the Church and allow the veneration of images of God and friends of God, sanctified by name and therefore overshadowed by the grace of the divine Spirit."⁶⁴

The series of treatises of Saint John of Damascus against the iconoclasts became the main document describing the position of iconodules in the eighth century.

Saint Theodore the Studite. Mosaic. Monastery of Nea Moni. Chios. Greece. 11th c.

Indeed it was these treatises that lay at the basis of the theology of the Seventh Ecumenical Council, which restored the veneration of icons. In the period after the council, when attacks on icons resumed with renewed strength, anti-iconoclastic literature was enhanced by the treatises of Saint Nicephorus of Constantinople and Saint Theodore the Studite (759–826).

The latter especially developed the teaching of Saint John of Damascus concerning the nature of the image (depiction) and the correlation between the image and its prototype (*first image*). In the thought of Saint Theodore, the image and prototype are not identical in essence, but they are identical in name:

The name "cross" is given to that on which Christ was lifted up both because of the signification of the word and because of the nature of the life-giving wood.

⁶¹John of Damascus, *Three Treatises*, 25.
⁶²Ibid., 95.
⁶³Ibid., 43.
⁶⁴Ibid., 30.

Iconographical Tradition in Byzantium

Its representation, on the other hand, is called "cross" because of the signification of the word, but not because of the nature of the life-giving wood. For it is made from some kind of wood, or gold, or silver, or stone, or some other material delineation. It shares the name of the prototype, as well as its honor and veneration, but it has no part in its nature.... In every case the copy is called by the name which signifies the prototype. This principle also applies to Christ and his icon.... It shares the name of its prototype, as it shares also the honor and veneration; but it has no part in the nature of the prototype. Therefore, by whatever names Jesus Christ is called, his image is called by the same names. If we should say that Christ is "the Lord of glory," in the same way his image is called "the Lord of glory" (1 Cor 2.8). If we should say that Christ is "the power of God and the wisdom of God," likewise also his image is called "the power of God" and "the wisdom of God" (1 Cor 1.24).... And by whatever names the inspired Scripture calls the Savior, we must be able to call his icon by the same names.[65]

Not only is it valid to give an image the name of its prototype but it is also proper to "name the prototype after its image."[66] However, the use of one name in relation to the image and its prototype is possible for the very reason that the image and prototype are ontologically different from one another. They are two realities not identical in nature and therefore they are not comparable or interchangeable. The name "Christ" may be used for both Christ himself and his icon, "yet there are not two Christs. It is not possible to distinguish one from the other by the name, which they have in common, but by their natures."[67]

In accordance with this approach the early Christian iconographical practice presupposed the presence of an inscription on any iconographic depiction. In the ancient Church there was no special service for the consecration of icons. The moment of an image's becoming an icon was considered to be the moment when the corresponding inscription was placed on it. It should be clear that this did not mean that *any* image bearing the inscription of the name of God or the name of a saint would automatically become an icon. It was necessary to observe other conditions as well. Of these the most important was the artist's faithfulness to the iconographical canon. But without an inscription, an icon, prepared according to all the rules of the art of iconography, was not perceived to be an icon.

[65] Theodore the Studite *Second Refutation of the Iconoclasts* 17; in Catherine P. Roth, tr., *On the Holy Icons* (Crestwood, NY: St Vladimir's Seminary Press, 2001), 51–52.
[66] Ibid., 32.
[67] Ibid., 28.

Characteristically, Byzantine iconoclasts paid special attention to the absence in the practice of the Church of a special service for consecrating icons. But they drew from this fact a false conclusion. "The impious institution of the false-named icons," they wrote, "has no foundation in the tradition of Christ, the apostles or the fathers. Nor is there a holy prayer to sanctify them and change them from ordinary into holy objects, but they always remain regular objects." The iconodules responded in this way:

> A holy prayer is not read over many of the objects which we acknowledge to be holy because they are filled with holiness and grace by the virtue of their names.... In such a way the very image of the life-creating cross, although it is not customary to read a particular prayer to consecrate it, is considered by us worthy of veneration and serves as sufficient means for us to receive a blessing.... The same relates to icons. In designating to them a well known name, we ascribe honor to their prototypes; kissing them and bowing down reverently before them, we receive a blessing.[68]

The iconoclasts asked this question: If a name makes an image holy, should one bow down to the image itself or to the inscription? Saint Theodore the Studite answered this question by explaining that in veneration, the inscription is inseparable from the image in the way that a name does not become separated from an object:

> That is rather like asking, "Is it right to venerate the Gospel book or the title on it? The representation of the cross or the inscription on it?" I might add also in the case of our own kind, "the man, or his name?" perhaps of Paul and Peter and each of the individuals of the same species. Would not that be stupid, not to say ridiculous? What is there, of all the things before our eyes, that is nameless? How can the thing which is named be separated in honor from its own appellation, so that we may offer veneration to the one and deprive the other of it? These are relationships, for a name is by nature the name of something which is named, and a sort of natural image of that to which it is applied. Therefore the unity in veneration is not divided.[69]

The identification of an image-icon with its name is encountered in the texts of iconodules many times. For instance, Saint John of Damascus cites the words of Stephen Bostrenus: "An image is a name and likeness of the one whom it represents.

---

[68]Seventh Ecumenical Council, Acts VI, in *Acts of the Ecumenical Councils*, vol. 4 (St Petersburg: 1996), 540–541.
[69]Theodore the Studite *First Refutation of the Iconoclasts* 13, in Roth, trans., *On the Holy Icons*, 34–35.

Iconographical Tradition in Byzantium 147

Thus both by writing and by engraving we are ever mindful of our Lord's sufferings, and of the holy prophets in the old law and in the new."[70] Iconodules also referred to the words of Saint John Chrysostom regarding the depictions of Saint Meletius of Antioch, which residents of Antioch drew on signet-rings, stamps, rocks, cups, and walls of rooms "so as not only to hear the holy name but also to see it everywhere."[71]

According to the teaching of the iconodules, there are two types of depictions: those made "through words written in a book" and those made "through sensual contemplation."[72] Literary symbols of the divine reality belong to the first type whereas visible depictions of the divine reality belong to the second type. The first type sanctifies our lips and hearing while the second type sanctifies our sight. In the Acts of the Council of Constantinople of 842 it is said, "Memory eternal to the faithful who proclaim and evangelize that an equal benefit is brought by the proclamation through the word as by the confirmation of the truth through icons."[73]

The essays of Saint John of Damascus, Saint Nicephorus of Constantinople, Saint Theodore the Studite, and other confessors of the veneration of icons became a manifesto of the Church in the struggle against the first "reform" movement in its history, which cost the Church many human lives. Moreover, many works of art were lost forever. Assessing the results of the iconoclastic crisis, Leonid Ouspensky wrote:

> The final toll of iconoclasm was heavy. During that period, everything that could be destroyed was destroyed, and this is why we have so few icons from the early centuries. "Wherever there were images," a contemporary says, "they were destroyed by fire or thrown to the ground, or effaced with a coating." . . . .State servants were sent to the most remote provinces to find and destroy works of sacred art. A great number of Orthodox were executed, imprisoned and tortured, and their properties were confiscated. Others were banished or exiled to faraway provinces. In short, it was a real catastrophe. Before iconoclasm, the Orthodox often had no clear awareness of the importance of sacred art. But the violence of the persecutions and the steadfastness of the confessors in venerating icons emphasized once and for all the importance of the sacred

---

[70]John of Damascus *Apologia against those who Decry Holy Images* 3, testimony 27. <http://www.fordham.edu/halsall/basis/johndamascus-images.asp#PART I>

[71]John Chrysostom, *Laudatory Homily in Praise of Meletius* (Works, vol. 2, 558–559).

[72]John of Damascus, *Apologia* 1, 13.

[73]Cited in F. Ouspensky, *Synodikon for the Sunday of Orthodoxy* (Odessa, 1893), 6–7.

image. . . . In the heat of battle, the Church found words capable of expressing the richness and depth of its teaching. Its profession constitutes a treasure we have inherited, one which is of particular importance to our time.[74]

Decorative Painting of Byzantine Churches. Basic Iconographical Types

The Church's final victory over Iconoclasm resulted in a new golden age in religious art. Artists had been in the grip of prohibitions and needed to be content with themes of vegetation and animals. Now these artists undertook with renewed energy the restoration holy images in churches where they had been destroyed. Between 843 and 847 Empress Theodora restored the image of Christ over the *Chalke Gate* of the Great Palace in Constantinople. Between 843 and 855 a mosaic of the Mother of God with the Infant Christ in her arms and archangels beside her was completed in the apse of Hagia Sophia. The mosaic contained an inscrip-

The Mother of God Seated on a Throne. Mosaic. Hagia Sophia in Constantinople.

[74]Ouspensky, *Theology of the Icon*, vol. 1 (Crestwood), 144–145.

tion, almost completely lost today, which read, "These images, which were destroyed by the deceivers, have been restored by the pious rulers."[75] The image of the Mother of God, together with the image of Christ Pantocrator, was to occupy a central position in the church's arrangement of murals in the post-iconoclastic period.

When building new churches, special attention was paid to the artistic arrangement of the church interior. By the middle of the ninth to the end of the twelfth century Orthodox churches were understood to be buildings whose walls are almost completely covered with painted images. Earlier, churches in the pre-iconoclastic period had been decorated with mosaics and frescoes, but generally images were found only in the sanctuary apse, in the space under the dome, and on the upper tiers of the walls, while the lower tiers remained without images. In the post-iconoclastic period the walls of churches came to be decorated by several rows of images while the lowest row of images might lie directly at the eye-level of an onlooker.

Theotokos "Orans." Mosaic. Saint Sophia Cathedral in Kiev. 11th c.

In the post-iconoclastic period, the arrangement of murals in Byzantine churches acquired strict canonical traits. In pre-iconoclastic churches, the *Ascension* composition occupied a special place: Christ in a circle, sitting on a rainbow, with the Mother of God *Orans* and the Twelve Apostles. This composition could be found in either the sanctuary apse or the central dome. In the post-iconoclastic period, a change in the dome's shape (its diameter was considerably reduced while the dome became taller), resulted in the break-up of the multi-figure composition into several compositional fragments. The half-figure of Christ Pantocrator in a medallion ended up in the dome while the apostles were brought into the drum of the dome. The "Orans" image became the arrangement's central element in the sanctuary apse.[76]

The dome and apse are two thematic centers of mural painting and constitute a dominant and subdominant. The painting of the dome imparts a particular tone to the entire church and the painting of the apse is always connected with the painting of the dome. When Christ is depicted in the dome, the Mother of God "Orans" is normally depicted in the apse, while the twelve apostles are depicted in the drum

---

[75] Lazarev, *Byzantine Painting*, 96.
[76] Ibid., 98.

of the dome and the four evangelists in the pendentives. But when the depiction of Christ the Pantocrator is found in the apse, the Mother of God with the Infant Christ may be depicted in the dome. Sometimes a depiction of Pentecost is found in the dome: in the center is the "throne of preparation" from which emanating tongues of flame descend upon the twelve apostles, while the multitudes of nations harkening to the apostles are depicted on the walls of the dome's drum and in the pendentives. When there are sixteen windows rather than twelve, prophets are depicted in the church's dome in the place of apostles.

The theme of the mural in the sanctuary apse is generally connected with the Eucharist. Scenes from the Old Testament may be found beneath the depiction of "Orans." These are perceived as prototypes of the Eucharist: Cain and Abel, the sacrifice of Abraham, Melchizedek with bread and wine, Moses and the burning bush. The central register often contains the composition "Communion of the Apostles." In the center of the composition is Christ at the altar. In one of his hands is bread, in the other is a cup with wine. The apostles, beginning with Peter and Paul, approach him from both sides. Christ is often depicted twice in this composition, in which case he stands half-turned to the apostles. The lower register of murals in the sanctuary apse is usually occupied by depictions of hierarchs. Closer to the center are the creators of the liturgies, Saint Basil the Great and Saint John Chrysostom, and also Saint Gregory the Theologian, Saint Athanasius of Alexandria, Saint Cyril of Alexandria, Saint Ignatius the God-bearer, and others.

The composition "Annunciation" is often found on the pillars or side walls of the sanctuary apse. On the left side is the archangel who, in profile to the viewer, faces the Theotokos. On the right side is the Theotokos who is either turned to face the viewer or shown in three-quarters view.

The central space of the church is usually painted in several registers whereby each register represents a thematic "collection" of subjects arranged from left to right in a circle according to chronological order. The "festal" row may include twelve compositions: "Annunciation," "Nativity of Christ," "Meeting of the Lord," "Baptism of Our Lord," "Transfiguration," "Raising of Lazarus," "Entry of the Lord into Jerusalem," "Crucifixion," "Descent into Hades," "Ascension," "Pentecost," and "Dormition." Often two registers of murals are found in place of the "festal" register. Scenes from the Gospel and the events of Christ's life are depicted in one register, while the other register depicts scenes from the life of the Theotokos. When a church is dedicated to a particular saint, a separate register may show scenes from the life of the saint.

Iconographical Tradition in Byzantium

Saints are also generally depicted in registers, in keeping with the Church's established categories for the ranks of saints. Sainted bishops are depicted in one register, while venerable saints are found in another and martyrs in still another. Head-and-shoulder depictions of saints are often found in medallions. There was nothing arbitrary about the selection of the images of saints. Generally a great deal of attention was paid to saints who were especially venerated in a particular region. Venerable fathers held an important place in the murals of monasteries. Venerable saints were holy monks whose images served as a source of inspiration for monastics.

Images of Christ and the Mother of God predominated in the artistic decoration of Byzantine churches. Parallelism is observed between these images and their placement in the church. Scenes from the life of the Mother of God may be found in a register together with scenes from the life of Christ. (In the church calendar, feasts of the Theotokos synchronize with feasts of the Lord in a similar way.)

The iconography of Christ in the Orthodox East is marked by great diversity. It has already been noted that as far back as the wall paintings of the Roman catacombs there were three pictorial types of Christ: *symbolic*, *antique* (depicted as a young man with short hair and without a beard), and *iconic* (depicted as a middle-age man with a beard and long hair). In the fifth and sixth centuries yet another type, conventionally called *Semitic-Palestinian*, is sometimes encountered. In this type, Christ is presented as a young man with a short beard and short, wavy hair. In particular,

Christ the Priest. Mosaic. Saint Sophia Cathedral in Kiev. 11th c.

this type is seen in one of the miniatures of the of the Rabbula Gospels, in an icon of Sinai from the seventh century, on coins of Emperor Justinian, in the mosaic "Christ the Priest" of Saint Sophia Cathedral in Kiev (1040s), and on a fresco of Manuel Panselinos in the Protaton on Mount Athos. Subsequently the Semitic-Palestinian type practically disappeared and only a few symbolic depictions of Christ have survived. The *antique* type was transformed into the Savior-Emmanuel and the *iconic* type became universal and famous by the name Pantocrator ("Almighty").

Images of Christ Pantocrator are so numerous and diverse that to unite them into a single group can be done only in a very general sense. A common trait in all these images is that Christ is always depicted frontally. His right hand is raised

Christ Pantocrator. Mosaic. Monastery of Hosios Loukas. Greece. 11th c.

Emmanuel. Fresco. Monastery of Dečani. Kosovo. 14th c.

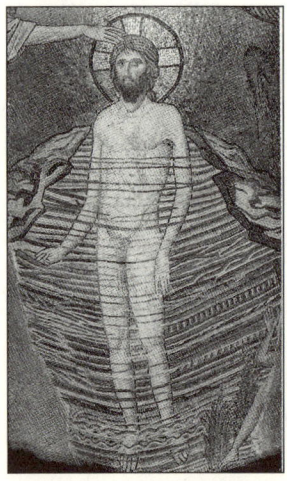

Christ. Fragment of a Mosaic. "Baptism of the Lord." Daphni Monastery. Greece. 11th c.

in a gesture of blessing, and the Gospel book, either opened or closed, is in his left hand. The Almighty may be depicted in full height and seated on the throne, from the waist up, or in a head-and-shoulders view. When depicted in the dome of a church, the image of the Pantocrator shown from the chest up is fitted into a circle. When depicted in the sanctuary apse, the image of Christ may be a head-and-shoulders view or from the waist up, or even in full height, depending on the shape of the apse and the arrangement of wall paintings.

The *iconic* type, famous by the name of Image Not-Made-By-Hands became widespread in the sixth century in connection with the discovery of the Edessa Image, which has already been described. Only the face of Christ on a cloth is represented, while in some cases the cloth is left out and only Christ's face is shown.

The image of the Savior-Emmanuel represents Christ as a child. Usually this image is placed inside a medallion supported by two angels.

The traditional clothing of Christ in the majority of compositions is the blue himation which covers his left shoulder and left arm while his right shoulder and right arm are covered with a dark red chiton with golden galloon (trim). The himation is sometimes white. In the "Transfiguration" scene all of Christ's clothing is white with gold finish. In some compositions of the passion cycle, Christ is depicted wearing a loincloth. This occurs primarily in the scene "Crucifixion" in which Christ is depicted hanging on the cross. The Mother of God is shown at the foot of the cross and to the left of the viewer while Saint John the Theologian is depicted on the right side as a young beardless man. Christ is also presented wearing a loincloth in the compositions "Descent from the Cross," "Lamentation," and "Burial." Christ is presented completely unclothed in the composition "Baptism of the Lord" in Ravenna's

Arian Baptistery (sixth century), in mosaics of the monasteries Hosios Loukas (middle of the eleventh century), and Daphni (end of the eleventh century), and also in several other cases. In later times he came to be depicted in these compositions wearing a loincloth.

In certain images thematically connected with the passion cycle, Christ is depicted as dead. This occurs in the scenes "Crucifixion," "Descent from the Cross," "Lamentation," and "Burial." The composition, famous by the name "Do not Weep for Me, Mother," is inherently connected with these scenes. (The name is borrowed from the opening verse of the irmos of the ninth ode of the canon on Holy Saturday.) In this image Christ is shown frontally and from the waist up, with the lower part of his body invisible in the tomb. The Savior's hands are folded, forming a cross over his waist. His head is tilted, his eyes are closed, and his torso is bare.

The iconography of the Mother of God is marked by more diversity than the iconography of Christ. In the apses of Byzantine churches, the Mother of God is often depicted as seated on a throne, facing forward, with the Infant Christ on her lap. The iconographic type *Hodegetria* (Guide) was developed from this composition in which the Mother of God holds in her arms the Infant Christ. She faces the viewer and with her right hand she indicates the Infant. The Infant also faces the viewer. His right hand is raised in a gesture of blessing, and in his left hand he holds a scroll.

"Orans" (One who is Praying) is widespread and one of the most ancient iconographic models. The Theotokos is depicted frontally and with raised hands. A variation of "Orans" is the image of the Theotokos as a part of the Deesis: a composition in which the Savior is depicted in the center and the Mother of God and Saint John the Baptist are shown on the sides. The Greek word *deesis* (δέησις) literally means *supplication*. In Rus' this type came to be mistakenly called *Deisus* which obviously refers to the central role of Jesus in the

Theotokos "Hodegetria." Mosaic. Monastery of Hosios Loukas. Greece. 11th c.

Theotokos "Orans." Icon. Yaroslavl. 8th c.

composition.[77] In this composition the Mother of God is usually presented with outstretched arms, but not in a frontal pose. Rather, she is half turned away from the viewer. Her face is turned to Christ. Other variations of "Orans" are depictions of the Theotokos from the waist up, with the Infant Christ in a medallion. This image was given the name *Nicopeia* (Giver of Victory) and first emerged in the seals of Emperor Maurice (582–602). It is especially encountered in the murals of the Monastery of Apa Apollo in Bawit (Egypt) and the Church of Santa Maria Antiqua in Rome (eighth century), as well as in murals of the sanctuary of the Church of Saint Sophia in Ohrid (during the 30s of the eleventh century).

In icons of the type "Eleusa" (Tenderness) the Theotokos is presented with her face turned towards the Infant, who tenderly clings to her cheek and embraces her around the neck. This type became widespread in Byzantium beginning in the twelfth century. In the opinion of Viktor Lazarev, "Tenderness" developed from "Hodegetria" as a result of the convergence of the heads of the Theotokos and Infant, which allowed him to clasp her neck with his arms and nestle up to her with his cheek.[78] A different version of "Eleusa" is the type called "Playful Child" which became famous in the beginning of the twelfth century in which the Infant Christ is shown playing with his Mother. In particular this type is seen in an icon of Mount Sinai dating from the twelfth century, in a fresco of the sanctuary screen of the church in Staro Nagoričine (Macedonia) painted in 1318, and in several Russian icons. *Galaktotrophousa* (Milk Giver), in which the Theotokos is presented breastfeeding the Infant, is considered to be yet another version of "Tenderness." This type first appeared in the third century in the Catacomb of Priscilla and was

Theotokos "Tenderness." Icon. Greece. 15th c.

"Milk Giver." Icon. Greece.

---

[77] The term "deisus," which lends to indicating the central role of Jesus in the composition, is also widely encountered in Russian art criticism. However, the use of this term in scientific literature should be considered incorrect because it represents an ancient Russian distortion of the Greek word "deesis" which has a different meaning altogether. The Greek "deesis" denotes the position of prayer of the Mother of God and John the Baptist who are turned towards Christ, who stands between them.

[78] Lazarev, *Byzantine Painting*, 284.

mentioned in the letter of Pope Gregory of Rome to Leo III the Isaurian.[79] It became widespread in the late Byzantine period.

Images of Christ together with the Mother of God are encountered in numerous scenes stemming from the Gospel, in the iconography of the feasts, in the passion cycle, and in a number of other compositions. It is impossible to provide here an overview of the entire multitude of these compositions. We will mention only that the iconography of feasts is closely related to the service texts for feast days. In some cases, when the celebrated event is not mentioned in the Gospel (for example, the birth of the Theotokos and her entry into the temple), the service texts become the sole basis for constructing an iconographical composition.

Angels are an indispensable element of many compositions of the festal row and passion cycle. The depiction of angels in Byzantine iconography also conformed to a particular canon. Most often, angels were presented in the form of genderless creatures (actually, they usually looked more like young boys than young girls) wearing light clothing and having multi-colored wings. The hair of angels is usually tied with a ribbon. Sandals are worn on their feet and often angels bear a walking stick with a cross on top. Angels may hold fans in compositions having a liturgical character. In many compositions, especially in the scene of the Dormition of the Theotokos, we see angels depicted from the waist up. In accordance with the vision of the prophet Ezekiel, cherubim are depicted having six wings. A human-like figure is completely covered by two wings turned downward while another two wings are raised over the head and yet another two wings are outstretched to the sides. Seraphim are depicted having many eyes in accordance with the same vision.

Archangel Gabriel. Fragment of a Mosaic. Annunciation. Daphni Monastery. 11th c.

The basic principles of the canonical depiction of a saint, be it a prophet, apostle, martyr, bishop, or venerable saint, were formulated by the sixth century and took shape once and for all in the post-iconoclastic period. As a rule, saints are depicted in frontal poses having halos around their heads and possessing the attributes of their rank.

An attribute of an apostle may be either a scroll or a codex in the left hand. Evangelists are always depicted with codeces. Sometimes an apostle holds in his

---

[79]See D. Ainalov, "Byzantine Monuments of Mount Athos," *Vizanatijski Vremennik* 6 (1899) 75.

The Betrayal of Christ. Fresco. Church of Saint George in Staro Nagoričine. Macedonia. 14th c.

Great Martyr Theodore the Recruit. Mosaic. Monastery of Hosios Loukas. Greece. 11th c.

hand the symbol of martyrdom, a cross. Beginning in the fourth century, a particular attribute of Peter is the keys (Mt 16.19). In particular, he is depicted with keys in his hand on the mosaic of the Church of Saint Constantine in Rome (middle of the fourth century) and on the well known Sinai icon (sixth century). The faces of apostles gradually acquired individual characteristics. For example, Peter is depicted with a short beard and short, curly, gray hair. Paul is depicted with a high forehead, a bald head, and a long, dark, cone-shaped beard. In scenes from the Gospel, John is presented as a beardless youth while in other compositions he is shown as a gray-haired elder with a balding head and a long beard. The twelve apostles, headed by Saints Peter and Paul, are figured in scenes of the Ascension, Pentecost, Dormition, the Last Judgment, and the Eucharist. The number of apostles usually does not change (there are always twelve), but their composition can vary somewhat. Often the evangelists Mark and Luke are figured in the group of twelve.[79] As the preeminent apostles, Peter and Paul are often figured in a separate composition. In the composition "Mystical Supper," and also in several other scenes from the Gospel (for example, the arrest of Jesus), Judas the Betrayer is depicted. He differs from the other apostles by the absence of a halo. Moreover, his face is usually depicted in profile.

Prophets are usually depicted wearing light clothing and holding scrolls in their hands. Sometimes a text from a book of the prophet is shown on an opened scroll. For example, the prophet Isaiah often holds in his hand a scroll with the words "Behold, the virgin shall conceive in the womb and shall bring forth a son . . ." (Is 7.14). Sixteen prophets are often depicted in the dome of a church or in medallions on the wall, as well as in the

---

[80] N. Kvlividze, "The Apostles: Iconography," in *Orthodox Encyclopedia*, vol. 3, 111.

sanctuary apse. Moses and Elijah must be included in the composition "Transfiguration."

Saint John the Baptist, the last of the prophets and the first of the apostles, is present in the compositions "Baptism of the Lord" and "Deesis." In the first case he lays his hand on the head of the Savior. In the second case he stands before Christ in a prayerful pose. Often the Baptist is depicted by himself. His face is marked by extreme asceticism; his beard and hair are disheveled; his body is covered by a hairshirt or in some cases a himation. Sometimes the forerunner holds in his hand a staff topped with a cross.

Saint Nicholas the Wonderworker. Mosaic. Monastery of Hosios Loukas. Greece. 11th c.

A hand cross is an indispensable attribute of martyrs. In the majority of cases martyrs are depicted in frontal poses. Portrait-icons of martyrs in medallions adorn the walls of churches. Sometimes the instruments of torture, known from the lives of the saints, are depicted on icons of martyrs. Some martyrs who belonged to the ranks of warriors during their lives are depicted in military uniforms holding weapons in their hands. In particular, in the mosaics of the monastery of Hosios Loukas, the great-martyrs Theodore the Recruit and Demetrius of Thessalonica are depicted holding spears in their right hands, shields in their left hands, and swords at their waists. Besides individual depictions of martyrs there are also paired depictions, such as the image of Saints Sergius and Bacchus, and also group depictions, such as the forty martyrs of Sebaste. In the latter case the martyrs are presented unclothed and drowning or already submerged in the water. Forty wreaths are seen over the heads of the martyrs.

Holy bishops are usually depicted wearing liturgical vestments—phelonions and omophorions. (In the late Byzantine period several hierarchs were depicted wearing a sakkos.) In compositions in the sanctuary apse, where bishops are lined up in a register around Christ and half-turned to him, they hold scrolls containing liturgical texts. Saint Basil the Great holds a scroll with a text from the liturgy attributed to him, and Saint John Chrysostom bears a scroll with a text from the liturgy bearing his name. In other compositions holy bishops are depicted in frontal view holding a closed Gospel book in the left hand. The faces of bishops have individual characteristics. Saint Basil the Great is depicted with short hair, a high forehead, and a long, dark beard. Saint Gregory the Theologian is depicted as bald with a wide, gray beard. Saint John Chrysostom and Saint Nicholas the Wonderworker are balding with short, curly, gray beards. Saint Cyril of Alexandria wears a cap with crosses (a mitre). In rare cases, for example in the murals of monastery churches, certain holy bishops may be shown wearing monastic clothing.

Deacons and presbyters are also depicted wearing liturgical clothing. Deacons wear sticharions with orarions and sometimes hold censers in their hands while priests wear phelonions. We shall note that in the ranks of the saints of the Byzantine Church there were very few presbyters and for this reason they are encountered extremely rarely in frescoes. Deacons, on the other hand, are encountered quite often.

Pious kings and queens are depicted wearing precious clothing and having crowns on their heads. Sometimes a king holds an orb (*globus cruciger*) in his left hand. The emperor Constantine and empress Helen are often presented standing next to the cross. Sometimes emperors and pious princes who accepted the monastic tonsure before death are depicted wearing monastic clothing. Emperors or their benefactors who are not included in the ranks of the saints, but who are related to the building or adornment of the given church, are often depicted in the narthex and sometimes in the main body of the church. In this case they may hold in their hands a model of the church.

Monastic clothing—a dark mantle, worn on top of a more lightly-colored garment —is attributed to monks, also called "venerable fathers." Some monastic saints are presented with their heads uncovered. In many cases the head of the holy monk is covered with a round or pointed hood. Sometimes the hands of venerable saints are raised to the sky, while in other cases they are raised to the level of the chest with palms turned to the viewers. (This gesture symbolizes the renunciation of the world and sinful passions.)

Holy women in Byzantine iconography are always depicted with their heads covered (a rare exception is Saint Mary of Egypt who is depicted half-naked and with uncovered short, disheveled hair.) The clothing of righteous Anna, the mother of the Most Holy Theotokos, is reminiscent of the clothing of the Theotokos herself. The myrrh-bearing women are depicted wearing similar clothing. Martyrs belong to a higher estate and are sometimes presented wearing rich clothing with crowns on their heads and holding crosses in their hands. The great martyrs Irene, Catherine, and Barbara are presented in this way in the murals of the monastery of Hosios Loukas.

The decorative arrangement of the interiors of churches became increasingly more complicated in the post-iconoclastic period. This was due to the fact that traditional compositions became richer, having additional figures and new, multi-

Iconographical Tradition in Byzantium

figured scenes. Aside from compositions which corresponded to the yearly cycle of church feasts, other multi-figure compositions became popular between the twelfth and fourteenth centuries, these were often thematically rooted in the pages of the Old Testament or in liturgical texts. These compositions, which included "Creation of the World," "Last Judgment" or "Second Coming," could be placed in the western part of the church or in the narthex. Each multi-figured composition was consistent with certain canonical norms from which an artist could not stray. However, considerable diversity was achieved even within the bounds of canonical rules. This was due to the use of a wide range of artistic means.

Byzantine Mosaics and Frescos of the Ninth Through Fourteenth Centuries

The period from the middle of the ninth through the fourteenth century was the time of the greatest flourishing of Byzantine mosaics and frescoes.

Among the earliest monuments of this period are the mosaics of the Church of Hagia Sophia in Thessalonica. The composition "Ascension" is placed in the dome of the church (880–885). Christ is depicted in the center in a medallion with a disproportionately large head, and seated on a rainbow. The medallion is supported by two flying angels wearing white clothing, having multi-colored wings. Directly below Christ, in the drum of the dome, the Mother of God is depicted in full height and with raised hands (Orans). On both sides of her are angels who indicate with their hands the rising Christ. Twelve apostles are placed in the same register, separated by tall trees with bare trunks and green tops. In the conch of the apse the Mother of God with the Infant Christ is depicted sitting on a throne (turn of the twelfth century). Remaining from the period of Iconoclasm is a cross depicted in the arch of the sanctuary bema.

Ascension. Mosaic. The Church of Hagia Sophia in Thessalonica. Greece. 4th c.

Empty Throne. Monastery of Hosios Loukas. Greece. 11th c.

An exceptional monument of Christian art from the era of the Macedonian Renaissance[81] is the mosaic ensemble of the monastery of Hosios Loukas (named for Saint Luke, a tenth-century hermit). These works date to the first half of the

---

[81] The Macedonian Renaissance is an epoch named for the ruling Macedonian Dynasty in Byzantium (867–1056).

eleventh century and have been magnificently preserved. Pentecost is depicted in the dome of the church. In the center of the composition is the "Empty Throne," on top of which is a dove, symbolizing the Holy Spirit, with its head in a golden halo. A tongue of flame descends from a medallion above each of the seated twelve apostles. The apostles are depicted seated on thrones and conversing with one another. Each apostle holds in his hand a Gospel book. Representatives of various nations are depicted in the pendentives, standing and heeding the apostles and wearing fanciful clothing. The conch of the sanctuary apse contains a depiction of the Mother of God sitting on a throne, with the Infant Christ. The Christological cycle consists of four compositions in the main body of the church in the pendentives of the dome above the tympanum of the dome ("Annunciation,"[82] "Nativity," "Meeting of the Lord," and "Baptism"), scenes of the passion in the narthex ("Washing of the Feet," "Crucifixion," "Descent into Hades"), and "Pentecost" in the small dome over the altar table. The remaining space of the church is adorned with numerous depictions of saints (about one hundred and fifty in all) with wide open, disproportionately large eyes and dark pupils. A considerable place among the saints is occupied by monastic saints, due to the monastic character of the building. Mosaics based on Old Testament subjects are preserved in the sacristy: Daniel in the lions' den, the Three Children in the furnace in Babylon.

Besides mosaics, several frescoes dating to the middle of the tenth and first quarter of the eleventh century are preserved in Hosios Loukas. In one of them Joshua the son of Nun is depicted wearing military clothing. A helmet is on his head and mail armor is seen on his body. He holds a spear in his left hand and wears a sword at his waist. The composition "Meeting of Christ with John the Forerunner" is placed in two arches. In the arch on the left-hand side the Forerunner is depicted turned towards Christ. He is wearing a coat with a wool lining and has a cross in his right hand while his left hand is outstretched to Jesus. In the arch on the right-hand side Christ holds a scroll in his left hand while his right hand is raised in a blessing gesture. The Forerunner is depicted standing on the ground while Jesus is walking towards him. In the composition "Entry of the Lord into Jerusalem," Christ holds a scroll in his hand and is seated on a donkey. A child who has climbed into a tree looks at Christ and crowds greet the coming Messiah with palm branches. In the scene "The Burial," Christ is depicted wrapped in a burial shroud and only his face with closed eyes can be seen. The mourning Theotokos bends over the body of Christ; Joseph and Nicodemus support his body with their

---

[82] This mosaic has not survived.

hands. The same composition contains another scene from the Gospel: two myrrh-bearing women are near the empty sepulcher on which an angel sits.

The mosaics which have survived in Hagia Sophia in Constantinople give but a partial picture of the arrangement of its interior.[83] Great significance was given in these mosaics to the images of Christ and the Theotokos and also to depictions of emperors and empresses. Mosaic depictions of the Mother of God on a throne with the Infant Christ sitting on her lap, completed in 867, survived in the conch of the sanctuary apse. The pose of the Mother of God is static while the figure is majestic. Her body, vested in a dark blue maphorion, is disproportionately large in comparison with her head. The faces of the Mother and Infant are rendered in antique traditions. The mosaic depiction of Christ on the throne with open gospel book dates to the beginning of the tenth century. Medallions with depictions of the Mother of God and an archangel are found on both sides of Christ. Bowing in pious prayer at the foot of the throne is Emperor Leo VI the Wise (reigned 886–912). A mosaic depiction of the Mother of God on a throne with the Infant Christ was created at the turn of the eleventh century. Emperor Justinian is present at her right side holding a model of the Church of Hagia Sophia and on her left side is Constantine the Great with a symbolic model of the city. A depiction of Christ on the throne with Emperor Constantine IX Monomachos (reigned 1042–1055) and Empress Zoe dates to 1044. Around 1118 a mosaic was created in which Emperor John II Komnenos and Empress Irene are depicted next to the Mother of God who holds the Infant Christ.

In terms of strength of expression, the most impressive of the surviving mosaic compositions of Constantinople's Hagia Sophia is the "Deesis," dating to 1261. In the center of the composition is Christ, wearing a blue himation, with his right hand raised in a blessing gesture and the gospel book in his left hand. Christ's expression has the mark of easy concentration. His nose is elongated; his lips are full. His eyes are asymmetrical as on the Sinai icon of the Pantocrator. His gaze is unfocused, and this feature creates the sensation of presence. At the same time it results in a certain distance between Christ and the one praying. The Mother of God and

Deesis. Mosaic. Hagia Sophia. Constantinople. 13th c.

---

[83]A somewhat better picture is given by the drawings of the Swedish engineer Cornelius Loos, made in 1710, and also by the illustrations of the Fossati brothers and von Salzenberg, made in the 19th century. See: Hatzidaki, Βυζαντινά ψηφιδωτά, p. 18.

Deesis. Fragment. Mosaic. Hagia Sophia. Constantinople. 13th c.

John the Baptist are half turned to the Savior. Their faces exhibit mourning and concentration.

The mosaics of the Cathedral of Saint Sophia in Kiev make up one of the most extraordinary monuments of Byzantine art from the first half of the eleventh century. The church's interior is on the whole oriented on Byzantine models. From the original ensemble of mosaics, occupying an area of six hundred and forty square meters (about 6,889 square feet), only about two hundred and sixty square meters (about 2,800 square feet) are preserved, but the surviving mosaics give a conception of the grandeur of the scheme and the perfection of its execution. A medallion with an image of Christ the Pantocrator is placed in the dome of the church. Beneath it are four figures of archangels (of which only one is partly preserved). In the drum of the dome, between the windows, are images of apostles (only a part of a figure of the Apostle Paul is preserved). The pendentives contained the four evangelists (only Mark has survived). In the arches, supporting the dome, were four medallions of which two are preserved—the Mother of God and Christ the High Priest, in the Semitic-Palestinian type of depiction of Christ—that is, with short, curly hair and a short, groomed beard. Medallions are placed in the cross arches with a depiction of the forty martyrs of Sebaste (fifteen medallions of the forty are preserved). The Mother of God "Orans" is depicted in full length in the conch of the apse. Her figure (with a height of nearly five and a half meters or about eighteen feet) dominates in the entire ensemble of the church's mosaics. The "Deesis" in three medallions is placed above the "Orans." In the middle register and under the "Orans" is "The Communion of the Apostles" (Christ is depicted twice), and in the lower register is the rank of holy bishops, and in the center of this deacons with artophorions are depicted in three-quarter view. These elements give the entire arrangement a most definite liturgical character.[84] The composition "Annunciation" is seen on the pillars before the sanctuary conch. Numerous depictions of saints are found on the walls of the cathedral. Figures of Christ, the Theotokos, and saints in compositions of Kiev's Saint Sophia are notable for their static and monumental character. Frontal poses predominate. Facial features of most of the personages are emphatically geometrical, eyes enlarged, lips full, and noses wide.

---

[84] G. Kolpakova, *Art of Ancient Rus': Pre-Mongol Period* (St Petersburg, 2007), 97–98.

Iconographical Tradition in Byzantium

The frescoes of the Church of Saint Sophia in Ohrid (Macedonia), dating to the period 1037–1056, are an exceptional example of Byzantine painting. The frescoes are marked by masterly execution, expressiveness of faces, and compositional diversity. The Theotokos is depicted in the conch of the sanctuary apse in a static pose, seated on a throne. On her arms, in an ovular medallion, is the Infant Christ. In the lower register is the "Communion of the Apostles." In the center of the composition is Christ, standing under the ciborium and turned with his face to the viewer. His right hand is raised in a blessing gesture and in his left hand he holds the bread. On either side of the Savior are two angels. On the right and left, apostles are lined up and approach the Savior. On the arch of the sanctuary apse is the grandiose composition "Ascension," in the center of which, in a medallion, Christ is depicted sitting on a rainbow. Four angels support the medallion. Rows of apostles and angels (one angel in each row) are situated on both sides of the medallion. Apostles are presented in dynamic poses with faces turned to the ascending Christ. Among the apostles is the Mother of God. Under each row is yet another row in which angels are depicted. The walls of the sanctuary apse are decorated with depictions of holy bishops, scenes from the Old Testament that have common themes with the Eucharist (especially the hospitality of Abraham), and scenes from the New Testament.

Theotokos on a Throne. Fresco. Church of Saint Sophia in Ohrid. Macedonia. 11th c.

The grandiose ensemble of mosaics of the Monastery of the Dormition of the Theotokos in Daphni (Greece) dates to the end of the eleventh century, the time of the so-called Comnenian Renaissance.[85] The image of Christ the Pantocrator is dominant in the ensemble. High, raised eyebrows and a gaze directed off to the side, the folds on the face, forehead, and neck, a powerful torso—all of this endows the image with a severity that was unusual by Byzantine standards. Sixteen prophets are depicted in the drum of the dome. The Mother of God with prophets bowing to her is depicted in the sanctuary apse. Much attention is given to the many-figured compositions dedicated to the major feasts of the Church. Acting personages are shown as dynamic and gracious figures and in the most diverse poses—full face, profile, half turn. Faces have an expression of calmness and concentration. Angels are featured in many compositions, and this creates the sensation of the constant

---

[85] Named after the Comnenian Dynasty (1057–1251).

Christ Holding a Sword. Fresco. Monastery in Dečani. Kosovo. 14th c.

presence of the heavenly powers in the life of man. The cycle of the Theotokos includes numerous compositions from the life of the Mother of God, including her nativity, entry into the temple, and dormition. Overall the mosaic ensemble is characterized by a striving to fully reflect the major events of the liturgical year. The thematic program of the mosaics is oriented not so much on the sequence of Gospel events as on the sequence of the Church calendar.

The murals of the Dormition Church in the village of Ateni (Ateni Sioni) date to the nineties of the eleventh century. Georgian monumental painting was genetically linked with Byzantium, but it had brightly expressive national features which are fully reflected in the murals of Ateni Sioni. The Mother of God "Nicopeia" with the Infant Christ is depicted in the conch of the sanctuary apse. On her sides are the archangels Michael and Gabriel. The composition "Eucharist" with apostles turning to Christ is found beneath this. Holy bishops are placed in the lowest register, while stylites are depicted in the spaces between windows. Among other depictions of the sanctuary apse are the Protomartyr Stephen and Venerable Romanus the Melodist and also patrons of the church including King David IV the Builder. A cycle containing eleven feasts is placed in the northern apse while in the southern apse are fourteen scenes from the life of the Most Holy Theotokos. The last judgment is represented in the western apse. The biblical rivers Nile, Pishon, Tigris, and Euphrates are personified and depicted in the form of young men on waves in the church's squinches, instead of the four evangelists.[86] The general style of the wall paintings suggests their belonging to Georgian masters. Dark colors are prevalent, silhouettes of figures are precisely outlined, images are distinguished by their monumental and static character and the heaviness of their shapes.[87]

During the twelfth and first half of the thirteenth centuries a number of mosaic ensembles in the Byzantine style were created in churches of Italy, in particular in the Sicilian towns of Cefalù, Monreale, and Palermo as well as in Venice and Rome. Mosaics of the sanctuary apse of the cathedral in Cefalù, dating to the first

---

[86]G. Abramishvili, "Ateni Sioni," in *Orthodox Encyclopedia*, vol. 3 (Moscow, 2001), 676.
[87]Lazarev, *History of Byzantine Painting*, 101.

half of the twelfth century, represent one of the most complete works of Byzantine art. In the words of one scholar, "From the very first glance these mosaics astound with the noble beauty of their purely Byzantine forms. Figures are marked by the strictness of proportions while the drawing has remarkable fortitude and the treatment of clothing is practically done with the elegance of antiquity."[88] The image of the Pantocrator in the conch is distinguished by a special refinement; the hair and beard are carefully modeled; the expression of his face is emphatically ascetical. Beneath the Pantocrator is situated a considerably smaller "Orans" and on each side of Christ is an angel. The lower registers of the sanctuary apse contain depictions of the apostles. Christ and the Mother of God are represented in strictly frontal poses while the figures of the apostles are depicted in various angles. The graphic character of the drawing as well as the exactitude and precision of line combine harmoniously in the mosaics of Cefalù with a pictorial expressiveness by which each image possesses its own characteristic traits.

In the mosaics of Italy the Byzantine influence coexists with the influence of Latin theology and local traditions. The composition "Second Coming," which includes four registers, is presented in one of the mosaics of the twelfth century in Torcello (Venice). Christ is depicted in the center of the upper row in an ovular medallion. He is seated with arms outstretched downward with the palms of his hands turned to the viewer. (He is showing the wounds from the nails on his hands.) From the medallion flows a stream of fire that divides the composition into the kingdom of the saved (to the left of the viewer—that is, by the right hand of Christ) and the kingdom of the condemned (by his left hand). At the sides of Christ are the Mother of God and Saint John the Baptist, while behind them is the assembly of angels. Apostles in white garments with Gospels or scrolls in their hands are depicted in the same register. Peter, according to tradition, holds keys. In the center of the second register is found the "Empty Throne" with an eight-ended cross standing in the background. Near the cross are two angels; Adam and Eve bow down at the foot of the throne. Angels are depicted opening the gates of Paradise to the righteous on the left side of the second register. On the right side are angels, plunging the heads of sinners into the eternal fire. Inside the flame, Satan is depicted in the form of a green creature with white claws, white hair and beard, sitting on a double-headed dragon. The left side of the third register is occupied by the depictions of the saved: holy bishops, martyrs, monastics, and women saints, turned in prayer to Christ. On the right side are the sinners condemned to torment, who are presented as naked.

[88]Ibid., 211.

The left side of the lower register is occupied with depictions of cherubim guarding the entry to paradise, the wise thief holding a cross at the gates of paradise, Abraham and Sarah with numerous descendants. On the right side various divisions of hell are presented. In its entirety the composition reflects not so much the Byzantine vision of the retribution of sinners in the after-life as the particular understanding of the Second Coming of Christ, the Last Judgment, and eternal torments which were characteristic of the Latin Middle Ages.

The mosaics of Saint Mark's Basilica in Venice, constructed according to the model of Constantinople's Church of the Holy Apostles, were created over the span of three centuries—from the eleventh through the fourteenth century. Masters, both Greek and of local origin, adhered to the tradition of church painting which had formed in Byzantium, but they also introduced elements characteristic of western art. A considerable part of the mosaics was damaged and remade in a later period. The mosaics of San Marco represent an ensemble which is extremely rich in composition and includes scenes having many figures, rendered with virtuosity. Often several scenes are united into a single composition. Scenes of the passion cycle which were created in different times are unified by an expressiveness and dynamism. In the scene of Judas' betrayal of Christ (1180–1190) the facial features of the negative personages (Judas, soldiers, high priests) are nearly grotesque while many of them are depicted in profile. In the scene of the agony at Gethsemane (thirteenth century), the sleeping apostles are depicted in a realistic manner. Each sleeps in a uniquely characteristic position. One holds up his head with his hand; another places his head on his lap; a third lies on his back while a fourth lies with his head leaning on the lap of a fifth, and so on.

On the ceiling of the western narthex of the church one finds the composition "Creation of the World" (first half of the thirteenth century), which illustrates the first two chapters of the Book of Genesis. (A similar composition is also found in the cathedral in Monreale, in Sicily.) In the center of the composition is a medallion containing ornamentation. The medallion is surrounded by three rows of images. The Creator is represented in the form of a child with a cross-in-halo and features prominently in the majority of the images. The "antique" appearance of Christ as the Good Shepherd is reborn in this image. The days of creation are symbolized as angel-like creatures wearing white garments. The heavenly firmament is presented as a circle containing six-pointed stars and the sun and moon with human faces. The history of Adam begins in the second register and continues in the third. Adam's basic facial features resemble those of the Creator to indicate that the creation of Adam was in the image and likeness of God. (In the mosaics of the cathedral in Monreale, where the Creator is presented with a beard and long hair, Adam also has a beard and long hair.) As for Eve, her facial features are similar to the features of Adam. The composition amazes not only by its perfection of artistic decision but also by the richness of its theological composition.

Creation of the Heavenly Bodies. Mosaic. Saint Mark's Basilica. Venice. 12th c.

In the period from the twelfth through the fourteenth century many churches of Asia Minor, Greece, Cyprus, Macedonia, Serbia, and other countries were adorned with frescoes.

An extremely rich collection of frescoes has been preserved in several churches of the Greek city of Kastoria (in the province of Western Macedonia). The churches of Saint Nicholas Kasnitzes, the Holy Unmercenary Physicians Cosmas and Damian, and the Monastery of Panagia Mavriotissa are marked by a particular richness of interior decoration.

Creation of the Beasts of the Earth. Mosaic. Saint Mark's Basilica. Venice. 12th c.

The murals of the Church of Saint Nicholas were created between 1160 and 1180. Prevalent are Gospel subjects and also scenes from the life of the church's patron saint. The builder of the church, Nicephorus Kasnitzes, and his wife Anna, are depicted on one of the frescoes, holding a model of the church. The murals of the Church of the Holy Unmercenary Physicians were created in a similar style in 1180. The composition "Lamentation of Christ" (a widely prevalent composition in the painting of Byzantine churches) is distinguished by its deep expressiveness. Inner restraint is present in the faces of the great martyrs whose images adorn the walls of the church. A striving towards realism and expression is prevalent in the murals of both churches. Faces are painstakingly outlined and poses are rhythmic and expressive. The drawing is precise and graphical. The style of the murals of the church of Panagia Mavriotissa, dating to the beginning of the thirteenth century, is somewhat different. Proper proportions are not always observed in figures that are marked by a certain angularity and faces are more schematic and conventional.

A most impressive ensemble of frescoes is preserved in the Serbian Church of the Holy Theotokos in Studenica (1208–1209), the Church of the Holy Apostles in Peć (1230–1240), the Church of the Savior in Mileševo (first half of the thirteenth century), the Church of the Holy Trinity in Sopoćani (the earliest frescoes date to 1265, while the later ones date to the thirteenth century and the forties of the fourteenth century), the Church of the Mother of God in Gračanica (around 1320), the Church of the Savior in Dečani (around 1348), and others. The Byzantine style combines in these frescoes with local influences. Traditional themes are prevalent in their subjects: scenes from the Old and New Testaments and images of ancient saints. Images of people who play an important role in the history of Serbia and her Church are also encountered: Saint Sava, King Vladislav and his brother Radoslav (in Studenica), King Uroš and his mother Anna (in Sopoćani). Several images from Serbian churches acquired universal fame—for example, the angel on the stone of the empty tomb from the murals of the church in Mileševo.

Of no lesser interest are the surviving frescoes in Macedonian churches of the same period: The Church of Saint Panteleimon in Nerezi (1164), the Church of Saint George in Kurbinovo (1191), the Church of the Theotokos Perivlepta in Ohrid (1295), the Church of Saint George in Staro Nagoričane (1317–1318), the Church of Saint Demetrius in the Monastery of Saint Mark (around 1370), and others. In the dome of the Church of Saint Panteleimon in Nerezi, Christ the Pantocrator is depicted while the half-figure "Orans" with the Infant Christ in a circular medallion is placed in the conch of the apse. The lower register of the apse is occupied by the composition "Eucharist" whose center is a prolonged altar table with bread and wine on it. Behind the table are two angels with fans next to a ciborium. Christ is depicted twice, on either side of the altar table, distributing communion to his disciples. On the walls of the sanctuary sainted bishops are depicted, who stand half turned to the viewer and holding scrolls in their hands. Before the sanctuary screen is the image of Saint Panteleimon, the heavenly protector of the church, in a carved marble case. The walls of the church are adorned with many-figured compositions depicting various scenes from holy Scripture. The compositions of the passion cycle, which include "Descent from the Cross" and "Lamentation of Christ," represent unsurpassed masterpieces. In terms of strength of expression they have no equals in Byzantine painting. In both scenes the Mother of God with a grieving face clings to the dead Christ. (Her grief is communicated in the lines of the eyebrows, highly raised to the center and lowered at the edges, as well as in the turn of the lips and in the eyes full of tears.) In the scene "Lamentation of Christ" the Theotokos holds the body of Christ with both arms; one arm clasps his neck and the other clenches his waist in such a manner that the Savior reclines on her bosom. (This unusual placement of figures emphasized the motherhood of the Theotokos—her blood connection with the Savior to whom she gave birth.) Saints John and Joseph with Nicodemus bow down before the body of the dead Christ in pious, prayerful poses. The half-figures of a pair of angels soar above the entire composition.

The church in Kurbinovo is small in size but amazes with the abundance of many-figured compositions rendered with virtuosity (art historians identify the style of three masters in these works). The major portion of the frescoes dates to the twelfth century, while some were created during the sixteenth century.[89] In the conch of the apse the Theotokos is depicted seated on a throne with the Christ Child playing in her arms. On either side of the Theotokos are the archangels Michael and Gabriel. The lowest register of the apse is occupied by depictions of sainted bishops. The composition "Ascension" is placed over the apse with Christ in a medallion, angels, the Theotokos, and apostles. On the sides of the apse is the composition "Annunciation." The archangel Gabriel is seen on the left side in a dynamic and graceful pose; the folds in his garment are outlined in detail. On the right side is the Theotokos, half-seated and in a no less unusual pose. Her head is turned to face the archangel and her bended knees are turned in the opposition direction. The walls of the church are adorned

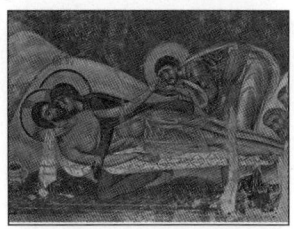

Lamentation of Christ. Fresco. Church of Saint Panteleimon in Nerezi. Macedonia. Middle of 12th c.

Theotokos with Infant Christ. Fresco. Church of Saint George in Kurbinovo. Macedonia. End of 12th c.

with a multitude of images of sainted bishops as well as great martyrs: the saints Thecla, Parasceva, Theodora, Barbara, Anastasia, and Catherine. Many-figured compositions are dedicated to the major feasts of the Church. The composition "Descent of Christ into Hades" stands out for its originality of composition and mastery of execution. Christ is presented in the center in a attitude of swift movement. In his right hand he holds Adam while in his left hand he holds the cross and the crown of thorns. His head is much inclined towards Adam. His himation is seen to be streaming in the wind. The figure of Christ is placed in a circle divided by eight rays of light and eight segments. The direction of the main lines

---

[89] See D.Trajkovska, *St Panteleimon at Nerezi: Fresco Painting* (Skopje, 2004), 53; C. Grozdanov, *Kurbinovo and Other Studies on Prespa Frescoes* (Skopje, 2006), 105–111.

which form the figure coincide with the direction of the rays of light, and this coincidence imparts an almost geometrical correctness and strict proportionality to the composition.

The frescoes of the Church of the Most Holy Theotokos and the refectory of the Monastery of Saint John the Theologian on the island of Patmos (Greece) date to the end of the twelfth and beginning of the thirteenth century.[90] Painted with remarkable mastery, these frescoes represent an exceptional example of monumental painting. One of the frescoes depicts the hospitality of Abraham, a subject from the wall paintings of the Roman catacombs and mosaics of Ravenna. However, in this case, the inscription Ἡ Ἁγία Τριάς (The Holy Trinity) appears over the three angels who sit in static poses. The angels on the right and left sides are shown half-turned while the angel in the middle is turned with his face to the viewer. The right hand of each angel is raised in a blessing gesture. In the left hands of the two angels on the sides are staffs while in the left hand of the angel in the middle is a scroll. The figure of the central angel occupies the central space. The angel is dressed in a blue himation and dark red chiton (these colors are characteristic of the garments of Christ), while the two other angels are dressed in bright himations and chitons. On the table lie three loaves of bread, three knives and a platter with the head and bones of a calf. Abraham is presented in the corner on the left-hand side of the composition carrying a platter, while Sarah is not present.

The church of the Protaton on Mount Athos (in Northern Greece) was covered with murals in around 1290 by the legendary artist Manuel Panselinos. (Information about him is preserved in the works of Dionysius of Fourna, the Athonite artist of the eighteenth century.) The iconographical arrangement of the church is divided into several thematic cycles, each one placed in its own register. The cycle of feasts includes the events from the life of Christ based on the Gospel. The cycle of the Theotokos is based on both the Gospel account and also the information stemming from church tradition. The culmination of the cycle of the Theotokos is the fresco of the Dormition which occupies the entire western wall of the central nave. It is the most multi-figured composition in the entire ensemble. The passion cycle is comprised of eight compositions which illustrate the final days, hours, and minutes of the earthly life of Christ. The paschal cycle includes four compositions dedicated to the appearance of Christ to the apostles after his resurrection. Seven compositions comprise the cycle that is linked with the feast of Pentecost and corresponds

---

[90]The frescoes of the Church of the Theotokos date from 1176–1180, while the frescoes of the refectory date to the beginning of the thirteenth century. Murals of the monastery's cathedral date to approximately 1600. See A. Kominis, ed., *Patmos: Treasures of the Monastery* (Athens, 1988), 57–69.

to the celebrations reflected in the service book called *The Pentecostarion*.[91] The walls of the church are adorned with numerous images of saints: forefathers and prophets, evangelists and other apostles, bishops and deacons, monks, warriors, martyrs, unmercenary physicians, and healers. Panselinos paid particular attention to the images of saints who originated in his home town of Thessalonica.

The art of Panselinos is distinguished by its particular spiritual depth, clarity, beauty of image, and brightness of color.[92] The artist has a tendency for symmetrical compositions, realism in portraits, and a sculptural quality in depicting the human body.[93] The influence of hesychasm is perceived in his art. His faces, whether that of Christ on the throne, the Theotokos on a throne, the great martyrs Theodore Stratelates or Theodore the Recruit, breathe with internal quietue and spirituality. Whether depicted individually or in multi-figured compositions, his depictions of Christ's face are exceptionally diverse. One of the frescoes, famous under the name "Christ Slumbering," depicts the Infant Christ lying on a pillow. The eyes of the Infant are opened but the expression of his face is sleepy and his head is upheld by his hand. In another fresco Christ is presented as a young man with short wavy hair and a short beard (Semitic-Palestinian type). An inscription reads: "Jesus Christ in another appearance" (ΙΣ ΧΣ ὁ ἐν ἑτέρα μορφῇ). In the composition "Descent into Hades," Christ is depicted leaning towards Adam whom he leads out of Hades. The features of the face of the Savior are marked by co-suffering and calmness. The faces and figures of Adam and Eve, on the contrary, are filled with dramatic effect.

One of the high points of representational art of the Palaeologan Renaissance[94] is the ensemble of mosaics of Constantinople's Chora Monastery (Kariye Camii). The church, built in the twelfth century, is a domed building to which three more buildings were added, each with its own dome: the narthex, exonarthex, and parecclesion. The church was adorned with mosaics in the beginning of the fourteenth century. Christ is depicted in a medallion in one of the domes of the church. Twenty-four forefathers are placed in rows around the medallion. In the dome of the narthex is the Theotokos, around whom sixteen forefathers are seen. In this way, all the forefathers of Christ mentioned in his genealogy (Mt

[91] This and other service books will be treated at some length in a forthcoming volume on church services.

[92] Αχειμάστον-Ποταμιανού, Τοιχογαφίες, p. 26.

[93] *Manuel Panselinos: From the Holy Church of the Protaton*: Art exhibit catalog (Thessaloniki, 2003), 40.

[94] The flourishing of fine arts in the epoch of the ruling Palaeologan Dynasty (1261–1453) is called the Palaeologan Renaissance.

Theodore Metochites. Mosaic. Chora Monastery Church. Constantinople. 14th c.

Christ "The Land of the Living." Mosaic. Chora Monastery Church. Constantinople. 14th c.

1.1–16) are presented in the mosaic ensemble of the two domes. The walls, arches, and pendentives of the narthex are adorned with numerous scenes of healings and miracles from the Gospel, episodes from the life of the Most Holy Theotokos, and images of saints. Images of Christ and the Theotokos dominate the ensemble of figures. In one of the mosaics of the narthex, Christ is depicted sitting on the throne. Kneeling at the foot of the throne is Theodore Metochites—the benefactor of the church and great *logothete* (first minister) of Emperor Andronikos II Palaiologus. He wears a tall hat and offers the Savior a model of the church. In another mosaic Christ is presented standing. At his right side is the praying Mother of God, half-turned towards Christ. In the lower part of the composition are small figures of the sebastokrator Isaac Komnenos and the Nun Melania (supposedly the step-sister of Emperor Andronikos II Palaiologus). In the lunette of the exonarthex is an impressive image of Christ "Χώρα τῶν ζώντων" (The Land of the Living).[95]

The monastery's mosaic ensemble is augmented by an ensemble of frescoes, created between 1315 and 1320, placed in the monastery's parecclesions. The semantic center of the ensemble, which includes several multi-figured scenes and numerous singular images of saints, is the composition "Resurrection" (Ἡ Ἀνάστασις). The traditional theme "Descent into Hades" (more precisely, the departure from Hades) is treated here with particular dramatic effect. In the center of the composition is a frontal depiction of Christ in white clothing. Christ is standing with broadly outstretched legs, grasping Adam in his right hand and Eve in his left hand. Adam and Eve are presented in dynamic poses. Adam is almost running towards Christ while Eve makes an effort to rise from the depths of Hades. On the right side of Christ (to the left of the viewer) are depicted John the Baptist and the righteous from the Old Testament with halos. On his left side (to the right of the viewer) are the Old Testament sinners led by Cain, the son of Eve, standing in an attitude of indecisiveness.

---

[95] This name alludes to Psalm 114.9 (MT 116.9), "I will walk before the Lord in the land of the living."

Byzantine Icons of the Ninth through Fourteenth Centuries

The post-iconoclastic period was a time of flourishing for Byzantine iconography. Precisely during this period icons painted on wooden panels became widespread and became an integral part of the church's interior. Panels for icons are made mostly from cedar and cypress. Icons may be of various sizes and shapes. As a rule, an ark is carved into an icon. It is a field of up to ten millimeters in depth with the same shape as the board. The icon's basic depiction is fitted into the ark, while the margin may be left empty or contain additional images.

As has already been stated, beginning in the eighth century icons were painted primarily using egg tempera: mineral paints, mixed with the yolk of an egg. The paint is laid onto the *levkas*, a layer of primer made from chalk and plaster (alabaster) powder dissolved in fish or animal glue. The paint may be laid on the *levkas* in several layers and the lowest layer, as as rule, consists of dark-colored paints, while lighter tones are added on top of the dark ones. The effect of creating volume is not due to laying shadows on top of light tones (as it is customary to do in secular painting), but, on the contrary, by adding light to necessary parts of the composition.

A collection of books known as *Hermeneia* (Gk. ἑρμηνεία—commentary) describes the technique of painting an icon which developed in Byzantium over many centuries. In the beginning of the eighteenth century, Dionysius of Fourna compiled the *Hermeneia* as the basis for the iconographic practice which had formed in a much earlier period (fourteenth through sixteenth centuries). A manual for the creation of an iconographic face is contained in the first part of the collection. According to the *Hermeneia*, painting a holy face requires many layers. It consists of seven layers of different colors, namely: base color, greige, body color, rouge, light body color, white, and highlights for shadows.[96] One at a time, layers of paint are applied in twelve stages. First the master applies a base color; then he paints the contour of the face and lays on greige, and on top of that, the flesh tone. Then creases are refined using flesh tone, and the space around the eyes and the protruding parts of the face are embellished with light flesh tone. White paint may be applied on these parts if necessary. In the concluding stage rouge is introduced

---

[96]Paint for the base color is prepared from a mixture of various amounts of green earth, yellow ochre, and white with the addition of a quarter measure of black. The result is a green color with a shade of gray. The body color is prepared from equal amounts of white, ochre, and cinnabar. The greige is a mixture of equal parts of the base color and body color, which results in a beige color. Rouge is prepared from a mixture of cinnabar and body color and the highlighting of shadows uses a reddish-brown color made from bole. The drawing of lines and contours uses a dark brown color.

"Deesis." Icon. Mount Sinai. 11th c.

and the shadowed parts are brushed on. Contours are gone over once again and creases may be redrawn if necessary, and the drawing of the forehead is refined with greige.[97] Separate rules existed for painting other body parts, clothing, and landscapes.

Gold played an important role in Byzantine iconography of the post-iconoclastic period. Many icons were painted against a gold background. For this purpose thin sheets of gold leaf were glued onto the primed panel and painstakingly smoothed out. Gold was used also for embellishing various elements of clothing. In this case a drawing was made on the icon using garlic juice, which possesses glue-like characteristics. A sheet of gold leaf was then laid on the surface and stuck to the surface of the icon in those places where the drawing was made with the garlic juice. Later, unneeded parts of the gold leaf were removed from the surface.

From the eleventh through fifteenth century gold was combined with white paint to create a unique system of conveying energy and sparkles of light in Byzantine icons. Light penetrates many icons of this period and illuminates images as if from inside. This light shines on faces, folds of clothing, and objects.[98] Thin brushstrokes of white are laid on top of the painted surface. This not only gives the image more relief (volume) but also an easy and light-bearing quality. A similar method was used in monumental painting.

A frontal depiction of Christ with figures of the Mother of God and John the Baptist in three-quarter turn are presented on an icon depicting the "Deesis" from Saint Catherine's Monastery on Mount Sinai (second half of the eleventh century). Images are painted against a background of gold. As is common for Sinai icons, halos are gilded in a way that creates for the viewer the sensation of a shining disc placed over the heads of the personages. The face of Christ, his neck and hands are covered with thin brushstrokes of white, illuminating the arches above the eyebrows, nose, upper part of the forehead, and fingers of the blessing hand. Gold is used for communicating the folds of clothing for Christ and the Mother of God. All three figures are static and breathe with inner calm. The gaze of Christ is fixed

---

[97] A. Yakovleva, "The *Hermeneia* of Dionysius of Fourna and the Iconographic Technique of Theophanes the Greek," in ed. O. Podobedov, *Old Russian Art of the 14th–15th Centuries* (Moscow, 1984), 10.

[98] O. Popova, *Aspects of Byzantine Art: Mosaics, Frescoes, Icons* (Moscow, 2006), 84.

directly on the viewer while that of the Mother of God is turned inward. We note that on these and other Byzantine icons (including the icon "Dormition") the Mother of God is never depicted as an elderly woman. Her face always preserves youth and harmony. Christ looks even older than his Mother on the Sinai icon just mentioned. Saint John the Merciful and Saint John of the Ladder are depicted on the edge of the icon in full height.

On the Sinai icon of Saint Nicholas (eleventh century) we encounter a man of middle age depicted from about the waist up. He has a tensely-concentrated expression on his face and a gaze turned to the side. He is shown with thin lips and creases between the arches over the eyebrows. This icon was painted against a gold background. A golden halo shines over the head of the saint. Owing to the combination of light brown tones and white paint, the face of the saint acquired volume and realism, and it is full of inner light. The beard and hair are covered with thin brushstrokes of white. The saint is dressed in a brown phelonion and a wide white omophorion with crosses. In his left hand he holds the gospel book which he points to with his right hand. Christ together with saints—warriors and healers—are depicted in medallions on the edges of the icon.

The icon of the Mother of God which received the name "Vladimir" in Rus' dates to the first third of the twelfth century. This icon came to Rus' from Byzantium in about 1131 as a gift to Yuri Dolgorukiy from the patriarch of Constantinople Luke Chrysoberges. In 1155 the icon was transferred to Vladimir and in 1395 to Moscow. At the present time the icon is kept in the Church of Saint Nicholas in Tolmachi on the grounds of the Tretyakov Gallery. The icon was altered more than once and the original image was covered over with several layers of later overpainting. In 1919 the layers of alterations were removed, and an image of most rare beauty and refinement was revealed. The Mother of God is depicted on the icon vested in a dark brown maphorion with a graceful golden edge. The gaze of the Mother of God's large almond-shaped eyes is fixed directly on the viewer. The expression of her face is soft and sorrowful; her eyebrows are slightly raised at the bridge of the nose and the lines of the nose and lips are rendered with grace and subtlety. The infant Christ embraces his Mother with his left arm around her neck and he presses his left cheek to the right cheek of his Mother. The lips of the Infant nearly touch the lips of his Mother, and this feature gives the composition a warm and intimate character. In terms of harmony of proportions, perfection of line, and expression, the image of the Vladimir icon of the Mother of God has no equal in all the art of Byzantine iconography.

Vladimir Icon of the Mother of God. Icon. Byzantium. 12th c.

Mother of God "Kykkotissa" Surrounded by Prophets and Saints. Icon. Mount Sinai. 12th c.

A completely different arrangement is seen in the image of the Mother of God and Infant Christ in an icon dating to the first half of the twelfth century, famous by the name "Kykkotissa" (from Kykkos Monastery in Cyprus), which is preserved in Saint Catherine's Monastery on Mount Sinai. Here the Infant is presented playing in the arms of his Mother. His pose is whimsical. His left leg is raised high and his left arm is concealed behind the folds of the Theotokos' clothing. In the right hand of the Infant is a scroll; the gaze of the Infant is directed at the viewer. The head and shoulders of the Theotokos are covered with a brown maphorion; her body is vested in dark blue chiton; her gaze is directed to the side. She supports the Infant with her left hand. It seems as if she is taking away his scroll with her right hand, and she touches the Infant's hair with her lips. The Theotokos sits on a golden throne with a red pillow. The lack of symmetry in the pose of the Theotokos underscores the element of playfulness which is the major theme of this icon. The figures of the Theotokos and Infant are arranged within an arch-shaped space. Depictions of the Savior together with the heavenly powers, prophets, and saints are seen on the edges of the icon.

Monastic spirituality exerted a significant influence on the development of the Byzantine art of iconography. Many iconographers were monks who strove to incarnate ascetic ideals in their works. The influence of monasticism was reflected in a certain spirituality and refinement in the images. Also, a number of iconographic subjects were connected with ascetic literature. One famous Sinai icon of the first half of the twelfth century is called "The Ladder." It owes its name and subject to the literary work of the same name by Venerable Saint John of the Ladder.[99] The icon's central element is a ladder that diagonally intersects the space of the icon. On top of the ladder is a semicircle on which Christ is present. Monks wearing light chitons and dark mantias ascend the ladder. Some of

---

[99] See vol. 1, 89–90 for more on this saint.

them are shown falling off the ladder, drawn into hell by demons. Saint John of the Ladder is at the head of the procession of saints ascending the ladder to Christ. Archbishop John of Sinai (who lived at the time the icon was painted) follows behind him. In addition to these two figures, twenty-three monks are presented, of whom six are shown to be falling and one is half-way buried in the ground. Does this reflect the view of Byzantine monks regarding the approximate percentage of the ratio between the saved and the condemned? Whatever the answer may be, the iconographer consigned the majority of the monks to the ranks of the saved.

Annunciation. Icon. Mount Sinai. 12th c.

The style of several icons and frescoes of the second half of the twelfth century is defined by art historians as "late Comnenian mannerism." This terminology points to the exaggeration and affectation of the poses chosen for figures in the icons. The Sinai icon "Annunciation" dating to the end of the twelfth century was painted in this style. The archangel Gabriel is presented in a unique pose. His face is depicted almost in three-quarter turn; the lower part of the figure is in half-turn and his torso is turned around to the side opposite the viewer. The sensation of the angel's lightness—as if he were walking on air—is heightened by the masterly use of gold to embellish his clothing. The Mother of God is depicted in a frontal pose. She sits on a throne and holds a spool of yarn in her hands. Her face is turned to the archangel. The fresco of the Macedonian church in Kurbino, described earlier, reveals a similar compositional arrangement for the scene "Annunciation."

Greatmartyr Catherine with Scenes from Her Life. Icon. Mount Sinai. Beginning of 8th c.

Several late Byzantine icons contain not only an image of a particular saint but also scenes from the saint's life. These are referred to as life icons of the saint. Marginal scenes with incidents from the life of the saint form a frame around the sides of the central image and are read in a clockwise fashion. Each scene is a miniature icon painted in accordance with the iconographic canon. Sometimes the scenes are arranged in a line and form a single sequence which reproduces the life of the saint in an order which strives to follow the chronology of the saint's life. The marginal scenes fit into the overall architectonics (organizational design and structure) of the icon. Whereas the basic image of the saint reveals the result of his ascetic activity, the marginal scenes illustrate the path along which the saint journeyed in life. Therefore, in these scenes, saints may be shown to be in motion. The Sinai icons of Saint Catherine (first quarter of the thirteenth century) and Saint Nicholas (beginning of the thirteenth century) are especially notable examples of icons bearing scenes from the lives of the saints.

Icons bearing images of the twelve feasts became widespread in the post-iconoclastic period. Such icons are often placed on the architrave of the sanctuary screen and are called the *epistyle* (from the Gr. ἐπίστυλον, Slav. *tyablo*). Often several icons of the epistyle are painted in a row on long boards. As a rule, the "Deesis" is placed in the center of the row of icons. A cycle of festal icons, dating to the end of the twelfth and beginning of the thirteenth century, is found on Mount Sinai. Another Sinai epistyle dates to the second or third quarter of the twelfth century and contains images depicting scenes from the life of the holy martyr Saint Eustratius.

One of the most expressive Byzantine icons is the image of Christ Pantocrator from Hilandar Monastery (third quarter of the thirteenth century) on Mount Athos.[100] The Savior's face depicted in this icon is not marked by perfect proportions. However, inner strength and spiritual energy combined with human warmth and attraction makes this image unique among artworks of its time:

> The Savior's image had never appeared so close to man in the history of Byzantine arts. Never was his image so closely compared to man, so commensurable with him. Never, let us permit ourselves to say, did his image appear so humanized. This was possibly the closest approach of the divine comprehension to human values. Byzantine religious consciousness . . . could not go further."[101]

Traces of the influence of the hesychastic controversies are seen in Byzantine icons of the second half of the fourteenth century.[102] The teaching of the hesychasts concerning the divine light, in the opinion of a number of art historians, found a direct reflection in iconography. They see this teaching reflected in the fact that in many Byzantine icons of that period, the faces of Christ, the Theotokos, and the saints were thickly modeled with white paint. One of these icons is the image

---

[100]Probably, the icon was placed on the sanctuary screen of old catholicon of the Hilandar Monastery. See *Icons of Hilandar Monastery*, 24.

[101]Popova, *Aspects*, 59.

[102]For a discussion of hesychasm, see vol. 1, pp. 125–129.

Iconographical Tradition in Byzantium

of Christ Pantocrator (1363), which may be found in the State Hermitage Museum. Another famous icon painted using a similar technique is the image of Saint Gregory Palamas (second half of the fourteenth century) found in the Pushkin State Museum of Fine Arts. In both cases white paint is applied on the faces in such abundance, especially around the eyes, that the sensation is created of inner luminescence. It is as if matter were pierced with light and shed light.

Several Byzantine icons are distinguished by exceptional expression and inner expressiveness. Primarily these are the icons of the passion cycle. Byzantine iconographers achieved great mastery in conveying grief and suffering. In icons entitled "Crucifixion" of the second half of the fourteenth century, the Mother of

Theotokos at the Cross. Fragment of an Icon. Crucifixion. Athens. Greece. 8th c.

God and Saint John, standing before the Savior's cross, are depicted in a state of profound sorrow. Sorrow is revealed in the expressions of their faces, their poses, and their gestures. In the icon "Crucifixion" preserved in the Byzantine Museum in Athens, the Mother of God is depicted with hands outstretched to Christ and eyes raised to his face; the eyebrows of the Theotokos are raised high at the bridge of the nose and lowered on the sides, which endows her face with an expression of deep sorrow. Owing to the skilful application of white paint, the eyes of the Theotokos appear filled with tears. No less expressive is John, standing on the other side of the cross with his hand raised in a gesture of astonishment. It seems that he silently asks the Savior the meaning of what is transpiring on Golgotha. Extremely expressive are the faces of other figures. Each face reflects a certain shade of sorrow. The face of the dead Christ is filled with inner strength and exudes quietude and repose.

Book Miniatures

Parallel to the development of monumental painting and iconographic arts in the period from the sixth through fourteenth century in the Christian East was the development of the art of book miniatures. The subjects of miniatures—which illustrated the codices of Holy Scripture and the works of the Church Fathers—normally corresponded to analogous icons. But in contrast to icons, miniatures were bound to illustrated texts and not to the church calendar. Therefore in book miniatures we encounter not only subjects seen in icons and frescoes but we also find completely original subjects characteristic of the tradition of manuscripts alone or even characteristic of a single individual manuscript.

The Flood. The Vienna Genesis. Circa 540. Italy.

One of the most ancient illustrated manuscripts is preserved in Austria's National Library in Vienna. It is a codex of the sixth century (around 540) containing the Greek text of the book of Genesis (Codex Vindob. theol. gr. 31). Twenty-four of the original ninety-six pages of manuscript have been preserved, the text of which is written in unique script.[103] The miniatures are placed on the lower part of the page below the text. Many of them are detailed compositions containing many figures. The great flood is presented in one of the miniatures. Rain is depicted using straight vertical lines of light-blue color in the upper part of the composition. In the lower part horizontal lines symbolize water. Drowning and already-drowned people are depicted in the water; their poses are diverse and expressive.

Another famous illuminated manuscript is the Rabbula Gospels, dating to 586. It contains the Syriac translation of four Gospels (the "Peshitta"), written in eastern Syriac script called 'Esṭrangēlā, on the highest quality parchment. The basic text of the Gospels is written in two columns in black or dark brown ink. Numerous notes under the text are set apart in red script. Individual figures from biblical history, the four evangelists, and scenes from the gospel are presented on the manuscripts' twenty-eight miniatures. The most interesting of these are the scenes of the "Crucifixion," "Ascension," and "Pentecost."

The scene "Ascension" is conventionally divided into two rows. Christ in white clothing appears in the upper row in the center. His figure is placed in a blue oval supported by the flame-red wings of cherubim. To the right and left of the oval are angels wearing white robes. In the lower row is the Mother of God surrounded by apostles. Two angels are turned to the apostles. One of them indicates with his hand the ascending Christ while the hand of the other angel is turned to the apostles.

---

[103] A. Džurova, *La miniature bizantina: I manoscritti miniati e la loro diffusione* (Milano, 2001), 23.

The crucifixion of Christ together with his resurrection is presented in the Rabbula Gospels as a unified composition and comprises two rows. In the upper row are three crosses, those of Jesus and the two thieves. Jesus on the cross is depicted in a long, dark, sleeveless chiton. The thieves wear loincloths. Near the cross of Jesus are two soldiers. One offers him a sponge with vinegar on a pole, while the other pierces his side with a spear. At a certain distance stand the Mother of God and other women. Next to the Mother of God is John the Theologian. Beneath the cross of Jesus are three soldiers who cast lots for his clothing. The resurrection of Christ is presented in the lower row of the composition. In the center is a miniature house depicting the sepulcher. Near it two soldiers are plunged down to the ground in fear. To the left of the tomb is an angel who proclaims the resurrection to two women, one of whom is the Mother of God. A scene depicting the appearance of Christ to Mary Magdalene appears on the right. In this way, several Gospel events which took place at different times are united in the composition.

While in the scene "Ascension" Christ is depicted as a middle-aged man with long hair and a cone-shaped beard, in several other miniatures he is presented as a young man with short hair and a short beard (Semitic-Palestinian style). In one case he is depicted sitting on the throne and conversing with four monks. In another case we see Christ vested in a dark chiton. The right hand of Christ is raised in a blessing gesture. The Savior's large dark eyes are directed off into the distance.

Only two illuminated manuscripts were preserved from the period of Iconoclasm. These are the *Sacred Parallels* of Saint John of Damascus, preserved in the National Library of France in Paris (Par. gr. 923), which dates to the first half of the ninth century, and the *Astronomical Tables* of Ptolemy, preserved in the Vatican Library (Vatic. gr. 1291), which were copied between 828 and 835. On the basis of these manuscripts it is difficult to form an opinion concerning the degree to which the art of book miniatures developed in the manuscripts of the iconoclastic period. It is possible that illustrated manuscripts in this period underwent the same destruction as icons, frescoes, and mosaics.

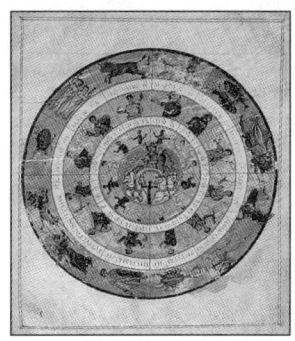

Helios, Months of the Year and the Cycle of Zodiac. Astronomical Tables *of Ptolemy.* Constantinople. 9th c.

The post-iconoclastic period was characterized by a flourishing of all forms of representational art including book miniatures. In the illustrations of several manuscripts, Christian themes are whimsically combined with antique motifs.[104] Concerning this, several researchers speak of the "double language" of Byzantine art—antique and Christian—reflected in manuscript miniatures.[105]

David is depicted on one of the miniatures of the Greek Psalter of the first half of the tenth century from the National Library in Paris (Par. gr. 139). He is playing a stringed instrument. Behind him is a maiden wearing antique clothing; she places her elbow on his shoulder. An inscription near her indicates that she symbolically depicts "Melody." Half-reclining is a partially unclothed male figure crowned with a laurel wreath who listens to the music. In another miniature from the same manuscript the prophet Isaiah is presented in a praying pose. Behind him is "Night" in the form of a woman wearing an antique tunic and a cloak thrown over her shoulders. (The figure of the woman and the folds of her clothing are reminiscent of the frescoes of Pompeii.) Opposite Isaiah is a symbolic depiction of "Morning" in the form of a young man bearing a torch.

Saint Luke the Evangelist. The Four Gospels or Tetraevangelon. Stavronikita Monastery. Mount Athos. 10th c.

Manuscript gospel books were adorned with images of the evangelists placed at the beginning of each of the four gospels. The evangelists are usually depicted sitting on short stools in front of a reading stand on which lies an opened book with the opening words of the gospel. On a small table by the reading stand is an ink well, a reed pen, and sometimes a compass. A symbolic architectural ensemble generally served as a background for the composition. The evangelists Matthew, Mark, and John are depicted in this way in the manuscript of the Four Gospels dating to 950–960 and preserved in the Library of Stavronikita Monastery (No. 43) on Mount Athos. Concerning Saint Luke, on his reading stand lays a closed book on which is a long scroll with miniscule text (it is evident that what is meant is that Luke first wrote a draft). Saint John the Theologian is often depicted dictating to his young disciple Prochorus, who writes the words of the Gospel on a scroll. Scenes from the gospel history which adorn manuscript gospels, in terms of composition often coincide with corresponding scenes on the walls of churches.

---

[104]V. Likhacheva, *Fine Arts: Culture of Byzantium, Second Half of the 7th–12th Centuries* (Moscow, 1989), 474. See Weitzmann, *Studies*, 176–223 for a more detailed discussion of the influence of antique art on Byzantine book miniatures.

[105]Galavaris, Ζωγραφική βυζαντινών χειρογράφων, p. 14.

Iconographical Tradition in Byzantium 183

Manuscripts containing the writings of the Holy Fathers often show depictions of the authors themselves. They are shown in diverse poses and various situations. The collection of liturgical orations of Saint Gregory the Theologian (Sinai Codex 339) from Saint Catherine's Monastery on Mount Sinai, which dates to 1136–1155, contains numerous images of the saint. The images are thematically connected with the contents of the orations. For example, an image of Saint Gregory giving alms to a crowd of poor people is found before his oration on the love of poverty. An image of Saint Gregory standing near a mountain on which the martyr Saint Mamas is sitting, appears at the beginning of an oration commemorating the martyr. A composition appears above the title of his "Invectives against Julian the Apostate" in which, in one corner Saint Gregory is depicted on a wooden armchair with a scroll in his hands while Julian is depicted in the opposite corner sitting on a stool, also holding a scroll. Between them are four male figures who symbolize those whom Saint Gregory is addressing in the oration.

Sometimes images of the people who ordered particular manuscripts appear in the manuscript collections. In a miniature of the codex from the years 1074–1078, which contains homilies of Saint John Chrysostom preserved in the National Library in Paris (Coislin, 79), Saint John is shown presenting a book to a client, Emperor Michael VII Doukas. On a miniature of a codex of the eleventh and twelfth centuries (No. 61) from the library of Dionysiou Monastery on Mount Athos, which contains the liturgical orations of Saint Gregory the Theologian, Saint Gregory is shown presenting the codex to an unknown client who is dressed in the clothing of an aristocrat. On a miniature of Sinai's Four Gospels, completed in about 1250 (manuscript No. 198), Saint John the Theologian is shown presenting the Gospel to Monk Herman, who is presented in the image of a kneeling young man with barely visible beard. He wears a dark mantia and a cap of the same color covers his head and ears.

Numerous manuscripts containing the lives of the saints are preserved from the late Byzantine period. In the beginning of the eleventh century systematic work was conducted in the Byzantine court in order to put the Church calendar into good order and to codify the lives of the saints. One of the results of this work was a manuscript now famous under the name "Menologion of Basil II" which is preserved in the Vatican Library (Vat. gr. 1613). The manuscript is made up of four hundred and thirty-nine pages (the format of a page is 363 x 287 mm/14.3 x 11.3 inches) and contains the lives of the saints from September 1 through February 28—that is, this is evidently the first of two volumes covering the entire liturgical year. Each page is divided into two halves. One half (either the upper or lower half) contains a miniature, while the other half contains a sixteen-line text that accompanies the miniature. Thus what we see is not so much an illustrated manuscript as a collection of miniatures with a short description of each composition.

Martyrdom of several saints. Menologion of Basil. 11th c.

The miniatures of the Menologion are extremely diverse in content. Sainted bishops in liturgical vestments, venerable saints in monastic clothing, soldiers in military uniforms, women saints in traditional garments of Byzantine women—all these are presented. Executions of martyrs are painted in numerous miniatures. In these images martyrs are crucified on crosses, beheaded, given to be devoured by beasts, burned, and cast into boiling water. Depictions are realistic and poses are diverse and full of dynamism. In their totality, the miniatures paint a grandiose picture of the history of the Church in the first centuries of its existence—a period of persecutions and mass heroism of Christians who gave their lives for their faith in Christ.

8

Russian Icons

Iconography in Rus'. Theophanes the Greek

R USSIAN CHURCH PAINTING of the eleventh through thirteenth century was closely connected with Byzantine painting. Numerous masters from Byzantium worked in Rus' in the pre-Mongol period, creating icons, frescoes, and mosaics. In the second quarter of the eleventh century a group of Byzantine masters worked in Kiev's Saint Sophia Cathedral. In the 1080s another group adorned the Dormition Cathedral of Kiev Caves Lavra. A disciple of the Greeks was Saint Alypius, the iconographer of the Kiev Caves who is mentioned in the Kievan Caves Patericon (Discourse 34).[1] Greek masters and their disciples also worked in Novgorod. An iconography studio was managed by Olisey Grechin at the end of the twelfth century. Byzantine influence is felt in the murals of Novgorod's Saint Sophia Cathedral (1108), the Cathedral of the Nativity of the Theotokos of Saint Anthony Monastery (1125), Saint George Church in Staraya Ladoga (last third of twelfth century), and also Mirozhsky Monastery in Pskov (40s of the twelfth century). The earliest of the existing Russian icons are marked with the clearly expressed influence of Byzantine iconogrpahy. This is seen primarily in the Novgorod icons "Savior Not-Made-By-Hands" and

"Angel with Golden Hair."
Icon. Novgorod. 12th c.

---

[1] Bishop Jonah (Zyryanov), "The First Russian Iconographer (On the 850th Anniversary of the Repose of Saint Alypius of the Caves)", in *Journal of the Moscow Patriarchate*, 9 (Moscow, 1964), 61–66.

"Angel with Golden Hair" which both date to the twelfth century. The faces on both icons are noble—enormous eyes, outlined with dark lines and gazes fixed to the side of the viewer.

During the period of the crusades the cultural links between Byzantium and Rus' were weakened, but in the first half of the fourteenth century they again became intense, and artists from Greece once again became guests in the Russian lands. In 1338 Isaiah Grechin created murals for Novgorod's Church of the Entry of the Lord into Jerusalem, and it is supposed that in 1363 Greek masters participated in the creation of wall paintings of the Church of the Dormition on Volotovo Field. The last quarter of the fourteenth century is marked by the activity of Theophanes the Greek.

In art history it is conventional to speak of several "schools" of Russian iconography: Novgorod, Pskov, Rostov-Yaroslav, Tver, and Moscow. The concept of *school* in the given case is used in an extremely conditional sense. Mostly, we are talking about several local traditions formed by the fourteenth century which gave icons, originating in one or another region, particular characteristics. The conditionality of the "school" concept is strengthened by the fact that, based on different indicators, a given icon may be consigned by some scholars to one school and by other scholars to another school. Nevertheless it is evident that the development of iconographic arts in Rus' took place around the large cities which were gaining significance as spiritual and cultural centers.

One of these centers was Tver. The principality of Tver emerged as an independent principality in the middle of the thirteenth century. In 1271 an episcopal throne already existed in Tver and in 1285 the construction of Holy Transfiguration Cathedral began—the first stone church in Rus' under the Tatar-Mongol yoke. Holy Transfiguration Cathedral became Tver's major religious center and the city itself began to be called the "House of the Holy Savior."[2] By the end of the thirteenth century Tver had already become a major center of iconography. The earliest of the existing Tver icons is the image of Saints Boris and Gleb, which dates to this period.[3] The icon is rendered in bright paints. The faces of the saints are abundantly covered with areas of white paint, and the clothing is adorned with silver tracery. Halos are white and the background is silver. Stylistically, the icon of the Savior Almighty (Pantocrator), dating to the end of the thirteenth and first

---

[2] L. Evseeva, I. Kochetkov, V. Sergeev, *Painting of Ancient Tver* (Moscow, 1983), 8–9.

[3] Several art historians actually attribute the icon to the Novgorod School since it was found in Novgorod's Saint Sabbas of Vishera Monastery. See N. Chernogubov, *The Icon of Boris and Gleb in Kiev's Museum of Old Russian Arts, Old Russian Arts of the 15th–16th Centuries* (Moscow, 1963), 285–290.

third of the fourteenth century and preserved in the Tretyakov Gallery, is similar to this icon. The face of Christ on the icon is expressive. Huge almond-shaped eyes exude light, conveyed by areas of white paint extending from the eyes as rays. Another image attributed to the same school is the image "Mother of God 'Hodegetria'" from the first quarter of the fifteenth century (Museum of Andrei Rublev). The opinions of art historians differ concerning the origin of an icon of Saint Peter, Metropolitan of Moscow (Tretyakov Gallery). Some see in it a work of the Tver School while others see in it the work of the Moscow School. The holy bishop is depicted in a white metropolitan's kukol having cherubim on top, a white omophorion with black crosses, and a sakkos made from material having rich ornamentation. The saint's countenance is aloof, absorbed, and somewhat sorrowful. His gaze is turned inward.

The Moscow School of iconography developed in parallel with the strengthening of Moscow as a large center of Rus' and later its main spiritual and political center. The oldest icons of the Moscow School are attributed to the first half and middle of the fourteenth century. These are the icons "Savior Oplechny" and "Savior 'Furious Eye'" from the Dormition Cathedral of the Moscow Kremlin. The first of these is painted in soft half-tones. Areas of white paint are absent. Light is equally distributed around the entire face of the Savior, as if illuminating the face from inside. The expression of the face is calm and gentle. On the second icon one sees the face of the Judge who gazes at the viewer with

Savior "Furious Eye." Icon. Moscow. 14th c.

wide open eyes having black pupils (from this comes the unusual name of the icon "Furious Eye"). The eyebrows of the Savior are raised sternly and deep creases cut through his forehead. Half circles under the eyes are made lighter by areas of white paint. Bright red lips, painstakingly traced out with cinnabar, only heighten the sensation of severity in the Savior's appearance. The "Don Icon of the Mother of God" (end of the fourteenth century) is attributed to the Moscow School. Some art historians attribute it to Theophanes the Greek or his school.[4] The icon belongs to the same type as the famous Vladimir icon, and the author's familiarity with

---

[4] See I. Grabar, *On Old Russian Art* (Moscow, 1966), 93, 104, 111; V. Lazarev, *Theophanes the Greek and His School* (Moscow, 1961), 63–67; I. Kochetkov, "Does the Donskaya Icon of the Mother of God Represent a Monument of the Kulikovo Battle?" in *Old Russian Arts of the 15th–16th Centuries* (Moscow, 1963), 36–40.

the Vladimir icon is evident. On the icon "John the Forerunner—Angel of the Desert" (end of fourteenth century) John is presented in a hair shirt, with a scroll in his left hand and wings behind his back. In accordance with tradition the hair and beard of the forerunner are disheveled. Not only the lips but also the nose is outlined with bright cinnabar which creates the sensation of a reflection of flame on the face of the Forerunner.

Theophanes the Greek stands apart from other iconographers of the second half of the fourteenth century. He was a legendary master who reared an entire pleiad of disciples. By the witness of Epiphanius the Most Wise, before his arrival in Novgorod, Theophanes painted murals in the Byzantine cities of Chalcedon, Galata, and Caffa (present-day Feodosia). Epiphanius calls Theophanes a "deliberate artist" and a "painter graceful in iconographs" and noted that while he worked he never referred to models and would "stand without rest, tongue conversing with those coming, his mind considering the distant and reasonable."[5] After arriving in Rus', Theophanes first settled in Novgorod, where in 1378 he painted the murals for the Church of the Holy Transfiguration on Il'yn Street, built four years earlier. Then he moved to Moscow. In 1395 Theophanes, together with a group of disciples, painted the murals of the Church of the Nativity of the Theotokos in Kolomna near Moscow. Chronicles state that the "masters were Theophanes the iconographer, Grechin Filosov, and Semen Cherny and their disciples."[6] In 1399 Thophanes together with his disciples painted the walls of the Moscow Kremlin's Cathedral of the Archangel and in 1405 together with Daniel Cherny and Andrei Rublev he painted the walls of the Kremlin's Annunciation Cathedral.

Of all the murals created by Theophanes, only the frescoes of Novgorod's Church of the Holy Transfiguration on Il'yn Street have been preserved up to the present day. They give a conception of the uniqueness of his almost "impressionistic" style which is equal to nothing either in Byzantine or Russian painting. Theophanes' style is distinguished by its schematic and precise drawing, correct proportionality, sparing use of hachures, and deep inner expression. Red-brown tones are prevalent in his range of colors. White is used in thick brushstrokes, and this technique endows faces and compositions with an inner light-bearing quality.

The image of Christ Almighty (Pantocrator), placed in the calotte of the dome, dominates in the ensemble of murals. Large, round, wide open eyes with exaggerated pupils, directed straight at the viewer, give particular strength to this image.

[5]Lazarev, *Theophanes*, 113.
[6]V. Briusova, *Andrei Rublev* (Moscow, 1995), 10.

Areas of white over and under the eyes create what seem to be luminous halos around each of them. The exact expression that the face of the Pantocrator once showed is impossible to determine with certainty, because a very essential part has been lost: the mouth. The inscription around the medallion proclaims: "O Lord, look down from heaven to the earth, to hear the sighs of the fettered and to loose the sons of the slain, to proclaim the name of the Lord in Zion" (Ps 101.19–21).

Christ Pantocrator. Fresco in the Dome of the Church of the Savior on Il'yn Street in Novgorod. Theophanes the Greek. Beginning of 15th c.

Depictions of the archangels Michael, Gabriel, Uriel, and Raphael are placed beneath the medallion in the drum of the dome. Between them are two cherubim and two seraphim. Pairs of figures of the righteous of the Old Testament—Adam, Abel, Seth, Enoch, Noah, Melchizedek, Elijah, as well as Saint John the Baptist— are placed in the spaces between the windows. The faces of the righteous are majestic and severe. Adam is depicted in the form of an elder having long gray hair and a long beard. His right hand is outstretched to the side while his left hand is raised and turned with open palm to the viewer. Abel is presented in the form of a young man with a face of proper antique proportions. His eyebrows somewhat form a frown while his eyes look at the viewer. Thin expressive lips, painted with but a few brushstrokes, are pressed close together. His head is set on a powerful and tall neck. The face and neck are abundantly covered with white brushstrokes. Noah is depicted in the form of an elderly, balding man and holds a model of the ark.

Frescoes in the northern chamber in the gallery are well preserved. The central place is occupied by the composition "Hospitality of Abraham," in which three angels are depicted seated around a semi-circular table. Sarah stands before them holding bread (the figure of Abraham has been lost). The angel in the middle symbolizes Christ. Over his head is a cross-in-halo with the inscription O ΩN (*Ho ōn*—He who is). His image bears a certain resemblance to the image of Abel—the same youthful traits, the same correctness of proportions, powerful and tall neck, the same thick areas of white paint on the face and neck. The expression of the face of this angel, however, is gentle and devoid of severity. The corners of the lips are raised asymmetrically. The wings of the angel are stretched out over the other two angels whose faces are directed at the viewer. An inscription over the composition reads: "Holy Trinity."

Images of stylites—saints who lived atop large columns and who embody in themselves the Byzantine ideal of extreme asceticism and mortification of the flesh—are extremely expressive. The faces of stylites are concentrated and their gestures laconic. Their eyes sometimes appear not to have pupils, and sometimes the eyes are left out and merely suggested by a few schematic brushstrokes. The ideal of the utmost asceticism is embodied in the image of Saint Macarius of Egypt. The saint is presented almost completely devoid of the physical characteristics of an earthly man. He has no clothing, no eyes, lips, or ears. His entire body is completely covered with white hair. Two arms raised in a gesture of prayer and turned with palms outstretched to the viewer make up the central element of the figure. The entire expressiveness of the image is concentrated in this gesture which symbolizes the renunciation of the world with all its vanity and passions.

Scholars note the indisputable familiarity of Theophanes the Greek with the teaching of the Byzantine hesychasts.[7] This familiarity is expressed, in particular, in his treatment of light. "The compositions and individual figures of the frescoes of the Church of the Holy Transfiguration on Il'yn Street, as in no other murals, are filled with light. Theophanes understands and treats light not only as a means, but primarily as a power which acts upon a person from inside and which forms, enlightens, and transforms his entire countenance." Light "may flow forth abundantly or may become very fine streams. It may be painted in ideally straight lines, in triangles, in sharp strokes and in small dabs made with precise strokes of the brush."[8] Highlights are made in a rigid sequence which strengthens the very features of the face and elements of the figure that need to be accentuated.

The icon "Transfiguration of the Lord," painted about 1403 and preserved in the Tretyakov Gallery, is attributed to Theophanes the Greek. The creator of the icon uses white and gold colors with virtuosity to convey light. The figure of Christ dominates as the icon's absolute center of light. Christ is depicted in a white chiton with a trim of gold hatching. Four powerful white-gold rays form a four-pointed star that emanates from the body of Christ. The figure of Christ fits into a light blue circle, over which golden beams of light and stars are depicted in the form of radii. The face of Christ is covered with bold strokes of white paint in such a way that a sensation of inner luminescence is created. Elements of the clothing of Elijah and Moses are trimmed with white paint as are the three apostles

---

[7]Lazarev, *Theophanes*, 29–30, 22–24. D. Obolensky, *The Byzantine Commonwealth* (London, 1971), 356–357.

[8]L. Livshitz, *Monumental Painting of Novgorod in the 14th–15th Centuries* (Moscow, 1987), Novgorod, 23.

who fall down in trepidation before the appearance of divine glory. Elements of the landscape are also covered with lightly executed strokes of white paint. All of this creates the sensation of space illumined with light emanating from the transfigured Savior.

Saint Andrei Rublev and the Development of the Iconostasis. The Iconography of the Holy Trinity

The Venerable Andrei Rublev (c. 1360–1427) occupies a central place in the history of Russian iconographic arts. His creative work is synonymous with the greatest mastery of iconography, a standard of perfection, and a model for all subsequent masters.

Andrei Rublev's name was first mentioned in the chronicles in connection with the adornment of the walls of the Annunciation Cathedral in the Moscow Kremlin. "In the year 6913 (1405), in the spring, the adornment of the stone church of the Holy Annunciation in the court of the Great Prince was begun, not the one which stands today, and the masters were the iconographer Theophanes the Greek and Prochorus the elder from Gorodets, and the monk Andrei Rublev, and in the same year they finished it." In 1408 the chronicler noted, "In the same year on May 25 the masters Danilo the Iconographer and Andrei Rublev began to cover in images the great stone cathedral of the Holy Theotokos in Vladimir by the order of the Great Prince."[9] We may conclude from the chronicler's meagre indications that Andrei Rublev, in contrast to Theophanes the Greek and other iconographers mentioned, was a monk; second, for a time he worked together with Theophanes the Greek; and third, by the first decade of the fifteenth century he became one of the leading Russian iconographers to whom princes assigned great responsibility in the painting the murals in the churches.

Angel—Symbol of the Evangelist Matthew. Miniature. Gospel. Khitrovo. 14th–15th c.

One may presume that Rublev worked in all known types of the iconographic arts. He created frescoes, icons, and possibly book miniatures as well. Several scholars consider him to be the author of the miniatures of the famous Khitrovo Gospels,[10] a manuscript prepared for the Dormition Cathedral of the Moscow

[9] Cited in Briusova, *Rublev*, 10.
[10] Russian State Library, ф. 304, III, No. 3/M, 8657.

Kremlin at the turn of the fifteenth century. Among Rublev's works are the iconostasis and frescoes of Zvenigorod's Dormition Church in Gorodok, the frescoes of the Dormition Cathedral in Vladimir, the frescoes of the Church of the Birth of the Theotokos in Savvino-Storozhevsky Monastery, the iconostasis and frescoes of Trinity Cathedral of Holy Trinity–Saint Sergius Lavra, and icons from the iconostasis of Annunciation Cathedral of the Kremlin.[11]

The time in which Andrei Rublev lived coincided with the introduction of large iconostases in Zvenigorod, Moscow, and other cities of Rus'. We recall that Byzantium did not have iconostases according to the Russian understanding of the term. In Rus' the iconostasis took on the central meaning and importance in the interior decoration of churches. This was linked to the development of wooden church architecture in the Mongol and post-Mongol periods. Insofar as the walls of wooden churches were not covered with images, the basic thematic accent was transferred to the iconostasis, which facilitated its development. Later multiple-tiered iconostases were placed in stone churches, many of which were not covered in frescoes at all. Furthermore, it is well known that the number of tiers increased over the span of centuries. By the fifteenth century triple-tier iconostases had appeared. In the sixteenth century four-tier iconostases appeared and in the seventeenth century iconostases having five, six, and seven tiers had appeared. The lower register of such iconostases (art historians call it the *Deesis row*) gradually grew in size. The Zvenigorod Deesis attributed to Andrei Rublev consists of icons nearly 160 cm (63 inches) in height on which figures are depicted in full height. The iconostasis of the Annunciation Cathedral of the Moscow Kremlin was created in this period and consists of three tiers. The height of the icons of the lower tier is nearly 210 cm (82.7 inches). In the iconostasis of Vladimir's Dormition Cathedral (1408) the height of the icons of the lower row is 313 cm (123.2 inches).

*Archangel Michael.
Icon. Zvenigorod Deesis.
End of 14th c.*

Several icons of the Zvenigorod Deesis have miraculously survived in their entirety. Painted in about 1393–1394, they were originally a part of the lower row of the iconostasis of Zvenigorod's Dormition Cathedral in Gorodok. However, in the beginning of the

---

[11] Opinions of researchers considering the dating and authorship of a large number of works attributed to Andrei Rublev vary. See Briusova, *Rublev*, 15, 24, 66.

seventeenth century a new iconostasis was built in its place and the old icons were placed on the walls of the church. In the eighteenth century traces of these icons disappeared. The majority of them were evidently used as wood to burn for heating. However, in 1918, three icons—"Savior," "Archangel Michael," and "Apostle Paul"—were discovered by conservators under a pile of logs in a shed in Zvenigorod.[12] In the opinion of most scholars, these icons were part of the original Zvenigorod Deesis and are the work of the hand of Andrei Rublev.

Savior. Icon. Zvenigorod Deesis. End of 14th c.

The Zvenigorod Deesis is a masterpiece of iconographic art and one of the most expressive images of Christ in the history of icon painting. On the icon before us appears a man with subtle facial features, breathing with calm and balance. His eyes have an almond shape and are outlined on the top by a thin black line. The gaze is directed straight at the viewer. The eyebrows are thin and slightly rounded. The arches over the eyebrows and the spaces under the eyes are delicately made lighter with white paint, endowing the face with volume and plasticity. The nose is long and thin; the lips are small and full, painted with bright cinnabar. The hair is thick and falls onto the shoulders. The mustache is thin and graceful; the beard is not long; the neck is high and full. This "Russian Christ" depicted on Andrei Rublev's icon substantially differs from Byzantine prototypes, primarily by the emphatically idealized image and the refinement of its features. (The size of the eyes, nose, and mouth in relation to the overall size of the face is significantly smaller than what is seen on similar Byzantine icons.) Another unique feature is the gentleness and harmony of the image in which severe and bold asceticism are absent.

The Apostle Paul. Icon. Zvenigorod Deesis. End of 14th c.

The most famous example of Andrei Rublev's creative work and perhaps the most famous Orthodox icon ever painted is the "Holy Trinity" from the iconostasis

---

[12]Grabar, *Art*, 191.

"Trinity." Fragment of an Icon. 14th c.

of the Trinity Lavra at St Sergius. The basis of the subject is the well known iconographic type "Hospitality of Abraham." This subject was encountered before in the Roman catacombs in the Via Latina (between the second and fourth centuries), in the mosaics of Rome's basilica of Santa Maria Maggiore (first half of the fifth century), and in the mosaics of Ravenna's basilica of San Vitale (first half of the sixth century). The subject can be traced back to the biblical account of the appearance of three men to Abraham. As such, it is an iconographic depiction of a specific event from the Bible. In the second millennium, the custom emerged of writing the words Ἡ Ἁγία Τριάς (The Holy Trinity) as an inscription on the "Hospitality of Abraham." This inscription is present on one of the miniatures of a Greek Psalter of the eleventh century. On this miniature, the head of the angel in the middle is crowned with a cross-in-halo. The angel is turned frontally to the viewer while the other two angels are depicted in three-quarter turn. The same type of depiction is encountered on the doors of the Church of the Nativity of the Theotokos in Suzdal (*c.* 1230) and on a fresco executed by Theophanes the Greek in Novgorod's Church of the Holy Transfiguration on Il'yn Street. The cross-in-halo indicates that the angel in the middle is identified with Christ.

Icons of the Trinity existed in the period preceding Andrei Rublev; in these the central angel was depicted in three-quarter turn and without Abraham and Sarah present. Indeed this is the iconographic type adhered to by Andrei Rublev in creating his "Trinity." As the basis of his image he used a type that had been almost completely abstracted from the initial subject ("Hospitality of Abraham") and that best lends itself to emphasizing the equality of the three hypostases of the Trinity.) The cross-in-halo is absent above the head of the angel in the middle (this is true, at any rate, in the particular appearance of the icon which has been preserved up to the present day). The effect is to deprive the angel of its central significance and to make his identification with Christ unnecessary. Art historians express various opinions concerning the question of which angel represents which Person of the Holy Trinity.[13] By all appearances, though, it is not a question of depicting the

---

[13] A summary of this question is found in Hieromonk Gabriel (Bunge), *Another Comforter: Saint Andrei Rublev's Icon of the Most Holy Trinity* (Riga, 2003), 91–102. The author of this work identifies the angel in the middle with the Son, the angel on the left with the Father, and the angel on the right with the Holy Spirit.

Persons of the Holy Trinity at all: Rublev's "Trinity" is a symbolic depiction of the *three-fold nature* of the Godhead, which had already been indicated by the Stoglav Council (also known as the Hundred Chapter Council). After all, the visitation of Abraham by three angels was not an appearance of the Most Holy Trinity, but was merely a "prophetic vision of this Mystery, which over the course of centuries would be gradually revealed to the faithful thinking of the Church."[14] According to this thought, it is not the Father, Son, and Holy Spirit appearing before us on Rublev's icon, but three angels symbolizing the pre-eternal council of the three Persons of the Holy Trinity. The symbolism of Rublev's icon is somewhat akin to the symbolism of early Christian painting, which kept profound dogmatic truths hidden under simple but spiritually significant symbols.

The symbolism of the icon and its spiritual significance is linked with the ideas on which the monastic community of Saint Sergius of Radonezh was built. He dedicated his cloister to the Holy Trinity, seeing in the love between the hypostases of the Trinity the absolute spiritual-moral reference point for a monastic community. A disciple of Saint Sergius, the Venerable Nikon of Radonezh, commissioned the icon of the Trinity from Rublev. An image in praise of Saint Sergius "ought to have emphatically borne a conceptual, philosophical character, in contrast to existing depictions of the Trinity."[15] At the same time, like its prototype the "Hospitality of Abraham," Rublev's "Trinity" is a eucharistic image symbolizing the bloodless sacrifice. This notion of the icon was emphasized by its being placed in the lower register of Trinity Cathedral's iconostasis, near the royal gates.

Dionysius and the Subsequent Development of Russian Iconography

The second half of the fifteenth century was marked by the activity of Dionysius (*c.* 1450–*c.* 1520), an outstanding icon painter and layman who worked together with his sons. The most impressive example of his creative work is the ensemble of frescoes of Ferapontov Monastery. Dionysius' images are devoid of the dramatism characteristic of many Byzantine images of saints found on murals. Figures are festive and static; faces are calm and illumined. Our attention is drawn to the intentional distortion of the human body's proportions. For Dionysius the ratio

---

[14] Gabriel (Bunge), *Comforter*, 17.
[15] A. Saltykov, "Iconography of Andrei Rublev's 'Trinity,'" in *Old Russian Arts of the 14th–15th Centuries* (Moscow, 1984), 81.

"The Uncircumscribed Word was Wholly Present among Things Below." (Akathist. Ikos 8.) Ferapontov Monastery. Dionysius. Beginning of 14th c.

Adoration of the Magi. (Akathist. Ikos 5.) Ferapontov Monastery. Dionysius. Beginning of 14th c.

of head to body is approximately 1:9 or even 1:10.[16] This creates a sensation of elongation and lightness of the figures. A significant place in the ensemble of Ferapontov Monastery is occupied by many-figured compositions such as "Last Judgment," "Akathist," and "Seven Ecumenical Councils." In Dionysius' range of colors, light tones such as light blue, lilac, light brown, and gold-beige are prevalent.

The composition "Akathist" is a series of illustrations for the Akathist to the Most Holy Theotokos, a work of Byzantine poetry created by an unknown author in the sixth or seventh century.[17] Each fresco corresponds to an ikos or kontakion of the akathist and reflects its contents. Similar compositions are encountered in churches of Greece and Serbia of the thirteenth and fourteenth centuries. However, according to the opinion of scholars, the "independence and sovereignty of Dionysius' embodiment of the Akathist are self-evident when compared to earlier surviving fragments executed by his predecessors."[18] Scenes from the life of the Theotokos pass in sequence before the viewer's gaze, and several scenes are encountered many times in different versions. In particular, the composition "Annunciation" is presented four times. In the first case (ikos 1) the angel is presented having come down from heaven; the Theotokos stands at full height. Her gesture expresses amazement. In the second case (kontakion 2) the angel stands before the Theotokos and she, seated, converses with him. The gesture of her right hand expresses astonishment. In the third case (ikos 2) the angel, dressed in a different color, stands before the Theotokos and she

---

[16] The usual proportion is 1:8 when the head is taken without the neck (from the top of the head to the bottom of the chin), or 1:6, if one considers the head to include the neck (from the top of the head to the level of the shoulders.)

[17] Some scholars suppose the author of the Akathist could have been Saint Roman the Melodist. See Wellesz, *the Akathistos Hymn* (Copenhagen, 1957); Idem. *A History of Byzantine Music and Hymnography*, 2nd ed. (Oxford, 1961), 191–197 and S. Averintsev, *Poetics of Early Byzantine Literature* (Moscow, 1997), 243–249 for more concerning the Akathist.

[18] E. Danilova, "Praise to the Theotokos Who Makes Exhortation to Those in Abiding in Darkness," in *Akathist to the Most Holy Theotokos—Dionysius the Iconographer; Photographs of Yuri Holdin* (Moscow, 2007), 158.

answers him, having risen from her seat. This time the gesture of her right hand expresses agreement with the words of the angel. In the fourth scene (kontakion 3) the Theotokos again sits before the standing angel. Both of her hands are raised. In this way the painter uses gestures and poses to convey the dynamism of the conversation between the Theotokos and the angel, a dynamism that ranges from amazement to humble consent before the will of God. In its entirety the composition "Akathist" is a grandiose hymn to the Theotokos and witnesses to the profound reverence paid to the Mother of God in Rus'.

The frescoes of Dionysius are a crowning conclusion to the period that art historians consider the golden age of Russian iconography.[19] The next two centuries were marked by the gradual departure of iconographers from strict adherence to canonical models. The color range of frescoes and icons changed. Artists of the sixteenth and seventeenth centuries leaned towards darker tones than their predecessors had used. Iconography became more complicated in turning to compositions which had been little known or totally unknown. These include such compositions as "It is Truly Meet," "Come, People, Let us Worship the Godhead in Three Hypostases," "In the Tomb in the Flesh," "Only-Begotten Son."[20] Influenced by western religious painting, depictions of God the Father as a gray-haired elder appeared in Russian icons of this period. In particular, God the Father is depicted sitting on the throne in the icon "Fatherland." The Infant Christ sits on his lap. The Holy Spirit in the form of a dove soars over the figures of the Father and the Son. Another composition, given the name "New Testament Trinity," presents God the Father and Jesus Christ sitting on two thrones with a dove soaring between them.

The use of the composition "New Testament Trinity" can be seen in the four-part icon from Annunciation Cathedral in the Moscow Kremlin. The upper left-hand part of the icon is titled "And God Rested on the Seventh Day." In the center of the composition, God the Father rests on a bed and beholds the world created by him. Next to him in medallions are the Mother of God with the Infant Christ and the Holy Spirit in the form of a dove. Further, in separate windows, are numerous allegorical subjects including the crucified Christ with cherubim's wings in the bosom of the Father. The upper right-hand portion is called "Only-Begotten Son and Immortal Word of God." Here Christ Emmanuel is depicted inside the heavenly sphere, supported by two angels over whom God the Father is exalted. The figure of God the Father dominates, and in the lower left-hand portion is "Come,

---

[19] E. Danilova, "Concerning Dionysius and His Age," in Yuri Holdin, *Frescoes of Russia: Dionysius, the Golden Age of Iconography, 14th–15th Centuries* (Moscow, 2006), 59.

[20] Buseva-Davydova, *Church Arts*, 549.

"In the Tomb in the Flesh." Fragment of Four-Part Icon. Annunciation Cathedral of the Moscow Kremlin. Middle of 16th c.

Let Us Worship the Godhead in Three Hypostases." The central medallion of the lower right-hand portion, "In the Tomb in the Flesh, in Hades with the Soul as God," presents the "New Testament Trinity." In all cases, God the Father is depicted in the form of an elder with white hair and a cone-shaped beard, wearing a white garment. In his halo is fitted an eight-pointed star. In its entirety the icon represents a multifaceted allegorical composition which only partially reproduces canonical subjects. This icon gives a visual illustration of the general trend which began to show in the sixteenth century and which continued in the seventeenth century.

The Stoglav Council of 1551 drew attention to this trend. One of the questions posed at the council related to the iconography of the Holy Trinity. The council indicated that various types of depictions of the Trinity existed. "On icons of the Holy Trinity, some represent a cross in the nimbus of only the middle figure, others on all three. On ancient icons and on Greek icons, the words "Holy Trinity" are written at the top, but there is no cross in the nimbus of any of the three. At present, "IC XC" and "The Holy Trinity" are written next to the central figure."[21] The council decreed that "painters must paint icons according to the ancient models, as the Greeks painted them, as Andrei Rublev and other renowned painters made them. The inscription should be: 'Holy Trinity.' Painters are in no wise to use their imagination."[22] The decree did not overtly make mention of uncanonical depictions of the Trinity but indicated that the general criterion for iconographers ought to be Rublev's "Trinity" and the icons of ancient Greek masters. In the opinion of George Ostrogorsky, the council attempted in this way "to cut off any attempt to depict God the Father on icons of the Trinity as was done in the West."[23]

Just two years after the Stoglav Council, however, in a dispute with the chancellor of the foreign office (the *diak*) Viskovatiy, the hierarchy of the Russian Church in the person of Metropolitan of Moscow Macarius (1542–1563) took a position of active defense of the new trend in the art of iconography. Ivan Viskovatiy, an influential state figure who was later accused of treason and executed by the order of Ivan the Terrible, drew attention to a number of iconographic subjects of an

---

[21] From the Stoglav Council, quoted in Ouspensky, *Theology*, 291.
[22] Cited in Ouspensky, *Theology*, 291.
[23] Georges Ostrogorsky, *Histoire de l'état Byzantin (Paris, 1956)*, 402.

allegorical character which did not correspond with ancient canonical models. He objected in particular to the depiction of God the Father. He objected to the depiction of Christ "in the image of an angel," having wings, wearing a warrior's armour, wearing the garment of a king and a hierarch's omophorion. He objected to the depiction of the Holy Spirit "in the image of a bird." Not without basis did Viskovatiy perceive "Latin sophism" in depictions of this sort. At a council convened by Metropolitan Macarius in 1553–1554, Viskovatiy's charges were studied and rejected and his writings were declared to be blasphemous. Church authorities that not long before had called for the strict adherence to ancient iconographical models now embarked on a path of justifying the existing practice. "There was a gradual departure from the Orthodox view of the icon," writes Leonid Ouspensky; "The art trend championed by the Council of 1553–1554 would gradually

Kikkskaya Icon of the Mother of God. Icon. Simon Ushakov. 1668.

cease to recast foreign borrowings into an artistic language proper to Orthodoxy. This would subsequently lead to a direct imitation of the West, and to a break with the Tradition."[24]

This break did not take place right away. In icons of the "Godunovsky" and "Stroganovsky" style (end of sixteenth century) and later in icons of Simon Ushakov (second half of the seventeenth century), a living connection still remained with traditional Russian icon painting amid all the stylistic novelties that appeared under the influence of western painting. At the same time, the influence of western religious painting increased, and uncanonical subjects became more widespread. This forced the Council of Moscow of 1666–1667 to consider the question of whether depictions of God the Father in the form of an elder and the Holy Spirit in the form of a dove (with the exception of the composition "Baptism of the Lord") were to be permitted or not. The council decreed as follows:

> We decree that from now on the image of the Lord Sabaoth will no longer be painted according to senseless and unsuitable imaginings, for no one has ever seen the Lord Sabaoth (that is, God the Father) in the flesh, . . . the Lord

[24] Ouspensky, *Theology of the Icon* (Crestwood), 323.

Sabaoth (that is, the Father) with a white beard, holding the only-begotten Son in his lap with a dove between them is altogether absurd and improper, for no one has ever seen the Father in his divinity. Indeed, the Father has no flesh, and it is not in the flesh that the Son was born of the Father before all ages. . . . And the Holy Spirit is not, in his nature, a dove: He is by nature God. And no one has ever seen God, as the holy evangelist points out. Nonetheless, the Holy Spirit appeared in the form of a dove at the holy baptism of Christ in the Jordan; and this is why it is proper to represent the Holy Spirit in the form of a dove, in this context only. Anywhere else, those who have good sense do not represent the Holy Spirit in the form of a dove.[25]

Neither the Stoglav Council nor the Great Council of Moscow were able to stop the development of Russian iconographic arts in the direction of a greater tendency to western models. Collections of Flemish engravings and illustrated Bibles, printed in the West, became widespread models for iconographers beginning in the middle of the seventeenth century. Subjects were borrowed from these for icons and frescoes, including "Resurrection of Christ" in which Christ is emerging from a cave holding a banner. (Previously, the only canonical image of the resurrection of Christ was the "Descent into Hades.") The faces on many icons of the second half of the seventeenth century became more realistic and "lifelike."[26]

In the sixteenth and seventeenth centuries the custom of enclosing icons in setting frames—metal *rizas* adorned with precious stones—became widespread. Generally such rizas covered the entire icon and left only traces of the face and hands. Precious setting frames for icons were given as gifts by tsars, boyars, and wealthy parishioners of monasteries and churches. In particular, Boris Godunov gave to the Trinity-Saint Sergius Lavra a setting frame for the icon "Trinity" painted by Saint Andrei Rublev. Under this framework, to which Tsar Michail Romanov added decorations, the icon was hidden from the eyes of viewers for three centuries. Other miraculous and venerated icons were enclosed in precious rizas, including the Vladimir icon of the Mother of God. Simple metal frameworks without precious stones were made for inexpensive and lesser known icons.

---

[25]Ibid., 371–372.
[26]Busevea-Davydova, *Church Arts*, 551–552.

Post-Petrine Period.
Academic Painting in Orthodox Churches

During the thirteenth through nineteenth centuries many Russian iconographers continued to work with a focus on old models. However, this focus was merely formal. Icons from this period preserved the connection with traditional subject matter and composition but the images themselves were painted in a manner that had little in common with icon painting of old. Ancient iconographic traditions were preserved only in Old Rite circles in which the development of church arts came to a halt and was preserved according to the standards of the end of the seventeenth century.

The reforms of Peter the Great affected all aspects of life in society and the making of icons was no exception. In 1711 the iconography studio at the Moscow Kremlin's Armory was closed. In its place a "Palace of Arts" became active in Saint Petersburg and attracted masters from all parts of Russia for icon-making. The "Office of Church Affairs," a state ministry overseeing religious matters, was charged with control over these iconographers.

Religious painting in the western "academic" style was a new direction that developed in parallel with iconography in the post-Petrine period. This trend was significantly strengthened in the second half of the eighteenth century and came to dominate in the murals of churches in Saint Petersburg and Moscow in the nineteenth century. Artist-academicians fully broke with the iconographical canon and rejected traditional techniques of painting in tempera on panels. They worked in oil paints on canvas and focused on paintings by Renaissance artists in their works. In 1757 the Academy of Arts opened in Saint Petersburg and became the major center where the aesthetic standards were to be worked out not only for secular painting but also, to a significant degree, for church painting. Many people who held managerial posts in the academy combined their activities as free lance artists with mural painting in churches and the painting of icons for iconostases.

A typical representative of the academic trend in church painting was Vladimir Borovikovsky (1757–1825), a Russian artist of Little-Russian origin. In 1784 he completed an iconostasis for Trinity Church in Mirgorod and in the 1790s he painted icons for churches in Arpachevo of Tver Province, the Monastery of Saints Boris and Gleb in Torzhok, and Saint Joseph Cathedral in Mogilyev. From 1804–1811 he created a number of images for Saint Petersburg's Kazan Cathedral. Borovikovsky's creative works have no connection with the traditional art of iconography. They

Theotokos with Infant. L. B. Borovikovsky.

Lord of Sabaoth. A. T. Markov. Mural of Christ the Savior Cathedral in Moscow. Photograph from beginning of 20th c.

represent images of religious painting created on the basis of western models. His painting "Mother of God with Infant," preserved in the State Tretyakov Gallery, is a typical example of academic realism. The image is painted from live models in a sentimental manner. The Theotokos is presented in the form of a girl of Jewish origins with open neck and a veil draped on her hair. The Infant has long curly hair and resembles a girl. He sits on his Mother's lap and looks with sadness at the viewer.

The influence of Italian Renaissance religious painting, especially that of Raphael and Michelangelo, had a determining impact on the creative work of another painter, Fyodor Bruni (1799–1875)—an Italian by ancestry and a Catholic by faith. To Bruni belong the murals or sketches for murals of Saint Isaac's Cathedral and Kazan Cathedral in Saint Petersburg as well as a number of paintings based on religious subjects. Characteristic of his paintings are an accentuated sentimentality, which aroused the indignation of some of his contemporaries and the delight of others. One of the admirers of Bruni's work described the "Russian Madonna" created by him in this way: "For his Madonna, Bruni manages to find a new image and a new position. He has portrayed her with the features of a maiden. In these dreamy, languorous eyes, in the paleness of the coloring, in the ethereal lines of the body, in this not yet developed youthfulness which had even been censured as a vice—you see the features of a northern, I would say Russian, Madonna, the concept and the image of whom were born on the banks of the Neva."[27] Leonid Ouspensky bitterly commented, "This mixture of sublimated eroticism and vulgar triteness had replaced the icon."[28]

Bruni's monumental frescoes in Saint Isaac's Cathedral, which include the "Great Flood," "Sacrifice of Noah," and "Vision of Prophet Ezekiel," stand side-by-side with the works of Karl Bryullov (1799–1852), the artist of "The Last Day

---

[27] A. Grishtennko, "The Russian Icon as Pictorial Art" (in Russian), *Voprosy zhivopisi* III (Moscow, 1917), 12, cited in Ouspensky, *Theology*, 437.

[28] Ouspensky, *Theology*, 437.

of Pompei." In particular, the grandiose dome of the cathedral (the area of the dome comprises eight hundred and sixteen square meters (about 8,783 square feet) belongs to Bryullov's hand. The creative work of Bruni, Bryullov, and other academic painters is in accordance with the peculiarities of the churches of Saint Petersburg, which were built according to western models in the baroque or classical styles, but, as with the churches themselves, are marked by a complete departure from ancient traditions. The activity of artist-academicians in the field of iconography amounted to an implantation of western secular aesthetic standards in Russian religious soil.

The murals of Christ the Savior Cathedral were executed in the academic style in 1875–1883. Leading members of the Russian Academy of Arts participated in this grandiose project under Bruni's direction, including: V.P. Vereschagin, N.A. Koshelev, I.N. Kramskoi, V.E. Makovsky, A.T. Markov, T.A. Neff, I.M. Prianishnikov, E.S. Sorokin, V.I. Surikov, and G.I. Semiradsky. They painted using oil paints on lime plaster. In the central dome of the cathedral, the artist Markov depicted a gigantic Lord of Sabaoth (God the Father) with a thick mustache raised on the sides and fluttering gray hair and outstretched hands. Before the face of Sabaoth, at the level of his beard, soars a dove, symbolizing the Holy Spirit. On the lap of Sabaoth sits the Infant Christ. Under the legs of Sabaoth are three cherubim who appear to be flying off in different directions. As with other compositions of Christ the Savior Cathedral, "New Testament Trinity" in the dome of the Cathedral is a striking illustration of the radical break with iconographic tradition that is characteristic of all Russian academic painting.

Appraising the "academic" period in the history of Russian iconographic arts, Viktor Vasnetsov said:

> Our secular art—painting and sculpture—was born in the beginning of the eighteenth century under the pressure of the European Enlightenment. The influence of European art is reflected both in our iconography and, alas, not to its benefit. . . . In iconography . . . not only did the European influence not contribute anything exceptional, it brought our religious art to an almost complete collapse, turning it into a formal, lifeless art, academic in its naturalism, which used live models and mannequins in depicting the saints. Although some—Losenko, Borovikovsky, and others—tried to create an image in the Italian manner, it was of course not iconography in the true sense.[29]

---

[29]Viktor Vasnetsov, "Concerning Russian Iconography" in *The Acts of the Sacred Council of the Orthodox Russian Church of 1917–1918*, vol. 5 (Moscow, 1996), 46–47.

In the second half of the nineteenth century many churches continued to be decorated in the academic style, but the people's interest in traditional icons was not extinguished. An icon industry developed in parallel with the activity of artist-academicians, and icon-making moved to the production line. The biggest centers of conveyor-line icons were the Suzdal villages of Kholuiy, Mstera, and Palekh. One characteristic of the manufacturing of icons was the clear-cut division of labor. Each icon was painted not by a single master but by a group in which each participant in the process was responsible for one or several operations. One master prepared the plaster, another worked it onto the board, a third made the sketch, a fourth added the clothing and landscape, a fifth painted faces and hands, etc. In just one day a master could place plaster on five-hundred panels for icons and a "face painter" (artist responsible for painting faces and hands), could execute his work on twenty-five to fifty icons. At the beginning of the twentieth century, three thousand four hundred and sixty-five people lived in Mstera, of whom eight hundred were involved in the iconography industry. Fourteen studios were used for preparing icons, twenty-four specialized in the treatment of copper and silver foil for frameworks, while ten studios prepared the frameworks themselves.

At the turn of the twentieth century people began to consider ancient icons valuable relics and began to collect them and clean them by removing layers of soot and overpaintings. This was the reason for a surge of interest in icons that, for the first time in many centuries, appeared before viewers in something approaching their original conditions. The discovery of ancient icons enabled a partial change in attitude of artist-academicians to icon painting. While a "Neo-Russian" style emerged in church architecture, an analogous style appeared in church painting.

Son of God. V.M. Vasnetsov. Study for a Mural of St Vladimir Cathedral in Kiev.

Viktor Vasnetsov (1848–1926) is considered to be the founder of this new movement in church painting. In 1885–1886, together with other masters, he executed the murals of Saint Vladimir Cathedral in Kiev. Creating images of Christ, the Theotokos, and saints, Vasnetsov oriented his work not on the religious painting of the Renaissance but rather on Byzantine and Old Russian monumental painting, while striving to avoid direct copying or stylization of ancient models. In Vasnetsov's icons and frescoes, motifs of folklore combine with elements of the "modern" style. Many of Vasnetsov's works had a great influence on other artists and were copied numerous times on iconostases and on walls of churches at the turn of the twentieth century. One of his most popular images is the Mother of God with Infant from the central apse of Saint Vladimir Cathedral (the artist used his wife and son as his models). The Mother of God is depicted in the form of a young woman in a blue garment who seems to approach the viewer. In her arms is the Infant Christ with bare shoulders and hands raised as if outstretched to the viewer.

Mikhail Nesterov (1862–1942) also participated in painting the murals of Saint Vladimir Cathedral. To him belong four iconostases in the side naves, the compositions "Nativity," "Resurrection," "Theophany," and images of Saints Boris and Gleb, Princess Olga, and several other saints. In the 1910s Nesterov painted the murals of the Holy Protection Cathedral of the Martha and Mary Convent in Moscow. Compositions having

Mother of God with Infant. V.M. Vasnetsov. Fragment of a Mural of St Vladimir Cathedral. Kiev. 1885.

canonical themes ("Protection of the Theotokos," "Annunciation," "Resurrection of Christ," "Christ with Martha and Mary") are found together with paintings depicting unconventional subjects. One of these paintings is "The Way to Christ." In it, Christ, dressed in a white garment, walks amidst a Russian landscape in springtime surrounded by birch trees, a lake, fields, and meadows. A crowd of children, adults, and injured people move towards him. Sisters of the convent help people to approach the Savior. As in Vasnetsov's paintings, the influence of the "modern" style, combined with accentuated Russian decoration and folklore, is noticeable in Nesterov's work. The Church of the Protection was closed in 1926. Later it was used to house a Soviet health education club. Nesterov's frescoes were painted over, and a statue of Stalin was placed in the sanctuary. In the post-war era the church was used as restoration studios. Not until the beginning of the twenty-first century were the Nesterov's murals restored.

Russian Icons in the Post-Revolutionary Period

Russia's iconographic tradition was interrupted for many decades following the Russian Revolution in 1917. During the years of the "Red Terror" and subsequent decades in which the Church was persecuted, thousands of churches on the territory of the entire USSR were wiped off the face of the earth. Murals perished

Igor Grabar. Self-portrait.

Viktor Lazarev.

along with them, and some of these represented significant artistic value. During the revolutionary years icons underwent systematic, often public destruction. They were broken into pieces and burnt on open fires. It is impossible to make a tally of the number of icons which disappeared without a trace during Soviet times. Certainly the overwhelming majority of icons that had been in Russia before the Revolution disappeared. Some icons were taken out of the country and were put up for open sale in the West. The export of icons continued during the Great Patriotic War[30] and subsequent years.

At the same time Soviet authorities soon realized that ancient icons represented a significant material and cultural treasure. Therefore, the cleaning and restoration of icons continued after the Revolution. The All-Russian Artistic-Scientific Restoration Center was created by 1918, and one of its tasks was to find and restore ancient icons of artistic value. It is true that in the 1930s, when the campaign against religion was intensified, secular art criticism was declared to be dangerous and many art historians were repressed. In 1934 the Restoration Center was closed since its work was declared to be "too narrow, apolitical, and lacking in public benefit." But in 1944 the work of the center was resumed, and in 1960 it was named after Igor Grabar. The center had branches situated in many Moscow churches. As a result, the churches themselves were saved from destruction and many monuments of ancient icon painting were restored. Valuable collections of restored icons were housed in the Tretyakov Gallery, the Pushkin Museum of Fine Arts, the State Hermitage Museum, and other large artistic collections of the USSR. Some icons were exhibited in museums of atheism.

Research on icons, which began before the Revolution by N.P. Kondakov, D.V. Ainalov, and other scholars, continued during Soviet times. Books by the art historians M.V. Alpatov and V.N. Lazarev, dedicated to monuments of Byzantine and Old Russian art, were published in small numbers and were available only to specialists.

---

[30]The Russian term for World War II—Ed.

Art historians did not generally travel abroad, and for that reason they were required to research monuments of Byzantine art without seeing them first-hand but by viewing photographs, reproductions, and descriptions. Books written by iconography experts underwent especially painstaking censorship since the very subject of these books was perceived to be potentially dangerous. In the 1960s a new generation of art historians emerged and was able to work in less strained conditions. Albums with reproductions of icons began to be published and sold. The number of publications dedicated to Old Russian iconography grew considerably.

"Holy Trinity." Monk Gregory (Kroug). Mural in Saint Seraphim of Sarov Church. Montgeron, France.

In Russian circles abroad, the work of studying icons continued not only from a purely formal and technical perspective, but also from a theological point of view. Leonid Ouspensky (1902–1987) made an outstanding contribution to the understanding of icons and their role in the life of the Church. He is the author of a major study entitled *Theology of the Icon in the Orthodox Church* which was published in the French language in 1960. Ouspensky was not only a theoretician of the study of icons but also a practitioner of iconography. Numerous icons in the Orthodox churches in Paris were painted by him. Another notable iconographer of the Russian diaspora was the monk Gregory (Kroug; 1907–1969).

Kazan Mother of God. Monk Gregory (Kroug).

Together Ouspensky and Kroug painted the murals of a major stronghold of the Moscow Patriarchate in Paris, the representation Church of the Three Hierarchs, which is a church converted from a garage. Painting the murals of this church, located on the ground floor with a low flat ceiling, presented itself as a difficult task for the icon painters. They managed to succeed, however, and placed murals of gospel subjects along the entire perimeter of the church under the ceiling. Ouspensky and Kroug created their own style of icon painting which was oriented on Old Russian models only in general characteristics. Icons created by Ouspensky and Kroug are distinguished by their graphic quality in which the silhouettes of figures are clearly outlined and faces are rendered in a conventional, nearly impressionistic manner. The style of Ouspensky and Kroug was the dominant style in Russian emigré circles for several decades. Both artists had many imitators.

The rebirth of icon painting in the Soviet Union in the 1950s–1970s is linked to the name of the nun Juliana (Sokolova; 1899–1981)—an art historian, restorer, and instructor at the Moscow Theological Academy. Frescoes and icons in several churches of Trinity-Saint Sergius Lavra were executed under the guidance of Mother Juliana. The nun organized an iconography class at the theological academy, and this course continued even after her death.

The iconographic activity of Archimandrite Zinon (Teodor) was noteworthy in the life of the Russian Orthodox Church in the 1980s–1990s. After beginning by copying Old Russian icons, Father Zinon gradually devised his own iconographic manner based on Byzantine models but interpreted in the light of the spiritual experience of the artist. In the words of Archimandrite Zinon, the labor of an iconographer is not blind copying, not dry imitation of ancient models. At the same time, artistic freedom must be combined with faithfulness to the Church's canon:

> Icon painting is a service in the Church and not creative work in the sense that it is understood by secular artists. . . . Striving to penetrate as deeply as possible the mysteries of icon painting, one must examine the best examples, and only then, after spending time with that which has preceded you, can you contribute something yourself. Each icon painter in all times without fail contributed his personal spiritual experience to his creative work. But the Church's iconographic canons exist, and not one icon painter has either the authority or need to overstep them. The iconographic canon merely disciplines the creator of icons. The icon painter does not allow anything arbitrary or self-willed, because in the sphere of faith there are truths which are not subject to change. Therefore, cutting off one's own conceptions, one must continually strive towards the experience of the Church.[31]

After the fall of the atheistic regime in the beginning of the 1990s, when the full-scale rebirth of the Church began, the labor of iconographers was needed once again, as in ancient Rus'. Iconostases were created in thousands of newly opened churches and the walls of many new churches were adorned with frescoes and mosaics. In a short time iconography schools and studios appeared in Moscow and

---

[31] Archimandrite Zinon (Teodor), *Conversations with an Iconographer*, 3rd Edition (St Petersburg, 2003), 35–36.

other cities of the former USSR. Many of them were created by disciples and successors of Father Zinon, who continued to endure as the "leading icon painter in Russia" whose creative work "in many ways defines the path of development of the contemporary iconographical tradition and ecclesiastical arts in general."[32]

The largest centers of icon painting were the iconography school of the Moscow Theological Academy headed by Igumen Luke (Golovkov), and the Iconography Department of the Faculty of Ecclesiastical Arts of Saint Tikhon's University of Humanities headed by Archpriest Nikolai Chernyshev. The majority of contemporary Russian iconographers work in the Old Russian manner while some are focused on the Byzantine style. Many icons and frescoes are created in imitation of later models (eighteenth and nineteenth centuries), and some churches are decorated in the "academic" style. Lost murals are being restored in individual churches. In particular, the murals of Christ the Savior Cathedral, rendered in the academic style, were restored. (The restoration of the murals was accomplished by using black and white photographs of the original paintings and also by using color sketches that were preserved.)

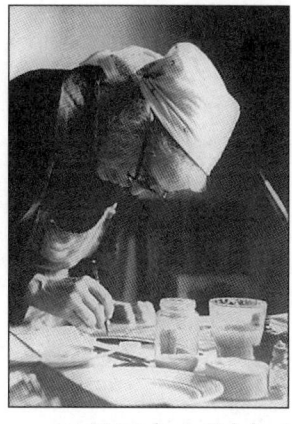

Nun Juliana (Sokolova) at Work.

Fr Zinon at Work in the Refectory of New Valaam Monastery in Finland.

Copying ancient models remains the most widespread method of work for contemporary icon painters. The obvious positive side of this method is that it helps to reproduce ancient icons painted in accordance with the Church's canon. But an iconographer cannot become a true creator of an icon by simply copying. A copy is a dead product, whereas ancient icons were living reflections of the spiritual world of the iconographer.

Alongside the copying of ancient icons by artists, serial "manufacturing" of icons has been growing in recent years. Several companies include the preparation of icons in their catalogs of services, together with the making of jewelry or decorative items, furniture, dishware, etc. One company, advertising its output on the internet, offers the customer a wide assortment of merchandise including "chess

---

[32]Irina Yazykova, *"Behold I Make All Things New": Icons of the 20th Century* (Moscow, 2002), 103.

Women Saints. Fragment of an Icon by Nun Juliana (Sokolova).

sets, spikenards, icons, lacquer boxes, billiard queues, and family crests." Another company promotes itself in this way: "We manufacture icons to order—high quality and low prices." The industrial manufacturing of icons is not a novelty; it appeared in Russia at the turn of the twentieth century. On November 25 (December 8), 1917, Viktor Vasnetsov spoke at the local congress of the Russian Orthodox Church:

> Over the past decades there have appeared images printed on tin plates by the manufactured paints of foreign companies such as "Bonacker" and "Giacco." . . . These images are sold everywhere in diocesan shops and monasteries. Such acceptance of factory-produced images, justified by the so-called deficit of hand-made icons—an "icon famine"—was obviously unjustified because, at this same time, it was necessary to artificially support the icon studios and masters of Palekh, Mstera, and others due to a work deficit. . . . A hand-created image is executed by a person with the indispensable participation of his soul. If only to a small degree, one can sense the creator's spiritual relationship to the depicted image, even in the case of the most meagre skill and lack of perfection in the icon's execution. At minimum, some spark of a prayerful mood in the human image is reflected. A factory-produced or machine-made image, no matter how precisely and perfectly it may convey a copied image of an original, is the product of a dead machine and a dead imitation. . . . To some degree it is even a *falsification*.[33]

The Russian artist's words, spoken at the height of revolutionary events, are still relevant today. Although the industrial manufacturing of icons may to some extent ease the "icon famine," it cannot and must not fully drive out the labor of the master-iconographer from the life of the Church.

---

[33] Vasnetsov, *Iconography*, 54.

9

The Meaning of Icons

AN EXCURSUS INTO THE HISTORY OF ICONS in Byzantium and Rus' was necessary in order to understand the meaning and significance of icons in the life of the Orthodox Church.

The Theological Meaning of Icons

Icons are primarily *theological*. Eugene Trubetskoi called icons "contemplation in color"[1] and the priest Pavel Florensky called them "a reminder of the first image on high."[2] Icons remind us of God—the first image in whose image and likeness every man is created. The theological significance of an icon hinges upon its communicating dogmatic truths that have been revealed to people in divine Scripture and the tradition of the Church.

The holy Fathers called icons the Gospel for the illiterate. Saint Gregory the Great, Pope of Rome wrote, "Images are used in churches so that those who do not have literacy, at least, looking at the walls, may read that which they are not able to read in books."[3] In the words of Saint John of Damascus, "An image is a reminder. What a book is to those who know reading and writing, images serve the same purpose for the illiterate, and whereas the word is for hearing, the image is for seeing. By means of the mind we enter into union with it."[4] Saint Theodore the Studite stressed, "That which is depicted in the Gospel by means of paper and ink is depicted on icons by means of various paints or some other material."[5] The sixth act of the Seventh Ecumenical

Seventh Ecumenical Council. Fresco. Dionysius.

---

[1] Trubetskoi, *Three Essays on the Russian Icon*, 2nd ed., (Moscow, 2007), 7.
[2] Priest Pavel Florensky, *Iconostasis* (2005), 79.
[3] Gregory Dialogus *Letters 9, 105: to Seren*. PL 77, 1027–1028.
[4] John of Damascus *Words in Defense* 1, 17.
[5] Theodore the Studite *Words in Accusation* 1, 10. PG 99, 340D.

Christ Pantocrator. Saint Catherine's Monastery. Mount Sinai. 13th c.

Council declared: "That which the word informs orally, painting shows silently through an image."

Icons in Orthodox churches play a catechetical role. "If one of the heretics comes to you saying, show me your faith, you take him to the church and place him before various types of holy images," says Saint John of Damascus.[6] At the same time an icon must not be perceived as a simple illustration of the events of the Gospel or the life of the Church. "Icons do not depict anything; rather, they reveal," says Archimandrite Zinon.[7] Primarily they reveal to people the invisible God, God who in the words of the evangelist, *no one has seen at any time*, but who was revealed to mankind in the Person of the God-Man Jesus Christ (Jn 1.18).

The image of Christ—God become Man—has special significance for Orthodox Christians. The iconographic appearance of Christ was definitively formulated in the period of the iconoclastic controversies. At the same time the theological basis of the iconographic depiction of Jesus Christ was formulated with extreme clarity, as expressed in the kontakion of the feast of the Triumph of Orthodoxy:

> The uncircumscribed Word of the Father became circumscribed, taking flesh from thee, O Theotokos, and he has restored the sullied image to its ancient glory, filling it with the divine beauty. This is our salvation we confess in deed and word, and we depict it in the holy icons.[8]

This text was written by Saint Theophanes, Metropolitan of Nicaea, one of the defenders of icon veneration in the ninth century. It speaks of God the Word, who through the incarnation made himself "circumscribed." Having taken upon himself fallen human nature, he restored in Man that divine image according to which Man was created. The divine beauty (Slavonic: *dobrota*) mingled with human impurity and saved Man's nature. This salvation is depicted on icons ("in deed") and in sacred texts ("in word").

---

[6] John of Damascus *Words in Defense* 1, 10.
[7] Zinon (Teodor), *Conversations*, 19.
[8] *The Lenten Triodion*, tr. Mother Mary and Archimandrite Kallistos Ware, Sunday of the Triumph of Orthodoxy. Matins. Kontakion (South Canaan, PA: St Tikhon's Seminary Press, 2002).

The Meaning of Icons

Byzantine icons do not merely reveal the man Jesus Christ, but—more precisely— God made flesh. In this way icons differ from Renaissance paintings which portrayed Christ "made man," humanized. Commenting on this distinction, Leonid Ouspensky wrote:

> The Church has "eyes to see" just as it has "ears to hear." This is why it hears the word of God in the Gospel, which is written in human words. Similarly, it always considers Christ through the eyes of the unshakeable faith in his divinity. This is why the Church depicts him in icons not as an ordinary man, but as the God-Man in his glory, even at the moment of his supreme humiliation. . . . This is precisely the reason why, in its icons, the Orthodox Church never represents Christ simply as a man who suffers physically, as is the case in western religious art.[9]

In the post-iconoclastic period the iconographic appearance of the Savior acquired the features it was to have later in Rus'. As before, Christ was depicted with a beard and long hair, in a brown chiton and blue himation; however, his face acquires more "iconic" features—less realism and more refinement and symmetry.

The icon of Christ—God who has become Man—is in fact an *icon of God* and the only admissible image from the perspective of the Orthodox tradition. Inadmissible is the depiction of God the Father, in accordance with the teaching of Saint John of Damascus: "Were we to make an image of the unseen God we would really transgress because it is impossible to make an image without a body, invisible, uncircumscribable, and without form."[10] Inadmissible from the perspective of the Church is also the depiction of the Holy Spirit, with the exception of the case when the Spirit is presented in the form of a dove in the context of one specific historical event—the baptism of our Lord Jesus Christ.

Canonically inadmissible is the earlier-mentioned icon "New Testament Trinity," also called "Fatherland," on which God the Father is depicted in the form of a gray-haired elder, the Son in the form of an infant in a

New Testament Trinity ("Fatherland") surrounded by saints and angels. Icon. Tula. 19th c.

---

[9] Ouspensky, *Theology*, vol. 1, 153.
[10] John of Damascus *Words in Defense* 2, 5.

circle, and the Holy Spirit "in the form of a dove." Despite the categorical prohibition of the Stoglav Council, the "New Testament Trinity" continues to figure in the icons and frescoes of many Orthodox churches, both old and newly rebuilt. Often a depiction of a dove in a triangle (or without a triangle) is seen, which implies the Holy Spirit. The theological inadmissibility of similar compositions is explained, according to the thinking of the fathers of the Stoglav Council, by the impossibility of describing the indescribable and depicting the invisible. Such a depiction can be nothing more than the fruit of human imagination.

These types of iconographic depictions not only fail to correspond with church canons, they conceal a spiritual danger within. These images may create for a person the impression that God the Father actually "looks" like a gray-haired elder and that the Holy Spirit looks like a dove. In this situation, the catechetical meaning of the icon is fully lost, and a mistaken, false notion about God is inspired—one that is not in accordance with Church tradition. The image "New Testament Trinity" is an attempt to depict that which cannot be depicted by using the fruit of human imagination, thereby turning God into an idol and the church service into idol worship.

Icons are inseparably connected with dogma and are inconceivable outside a dogmatic context. The basic dogmatic truths of Christianity—the Holy Trinity, the incarnation, the salvation and deification of man—are conveyed in icons by artistic means.

Many historical events from the gospel are treated in iconography primarily in a dogmatic context. For example, the resurrection of Christ is never depicted on canonically Orthodox icons. Rather, Christ's departure from Hades and his leading the Old Testament righteous out of Hades is depicted. The image of Christ emerging from the tomb, often with a banner in his hands,[11] is of extremely late origin and genetically linked with western religious painting. The Orthodox tradition knows only the image of Christ emerging from Hades, which corresponds with the liturgical understanding of the resurrection of Christ and the service texts of the *Octoechos* and *Lenten Triodion*, which reveal the event from a dogmatic perspective.

---

[11] This image, painted on glass and illumined from the inside with electric lamps, is found in some churches in the sanctuary at the high place, which witnesses not only to the tastelessness of the authors (and clients) of such compositions, but also to their ignorance or intentional ignoring the traditions of the Orthodox Church.

The Anthropological Meaning of Icons

Every icon is *anthropological* in its content. There is not a single icon on which a person is not depicted, whether the God-Man Jesus Christ, the Most Holy Theotokos, or one of the saints. Exceptions to this are merely symbolic images[12] as well as images of angels (but even angels are depicted on icons as man-like). There are no icons that are landscapes or still-lifes. Scenery, vegetation, animals, objects of everyday life—all of these things may be present on an icon if the subject requires it, but the main hero of every iconographic depiction is a person.

An icon is not a portrait and does not have pretensions of rendering the exact external appearance of saints. We do not know what ancient saints looked like, but we have at our disposal numerous photographs of people whom the Church has glorified in the rank of saints in the recent past. A comparison of a photograph of a saint with his icon visually demonstrates that the iconographer strives to preserve no more than the most general characteristic features of the external appearance of the saint. The saint is recognizable on the icon, but he is different. His features are refined and ennobled; he is given an iconic appearance.

An icon reveals a person in his transformed, deified condition. In the words of Archimandrite Zinon, an icon is "a revelation of the transformed, deified creation, that same transformed humanity that Christ revealed in his person."[13] Leonid Ouspensky stresses:

> The icon is the image of the man in whom the grace which consumes passions and which sanctifies everything is truly present. This is why his flesh is represented completely differently from ordinary corruptible flesh. The icon is a peaceful transmission, absolutely devoid of all emotional explanation, of a certain spiritual reality. If grace enlightens the entire man, so that his entire spiritual and physical being is filled by prayer and exists in the divine light, the icon visibly captures this man who has become a living icon, a true likeness of God.[14]

According to biblical revelation, Man was created in God's image and likeness (Gen 1.26). The image of God in Man was darkened and distorted by his fall in sin, but it was not completely lost. Fallen man is similar to an icon darkened by the passage of time and by soot, so that one must clean it in order for it to shine in its

---

[12]For example, the cross (without depiction of the crucifixion) or the "Empty Throne" (a symbolic depiction of God's throne).
[13]Zinon (Teodor), *Conversations*, 19.
[14]Ouspensky, *Theology*, vol. 1, 166.

Saint John the Forerunner. Icon. Russia. 20th c.

original beauty. This cleansing takes place thanks to the incarnation of the Son of God, who "assumed the image sullied in time of old"—that is, he restored the image of God, sullied by man, to its original beauty. This cleansing also takes place by the action of the Holy Spirit. But an ascetic effort is required from man himself that he may prove capable of containing God's grace—lest the grace of God be for him in vain.

Christian asceticism is the path to spiritual transformation. And icons reveal to us man transformed. Orthodox icons are teachers of the ascetic life no less than they are teachers of the dogmas of the faith. An iconographer consciously makes the hands and legs of a person finer than in this life, the attributes of the face (nose, eyes, ears) more elongated. In some cases (for example, in the frescoes and icons of Dionysius), the proportions of the human body are changed. All of these and other similar artistic methods are adopted in order to convey that spiritual change that human flesh undergoes by the ascetic effort of the saint and the transforming action of the Holy Spirit.

Human flesh depicted in icons differs strikingly from flesh depicted in paintings. This becomes especially evident when one compares icons with the realistic canvases of the Renaissance. Comparing Old Russian icons with paintings by Rubens in which obese human flesh is depicted in all its bare ugliness, Eugene Trubetskoi tells how icons stand to contrast a new meaning of life against the biological, brutal, beast-like life of fallen man.[15] He thinks that the most important thing for an icon is "the joy of the final victory of the God-man over the man-beast, the gathering of all mankind and all other creatures into the church." However, in the opinion of this philosopher, "man must prepare for this joy by strenuous efforts. He cannot become a part of God's church in his present state. There is no room in that church for the uncircumcised heart, the fat, complacent body. *That is why icons must not be painted from living people.*"[16]

Trubetskoi continues in saying that icons are a "prototype of the future man-within-the-church." Since "we cannot yet see this man but *only divine* him in present sinful people, an icon can represent him only symbolically." He asks the

---

[15] Trubetskoi, *Icons*, 36–38.
[16] Ibid., 21. Italics are the author's.

question, what does the "attenuated body" of iconic personages mean?

> It means outright rejection of the "biologism" that makes the body's gratification an absolute law justifying not only man's grossly utilitarian and cruel view of the lower creatures but also the right of any nation to wage bloody war on other nations if they happen to prevent it from getting its fill. The gaunt faces of saints in the icons oppose to this bloody reign of sated flesh not only "refined feelings" but also, and above all, a new norm of relationships. That is the kingdom that flesh and blood cannot inherit.[17]

Saint Mary of Egypt.
Icon. Russia. 21st c.

On an icon the saint is devoid of those bodily, fleshly characteristics which could elicit in the viewer passionate thoughts or associations. This in enabled, to a considerable degree, by the fact that for the majority of icons the body of the saint is completely covered with clothing painted according to particular rules. The clothing does not accentuate the body's contour but rather merely marks it symbolically. In some instances the saint may be presented completely or almost completely naked.[18] "In iconography, the clothed body is no more modest than the naked," remarks one contemporary theologian. "Here everything is filled with contrite devotion because it is inwardly holy, newly created, and pure."[19]

Icons of saints show not so much the process as the result, not so much the path as the destination, not so much the motion towards the goal as the goal itself. On an icon we see not a person struggling with the passions, but one who has already conquered them, not one seeking the kingdom of heaven, but one who has already attained it. Therefore, icons are not dynamic but static. The main hero of an icon is never depicted in motion. He either stands or sits. (An exception are the marginal icons of life icons of saints; here, as was mentioned earlier, a saint may be depicted in motion.) Secondary figures may also be depicted in motion; for example, the Magi on the icon of the nativity of Christ, or the heroes of multiple-figured compositions which have a deliberately auxiliary, illustrative character.

---

[17]Ibid., 21.

[18]In particular, Marcarius of Egypt, Mary of Egypt, Basil the Blessed, and other fools-for-Christ may be depicted naked.

[19]Archimandrite Vasileios of Stavronikita, Elizabeth Briere, trans., *Hymn of Entry: Liturgy and Life in the Orthodox Church* (Crestwood, NY: St Vladimir's Seminary Press, 1984), 87–88.

Saint George the Victory-bearer. Icon. Pskov. 15th c.

For this very reason the saint on an icon is never painted in profile but almost always in full-face view and sometimes, if required by the subject, in half-profile (three-quarters view). Only persons to whom reverence is not given may be depicted in profile. These are either secondary figures (such as the Magi) or anti-heroes, such as the betrayer Judas at the mystical supper. Animals on icons are also painted in profile. The horse on which Saint George the Victory-bearer sits is always depicted in profile, as is the snake the saint is striking, while the face of the saint is turned towards the viewer.

The same reason—the striving to show the person in his deified, transfigured condition—requires iconographers to abstain from depicting any bodily defects which were characteristic of the saint during his or her life. A person who was lacking one hand is depicted on the icon having two hands; a blind person is shown to be seeing and one who wore glasses "removes them" for the icon.[20] On ancient icons, it was not blind people who were depicted with closed eyes but rather dead people; for example, the Mother of God in the scene of the Dormition and the Savior on the cross. Theophanes the Greek depicted some ascetics and stylites with closed eyes, with eyes without pupils, and completely without eyes, but none of these saints had been blind. By depicting them in this way, it seems that Theophanes desired to emphasize that they completely died to the world and mortified in themselves "all the wisdom of the flesh."

According to the teaching of the Church Fathers, following the resurrection of the dead, people will receive their former bodies, but renewed and transfigured, similar to the body of Christ after he rose from the dead.[21] Man's new "glorified" body will be ethereal and have the semblance of light; however, it will retain the "image" of the material body which the person possessed during earthly life.[22] Accordingly, no defects of the material body, such as mutilations or signs of aging, will be characteristic.[23] In this very way the icon should retain the "image" of the material body without reproducing its bodily defects.

---

[20]It should be noted that the icons of Blessed Matrona of Moscow, on which she is depicted with closed eyes, in this way do not completely conform to the iconographic canon. Despite the fact that she was blind from birth, she ought to be depicted on icons as having sight.

[21]John Chrysostom *Commentary on 1 Corinthians* 41, 42, in *Works*, vol. 10, part 2, 425–426.

[22]Gregory of Nyssa *On the Making of Man* 27.

[23]Tertullian *On the Resurrection of the Flesh* 57.

Icons avoid naturalistic depictions of pain and suffering and do not present themselves with the goal of emotionally acting upon the viewer. Emotionality and anguish are totally foreign to icons. Precisely for this reason, Christ is depicted not as suffering but as dead on Byzantine and Russian icons of the crucifixion, in contrast to their Western counterparts. Christ's final words on the cross were: "It is finished" (Jn 19.30). The icon shows what occurred afterwards, not what transpired earlier; it shows not the process, but the result. It reveals what has been finished. Pain, suffering, agony—all that which attracted Western painters of the Renaissance in the image of the suffering Christ—all these remain behind the scenes in icons. Christ is presented dead in the Orthodox icons of the crucifixion but he is no less beautiful than on icons that depict him alive.

Theotokos on Deathbed. Fragment of the Fresco "Dormition." Cathedral of the Protaton. Mount Athos. 14th c.

The iconic face never depicts a particular emotional condition, be it joy or sorrow, anger or pain. The face of Christ driving the money-changers from the temple is just as calm as his face depicted on Mount Tabor, at the Mystical Supper, in the Garden of Gethsemane, at the trial before Pilate, or on Golgotha. Archimandrite Vasileios, igumen of the Iveron Monastery on Mount Athos, notes:

Crucifixion of Christ. Icon. Archimandrite Zinon. 2007.

> The Lord's face does not "shine" at the transfiguration more than in any other icon of him. . . . The Lord's expression is calm and divinely peaceful as he sits on the foal of an ass, entering Jerusalem on the eve of the Passion. Later, when he is mocked and buffeted in the courtyard of the High Priest, he keeps the same undisturbed tranquility, mingled with a deep sorrow at the consequences of sin for his creature. On the cross he preserves his serene glory from before the ages, which he had with God before the world was made (Jn 17.5). Upon the cross the Orthodox Church sees him as King of glory. And finally, when he is raised from the dead, there appears before us the same peaceful and, one might almost dare to say, sad face.[24]

---

[24] Archimandrite Vasileios, *Hymn*, 87, 88.

Venerable Saint Luke of Hellas. Mosaic of the Cathedral of Hosios Loukas Monastery. Greece. 10th c.

The major element of an icon's content is the face. Ancient iconographers differentiated *lichnoye* (personal) from *dolichnoye* (circumstantial). The latter, including the background, scenery, clothing, would often be given to a disciple or artist who was not yet a master, while the master himself painted the actual faces.[25] The *personal* was always treated with particular care and this part of the iconographer's labor was especially highly regarded. (A separate, higher price could be established for the *lichnóye* of a commissioned icon.) The spiritual center of the iconic face is the eyes which rarely look straight at the viewer; neither are they directed to the side. Most often the eyes appear to look "over" the viewer: not so much into his eyes but into his soul.

Lichnóye includes not only the face but the hands as well. On icons the hands often possess special expressiveness. Venerable (monastic) fathers are often depicted with raised hands and palms turned toward the viewer. This characteristic gesture,

---

[25]Irina Yazykova, *The Theology of the Icon* (Moscow, 1995), 21.

The Meaning of Icons

as on the icons of the Most Holy Theotokos Orans, is a symbol of the prayerful turning towards God. At the same time, it indicates the saint's renunciation of this world with all its passions and lusts.

The Cosmic Meaning of Icons

While a person is always the major figure of an icon, its background is often an image of the transformed cosmos. In this sense, icons are *cosmic* since they reveal nature—albeit nature in its eschatological, changed condition.

According to Christian understanding, the initial harmony which existed in nature before man's fall into sin was destroyed as a result of the fall. Nature suffers together with man and together with man awaits redemption. The Apostle Paul speaks of how "creation was subjected to futility, not willingly, but because of him who subjected *it* in hope; because the creation itself also will be delivered from the bondage of corruption into the glorious liberty of the children of God" (Rom 8.20–21).

"All of Creation Rejoices in Thee." Icon. Russia. 20th c.

Icons reflect the eschatological, apocalyptic, redemptive, and deified condition of nature. The traits of a donkey or horse on an icon are just as refined and ennobled as the traits of a person, and the eyes of these animals on icons appear to be human, not those belonging to donkeys or horses. We see in icons the earth and sky, trees and grass, the sun and moon, birds and fish, animals and creeping things, but all of these are subjected to the unified scheme and comprise a single temple in which God reigns. Eugene Trubetskoi writes that on icons like "Let Every Breath Praise the Lord," "Praise the Name of the Lord," and "All of Creation, Gladdened, Rejoices In Thee":

> We see all terrestrial creatures together, in a glorified vision of romping animals, singing birds, and even fish swimming in the sea. In all these icons, the architectural design to which *all creation* submits is represented by the image of a church, a *sobor*. Angels stream toward it, saints assemble in it, plants of paradise entwine it, and animals swarm before or around it.[26]

[26]Trubetskoi, 29–30. Italics are the author's.

Trubetskoi notes that in the literature depicting the lives of the saints, animals often surround a saint and trustingly lick his hands.[27] It is enough to recall Saint Gerasim of the Jordan, whom a lion served, and Saint Seraphim of Sarov, who fed a bear from his hands. Holiness transforms not only man but also the world around him, including animals which have contact with it since they, in the words of Saint Isaac the Syrian, sense the fragrance emanating from the saint, that which emanated from Adam before the fall. In holiness, that order of mutual relationship between man and nature is restored—an order that existed in the newly-created world and was lost through the fall.

Trubetskoi cites the famous words of Saint Isaac the Syrian about the "merciful heart" which is "a heart on fire for the whole of creation, for humanity, for the birds, for the animals, for demons, and for all that exists."[28] In these words the philosopher sees:

The Prophet Daniel in the Lions' Den. Mosaic. Cathedral of the Hosios Loukas Monastery. Greece. 10th c.

... concretely the new plane of being where the law of mutual gobbling is overcome at its very root, *in the heart of man*, through love and compassion. Conceived in man, the new relationship extends to the lower orders. A cosmic revolution takes place: *new creatures* originate in man's love and pity. These "new creatures" are shown in the icons: through the prayers of saints, God's church opens its portals to them, gives a place to their spiritualized image.[29]

By means of illustration, Trubetskoi refers to the Old Russian icon of the Prophet Daniel among the lions:

To an untrained eye it may seem naïve and the lions impossibly unrealistic as they gaze at Daniel with touching devotion. But in art the naïve often borders on genius. Actually, the unlikeness here

---

[27]Ibid.
[28]Isaac the Syrian *Homily 71*, in *Ascetical Homilies*, 507–508; translated at *http://cyberdesert.wordpress.com/2013/01/28/what-is-a-merciful-heart-st-isaac-the-syrian/*, where it is called Homily 81; Dec. 5, 2013.
[29]Trubetskoi, *Icons*, 30–31.

Creation of the World. Mosaic. Cathedral of Saint Mark. Venice. 13th c.

is quite appropriate and probably intentional. These lions are not supposed to look like the animals we know. They prefigure the new creatures, already aware of having come under a new, not the biological, law. It was the artist's task to depict a new way of life, still unknown to us, and of course he could do this only symbolically, not by copying *our* reality.[30]

In some rather rare instances, nature becomes not a background but the basic object of attention of a church artist. For example, this can be seen in mosaics and frescoes dedicated to the creation of the world. A beautiful example of this type is the previously mentioned mosaics of Saint Mark's Basilica in Venice (thirteenth century) on which the six days of creation are depicted inside a gigantic circle divided into numerous segments. In one of the segments we see the sun and moon with human faces inside a circle, symbolizing the starry sky. Four angel-like creatures symbolize four days of creation. In another segment we see Adam naming the animals. Horses, lions, wolves (or dogs), bears, camels, leopards, and hedge-hogs line up before him in pairs. In all segments the Creator is depicted in the form of

---

[30]Ibid., 31. Italics are the author's.

Descent of the Holy Spirit on the Apostles. Icon. Novgorod. 15th–16th c.

a young, beardless man with a cross-in-halo, holding a cross. This corresponds with the Christian understanding that Old Testament revelations of God were revelations of the Son of God.

In the mosaics of Saint Mark's Basilica and also in other icons and frescoes, both Byzantine and Old Russian, nature is sometimes depicted as animate. It has already been said that in the mosaic of the Ravenna Baptistery the Jordan River is presented in the form of an elder with long hair, holding a branch. In ancient icons of the baptism of our Lord two small human-like creatures, male and female, are often depicted in the water. The male creature symbolizes the Jordan while the female creature symbolizes the ocean (an iconographical allusion to Psalm 113, verse 3: "The sea saw it and fled; Jordan turned back"). Some perceive these figures as relics of pagan antiquity. Actually it is more likely that they witness to the iconographers' perception of nature as a living organism capable of containing divine grace and responding to God's presence. Descending into the waters of the Jordan, Christ sanctified the watery world, which joyfully greeted and received the incarnate God into itself. This truth is also revealed by the human-like creatures depicted on the icons of the baptism of the Lord.

On some Old Russian icons of Pentecost, a man wearing a king's crown is depicted in a dark niche near the bottom; over him appears the inscription "Cosmos." This image is sometimes interpreted as a symbol of the universe, enlightened by the action of the Holy Spirit through the preaching of the apostles. Eugene Trubetskoi sees in the "King-Cosmos" a symbol of the ancient cosmos, held captive by sin, against which a temple encompassing the whole world filled with the grace of the Holy Spirit is juxtaposed:

> From the very fact that Pentecost is counterposed to *King Cosmos* it is clear that the church in which the apostles are enthroned is seen as the *new universe* and *new kingdom*—the *cosmic ideal* that is to liberate the actual cosmos. In order to receive the royal prisoner, the church must coincide with the universe, must encompass not only a new heaven but also a new earth. The tongues of flame above the apostles show us what is understood as the force that must bring about this cosmic revolution.[31]

[31] Ibid., 31.

The Meaning of Icons

The Greek word "cosmos" signifies splendor, goodness, and beauty. In the treatise by Dionysius the Areopagite entitled *On the Divine Names*, beauty is treated as one of the divine names. According to Dionysius, God is the perfect Beauty "because beauty is communicated from him to all beautiful things in a manner appropriate to each, and because he is the Cause of the good organization and refinement of all things which, as light, radiates to all the beautifying teachings of his exuding radiance; and because he calls all things to himself—for this reason he is called Beauty."[32] All earthly beauty pre-exists in the divine Beauty as in its original cause.

In his book with the distinctive title *The World as the Realization of Beauty*, the Russian philosopher Nikolai Lossky wrote, "Beauty is the absolute value; that is, the value which possesses a positive meaning for all personalities capable of perceiving it. . . . Perfect beauty is the fullness of Being, containing in itself the totality of all absolute values."[33]

Nature, the cosmos, the entire earthly foundation is a reflection of the divine Beauty and this is precisely what icons are called to reveal. But the world communicates with the divine beauty only as far as it has not "submitted to vanity" and has not lost the ability to sense the divine presence. In the fallen world beauty coexists with ugliness. However, as evil is not a full-fledged "partner" of good, but is merely the absence of good—that which is opposite to it—so too ugliness in this world does not prevail over beauty. "Beauty and ugliness are not equally distributed in the world. Overall, beauty has superiority," confirms Lossky.[34] In icons there is an absolute prevalence of beauty and almost total absence of ugliness. Even a snake on an icon of Saint George and the demons in the scene of the last judgment have a less frightening and repulsive look than many of the personages of Bosch and Goya.

The Liturgical Meaning of Icons

Icons are *liturgical* because of the purpose they serve. They are an inherent part of the Church's liturgical space and an indispensable participant in the divine services. "Icons by their nature . . . are in no way images intended for personal pious

---

[32]Dionysius the Aeropagite *On the Divine Names* 4, 7. The English translation found at *http://www.ccel.org/ccel/dionysius/works.i.ii.iv.html* (Feb. 26, 2014), is slightly different.
[33]Nikolai Lossky, *The World as the Realization of Beauty* (Moscow, 1998), 33–34.
[34]Ibid., 116.

Icon in the Interior of an Orthodox Church.

reverence," writes Hieromonk Gabriel Bunge. "Their theological place is primarily the liturgy where the proclamation of the good tidings by the Word is made perfect by a proclamation of the good tidings by images."[35] Outside the context of the Church and the liturgy, icons lose their meaning to a considerable degree. Of course, every Christian has the right to hang icons in his home, but he has this right insofar as his home is an extension of the church and his life is an extension of the liturgy. Icons do not belong in museums. "It is ridiculous to think of icons in museums. An icon is not alive there, but exists only as a dried flower in a herbarium or as a butterfly stuck by a pin in a collector's box."[36]

Icons participate in the divine services together with the gospel book and other sacred objects. In the tradition of the Orthodox Church, the gospel is not only a book for reading—it is also an object to which liturgical reverence is rendered. During the divine services the gospel book is ceremoniously carried out of the sanctuary and venerated by the faithful. In just the same way, icons ("the Gospel in paint") are not only objects of contemplation—they are also objects of prayerful veneration. Icons are venerated; censing takes place before them; bows to the waist

---

[35] Hieromonk Gabriel (Bunge), *Another Comforter: Saint Andrei Rublev's Icon of the Most Holy Trinity* (Riga, 2003), 111.

[36] Yazykova, *Theology*, 33.

and to the ground are made before them. But Christians do not bow down to a painted board, but to the one whose image is depicted on it.

In our time, the most common icons are those painted on panels and commissioned individually for use both in churches and in homes. Such icons live their own lives and may be thematically unrelated to other icons. They are given and regiven as gifts, sold and re-sold, exhibited in museums, hung on walls in churches and in homes. One may photograph such icons, make reproductions of them and place them in albums, on the Internet, and in frames to be hung on walls. The making of commissioned icons has turned into a lucrative and far-flung business. Depending on the taste of the consignee, icons are painted in the Byzantine, Old Russian, "Ushakov," "academic," or some other style. Often icons are stylized in order to appear old—intentionally containing soot, cracks, and other signs of aging to look "authentic." This "technique" is essentially a violation of icons and a flagrant profanation of Church arts.

In the ancient Church, icons painted for a specific church as an inherent part of the church ensemble were most common. Such icons were not isolated objects but rather they were inseparably linked to other icons found in close proximity to them. An artist of the church would never think to stylize an icon according to a certain period of history or to give it an "antiquated" look. In every period, icons were painted in the style that was prevalent at that time. When a period changed, the style changed and aesthetic standards and technical methods changed as well. Only the iconographical canon, formed over many centuries, remained unchanged. All ancient iconography was strictly canonical and did not leave room for human imagination.

Ancient churches were adorned not so much with icons painted on panels as with murals. Frescoes were the earliest example of Orthodox iconography. Frescoes already occupied an essential place in the Roman catacombs. Churches began to be completely covered with frescoes from top to bottom and on all four walls in the post-iconoclastic period. The richest churches were adorned with mosaics as well as frescoes.

The most obvious distinction between frescoes and icons is that it is impossible to take frescoes out of a church. A fresco is permanently affixed to a wall and forever connected to a particular church; it ages with the church, is restored with it, and perishes with it. An icon can be taken out of a church and may be transported from one place to another and may be transferred from one church to another. In the period of neo-iconoclasm and resistance to God which began after the

Frescoes.

Russian Revolution of 1917, frescoes perished together with destroyed churches while icons perished outside of churches—on bonfires which blazed all over Russia. It was possible to save some icons that were taken out of churches as they found refuge in museums of ancient art or museums of atheism, in closed depositories and warehouses. The frescoes of demolished churches were irretrievably lost.

Inseparably linked with churches, frescoes comprise an organic part of the liturgical space. As with icons, the subjects of frescoes are in accordance with the thematic program of the yearly ecclesiastical cycle. During the year, the Church commemorates the major events from the history of the Bible and Gospel, the events from the life of the Most Holy Theotokos, and from Church history. Every day of the Church calendar is dedicated to the memory of certain saints—martyrs, bishops, monastic saints, confessors, right-believing princes, fools-for-Christ, etc. In accordance with this, murals may include depictions of Church feasts (both of the Christological cycle and the cycle of the Theotokos), images of saints, scenes from the Old and New Testaments. Together with this the events of one thematic row, as a rule, are placed in one register. Every church is conceived and built as a united whole and the thematic arrangement of frescoes both corresponds with the yearly liturgical cycle and reflects the specific need of the church itself. (For example, in a church dedicated to the Most Holy Theotokos, frescoes depict her life, while in a church dedicated to Saint Nicholas, the life of that saint is depicted.)

The organizational design and structure of the iconostasis possesses fullness and completion, while its themes, as noted earlier, correspond with the themes of the church's frescoes. The theological meaning of the iconostasis consists not in hiding something from the faithful. On the contrary, it consists in revealing to them the reality into which each icon is a window. In the words of Florensky, the iconostasis "does not hide something from the faithful . . . but rather the opposite: it indicates the mysteries of the sanctuary to them who are half-blind and opens an entrance into another world to those who are lame and maimed, the entrance which is closed by their own sluggishness, it shouts to them who have deaf ears things concerning the kingdom of Heaven."[37]

---

[37] Florensky, *Iconostasis*, 46.

High Multi-tiered Iconostasis. Archangel Cathedral. Moscow Kremlin. 17th c.

However, it is necessary to note that it was not characteristic for the ancient Church to perceive the laity as half-blind, deaf, lame, and maimed, as distinct from the clergy located within the sanctuary for whom, if one were to follow the same logic, the entrance into the other world is always open. And it is hard to disagree with those scholars who note that the transformation of the iconostasis into a deaf, impenetrable wall between the sanctuary and central part of the church had a negative effect on the liturgical tradition of the Russian Church. High many-tiered iconostases isolated the sanctuary from the main space of the church and encouraged a more profound break between the clergy and people of the church who were transformed from active participants in the divine services into passive listeners and viewers. The priests' exclamations reached the people from behind the deaf wall of the iconostasis with closed royal gates and drawn curtain and in no way made it possible for those praying to be drawn into this "common deed" which the Divine Liturgy and every divine service ought to be.

Icons reflect the liturgical life and experience of the Church. As in the liturgy, the boundary between past, present, and future is wiped away in icons. Events which took place at different times and persons who lived in different eras may be heroes of a single iconographical composition. Archimandrite Vasileios writes:

> What we have in the icon is not a neutral, faithful historical representation, but a dynamic liturgical transformation. In iconography, the events of salvation are not interpreted historically. . . . The Apostle Paul is represented in the icon as first among those present at Pentecost, even though he was not "historically" present. . . . The icon is a witness to liturgical life and to the unity of the Godhead. It is not the creation or improvisation of some genius. It does not serve merely artistic ends. It does not divide up history. For the world of the icon, distance in space and the passing of time do not exist. What the icon expresses is not the fragmentation characteristic of the present age, but the unifying power of the liturgy. [38]

The development of iconography, changes in iconographic styles, the emergence or disappearance of certain elements of church decoration—all this is inseparably connected with the liturgical life of the Church, with the level of eucharistic piety of the people of the Church:

> Icons are fundamentally rooted in the Church's eucharistic experience and are inseparably linked to it, as to the level of ecclesiastical life in general. When this level was high, ecclesiastical arts were also at a height; when ecclesiastical life was weak or in decline, of course a decline resulted in the ecclesiastical arts as well. Often icons turned into mere paintings of a religious suject and their veneration ceased to be Orthodox.[39]

Active participation in the divine services of all the faithful, both clergy and laity, was the norm for the early Christian Church. The eucharistic prayers in the ancient Church were read aloud and not secretly. The people, not the choir, responded to the exclamations of the priest. All the faithful approached the holy chalice, not only the clergy and those specially prepared for receiving communion. This experience of the church was facilitated by an open sanctuary, the absence of a visible wall between the clergy and people. A most important place was given to eucharistic themes in the murals of this period. A eucharistic subtext was present in early Christian symbols painted on walls such as: a chalice, fish, lamb, a basket with loaves of bread, grapevine, or a bird pecking at a bunch of grapes. In the Byzantine

---

[38] Archimandrite Vasileios, *Hymn*, 82–83. Italics are the author's.
[39] Zinon (Teodor), *Conversations*, 23.

Ancient Altar Screen. Church of the Apostles in Athens. Greece. 11th c.

period all church murals were thematically oriented towards the sanctuary, which remained open, as before; and the sanctuary was painted in images having a direct relationship to the Eucharist. These included the "Communion of the Apostles," "Mystical Supper," images of the authors of the liturgies (in particular, Saint Basil the Great and Saint John Chrysostom), as well as hymnographers of the church. All of these images should convey a eucharistic disposition upon the faithful and prepare them for full participation in the liturgy and the communion of the Body and Blood of Christ.

A change in the eucharistic consciousness in a later period, when communion ceased to be an inalienable element of every believer's participation in the Eucharist and the liturgy ceased to be a "common deed," led to the a pseudo-morphosis in the iconographic arts as well. The Eucharist became primarily the inheritance of the clergy, who preserved the custom of communing at every liturgy, while the common people began to commune infrequently and irregularly. Correspondingly, the sanctuary was separated from the main space of the church and the iconostasis wall grew between the communing clergy and non-communing laity and the murals of the sanctuary, dedicated to the Eucharist, became hidden from the eyes of the laity.

A change in the style of icon painting during certain periods was also connected with a change in eucharistic consciousness. In the Synodal period (eighteenth and nineteenth centuries) the custom took definitive hold in Russian ecclesiastical piety of communing once or a few times per year. In the majority of cases, people came to church in order to "stand" for the duration of the liturgy and not in order to commune of the Holy Mysteries of Christ. The decline in eucharistic consciousness fully corresponded with the decline in church art, which led to its being replaced by realistic "academic" painting, while ancient *znamenny* singing was replaced by *partesny* many-voiced singing. Church murals of this period retained but a distant thematic resemblance to their ancient prototypes. But they are totally devoid of all the basic characteristics of iconography which would distinguish them from ordinary painting.

The rebirth of eucharistic piety in the beginning of the twentieth century, the striving towards more frequent communion, attempts to surmount the barrier between the clergy and the people—all of these processes coincided chronologically with the "discovery" of icons and renewal of interest in ancient icon painting. Concurrently in the Russian Church low single-tier iconostases began to return, thus opening up to the faithful a view of the activities inside the sanctuary. Ecclesiastical artists of the early twentieth century began searching for ways to bring about a rebirth of canonical icon painting. This search continued among members of the Russian emigration in the creative work of such iconographers as the monk Gregory (Kroug). It continues in our day in the icons and frescoes of Archimandrite Zenon and other masters who are giving rebirth to ancient traditions.

For the sake of fairness it must be noted that many who are zealous for true icons and a eucharistic rebirth believe that it is precisely the traditional iconostasis that can play an important role. Leonid Ouspensky writes, "One of the most important results of the development of hesychasm in Russia—a period of the flowering not only of holiness and sacred art, but also of liturgical creation—is the iconostasis in its classical form."[40] Speaking of a five-tiered "Rublev" iconostasis, Ouspensky sees in it the striving "to make the meaning of the sacrament of the Eucharist more explicit." In this the "precision and power of expression proper to hesychasm"[41] are manifested.

[40]Ouspensky, *Theology*, 275.
[41]Ibid.

Exposing the meaning of every detail, the scholar emphasizes, "this iconographic structure of the iconostasis, the order of its rows, corresponds to the liturgical prayer immediately preceding the epiclesis: 'You and Your Only-begotten Son and Your Holy Spirit" brought "us from non-existence into being, and when we had fallen away" raised "us up again, and did not cease to do all things until You had brought us back to heaven and had endowed us with Your kingdom which is to come.'"[42] In other words, in Ouspensky's opinion, the classical iconostasis of the period of the flourishing of hesychasm and ecclesiastical arts is a visual illustration of that which the priest reads in the "secret" prayers.

Priest Pavel Florensky.

"The iconostasis therefore has more than merely a didactic meaning," concludes Ouspensky. "It represents the ontological link between sacrament and image, and shows this glorious body of Christ, the same real body given in the Eucharist and represented on the icon."[43] Considering such an important meaning of the iconostasis for the perception of the liturgy, the scholar supposes that only "when it is materially impossible to have a complete iconostasis in a church, it can undoubtedly be limited to the Deesis itself, or even to the single icon of Christ. However, deliberately to forgo the fullness of the iconostasis is to repudiate what the Church teaches through it."[44]

This same understanding of the classical iconostasis was discussed by Eugene Trubetskoi in his *Three Essays on the Russian Icon*[45] and by Priest Pavel Florensky in his work *Iconostasis*. For the perception of the liturgy, in the opinion of these scholars, the atmosphere of mystery plays a large role and is attained by the accompanying action of a many-tiered iconostasis with royal gates which alternately open and close the sanctuary to the view of the faithful, the presence of "secret prayers" read by the priest in the sanctuary, and other details of the church services. In the words of Trubetskoi, "All the beauty of Old Russian icon painting is but the translucent shell of this mystery, its rainbow-hued cover."[46]

---

[42] Ibid., 279.
[43] Ibid., 282.
[44] Ibid., 285.
[45] See Trubetskoi, *Three Essays*, 169–172.
[46] Trubetskoi, *Icons*, 92.

The Mystical Meaning of Icons

Icons are *mystical*. They are inseparably linked with the spiritual life of Christians, with their experience of communing with God, and their experience of coming into contact with the world "on high." At the same time, icons reflect the mystical experience of the whole fullness of the Church and not only of some of its individual members. An artist's personal spiritual experience cannot fail to be reflected in icons, but this experience is perceived through the experience of the Church and verified by it. Theophanes the Greek, Andrei Rublev, and other masters of the past were people who had deep inner spiritual lives. But they did not paint "from themselves." Their icons are rooted in the tradition of the Church in a most profound way that encompasses the whole experience of the Church, spanning many centuries.

Many great iconographers were great contemplatives and mystics. As witnessed by Saint Joseph of Volokolamsk who spoke of Daniel Cherny and Andrei Rublev:

> The venerable iconographers Daniel and his disciple Andrei . . . had as much virtue and zeal for fasting and the monastic life as was vouchsafed to them by divine grace and acquired more divine love than is exercised by those on earth, but always they lifted up their minds and thoughts to the ineffable and divine light. . . . On the very feast of the bright resurrection they were seated in the seats and had before them the all-venerable and divine icons, and gazing upon them intently they were filled with divine joy and brightness, and not only on that day when such were created but on other days, when it was not the custom to paint icons.[47]

The experience of contemplating the divine light, spoken of in this text, is reflected in many icons, both Byzantine and Russian. It especially relates to icons from the period of Byzantine hesychasm (eleventh through fifteenth centuries) and also to Russian icons and frescoes of the fourteenth and fifteenth centuries. Earlier we spoke of how artists conveyed the experience of contemplating the divine light by means of gold and white paint, illuminating the icon with inner light and making it light-bearing.

Icons grow out of prayer and without prayer an authentic icon cannot be made. "An icon is an incarnate prayer. It is created in prayer and for the sake of prayer as

---
[47] Joseph Volotsky, *Otveschanie liubozazornym*, 557–558.

The Meaning of Icons

a moving power which is love for God, striving towards him and towards the perfect Beauty."[48] Being the fruit of prayer, an icon is also a school of prayer for those who contemplate it and prayer before it. By all of its spiritual order an icon disposes us towards prayer. At the same time, prayer carries a person beyond the borders of an icon and places him before the face of the first image himself, the Lord Jesus Christ, the Mother of God, and the saints.

There are well known cases of people, during prayer, seeing the one depicted on the icon as living. For example, the Venerable Saint Silouan the Athonite saw the living Christ in the place of his icon:

Transfiguration of the Lord. Icon. Theophanes the Greek. 1403.

> "During vespers, in the church . . . to the right of the royal gates, where the icon of the Savior is situated, he saw the living Christ. . . . It is impossible to describe the condition in which he was at that time," spoke his biographer Archimandrite Sophrony. "We know from the words and writings of the blessed elder that the divine light shone upon him and he was taken from this world and in spirit transported to heaven where he heard unutterable speech and that at that moment he received what was like a new birth from above."[49]

Those who are depicted on icons appear not only to saints but also to ordinary Christians. In the narrative of the icon of the Mother of God "Unexpected Joy" it is told how "a certain outlaw had a rule of praying to the Most Holy Theotokos every day." Once during prayer the Mother of God appeared to him and cautioned him against his sinful life. Icons such as "Unexpected Joy" are known in Russia as "miraculously appearing" icons.

The question of the correlation between icons and miracles deserves special examination. In the Orthodox Church wonder-working icons are widespread and connected to cases of healing and deliverance from military danger. In Russia special veneration is given to the Vladimir, Kazan, Smolensk, Iveron, "Seeking Out of the Lost," "Joy of All Who Sorrow," and other miraculous icons of the Mother of God. For example, the deliverance of Rus' from the attacks of Mongol khans of Tamerlane in 1395, Akhmata in 1490, and Makhmet-Girei in 1521 is

---

[48]Zenon (Teodor), *Conversations*, 22.
[49]Archimandrite Sophrony (Sakharov), *Silouan the Athonite* (Essex, 1991), 13.

"Unexpected Joy." Icon. Russia. 20th c.

connected with the Vladimir icon. In the first case, the Mother of God herself appeared to the khan in his sleep and ordered him to leave the borders of Rus'. Soldiers of a people's volunteer corps headed by Kuzma Minin and Dmitri Pozharsky prayed before the Kazan icon of the Mother of God as they prepared for a decisive victory over the Poles who seized Moscow in 1612. During Napoleon's occupation the Kazan icon of the Mother of God protected Russian soldiers who prayed before it. The first major defeat of the French after the departure from Moscow took place on the feast in honor of the Kazan icon on October 22, 1812.

A phenomenon to which many people attribute special mystical significance has become widespread in Russia in recent years: myrrh-streaming icons. In our days icons exude myrrh in all places: monasteries, churches, and private homes. There are myrrh-streaming icons of the Savior, the Mother of God, Saint Nicholas, the Greatmartyr Panteleimon, Tsar and Passion-bearer Nicholas II, and many other saints. Both ancient icons and contemporary icons exude myrrh. Even reproductions and postcards on which icons are depicted are known to exude myrrh.

How are we to consider this phenomenon? First of all, it is necessary to say that cases of myrrh-streaming icons are an indisputable fact and have been recognized repeatedly. But facts and their interpretations are different things. Some people see in myrrh-streaming a sign of the nearing of apocalyptic times and the closeness of the coming of the antichrist. In this case it is no more than one's personal opinion which in no way stems from the essence of the phenomenon of myrrh-streaming. It seems that myrrh-streaming of icons is not a somber forecast of coming calamities but on the contrary, a revelation of the mercy of God sent for the comfort and spiritual strengthening of the faithful. An icon that exudes myrrh is a witness of the real presence in the Church of the one who is depicted on the icon. It is a witness to us of the closeness of God, the Mother of God, and the saints.

The theological interpretation of the phenomenon of myrrh-gushing requires particular spiritual wisdom and sobriety. Giddiness concerning this phenomenon is inappropriate and brings harm to the Church. The pursuit of a "miracle for the sake of a miracle" was certainly never characteristic of true Christians. Christ himself refused to give the Jews "a sign," emphasizing that the only true sign is his own descent into the grave and resurrection. The greatest miracle of the Church is the Eucharist, in which bread and wine are changed into the Body and Blood of the Savior. No less a miracle is the spiritual change which takes place in the faithful due to their participation in the mysteries of the Church. In order to acknowledge the meaning of these miracles spiritual eyes are needed, but myrrh-streaming icons, visible to the physical eyes, are given to those whose eyes are darkened by sin. Because of this, myrrh-streaming is regarded by some with greater veneration than even the Eucharist.

It is necessary to point out that not only icons painted in accordance with canonical norms may be wonder-working, myrrh-streaming, and "miraculously appearing," but icons executed in a pictorial and academic style and also depictions of a religious motif rendered in a manner far removed from the iconographical canonical norm as well.[50] But neither miracles nor myrrh-streaming or other similar phenomena in themselves change painting into iconography. With regard to iconography the Church always put forth as the major criterion that of canonicity, not wonder working. Ouspensky writes:

Montreal's Iveron Myrrh-gushing Icon of the Mother of God.

> The entire life of the Church is certainly based on a miracle, the miracle *par excellence* that gives meaning and structure to this life—the incarnation of God and man's deification. . . . It is precisely this miracle that is the norm of the life of the Church, a norm fixed in its canon, one which the Church places against the actual condition of the world. The entire liturgical cycle of the Church is defined by this: its annual cycle is based on the stages, the aspects of this fundamental, decisive miracle—and not on various specific miracles, even those worked by Christ himself. The Church lives not by what is passing and specific, but by what is immutable. Is this not the reason why, for the Church, miracles have never been a criterion in any domain whatsoever? Its life has never been ruled by them. It is significant that the conciliar decisions ordain that icons be painted not based on miraculous models (indeed, the miracles performed by an icon are an external, temporal manifestation, not an enduring display),

---

[50]In the Catholic Church there are famous cases of myrrh-streaming, tear-streaming, and blood-streaming in painted images and statues of the Most Holy Virgin, executed in the traditions of the Renaissance.

but in the same manner in which the ancient iconographers painted, that is, according to the iconographical canon.[51]

The Moral Meaning of Icons

In conclusion it is necessary to say a few words about the *moral meaning* of icons in the context of the contemporary opposition between Christianity and so-called "post-Christian" secular humanism. Ouspensky writes:

> The present situation of Christianity in the world is often compared to that of the first centuries of its existence . . . . But if, in the first centuries, Christianity stood before a pagan world, the world it faces today is a dechristianized world, the outcome of apostasy. It is before this world that Orthodoxy is "called to bear witness" to give evidence of the truth. It does so by its liturgy and its icon. Hence the need to regain awareness of the dogma of the veneration of icons and to express it in conformity to the needs of our present life, to the problems and questions of modern man.[52]

Image of the Holy Trinity. Modern Icon.

In the secular world individualism and egoism dominate. People are separated from one another, everyone lives for himself, and loneliness has become the chronic illness of many. The understanding of sacrifice is something alien to contemporary man as is the willingness to give one's life for another. The feeling of mutual responsibility for one another is becoming dull and its place is taken by the instinct for self-preservation.

Christianity speaks of man as a member of a unified collective organism which bears responsibility not only before itself but before God and other people. The Church binds people together in a single body whose head is the God-Man Jesus Christ. The unity of the body of the Church is a prototype of the unity to which all humanity is called, according to the eschatological perspective. In the kingdom of God people will be united with God and there will be love between them similar to the love which unites the three Persons of the Holy Trinity. The image of the Holy Trinity reveals

[51]Ouspensky, *Theology*, 476–477.
[52]Ibid., 508.

to mankind that spiritual unity to which it is called. And the Church will ceaselessly, despite all separation, individualism, and egoism, remind the world and every person about this high calling.

The stand-off between Christianity and the dechristianized world is particularly obvious in the field of morality. A liberal moral standard which denies the existence of an absolute ethical norm prevails in secular society. According to this standard, all things are permissible for man that do not contradict the law and violate the rights of other people. In the secular lexicon the notion of sin is absent and every person determines for himself the moral criterion on which he is oriented. Secular morality has repudiated the concept of marriage and marital fidelity and de-sacralized the ideals of motherhood and childbearing. Against these fundamental ideals secular morality has pitted "free love," hedonism, and the propaganda of vice and sin. The emancipation of women, their striving to be equal in all things to men, has led to a drastic drop in childbirth and an acute demographical crisis in the majority of countries which have adopted secular morality.

Mother of God. Image from the Sanctuary of the Church of Santa Maria e San Donato. Murano. 12th c.

Despite all the contemporary tendencies, the Church, just as centuries ago, continues to preach chastity and marital fidelity. The Church considers the highest calling of women to be motherhood and having many children is considered the greatest blessing from God. The Orthodox Church glorifies motherhood in the person of the Mother of God who is glorified as "more honorable than the cherubim and more glorious beyond compare than the seraphim." The image of the Mother holding on her lap the Infant Christ, who tenderly presses his cheek to her cheek—this is the ideal which the Orthodox Church offers to every Christian woman. This image, in a countless number of versions existing in all Orthodox churches, possesses a great spiritual power of attraction and moral strength. And despite all the spirits of the times, as long as the Church exists it will remind women of their calling to motherhood and childbearing.

Contemporary morality has de-sacralized death, turning it into a cheerless ritual lacking any positive content. People are afraid of death, ashamed of it, and avoid speaking of it. Some people prefer, not waiting for a natural end, to depart from life voluntarily. Euthanasia—doctor-assisted suicide—has become more and more widespread. People who have lived life without God die in the same aimless and empty way in which they lived—in the same spiritual void and godforsakenness.

During every divine service the Orthodox faithful ask God for a Christian ending to their lives, painless, blameless, and peaceful. They pray for deliverance from sudden death so as to have time to offer repentance and to die in peace with God and their loved ones. The end of a Christian's life is not death but a passing over into eternal life. A visual reminder of this are the icons of the Dormition of the Most Holy Theotokos, in which the Mother of God is depicted beautifully lying on her deathbed surrounded by the apostles and angels. Christ receives into his hands her most pure soul, symbolized by a young girl. Death is a transition to a new life, more beautiful than the earthly life, and at the threshold of death Christ receives the souls of Christians. This is the news which the image of the Dormition bears. And despite all materialistic notions of life and death, the Church will always proclaim this truth to humanity.

It could have been possible to discuss a number of other examples of icons which proclaim various moral truths. In fact, each icon bears in itself a powerful moral charge. Icons remind contemporary man that, apart from this world in which he lives, there is yet another world. Besides the values preached by a-religious humanism, there are yet other spiritual values. Besides the moral standards established by secular society, there are other standards and norms. Ouspensky wrote concerning the meaning of icons for the contemporary world:

> In our day . . . two completely different orientations of man and of his creativity confront one another: the anthropocentrism of a secularized, a-religious humanism, and Christian anthropocentrism. In this confrontation, the icon plays a leading role. The essential meaning of its "discovery" in our epoch does not lie in the fact that it is now appreciated and understood to a greater or lesser extent, but in the witness it offers to contemporary man: a witness to the victory gained by man over all discord and disintegration, a witness to another way of life that puts man in a totally different perspective in relation to his Creator and radically reorients his attitude toward the fallen world, gives him a different understanding, another vision of the world.[53]

---

[53]Ibid., 480.

PART THREE

Church Music

Section One: Liturgical Singing

Saint Vladimir's Seminary Chorale in 2013. New York.

BOTH CHORAL AND SOLO SINGING are given an important role in the Orthodox divine services. All the exclamations of the priests and deacons are pronounced in a singing voice. All passages from the gospel book, the book of the epistles, the Psalter, and other sacred books are also read in a singing voice—on a single note or a few neighboring notes. Unlike Catholic or Protestant traditions in which services are conducted in a "speaking voice," the Orthodox tradition has no services whatsoever that are not performed in a singing voice and there is no distinction between "sung Eucharist" (liturgy with singing) and "said Eucharist" (liturgy without singing). Two or three singers can always be found in the choir of even the most humble village church.

In this chapter we will first examine the background of Orthodox liturgical singing, whose early sources are found in the musical culture of ancient Israel and the music of ancient worship. The history of Orthodox liturgical singing itself began in the epoch of the early Christian Church and continued in Byzantium, Rus', the Balkans, and other regions in which Orthodoxy became the dominant Christian confession. In this exposition of the history of liturgical singing, we will also touch on its theological content because an understanding of liturgical singing, as is the case with icons, is not possible without understanding its theological context.

10

Background.
Music in Ancient Israel and Ancient Greece

Music and Song in the Old Testament

MUSIC AND MUSICAL INSTRUMENTS, songs and singers, choirs and orchestras are mentioned many times in the Old Testament. According to the Book of Genesis, the creation of stringed and wooden wind instruments took place at the dawn of human civilization. Jubal, one of Cain's descendants, "was the father of all those who play the lyre and pipe" (Gen 4.21). Timbrels were used together with the harp in order to express feelings of joy and amusement (Gen 31.27). Following Israel's exodus from Egypt, Moses sang a festive song to God (see Ex 15.1–18) and his sister Miriam "having taken a timbrel in her hand—then there went forth all the women after her with timbrels and dances" (Ex 15.20). Silver trumpets were used as signal instruments (Num 10.2–3).

A great number of musical instruments including percussion, stringed, and wind instruments were used during the time of King David both during divine services and outside of services. David himself was a musician; as a youth he "was playing on the harp with his hands" (1 Sam 19.9). By David's playing on the harp, the evil spirit departed from Saul (see 1 Sam 16.14–23).

David, who had been convinced of the salutary power of music while still a youth, later attached particular significance to the art of music. After becoming king over Israel, he implemented a liturgical reform and created an entire staff of Levite-musicians to provide professional accompaniment during liturgical ceremonies. He ordered the chiefs of the Levites to appoint their "brethren singers with musical instruments, lutes, harps, and cymbals, to sound aloud with a voice of joy" (1 Chron 15.16). During divine services, some of the Levites played "with brazen cymbals to make a sound to be heard," some "with lutes" and others "with harps . . . to make a loud noise" and still others "were sounding with trumpets

King David Playing the Harp. Saint Dimitry Cathedral. Vladimir. End of 12th c.

before the ark of God" (1 Chr 15.19–24). The chief of the Levites, Hananiah "was master of the bands because he was skilful"(1 Chr 15.22). This description "witnesses to a fully formed, advanced, and rather complicated group 'music making,' which required a certain professional training."[1]

Singing and the playing musical instruments accompanied the ark of the covenant while it was transported to Jerusalem. When the ark was brought up out of the house of Abinadab, the entire people congregated and "David and the children of Israel were playing before the Lord on well-tuned instruments mightily, and with songs, and with harps, and with lutes, and with drums, and with cymbals, and with pipes" (2 Sam 6.5). Transporting the ark from the house of Abinadab[2] to the city of David was accompanied by dances and the playing of trumpets. "David danced before the Lord with all his might" and the sons of Israel "brought up the ark of the Lord with shouting, and with the sound of a trumpet" (2 Sam 6.14–15).

In transferring the kingdom to Solomon, the elderly David made yet another liturgical reform when he considerably enlarged the staff of temple musicians. Of thirty-eight thousand Levites he appointed twenty thousand for service to God. Among these were "four thousand to praise the Lord with musical instruments which he made to praise the Lord" (1 Chr 23.5). Then David appointed the "sons of Asaph, and of Heman, and of Jeduthun, prophesiers with harps, and lutes, and cymbals. . . . All these sang hymns with their father in the house of God, with cymbals, and lutes, and harps. . . . And the number of them after their brethren, those instructed to sing to God, everyone that understood singing was two hundred and eighty-eight" (1 Chr 25.1, 6–7).

King David went down in history as the author of psalms—prayers intended to be sung by a choir. In his very first psalm, composed for the occasion of the transfer of the ark of the covenant to Jerusalem, David exclaimed, "Give praise to the Lord himself! Call upon his name; Make known his deeds among the peoples; Sing songs to him, sing praises to him . . ." (1 Chr 16.8–9). Singing songs and "singing praises" (i.e., vocal music performed either in a choir or solo), as well as the

---

[1]Vladimir Martynov, *History of Liturgical Singing* (Moscow, 1994), 21.
[2]Hebrew: Obed-edom—Ed.

Background: Music in Ancient Israel and Ancient Greece

playing of musical instruments, were the major elements that were to give shape to psalms as the major liturgical genre in ancient Israel. Dances and hand-clapping were sometimes added to these elements.

Various forms of singing (including odes, singing, exclamation, glorification, and praise) and various types of musical instruments, as well as hand-clapping during singing, are mentioned in the Psalter more than once:

> Give thanks to the Lord on the lyre; sing praises to him on a ten-stringed instrument. Sing to him a new song; sing praises beautifully with a shout (Ps 32.2–3).

> Oh, clap your hands, all you nations; shout to God with the voice of rejoicing. . . . God ascended with a shout, the Lord with the sound of the trumpet. . . . Sing praises to God; sing praises; sing praises to our King; sing praises (Ps 46.2; 6–7).

> I will incline my ear to a parable; I will open my riddle on the harp (Ps 48.5).

> Awake, my glory; awake, harp and lyre (Ps 56.9).

> Shout to God, all the earth; sing now to his name; give glory to his praise (Ps 65.1–2).

> Truly, I will give thanks to you with the instrument of a psalm, O God; I will sing to you with the lyre, O Holy One of Israel (Ps 70.22).

> Rejoice greatly in the living God. Take up a psalm and sound a timbrel, a pleasant psaltery with a harp; Sound a trumpet in the new moon on this honorable day of our feast (Ps 80. 2–4).

> It is good to give thanks to the Lord and to sing to your name, O Most High, to proclaim your mercy in the morning and your truth at night, on the harp of ten strings, with an ode on the lyre (Ps 91.2–4).

> Come, let us greatly rejoice in the Lord; Let us shout aloud to God our savior; Let us come before his face with thanksgiving, and let us shout aloud to him with psalms. (Ps 94.1–2).

> O, sing a new song to the Lord, sing to the Lord, all the earth (Ps 95.1).

Sing to the Lord on a lyre, on a lyre and with the voice of a psalm; with trumpets of metal and the sound of a trumpet of horn, shout aloud before the Lord our King (Ps 97.5–6).

Shout aloud to the Lord, all the earth: Serve the Lord with gladness; enter into his gates with thanksgiving and into his courts with hymns (Ps 99.2, 4).

Awake, lute and harp; I shall awake early in the morning. I will give thanks to you among the peoples, O Lord, and I will sing to you among the Gentiles (Ps 107.3–4).

Sing to the Lord a new song, his praise in the assembly of his holy ones. . . . Let them praise his name with dance; with tambourine and harp let them sing to him . . . The high praise of God shall be in their mouth (Ps 149.1, 3, 6).

Praise him with the sound of a trumpet; praise him with the harp and lyre; praise him with timbrel and dance; praise him with strings and flute; praise him with resounding cymbals; praise him with triumphant cymbals (Ps 150.3–5).

Musical instruments are mentioned also in the inscriptions that preface the psalms; for example, "on stringed instruments" (see Ps 4.1; 53.1; 54.1; 66.1; 75.1); "on wind instruments" (see Ps 5.1); "on an eighth" (see Ps 6.1; 11.1); "on a stringed instrument" (see Ps 60.1); "on a wind instrument" (see Ps 52.1); "on a musical instrument Shoshan" (see Psalm 44.1); "on a musical instrument Alamof" (see Ps 45.1); "on a musical instrument Shushan Eduf" (see Ps 59.1); "on Shoshannim" (Ps 68.1); "on Gef instrument" (see Ps 8.1; 80.1; 83.1). From these inscriptions it is reasonable to assume that some psalms were performed with the accompaniment of a single instrument and others with the accompaniment of a group of instruments.

It must be noted that in translating the Old Testament into modern languages the names of musical instruments are rendered in a very approximate manner by using analogies with instruments used in our own time. In the original Hebrew text of the Bible there are twenty-nine names of various musical instruments. Of them twenty-one have been typologically identified by contemporary scholars. All musical instruments used by ancient Hebrews are divided into three categories: wind, stringed-pizzicato, and percussion instruments. The group of wind instruments included various types of horn (*shofar, keren, yubel, karna*), the trumpet (*khatsotsra*), and wooden wind instruments (*khalil, ugab, mashrokita*). The group of stringed instruments includes lyres (*kinnor, katros*), harps (*nebel, sabbkha*), zithers

Background: Music in Ancient Israel and Ancient Greece

(*asor*), and lutes (*psanterin*, from the Greek *psaltirion*, ψαλτήριον). The percussion group includes various types of drums, bells, and cymbals (*tof, menaanim, shalishim, tseltselim* or *metsiltaim, mtsillot* and *paamonim*).[3]

Each of these instruments was rather primitive and could produce only one or a few sounds. As their basic function was to accompany choral or solo singing, the instruments had an auxiliary significance. The sound of musical instruments blended with the singing of the choir during festive liturgical ceremonies and often increased the power of human voices. In particular, the description of the consecration of the temple in Jerusalem by King Solomon makes reference to this:

> ... when the priests went out of the holy place ... all the singing Levites—all of them[4] ... of them that were clothed in linen garments, with cymbals and lutes and harps, were standing before the altar, and with them a hundred and twenty priests, blowing trumpets. And there was one voice in the trumpeting and in the psalm-singing, and in the loud utterance with one voice to give thanks and praise the Lord; and when they raised their voice together with trumpets and cymbals, and instruments of music, and said, Thanks to the Lord, for he is good, for his mercy endures forever.[5] Then the house was filled with the cloud of the glory of the Lord. And the priests could not stand to minister because of the cloud: for the glory of the Lord filled the house of God (2 Chr 5.11–14).

How literally should we understand the expression "there was one voice"? Does it mean that the voices of the singers and musical instruments sounded in unison? Or is this a simple metaphor used to emphasize that "the ensemble, considerable in size and quite diverse in its collection of instruments and timbrels, sounded very harmonious and organized as if it were a single voice or a single instrument"?[6] Unfortunately, it is not likely that we will ever have a precise answer to this question because concrete samples of ancient Hebrew musical arts have not survived.

However, there is a sound basis to assert that despite the presence of diverse musical instruments, their playing, which accompanied singing, was not at all

---

[3]Yelena Kolyada, David J. Clark, trans., *A Compendium of Musical Instruments and Instrumental Terminology in the Bible* (London and Oakville, CT: Equinox Publishing: 2009), 28. See also Archpriest Vasily Metallov, "Music and Musical Instruments of the Ancient Hebrews" in *Readings of the Society of Lovers of Ancient Written Languages* (1912), Nos. 6, 7, 8.

[4]The fact that all two hundred and eighty-eight psalm-singing Levites participated in the ceremony is emphasized here.

[5]An allusion to a specific psalm sung during the consecration of the temple (Psalm 135).

[6]Martynov, *History*, 22.

similar either to what is well known today by the name *polyphony* or to homophonic-harmonic music. In ancient Israel the principle of *single-voice* (unison) lay at the foundation of singing and the playing of music instruments; melody was created from an extremely limited quantity of sounds. Such music naturally developed from psalmodic cantillation—the intoned reading of prayers or sacred texts. According to one scholar, the most characteristic elements of ancient Hebraic music were:

> . . . a *"single-voice"* character, the result of being founded in a vocal origin; the presence of characteristic "melodic models"; *improvisationality* . . . and the huge role of melismatic *ornamentation*, which is linked with the oral transmission of tunes; characteristic division of tunes into *psalmodic recitation* and vividly expressive, rhythmic, well-defined tunes of a hymnodic character linked with dancing and marching, which were accompanied by hand-clapping, dances, and keeping the beat on small drums.[7]

The given conclusion is based on research conducted at the dawn of the twentieth century by Jerusalem's cantor Abraham Zevi Idelsohn who learned singing in the synagogue communities of Yemen and several regions of the former Assyro-Babylonian kingdom. "As if frozen in time," these communities "preserved the traditions of temple music from the time of the first temple in a fully untouched state. The simple, strict, and exalted melodies of these communities' songs, rarely departing from the boundaries of the perfect fourth and built on the steps of diatonic harmony with avoidance of half steps, have very little in common with contemporary singing in synagogues."[8]

The period of the Babylonian captivity was a time of spiritual and cultural decline for the Israelites. Without a doubt, this decline affected music as well, including singing in divine services. This was reflected in the words of a psalm:

> By the rivers of Babylon, there we sat and wept when we remembered Zion. Upon the willows in her midst, we hung up our musical instruments; for there our captors asked us for words from our songs, and those who carried us off said to us, "Sing us the songs of Zion." How shall we sing the Lord's song in a foreign land? (Ps 136.1–4).

---

[7]R. Gruber, *General History of Music*, 1, 2nd edition (Moscow, 1960), 86–87. All italics are the author's.

[8]Martynov, *History*, 26.

Background: Music in Ancient Israel and Ancient Greece

It is evident that for the Jews music was inseparably linked with the divine services, and the divine services were linked with the temple and in a wider sense with the homeland, Israel. Jews neither had nor could even imagine a musical culture separate from the temple and the homeland. Moreover, the phrases "songs of Zion" and "the Lord's song" are synonymous which indicates that secular music *as such* did not exist in the understanding of the ancient Jews. All music, whether during divine services or not, was of a religious character.

The return from the Babylonian exile and the restoration of the temple called to life a new flourishing of musical arts. The divine services of the period of the second temple were distinguished by no less majesty than those during the reigns of David and Solomon. In the Book of Wisdom of Jesus, the Son of Sirach, the festive offering of sacrifice during the time of the High Priest Simon II, the Son of Onias II (*c.* 230–195 BC) is described:

> There was Simon, the high priest and son of Onias, who repaired the house during his life and strengthened the temple in his days. . . . When he received the portion from the hands of the priests while standing by the hearth of the altar, a crown of brethren surrounding him. . . . Finishing the services at the altars and arranging the offering to the Most High, the Almighty, he stretched out his hand to the cup and poured a libation of the blood of the grapes. He poured it out on the foundation of the altar, a fragrant scent to the King of all, the Most High. Then the sons of Aaron cried out, sounding out the trumpets of hammered work, a great noise to be heard as a remembrance before the Most High. Then all the people hastened in common and fell with their faces on the ground to worship their Lord, the Almighty God, the Most High. The singers also praised him with their voices, and their song was sweetened with a variety of sounds. The people also prayed to the Lord Most High, in prayer before the Merciful One, until the order of the Lord was ended and they finished his liturgy (Sir 50.1, 12, 14–19).

Musical Arts of Antiquity

While our information about the musical culture of Israel is extremely scant, being drawn mainly from individual references in the Bible concerning music, musicians, and musical instruments, the situation is considerably better in relation to the musical arts of antiquity. First of all, numerous musical tracts survive, and these give a fairly full picture of the attitudes of the ancient Greeks concerning music. Second, images of musical instruments may be seen on amphoras and vases, bas-reliefs and frescoes, and these images allow for the reproduction of their external appearance. (Also, a certain number of musical instruments have been discovered during excavations, such as in Pompeii, for example.) Third, individual samples of antique musical compositions have been preserved. These were written down using letter notation and have been deciphered, albeit somewhat tentatively.

Music played an important role in the life of the ancient Greeks. There existed solo music and ensemble music, instrumental and choral. Dances, feasts, theatrical presentations, community celebrations, athletic contests (especially the Olympic Games), and funerals were all accompanied by music. Music sounded even on the battle field. It is well known, for example, that the Spartans entered into battle with a song sounding under the accompaniment of the *aulos*.

Scenes from the Cult of Dionysus. Greek Vase.

Worship services in pagan temples and various "mysteries" were accompanied by choral singing and the playing of musical instruments. In particular, trumpets, flutes, lyres, and percussion instruments were sounded during the performance of the Eleusinian Mysteries.[9] Playing the flute accompanied the sacrificial offering in honor of Apollo, who was considered the protector of musicians and poets. The use of cymbals and bells was characteristic of the cult of Dionysus. The participation of musicians in pagan cults is spoken of in literary sources and seen in painted images as well as bas-reliefs and sculptures preserved from the era of antiquity. There is a depiction of a sacrificial offering to Dionysius on a Greek vase exhibited in the National Archeological Museum of Naples. In the middle is seen an altar with a burning fire. Behind it a priestess prepares to sacrifice an animal, and to her left two dancing women hold cymbals and bells. On one of the friezes of the Parthenon a depiction of a cultic procession is seen, and four flutists and four *kitharodes* participate in the procession.[10]

Maenad Playing a Double Aulos. Cup. AD 410.

---

[9] Dieter Lauenstein, *The Eleusinian Mysteries* (Moscow, 1996), 232.
[10] Johannes Quasten, *Music and Worship in Pagan and Christian Antiquity* (Washington, 1983), 3–4.

As in ancient Israel, stringed, wind, and percussion instruments were used in ancient Greece. The *kithara* and the lyre (whose predecessor was the *phorminx*), were types of stringed-plucked instruments. Originally the kithara had four strings but by the middle of the seventh century BC it had seven and later the number of strings increased to eighteen.[11] A common type of wind instrument was the double aulos—two conical pipes made from reed or wood (sometimes even from bone or metal). The musician would blow into both pipes simultaneously, producing higher sounds from the pipe on the right and lower sounds from the pipe on the left. Instruments such as the flute were popular, including the multi-barreled "flute of Pan"—an instrument consisting of several pipes of different length. Each pipe could produce only a single particular sound. Several types of trumpet, prepared from the horns of animals, copper, iron, or ivory, were used during military operations and also to accompany several cultural ceremonies. Percussion instruments included various types of drums and bells including timbrels, sistra, cymbals, crotala (similar to castanets), and others.

As in other ancient musical cultures, vocal music played a central role in Greece. The art of rhapsody (Gk. *rhapsodos*, ῥαψωδός) was greatly popular. This literally signifies the "one who stitches together songs" and combined both composer and singer in a single person. Good singing was extremely prevalent. Men's, women's, and youth choirs all existed. Solo and choir singing could alternate in musical-choreographical compositions; antiphonal singing was used and music was accompanied by dancing. (For example, the odes of Pindar were performed in this way.)

Unlike ancient Israel, from which no examples of musical-theoretical thought have survived, a huge significance was attached to the theoretical arrangement of acoustic phenomena in ancient Greece. Philosophers, historians, and mathematicians all wrote about music. In the ranks of special musical-theoretical tracts belong, in particular, *The Elements of Harmony* by Aristoxenus (354–300 BC), *On Music* by Pseudo-Plutarch (AD 45–125), *Harmonics* by Claudius Ptolemy (AD 83–161), and the commentaries of Porphyrius (254–203) on the essay *Divisions of the Canon* by Pseudo-Euclid. The works of Plato and Aristotle contain discussions concerning music. An excellent example is the treatise *Against the Musicians* by Sextus Empiricus. The treatise seeks to make a criticism of the major postulates of antique music theory. Antique music theory continued to develop even in the Middle Ages in the West. In particular, Saint Augustine (*c.* 354–430), Boethius (480–524), and George

---

[11]Gruber, *History*, vol. 1, 94.

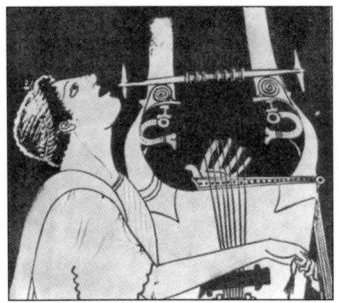

Kitharode. Amphora. 490 BC.

Pachymeres (1242–c. 1310) were authors of treatises dedicated to the music theory of antiquity.

The terminology of antique music is connected with playing plucked stringed instruments. The sound of a particular pitch—the lowest building block of a musical phrase—was given the term *tonos* (τόνος—tone), originating from the verb *teino* (τείνω—to pull, stretch). The understanding of a tone indicated the particular tension of the strings of a lyre or kithara; a difference between the tones arose due to the different tensions of strings. The distance between two neighboring tones was given the term *diastema* (διάστημα—interval). Some intervals were perceived as consonance while others as dissonance. "Musicians refer to the first and smallest consonant intervals as a perfect fourth. The next largest is called a perfect fifth and larger yet is a perfect octave. In this same way the smallest dissonant interval is called diesis,[12] the second is called a semitone, which is double in relation to diesis, and the third is called a tone, double in relation to the semitone."[13]

Consonances, including three or four neighboring sounds, were called, correspondingly, trichords (Gk. *trichordos*, τρίχορδος—literally "three-stringed") and tetrachords (Gk. *tetrachordos*, τετράχορδος—literally "four-stringed"). The term "symphony" (Gk. *symphonia*, συμφωνία—"consonance," or "agreement") could be used to signify a tetrachord.

The tetrachord was the basic constructional element of the musical phrase. According to Plato, "all harmonies are formed from four sounds."[14] The principle of the tetrachord was applied to all types of music—not only instrumental but vocal as well.

The main difference between ancient Greek music and contemporary western European music lies precisely in the principle of the tetrachord. As Evgeny Gertsman emphasizes, "in antiquity all sonar space was differentiated in tetrachords while contemporary musical thought subdivides into octaves. In the first case all the harmonic steps are separated from one another by a perfect fourth while in the second—by a perfect octave."[15] Therefore, even in the rare cases when it is

---

[12] A quarter tone.
[13] Sextus Empiricus *Against the Musicians* 4 (*Essays*, vol. 2, 200).
[14] Plato *The Republic* III 400.
[15] Evgeny Gertsman, *Antique Musical Thought* (Moscow, 1986), 38.

Background: Music in Ancient Israel and Ancient Greece

possible to reproduce samples of ancient Greek music, the hearing of the contemporary person is not capable of perceiving the logic of the musical thought of ancient authors. In Gertsman's opinion, artistic contacts are impossible between civilizations that are as separated as the civilizations of antiquity and contemporary Western Europe:

> (This is) due to changes that took place in the language of music, which has been so greatly modified since ancient times that it has changed into a completely new system of expressing information and intonation. In the best case our contemporary can hear a series of sounds placed in an order and pitch set by an ancient composer. The functional connections between (the sounds) and the logic of the musical material's motion—the very content of the work—remains out of reach.[16]

Tetrachords are conjoined between themselves either "by division"—that is, with the help of a single dividing tone (such that two tetrachords comprise an octave), or "by joining"—without such a dividing tone (such that the upper sound of the lower tetrachord became the lower sound of the upper tetrachord). The maximum number of tetrachords joined in a "Perfect System" was five and encompassed the musical space of two perfect octaves and a perfect fourth. This space corresponded with what the ancient Greeks considered to be the maximum range of the human voice (Gk. *topos fonis*, τόπος φωνῆς— in the expression of Cleonides). "It was thought that the human voice, if one considers its lowest and its highest tone, is equal in register to that which we would now call two octaves while Greek music theorists called it five tetrachords, one directly following the next, beginning from the lowest and ending with the highest tone."[17]

"The Perfect System" was comprised of five tetrachords: lower, middle-range, disjunctive, upper, and conjunctive. Translated into contemporary musical notation this system appears in the following way[18]:

| Low Tetrachord | Middle Tetrachord | Dividing Tetrachord | Upper Tetrachord | Connected Tetrachord |

---

[16]Ibid., 15.
[17]Aleksei Losev, *History of Ancient Aesthetics: Early Hellenism* (Moscow, 2000), 623.
[18]Gertsman, *Thought*, 71.

The lowest sound of the system was called *proslambanomenos* (προσλαμβανόμενος, from Gk. *proslambano*, προσλαμβάνω—to take to oneself, to join) and was not a part of the tetrachords.

The Perfect System was divided into two smaller systems—the greater and lesser. The Greater Perfect System was identical to the Perfect System except for the three upper sounds, which were absent in it (that is, there was no tetrachord connected to it). The Lesser Perfect System was comprised of three tetrachords:

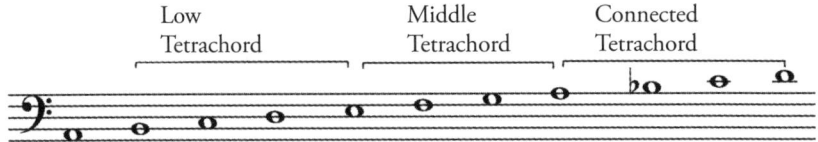

The basic and most ancient core of the Perfect System were two tetrachords—the middle tetrachord and the dividing tetrachord. Similar tetrachords were added in a later period. This is shown by the fact that the names of the sounds found in the later elements are the same as the names of the sounds of the two central tetrachords.

For an understanding of the meaning and logic of the cited scales it is above all necessary to consider the melodic identity of the steps which have the same names as each of the tetrachords. In the consciousness of the ancient Greek the first step of the low tetrachord was identical to the first step of the middle tetrachord while the second step of the dividing tetrachord was identical to the second step of the upper tetrachord. (In exactly the same way, in the consciousness of the contemporary European, "*do*" of the second octave is identical to the "*do*" of the first octave, and "*mi*" of the first octave is identical to "*mi*" of the second octave). In this way, in two tetrachords conjoined "by unison," chords of perfect fourths are melodically identical, while in tetrachords conjoined "in disjunction," these became perfect fifths.[19]

It is necessary also to bear in mind that for the ancient Greeks the concept of a scale's absolute pitch did not exist. Each human voice could encompass the space of several tetrachords, but the low sound (Gk. *proslambanomenos*, προσλαμβανόμενος) was unique to each voice. Exactly the same situation existed with musical instruments whose strings were tuned in relation to the pitch of one of its strings, but

---

[19] In the Lesser Perfect System cited above, melodically identical (in rising order) are: 1. "B, E, A"; 2. "C, F, B-flat"; 3. "D, G, C." In the contemporary system melodically identical are: 1. "B, E, B, E, A" 2. "C, F, C, F, B-flat' "; 3. "D, G, D, G, C"; 4. "E, A, E, A, D."

Background: Music in Ancient Israel and Ancient Greece

an absolute pitch for the string did not exist. It stands to reason that in the case when several human voices and/or several musical instruments were sounded, the low sound of the entire ensemble was the same, which imparted smoothness and harmony to the ensemble.

It is also important to bear in mind that the cited scale relates to the diatonic type (manner, inclination) in which each tetrachord is comprised of the sequence *semitone—tone—tone*. Besides the diatonic type, there were also the chromatic and enharmonic types. The first was built on the basis of the sequence *semitone—semitone—tone-and-semitone*, while the second included two quarter-tones and one interval in two tones.

Finally, it is necessary to bear in mind for the benefit of the reader (and in view of the comparison with scales of Old Russian Church singing that will follow) that the scale cited above is presented in the form of a sequence from the lower sounds to the higher ones, while the ancient Greeks themselves constructed tetrachords and octave scales in the opposite order—from the higher to the lower. This was connected to the general aesthetic arrangement in which the movement of melody from the higher sounds to the lower ones was perceived as more beautiful than the movement in the opposite direction. Aristotle discussed this in one of his treaties:

> The high note is *worse* than the low one.[20]

> Why does the low sound have more significance than the high one? Because the low one is *greater*: it resembles a blunt corner, while the higher sound resembles a sharp one.[21]

> The lower sound is *great* because it is *strong*.[22]

> Why is the (movement) from top to bottom more beautiful than the movement from bottom to top? . . . Because *the lower sound in comparison with the high sound is more noble and more noble-sounding.*[23]

In order to determine the interval connecting the extreme sounds of two conjoined tetrachords, the term *dia pason* (διὰ πασῶν—literally "through all") is used,

---

[20] Pseudo-Aristotle, Problems XIX 26.
[21] Ibid., 8.
[22] Ibid., 12–13.
[23] Ibid., 33. All four citations are translated from the Russian translation of A.F. Losev in his book *History of Ancient Aesthetics: Early Hellenism* (Moscow, 2000), 668. Italics appear as they do in Losev's translation.

Scene of a Feast. C. 480 BC. Munich. Glyptothek.

Scene of a Feast. Beginning of Fifth Century BC. British Museum.

from which the contemporary Russian word *diapason* (range) is derived. For two tetrachords conjoined "in conjunction," the term indicated a major seventh. For two tetrachords conjoined "in division," *dia pason* (διὰ πασῶν) formed a perfect octave.[24] The understanding of "range" was above all necessary to determine the overall volume of sounds whose extraction was possible for stringed-pizzicato instruments (the lyre and kithara). The most common number of strings for a musical instrument was seven, which also comprised a full "range" of the instrument which included two tetrachords conjoined "in conjunction."

The basis of musical thought for the ancient Greeks was unison—the sounding of different voices in a single tone. The understanding of "harmony" (Gk. *harmonia*, ἁρμονία) was not of the simultaneous combination of several sounds of different pitch but rather of the combination of neighboring sounds in the framework of a single melodic line. Such an aesthetic standard was linked, primarily, to the vocal nature of antique music.[25] At the basis of this music lay the human voice, whose range does not exceed four or at the most five tetrachords. A choir was considered to be a human voice strengthened by other similar voices. The playing of musical instruments also was perceived as an acoustic strengthening of the human voice: the range of musical instruments corresponded to the range of the voice.

Did singing with two or three voices exist in antiquity? Some scholars suppose that voices of different ranges (for example, men's and women's) could sing in a perfect octave.[26] As we have seen, the perfect octave, together with the perfect fourth and perfect fifth, was considered to be a "consonant" interval[27], and therefore the making of melody in parallel octaves could be perceived as unison. Furthermore, the design of several musical instruments invites the supposition that two different sounds were made simultaneously. Consequently, singing in two voices existed in

[24]Gertsman, *Thought*, 71.
[25]See Losev, *Aesthetics*, 697.
[26]Losev, *Aesthetics*, 697.
[27]Gertsman, *Thought*, 87.

Background: Music in Ancient Israel and Ancient Greece

the music of ancient Greeks (at least in instrumental music). In particular, musicians could make double notes while playing the double aulos.

The understanding of the ancient Greeks concerning modes deserves special attention. In contemporary musicology the term *mode* is used to denote the various principles of sound organization within the framework of a single octave. Moreover, in the early stage of development of ancient Greek music, differences in modes indicated the various locations of sounds within a single tetrachord. Three basic variants of constructing a tetrachord in the framework of diatonic scale existed: 1. Lydian (tone—tone—semitone) (or step, step, half-step); 2. Phrygian (tone—semitone—tone); 3. Dorian (semitone—tone—tone). Translated into contemporary musical notation, these tetrachords appear in the following way:

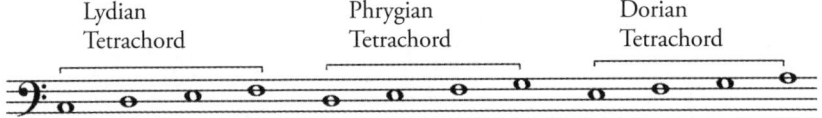

These were the very tetrachords which comprised the original Greek mode (*mode* in the Greek language was signified by the term *genos* (γένος) which literally means *generation*). Ptolemy calls tetrachords "accords of perfect fourth," adding to them also four "accords of perfect fifth" (semitone—tone—tone—tone; tone—tone—tone—semitone; tone—tone—semitone—tone; tone—semitone—tone—tone.)[28] From the cited tetrachords and pentachords—in their conjoining one to another—octave constructions were developed which are now called melodies and which were called "octave types" (Gk. *dia pason eidi*, διὰ πασῶν εἴδη) by ancient Greek theorists. Cleonides, the author of *Introduction to Harmonics*, considered there to be seven "octave types" or modes: Mixolydian, Lydian, Phrygian, Dorian, Hypolydian, Hypophrygian, and Hypodorian.[29]

Ancient Greek music theory examined in each of the modes a special, unique-to-itself spiritual-moral content, a special character called *ethos* (ἦθος). In particular, the Dorian mode, as a brave and festive, was juxtaposed with the Phrygian mode as ecstatic and sensual. But the views of musicologists and philosophers concerning the ethos of certain modes essentially differ from one another. So, for example, Plato considered that the Mixolydian mode, the strict Lydian, and several other modes were marked by lamentations and therefore "they need to be removed"

---

[28]Gertsman, *Thought*, 77.
[29]See Gertsman, *Thought*, 69–70.

Procession in Honor of Dionysus.
Detail of a Frieze.

since "they are not useful even for women, who should be decent; all the more so they are not useful for men." Ionian and Lydian modes, according to Plato, "make one effeminate and are akin to drinking songs": these modes should not be used by warriors. The only admissible modes are Dorian and Phrygian.[30] As usual, all of these assertions of Plato were attributed to the lips of Socrates.

Aristotle, on the other hand, deemed only the Dorian mode to be of use in education, as well as perhaps a few of the other modes "if approved by those concerned with the teaching of philosophy and musical education." Aristotle believed that "Socrates in the *Republic* is not correct when he asserted that only the Phrygian mode is on the same level as the Dorian mode; the more so as he excludes the flute from among musical instruments. After all, the Phrygian mode can be compared to the flute: both have an orgiastic, passionate character." The Dorian mode, in the words of Aristotle, "is marked by the greatest peacefulness," and it "for the most part differs by its courageous character." Aristotle deemed also that "for people exhausted by the many years of life, it is not easy to sing in tense modes; for such people nature itself suggests the necessity of turning to songs composed in languid modes. For this reason several experts of music issued a basic reproach to Socrates for not teaching the languid modes." Aristotle considered another mode unfairly excluded by Socrates from the process of education to be the Lydian mode "which is decent for children for the very reason that it enables, aside from education, the development of good manners."[31]

Rhythm was given an important constructive significance in ancient Greek music. Prosodic rhythm was employed for vocal music, formed in accordance with poetic measures based on the principle of alternating long and short syllables.[32] In this music one measure (we may conditionally call it a quarter) corresponded

---

[30]Plato *The Republic* III 398e–399b.
[31]Aristotle *Politics* VIII 7, 1341b–1342c.
[32]A binary measure—pyhrric—contained two short syllables. Ternary measures included the *iamb* (one short followed by one long syllable), *trochee* (one long followed by one short) and *tribrach* (three short syllables). Quaternary measures were the *dactyl* (one long syllable followed by two short syllables), the *anapaest* (two short syllables followed by one long syllable), and the *spondee* (two long syllables). See Zacharias Paschalidis, *Byzantine Church Music: Brief Theory and Practice* (Moscow, 2004), 34.

Background: Music in Ancient Israel and Ancient Greece

to each short syllable while a double measure (we will call it a half) corresponded to each long syllable.

In the conception of the ancient Greeks, rhythm possessed its own character and ethos—its own moral content. In discussing various rhythms, Plato asserted that "it is not necessary to seek out their diversity and their many possible dimensions; rather, it is necessary to determine which rhythms correspond to a humble and courageous life." Some measures "are befitting of expressions of meanness, insolence, insanity, and other wicked characteristics," while others "must be left for the expression of the opposite states." In Plato's opinion, there exists "an accordance between comeliness and rhythm, on the one hand, and ugliness and lack of rhythm, on the other."[33]

To make a record of works of music in Ancient Greece there existed notational signs (*semeia*, σημεῖα), which appeared around the third century BC (some scholars even ascribe the invention of musical notation to the seventh century BC). At the basis of the notation lay the combination of letters or special signs which helped to indicate the distance between sounds.[34] Ancient letter notation existed right up to the end of the age of antiquity (that is, up to and including the fourth century), and in the opinion of some scholars, right up to the late Byzantine age; that is, up to the eighth and ninth centuries[35] when another type of notation—neume notation—was already in use.

More than fifty papyri containing fragments of notational records of ancient music have survived to the present day. The majority of these date to the period beginning in the third century BC through the third century AD. Many fragments have been deciphered, although transcriptions are always more-or-less hypothetical. In all cases we are dealing with samples of unison music. The structure of the melodies is tetrachordal; that is, the music "steps in place" on a few neighboring sounds. A descending motion is prevalent in the melody while its rhythm is determined by the rhythm of the verse.

A survey of ancient music theory was necessary because the basic elements of ancient Greek music were to be preserved in early Christian music and Byzantine musical arts. Moreover, several of these elements were later to be incorporated into ancient Russian church singing. The discussion that follows concerns these subjects.

---

[33] Plato *The Republic* III 399e–400c.

[34] Two different methods of notation were used for instrumental and for vocal music: in the first case notation consisted of signs while in the other it consisted of letters. Letter notation reproduced sound-pitch fluctuations in the melodic line but did not indicate its rhythmic characteristics.

[35] See Evgeny Gertsman, *Mysteries from the History of Ancient Music* (St Petersburg, 2006), 386–388.

II

Early Christian and Byzantine Church Singing

Early Christian Music. The Teaching of the
Holy Fathers Regarding Music and Singing

THE AVAILABLE INFORMATION CONCERNING early Christian music is so scant and fragmented that it is possible to form only a very general and most approximate picture concerning it. In view of the complete absence of musical manuscripts from the period from the fourth through the ninth century, it is impossible to establish the degree to which early Byzantine singing derived from Hebrew music or the music of late antiquity.[1] Nevertheless, the very fact that it did indeed derive from earlier sources hardly needs to be argued.

One may suppose that in the community of Christ's disciples one sang melodies that were characteristic of the synagogue and temple worship of the time. When the Savior and his disciples celebrated the Mystical Supper, "when they had sung a hymn, they went out to the Mount of Olives" (Mt 26.30). The words "when they had sung a hymn" (Gk. *hymnesantes*, ὑμνήσαντες) indicates the singing of a certain well known hymn, most likely a psalm. There can be no doubt that at this stage in the disciples' community, they did not have their own melodies, different from those which were heard at the divine services of the Jews.

A little more than a quarter century after the Mystical Supper (*c.* 61–63), the apostle Paul, addressing the Christians in Ephesus wrote: "And do not be drunk with wine, in which is dissipation; but be filled with the Spirit, speaking to one another in psalms and hymns and spiritual songs (ψαλμοῖς καὶ ὕμνοις καὶ ᾠδαῖς πνευματικαῖς), singing and making melody in your heart to the Lord . . ." (Eph 5.18–19). Paul gave the same advice to the Colossians (Col 3.16). This concerns three musical genres—psalms, hymns, and spiritual songs (odes). It is hardly possible now to establish with certainty what difference existed between these genres. It is fully probable that the term *psalms* indicated the Old Testament psalms while the

---

[1]Alexander Lingas, *Byzantine Empire: Church Singing* (Moscow, 2004), 355.

terms *hymns* and *songs* related to works of early Christian poetry and music. Some suppose that psalms were performed in the ancient Hebrew language while hymns and spiritual songs were performed in the Greek language.[2] However, the use of two languages simultaneously during early Christian divine services does not seem very likely to us. (Without a doubt, Christians—for whom the Greek language was the basic language—would use psalms translated in the Septuagint and not in an unknown original language.)

The term "psalm" is used also in other epistles of the apostle Paul. In one of them he writes, "Whenever you come together, each of you has a psalm, has a teaching, has a tongue, has a revelation, has an interpretation . . . " (1 Cor 14.26), Here the "psalm" is viewed in the same vein as other products of the creative work of individual Christians. Is it possible that the text of a psalm was composed by the Christian himself? Or that a member of the community took an Old Testament psalm and independently set it to music? Or, finally, could it be that a member of the Church community was permitted (or requested) to perform a particular psalm by using an established melody or even an element of improvisation before delivering a teaching or speaking in an unknown language?

We are inclined to accept the third possibility. After all, it is evident that the solo singing of psalms played an important role in the Christian divine services during the times of the apostle Paul. His mention of psalms in the given context is surely connected with this. But no less evident is that improvisation was widely practiced in the early Christian Church. Texts of prayers as well as tunes could emerge spontaneously, at the moment of utterance or singing. Tertullian wrote, "After the washing of hands and the lighting of lamps, each is invited to the center to praise the Lord in songs, each one as he is able—from Holy Scripture or from his heart."[3] Praise in songs "from Holy Scripture" is nothing other than the reading of psalms while praise in songs "from one's heart" is improvised singing.

If the same melodies heard in the temple or synagogues were used in the Judeo-Christian community during the performance of psalms, what melodies were used by Christians who emerged from pagan roots and were not acquainted with Jewish tradition but were raised in the traditions of ancient Greek music? There is solid reason to suppose that melodic intonations characteristic of ancient Greek music were used during the performance of Christian hymns prior to the emergence of specifically Christian melodies. Christian melodies would have resembled antique

---

[2] Andrew Wilson-Dickson, *The Story of Christian Music* (Moscow, 2001), 29.
[3] Tertullian *Apology* 39.

singing in their intonational structure when they began to appear. And prior to the appearance of Byzantine neume notation, it was possible to write down such hymns by using antique letter notation.

An excerpt from a hymn to the Holy Trinity discovered on an Egyptian papyrus from the third century (Papyrus Oxyrhynchus 1786) serves as a confirmation of this. This hymn is a simple diatonic melody in the Dorian mode, written in antique letter (vocal) notation. The question of the melody's origin remains unanswered: is it a Christian melody, written in antique letters, or a pagan melody with a Christian text? And another question remains: is the hymn intended for liturgical use or for singing in a domestic setting? The former suggestion seems more likely but the answer is not clear. Whatever the case, the hymn to the Holy Trinity is the only sample known to scholars in which Christian music is set to antique musical letter notation.[4]

No information exists concerning the use of musical instruments during early Christian divine services and there are convincing reasons to believe that the Church in the East most consciously rejected the use of instruments at the earliest stage of its existence. There are several reasons for this.

First, musical instruments were viewed as tools necessary only for people who did not possess a good voice. In the words of Gregory of Nyssa, "A person who has been instructed in music but because of a physical imperfection does not possess his own voice, who wishes to show his skill, resorts speedily to artificial voices for melodies—the flute and lyre—and in this way he makes his skill evident to others." Indeed in the sounding of the human voice, "it is as if the music of the flute and lyre are mixed and simultaneously emit a concerted sound."[5]

Second, music in churches was perceived as something auxiliary and secondary in relation to uttered words. For this reason, musical instruments, incapable of reproducing words, were rejected as completely unneeded. Saint Gregory of Nyssa wrote: "From musical instruments only sounds can be delivered to a person's hearing, but with singing the melody of the tune as well as the individual words are simultaneously heard; words are necessarily lost when instruments are played alone."[6]

---

[4]See A.W.J. Hollemann, "Oxyrhynchus Papyrus 1786 and the Relationship between Ancient Greek and Early Christian Music," *Vigiliae Christianae* 26. No 1 (1972), 1–17; Gertsman, *Mysteries of History of Ancient Music* (St Petersburg, 2006), 342–344.
[5]Gregory of Nyssa *On the Making of Man* 9. PG 44, 149C.
[6]Idem, *Concerning the Inscriptions of Psalms* 2, 3. PG 44, 495D–496A.

Third and last, in the understanding of Christians converted from paganism, musical instruments were closely linked with pagan worship and the cultural tradition rejected by them when they became Christians. This is confirmed by numerous references in early Christian authors concerning musical instruments as fixtures of pagan worship and indecent feasts. Saint Clement of Alexandria, in particular, wrote:

> For revelry is an inebriating pipe. . . . For if people occupy their time with pipes, and psalteries, and choirs, and dances . . . they become quite immodest and intractable, beat on cymbals and drums, and make a noise on instruments of delusion . . . Let the pipe be resigned to the shepherds, and the flute to the superstitious who are engrossed in idolatry. For, in truth, such instruments are to be banished from the temperate banquet, being more suitable to beasts than men, and the more irrational portion of mankind. For we have heard of stags being charmed by the pipe, and seduced by music into the toils, when hunted by the huntsmen. And when mares are being covered, a tune is played on the flute—a nuptial song, as it were. . . . For the various spells of the broken strains and plaintive numbers of the Carian muse corrupt men's morals, drawing to perturbation of mind, by the licentious and mischievous art of music.[7]

In Clement's words, "man is truly a pacific instrument; while you will find, if you investigate, that other instruments are warlike." Various nations used musical instruments for the rousing of a bellicose spirit but "the one instrument of peace, the Word alone by which we honor God, is what we employ. We no longer employ the ancient psaltery, and trumpet, and timbrel, and flute, which those expert in war and contemners of the fear of God were wont to make use of also in the choruses at their festive assemblies."[8]

No less categorical in his rejection of musical instruments was Saint Basil the Great. For him the playing of the lyre is synonymous with obscenity and depravity:

> Let this be heard by those who possess at home psalters and lyres in the place of the Gospel! The prophet appeals to them as if to those already dead, in co-suffering of love lamenting their death. "Woe to them," he says, "(who) drink wine with harp, and psaltery, and drums, and pipes."[9] And you have a

---

[7]Clement of Alexandria *Pedagogue* 2, 4. <http://www.ccel.org/ccel/schaff/anf02.vi.iii.ii.iv.html>, Jan. 24, 2014.
[8]Ibid.
[9]Is 5.11–12 (LXX). These verses are cited in the twenty-second canon of the 7th Ecumenical Council,

lyre adorned with gold and ivory lying on some exalted altar, like some kind of carved image or idol of demons. And some poor woman, rather than learning how to operate a spindle, by the necessity of slavery, is taught by you how to stretch her hands out to a lyre for which you, perhaps, paid money and gave it for the teaching of some other woman who first with her own body served all sorts of obscenities and now for young virgins became a teacher of such things . . . There she is with the lyre; she lays it on her fingers in order to extract its sounds; her hands are bare, her face without shame. The whole assembly of those feasting turns towards her; all eyes focus on her; ears are pricked awaiting a sound; noise is quieted; laughter ceases; not an idle conversation can be heard where hitherto one tried to rise above the another; all in the house are silent, enchanted by the sweet and passionate playing . . . A pitiful spectacle for the eyes of the chaste—the woman sits not behind a weaver's loom but with a lyre in her hands; she is known not by her own husband but is seen by strangers; she has made herself common property; she sings not a psalm of confession but adulterous songs; she prays not to God but makes haste to Gehenna; she strives not to the church of God but rather expels others from it along with herself![10]

Muse Playing the Kithara. Amphora. 445 BC.

Neither did Western authors spare expressive words in denouncing the playing of musical instruments. At the turn of the fourth century, Arnobius wrote about musicians in the following way:

> That they should swell out their cheeks in blowing the flute; that they should take the lead in singing impure songs . . . and raising the loud din of the castanets,[11] by which another crowd of souls should be led in their wantonness to abandon themselves to clumsy motions, to dance and sing . . . raising their haunches and hips.[12]

which states that it is inadmissible for Christians to partake of food "with satanic songs and with female singers and licentious soundings."

[10] Basil the Great *Commentary on Exodus* 5.11.
[11] Castanets are a type of percussion instrument.
[12] Arnobius *Against the Heathen* 2, 42. http://www.intratext.com/IXT/ENG1008/_P2.HTM. Jan. 24, 2014.

Authors of the fourth century, including Basil the Great, Gregory the Theologian, and John Chrysostom, insist that the playing of musical instruments is unbefitting of Christians in their daily lives at home and all the more so at church. Only a living human voice should sound in the temple of God where the human body replaces the organ and psaltery:

> Let us replace timbrel with spiritual songs, outrageous cries and songs with psalmody, theatrical hand-clapping with thankful hand-clapping and the harmonious movement of hands.[13]

> Here neither psaltery nor tightened strings are needed, neither a bow nor skillfulness, neither some type of musical instruments; but, if you like, it is possible to make oneself a psaltery, mortifying the members of the flesh and tuning the body in harmony with the soul.[14]

> After arising, they[15] immediately stand in a row and sing prophetic hymns with great agreement and melodic harmony. Neither harps, nor pipes, nor any other musical instrument produce such a sound as can be heard in the profound silence and in the desert when these holy people sing. And the songs themselves are fruitful and executed with the love of God.[16]

> Singing by itself is not pleasing to infants (νηπίοις);[17] but singing accompanied by lifeless instruments, dancing, and rattling is. Therefore the use of such instruments is prohibited in churches as well as everything else that is characteristic of children. Only pure singing is permitted because it is pleasing to the soul.[18]

The Church Fathers concluded that the use of instruments in Old Testament worship was possible because of God's "condescension" to the spiritual sickness of the ancient Jews. In the Church of the New Testament, however, musical instruments ought to be replaced with praise, which the Christian sends up with all his being and with all his organs of soul and body. Saint Clement of Alexandria had already interpreted the reference to musical instruments in the psalms allegorically.

---

[13] Gregory the Theologian *Homily no. 5*, 35. SC 309, 366–368. (*Works*, vol.1, 141.)
[14] John Chrysostom *Commentary on Psalm 41* 2. (*Works*, vol. 5. Book 1, 153.)
[15] The monks.
[16] John Chrysostom *Commentary on 1 Timothy* (14.4). PG 62, 576.
[17] νηπίοις, i.e., "fools."
[18] Pseudo-Justin, *Answers to the Orthodox* PG 6, 1354C. This essay is considered spurious (written around AD 400).

In this way, the "sound of a horn" refers to the resurrection of the dead; psaltery refers to the human tongue; the zither refers to the mouth; timbrel refers to the Church; the organ refers to the body; and strings refer to the bodily nerves.[19] Building upon this same allegory, Saint John Chrysostom wrote:

> So just as he urges the Jews to praise God with all the instruments, so he urges us to do so with all our bodily parts—eye, tongue, hearing, hand. . . . Then it is that a person becomes a tuneful lyre, offering to God a kind of harmonious and spiritual melody. Those instruments were entrusted to them at that time for that reason, on account of their frailty and to temper their spirits in line with love and harmony. . . . To cope with their sluggishness, indifference and despondency, God planned to awaken them by this device, injecting the sweetness of the music into the stiffness of their resistance. What is the meaning of "with meaningful cymbal?" (Ps 150.5). He utters the psalms to this effect: they did not recite them simply with a cymbal, nor simply with a lyre; instead, as far as possible they conveyed the meaning of the psalms through cymbals, through trumpets, through lyres, and their zeal and effort in doing this resulted in considerable benefit to them.[20]

Saint Basil the Great indicates that from many musical instruments, King David chose the psaltery for the purpose of accompanying the psalms, "showing with this . . . that it is characteristic of the grace from above, from the Spirit, since it is the only musical instrument whose sound is emitted from the upper part." Saint Basil notes that "sounds of the kithara and lyre are made by hitting the lower part of the strings and the source of stringed rhythms on the psaltery is fixed on the top, so that we would also be inclined to the higher things and not be drawn to the passions of the flesh in submitting to a melody's charm." In this way, "with profound wisdom the prophetic word instructed us by the very structure of an instrument that the way upward is not difficult for souls that are disciplined and harmonious."[21]

All of the above-cited references by authors of the early Church contain criticism of musical instruments not in and of themselves but as inherent attributes of pagan worship or festive pastimes. For this reason instruments were not permitted

---

[19]Clement of Alexandria *The Instructor* 2,4.
[20]John Chrysostom *Commentary on Psalm 150:2*, PG 55, 497–498. In English: St John Chrysostom, *Commentary on the Psalms,* Robert Charles Hill, tr., vol. 2 (Brookline, MA: Holy Cross Orthodox Press, 1998), 382–383.
[21]Basil the Great *Commentary on Psalm 1* (The text is a translation of T. Miller's translation found in the Russian text of the book *Musical Aesthetics*, 105).

in Christian divine services. The musical program of early Christian worship was exclusively vocal and, as we have seen in the citations above, it was the result of a conscious choice made by the Church. The human voice was perceived as an instrument created for praising God and the use of this instrument alone was permitted during worship services.

What were the main characteristic features of church singing according to the teaching of the Fathers of the ancient Church? Above all church music should possess a restrained and prayerful character and should not contain any element of amusement and passion. Clement of Alexandria wrote:

> Let our songs be hymns to God. . . . For temperate harmonies are to be admitted; but we are to banish as far as possible from our robust mind those liquid harmonies, which, through pernicious arts in the modulations of tones, train to effeminacy and scurrility. But grave and modest strains say farewell to the turbulence of drunkenness. Chromatic harmonies are therefore to be abandoned to immodest revels, and to florid and meretricious music.[22]

Saint Gregory of Nyssa. Fresco. 14th c.

In the words of Saint Gregory of Nyssa, "our melodies are created according to other laws than those of people who are ignorant of our wisdom. . . . An unsophisticated melody mingles with divine words so that the very sound and motion of the voice might express a hidden meaning in the words, whatever it may be."[23] The saint's reasonings on music and its meaning for the spiritual life of Christians are interesting:

> Music is fundamental to our very nature. . . . For this very reason the great David added melody to moral teaching. It was as though he watered exalted dogmas with the sweetness of honey, opening up to our nature the possibility of contemplating and healing ourselves in some way . . . Perhaps music is nothing other than a call to a more exalted way of life, which instructs those who are devoted to doing good deeds not to allow in their disposition anything unmusical, uncomely, unharmonious, not to tighten strings more than is necessary lest they break from unnecessary tension, but also not to weaken the strings in pleasures that violate good measure. . . . Generally music teaches how to

---

[22]Clement of Alexandria *The Instructor* 2, 4. <http://www.ccel.org/ccel/schaff/anf02.vi.iii.ii.iv.html.>
[23]Gregory of Nyssa *Treatise on the Inscriptions of the Psalms* 1, 3. PG 44, 444CD

tighten and weaken strings at the proper time and to be watchful that in our way of life the proper melody and rhythm may be steadfastly preserved, avoiding both excessive slackness and unnecessary tension.[24]

The conformity of the melodic makeup of church singing to the way of life prescribed for Christians in the Gospel makes this singing authentically "church singing" that possesses the necessary spiritual and moral charge. For this very reason all perversion and theatricality, all wretchedness and garishness, should be eliminated from church singing. The seventy-fifth canon of the Sixth Ecumenical Council proclaimed:

> We wish those who attend church for the purpose of chanting neither to employ disorderly cries and to force nature to cry out aloud, nor to foist in anything that is not becoming and proper to a church; but, on the contrary, to offer such psalmodies with much attentiveness and contriteness to God, who sees directly into everything that is hidden from our sight.[25]

Singing in church, according to the Church Fathers, should be strictly conducted in unison, reflecting that unity which Christians acquire in the Church, the body of Christ. Saint Ignatius the God-bearer wrote in the second century: "Compose of yourselves a single choir so that, agreeably disposed in oneness of mind, harmoniously beginning a song to God, you may sing it to the Father through Jesus Christ *with one voice*."[26] In the fourth century Saint Athanasius of Alexandria, speaking concerning the divine service in Alexandria, noted that "a single voice is raised up from the many people assembled and calling out to God."[27] In the words of Saint John Chrysostom, "*one voice* should always be heard in the church, because it is one body. For that reason the reader reads by himself . . . and the singer sings by himself; and when all exclaim, their voice is uttered *as if from one mouth*."[28] In the fifth century the author of the *Corpus Areopagiticum* speaks of the "conformity of sound in the divine hymns" which "by means of a unified and single-voiced holy choir" establishes "oneness of mind both in relation to God and in relation to ourselves and each other."[29]

---

[24] Ibid., AB. (Cited in *Musical Aesthetics*, 108–109).
[25] *Rules of the Orthodox Church*, vol. 1 (Moscow, 2001), 566. English translation at <http://www.intratext.com/ixt/eng0835/_P43.HTM>, April 30, 2014.
[26] Ignatius the God-bearer, *Epistle to the Ephesians* 4.
[27] Athanasius of Alexandria, *Apology to Constantine the Emperor* 16. PG 25, 616 (*Works*, vol. 2, 54).
[28] John Chrysostom *Commentary on 1 Cor* 36.6, PG 61, 315 (*Works*, vol. 10, Book 1, 375).
[29] Dionysius the Areopagite *The Ecclesiastical Hierarchy* 3, 3, 5. In all citations in the present paragraph, the italics are our own.

These words show that church singing was conducted in unison not because of any lack of development in the musical arts, but rather because the voices of many people should be united in a single expression of praise to God. Choral singing was perceived not as many voices and many sounds but rather as a single voice sounding from many mouths.

Special professionally trained singers and choirs did not exist when Christian worship services were at the very earliest stages of development. The entire community participated in singing and ordinary members of the community could perform in the role of soloists. The situation gradually changed because the divine service became all the more ceremonial and texts and music acquired a fixed character. Professional singers and choral ensembles became a normal phenomenon in the Christian East after the Edict of Milan issued by Emperor Constantine. The church canons that regulate the duties of readers and singers date exactly to this time. The fifteenth canon of the Council of Laodicea (367) forbids singing in church for all except "canonical singers (κανωνικῶν ψαλτῶν) who ascend the ambo and sing from the books,"[30] (which suggests the fixation of the text and possibly even the melody of the performed hymns). A canonical singer was a person placed in this service by the bishop through the laying-on-of-hands (*cheirothesia*, χειροθεσία). In this way, singers as well as readers were members of the clergy.

Several types of choral singing existed in the early Christian Church. First, the most widespread type was the singing of the entire choir in unison. In particular, hymns of the eucharistic and non-eucharistic divine services were performed in this manner (e.g., "Holy, Holy, Holy," "O Gladsome Light"). Antiphonal singing was widespread; in this style the choir was divided in half and verses from the psalms were performed in alternating fashion by both halves of the choir. There existed also responsorial singing in which the basic melodic phrases were undertaken by the soloist while the choir either repeated them or performed a particular refrain at the end of each phrase.

In the fourth and fifth centuries church music developed simultaneously in both the Christian East and West. There is evidence of direct borrowing of eastern melodies by western churches. In his *Confessions*, Saint Augustine discusses how, not long before his conversion to Christianity, "the church of Milan had only recently begun to employ this mode of consolation and exaltation with all the brethren singing together with great earnestness of voice and heart." The introduction of hymns into the divine services was connected with the persecutions

---

[30]Canon 15 of the Council of Laodicea. Cited in *Canons of the Orthodox Church*, vol. 2, 92.

Early Christian and Byzantine Church Singing

of Saint Ambrose of Milan by the secular authorities. Fearing for his life, a crowd of people spent nights in prayer in the church: "At that time the custom began, after the manner of the Eastern Church, that hymns and psalms should be sung, lest the people be worn out with the tedium of lamentation. This custom, retained from then till now, has been imitated by many, indeed, by almost all thy congregations throughout the rest of the world."[31]

Saint Augustine. Fresco. Lateran. 6th c.

As asserted by Augustine, church singing came to the Christian West from the East in this way. In the same work Augustine states that "Athanasius, bishop of Alexandria . . . required the readers of the psalm to use so slight an inflection of the voice that it was more like speaking than singing."[32] He is referring to psalmodic *cantillation*—the reading of holy texts in a singing voice—from which church music was born. The tradition of cantillation as the basic means of reading Holy Scripture in the church was shared by both East and West.

Saint Augustine was one of the pastors of the ancient Christian Church who recognized the importance and usefulness of church music, its beneficial influence on the soul of a person. Twice he mentions the tears he shed during the performance of church hymns.[33] In the words of Augustine, "our minds are more devoutly and earnestly inflamed in piety by the holy words when they are well sung; poor singing does not render this effect. And I recognize that all the diverse affections of our spirits have their appropriate measures in the voice and song, to which they are stimulated by I know not what secret correlation." And although Augustine considered that the content of the singing is of greater importance than the singing itself, nonetheless when "it is sung with pure voices and in a tune fully appropriate," the usefulness of such singing is evident.[34]

---

[31] Augustine *Confessions* 9, 7. <http://www.ccel.org/a/augustine/confessions/confessions-bod.html> May 1, 2014.
[32] Ibid., 10, 33.
[33] Ibid., 9, 7 and 10, 33.
[34] Augustine *Confessions* 10, 33. We note that to Saint Augustine belongs a special treatise *On Music* in which he develops the basic postulates of antique musicology.

Byzantine Church Music

The development of church music in Byzantium in the period between the sixth and eighth centuries led to the formulation of a musical system called the *Octoechos*. In a future volume we shall discuss the Octoechos as a collection of divine service texts divided into eight modes.[35] In the current section we will examine the basic organizational principles of the melodies of the eight tones which comprised the basis of Byzantine church music.

First, what constitutes the difference between one mode and another? Research offers two perspectives to this question. Several scholars consider that the main difference lies in the fact that each mode uses its own melody with its own characteristic scale. This perspective rests on the fact that the modes of the Octoechos—four basic and four plagal modes—bore the names of ancient Greek melodies: first mode—Dorian, second—Lydian, third—Phrygian, fourth—Mixolydian, plagal of the first—Hypodorian, plagal of the second—Hypophrygian, plagal of the third—Hypolydian, plagal of the fourth—Hypomixolydian.[36]

Other scholars consider that the difference between modes consists not in a difference of scales but in the fact that each mode possessed its own characteristic inventory of melodic formulae from which a melody was then "patched together." In contemporary musicology this technique bears the name *cento* (i.e., patchwork; or in Russian, *popevochnii*). Egon Wellesz was one of the first to reveal the existence of this technique in ancient church singing. He discovered this compositional principle in the melodies of the eighth-century Serbian Octoechos that he was researching and later concluded that cento technique was used both in Byzantine church music and in western European Gregorian chant:

> Analyzing the musical structure of melodies that belong to one of the eight modes, I discovered that the melodies of each mode are constructed on a known number of formulae which characterize the given mode. In other words, it is not the "range" which served the basic composition in early Christian and Byzantine hymnography, but a group of formulae, whose totality comprised the material of each mode.[37]

---

[35]In the forthcoming vol. 4 of the English translation, which will deal with the the Divine Services; or, in the Russian original, vol. 2, pp. 234, 403–413.

[36]Evgeny Gertsman, *Development of Musical Culture. Culture of Byzantium. VIII–1st Half of XV Centuries* (Moscow, 1991), 562.

[37]Egon Wellesz, *A History of Byzantine Music and Hymnography*, 2nd edition (Oxford, 1961), 71. Concerning "popevechnaya" technique in Gregorian chant, see P.D. Johner, *Wort und Ton im Choral* (Leipzig, 1953), 175–177.

This perspective is accepted today by the majority of researchers of Byzantine music. It is confirmed by the fact that the scales of some modes (at least when the hymns of these modes are transcribed into contemporary line notation) turn out to be identical since certain melodic formulae are used for certain modes but not for others.

The system of eight tones in Byzantium was formed over time. According to the hypothesis of several scholars, it originated in the early Christian Church's custom of performing, during each of the first eight days of Pascha, the divine service texts in a special melody or mode specific to that particular day. Later the eight-day cycle of melodies was expanded to eight weeks of the Paschal cycle—from Pascha to Pentecost, and later to the entire Church year.[38]

One of the main goals of creating the Octoechos system was the "canonization" of all musical material suitable for use in the Church. Such a canonization could not have been the work of individual persons, even as Church tradition ascribes an important role in the formulation of the Octoechos to Saint John of Damascus. The selection of melodic formulae was realized over the span of a prolonged period and was the result of the activity of many generations of singers and *domestiki* (church choir directors). From the point of view of the secular musicologist, it was a spontaneous process. But from the point of view of a churched person, this process was directed by the Holy Spirit, under whose action the collective mind of the Church selected that which was appropriate from the vast range of musical material at its disposal while rejecting that which was not suitable.

An important constitutive element of Byzantine singing was the system that allowed a singer, with no particular difficulty, to set various texts to music according to the model of earlier texts set to music. Such examples were called *automelon* (plural *automela*—αὐτόμελον, -α, Sl. *samopodoben*), while songs constructed according to their model were called *prosomoia* (singular, προσόμοιον, -α, or in the Slavic languages, *podoben*, plural *podobny*).[39] Some genres of liturgical poetry and music, such as the canon, were constructed according to the principle of alternating automela and prosomoia (podobny): the irmos emerged in the role of the automelon and the troparia were performed in the role of the prosomion (podoben).

---

[38]Martynov, *History*, 48–49.

[39]A third type of hymn—the *idiomelon* (plural *idiomela*—ἰδιόμελον, -α, Sl. *samoglasen*)—is meant for use on more solemn or festive occasions. The original Greek text of such hymns does not conform to the metrical patterns of any of the prosomia (podobny), and thus each idiomelon has its own unique and often quite elaborate melody in Byzantine and Znamenny Chant.—Ed.

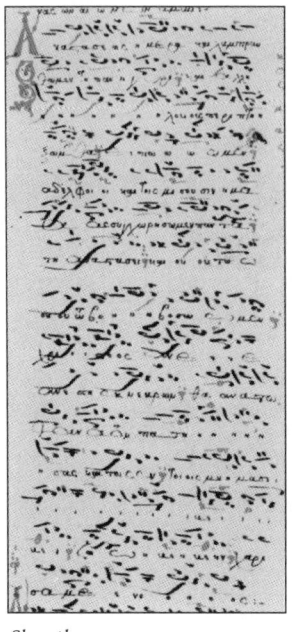

Slavnik.

Because of the strength of these particularities, Byzantine church music practically eliminated any possibility of a composer's activity in the sense in which we understand the term "composer" in our time. Byzantine melodists compiled and organized church music but in no way did they compose music as we understand it today. Melodists did not compose original music; they merely arranged songs from an already prepared inventory of melodic formulae and assembled them in a way similar to the ancient Greek rhapsodies.[40] The labor of the melodist was similar to that of a maker of mosaics who creates an image from previously prepared pieces of multi-colored smalt. The melodist's labor may also be compared to the work of an iconographer who creates an original image by strictly following a particular canon. "However it would be a mistake to consider that this method of composition deprived the singer-composer of every possibility for creative work," notes one scholar. "Such a method of creative work protected church arts from the introduction of a foreign and alien aesthetic and drew the artist towards certain norms and an artistic standard and did not allow one to stoop to a lower level."[41]

A special means of notation was required to write down such music, one that would differ from the system used in antiquity and would allow for any musical content to be noted. Some hold the opinion that written notation "does not bear any 'ideological weight'. It is merely a means of recording musical material.... With the use of notation one can record both blasphemous ditties as well as exalted liturgical hymns. Musical notation lies outside the realm of ideology."[42] It is difficult to agree with this opinion when discussing Byzantine or Old Russian *znamenny* notation. It is impossible to record "blasphemous ditties" by means of this type of notation because it was created precisely and exclusively for the purpose of recording church hymns. It is true that antique letter notation was ideologically neutral: surely for this reason it was used for recording pagan hymns while in the

---

[40] We note, however, that the original sense of the Latin word *compositor* from which our *composer* is derived, was "compiler" or "arranger."

[41] T. Vladyshevskaya, *Byzantine Musical Aesthetics and Influence on the Culture of Song in Ancient Rus': Byzantium and Rus'* (Moscow, 1989), 147–148.

[42] Gertsman, *Mysteries*, 344.

Early Christian and Byzantine Church Singing

third century it was used in recording the Christian hymn to the Holy Trinity. Contemporary line notation is also ideologically neutral since one can record any type of music at all with it. But Byzantine notation was not ideologically neutral and in this lay its power to secure. It protected church singing from the penetration of foreign, secular, and non-church elements.

Neume notation was by its nature a system of intervals. Its main object was not an individual sound (note) but a movement from one sound to another. A melody, noted by Byzantine neumes, is perceived not as a series of individual sounds, one succeeding the next, but as an uninterrupted movement of the voice reflecting the prayerful bursts of the human soul.

The purpose of neume notation was of a most auxiliary nature. It merely allowed the singer to call to mind familiar musical material. Its characteristic feature was the ability to use special signs to visually establish the overall movement of intonational patterns without specifically determining the pitch of the intoned melody. Therefore, rather than reading a melody marked with neumes, it was necessary to listen to the melody. The oral tradition had a decisive importance in this; that is, mastering the intonation by learning from the voice of the teacher. In this way, notation was merely an addendum to the oral tradition. Without oral tradition, notation could be nothing more than a script that could not be precisely interpreted. For this very reason songs recorded in Byzantine notation are not subject to precise deciphering.

Vladimir Martynov explained the peculiarities of neume notation, its theological meaning, and how it fundamentally differs from letter notation and contemporary staff notation:

> The neume does not express the precise pitch and duration of the sound but conveys the mystical and elusive dynamic essence of the intonation. Neume notation establishes the melody's specific intonational outline in all its actual fullness while letter notation or staff notation transforms the living continuity of the intonational outline into a purely external speculation and breaks down the united outline into a number of disconnected "points" or moments. The absence of exact indications of pitch and duration of sound, characteristic of neume notation, implies the necessity of teaching and oral tradition without which recording music with neumes cannot be understood at all. This feature of neume notation, which many scholars view to be its shortcoming, in fact reveals its deeper aspects of Orthodox consciousness. This gave birth to such

phenomena as spiritual elders, absolute obedience, and the renunciation of one's own will, which developed into special and distinctive conceptions of rearing and training. Creative works in a cathedral require that their creators have personal communion in the body of the Church; in the same way, a student can understand the meaning of neume notation only through personal contact with a teacher-elder.[43]

Byzantine notation underwent a particular evolution throughout its entire history. *Ekphonetic* notation for the reading of psalms was the predecessor of song notation. It consisted of marks that indicated a voice's rise or fall during reading. The earliest examples of recorded church singing, conventionally grouped under the name *paleobyzantine notation*, are well known in manuscripts beginning in the ninth century. In the twelfth century a new type of notation called *Middle Byzantine* became widespread. It allowed for the recording of church music with great exactitude. The Middle Byzantine system of notation contained fourteen basic marks (Gk. *phonai*, φωναί) and each one signified the movement of a particular number of intervals. Besides this, auxiliary marks called *martyriai* (μαρτυρίαι) were used, and these indicated the sound's pitch, modes, and the modulation from one mode to another. Yet another group of marks is called *large hypostases* (Gk. *megalai hypostaseis*, μεγάλαι ὑποστάσεις). Some of these indicated the change of the sound's duration while others indicated the sound's special character (pauses, decelerations, accelerations) and still others were short melodic formulae.[44] Later versions of Byzantine notation are called *late-Byzantine* and *post-Byzantine* (from the beginning of the fifteenth century until 1814).[45]

It is not clear to what extent the legendary Byzantine hymnographers and melodists—Saint Roman the Melodist, Saint John of Damascus, and Saint Cosmas of Maiuma—and others created not only texts but also music itself. Information, especially concerning Saint Roman the Melodist, suggests they were singers. As for others, however, information supporting this assertion is lacking.

As in antiquity, various forms of choral singing, including responsorial and antiphonal singing, were used in Byzantine liturgical song. The role of the soloist in responsorial singing was performed by the canonarch (Gk. *kanonarches*, κανονάρχης). Originally this term was used to describe a monk who called other monks to the service by striking *kolotushki*, but by the time of Saint Theodore the

---

[43]Martynov, *History*, 54.
[44]Gertsman, *Culture*, 528.
[45]I. Arvanitis, "Byzantine Notation," in *Orthodox Encyclopedia*, vol. 8 (Moscow, 2004), 361.

Studite the term was used to refer to the singer-soloist whom the choir would follow. In antiphonal singing two choirs were located in two choir sections, on the right side and on the left side, and they sang in alternating fashion. In some cases (especially during the performance of the *katavasia* of the canon during Matins) members of the two choirs would descend to the center of the church in order to sing together, after which they would return to their respective choir stations.

The choir was directed by the *domestik*—a church choir director who demonstrated to the singers the motion of the melody by using special chironomic signs. Often the duties of the canonarch and domestik were combined and performed by a single person. The domestik needed not only to have a mastery of music but also to have a perfect knowledge of the Church's service order book (*Ustav* or *Typikon*) insofar as it was his duty to select the songs to be used for each service. When there were two choirs, each choir had its own domestik.

As a rule, only men's choirs participated in Byzantine divine services. The absence of women in the church choir was stipulated by general instructions that date back to the Apostle Paul who wrote, "Let your women keep silent in the churches" (1 Cor 14.34). In parish churches and cathedrals men were charged with the duties of singing and they received a blessing for this service from the bishop through the laying-on-of-hands (*cheirothesia*).

Exceptions to the rule did exist, however. In women's monasteries, for example, the duty of singing lay with the sisters of the cloister. It is well known that Saint Ephraim the Syrian (fourth century) created sisterhoods in Edessa whose members participated in singing in the choir.[46] Egeria (*c.* 386) mentions the participation of virgins in singing the psalms and antiphons in Jerusalem's Church of the Resurrection.[47] Blessed Theodoret[48] (fifth century) refers to a choir of virgins under the direction of Publia. Saint Ambrose of Milan stated that women can participate in the singing of psalms because it "is appropriate for any age or gender."[49]

On the other hand, Saint Cyril of Jerusalem considered that women may be permitted only to open their mouths, without uttering sounds, during the singing of psalms.[50] And Saint Isidore of Pelusium considered that women were allowed to sing in church in apostolic times but later this permission was taken away because "they turned divine teachings into something opposite them and it became the cause of relaxation and sin. They did not acquire tenderness from the divine hymns

---

[46] For more concerning the participation of women in choral singing, see Quasten, *Music*, 75–87.
[47] Egeria *Pilgrimage* 24 1; CSEL 39, 71.
[48] Theodoret *Church History* 3, 19, 2.
[49] Ambrose of Milan *Commentary on Psalm 1*; PL 14, 925.
[50] Cyril of Jerusalem *Catechetical Lecture* 14; PG 88, 356.

and the sweetness of the melody aroused passions in them because they did not see in it anything more than theatrical music."[51]

While women's choirs were an exception to the rule and existed for the most part only in places where women lived together (sisterhoods and women's monasteries), evidently choirs of boys were much more commonly permitted. Sources from the fourth century mention the participation in the divine services of children,[52] although professionally trained children's choirs are not mentioned in any of the sources. Later sources make reference to the existence of special choir schools for boys as well as boys' singing during divine services under the direction of an older director.[53] Boys were also permitted to participate in Byzantine divine services as soloists both in singing and reading. Boys who had reached the age of eight years could fulfill the duty of reader according to a decree issued by Emperor Justinian in 546. *Lectores infantuli* (boy-readers) existed in the Western Church as well.[54]

A principle inherited from antique vocal music dominated for several centuries in Byzantine singing. In accordance with this principle one syllable corresponded to one sound. The melody is completely subject to the text in this style of singing.

The formation of a somewhat different principle is observed in manuscripts of the ninth century: one syllable corresponds to one neume, where a neume could contain two or three sounds.[55]

A new style of singing which received the name *kalophonia* (καλοφωνία— literally, "beautiful sounding") became common in the twelfth century and by the end of the thirteenth century had become the leading style. The influence of Turkish *melos* (melody) is seen in the emergence of this style.[56] Music dominates over the text in the kalophonic style. Widely employed is the melismatic technique including various forms of *jubilus* (prolonged melodic formulae sung on a single syllable). Several examples of kalophonic singing show that words may be repeated; also, meaningless syllables may be placed between the syllables of individual words. These include: *a*/α, *ne*/νε, *na*/να, *te*/τε, *ri*/ρι, *re*/ρε, and so forth. Groups of such

---

[51] Isidore of Pelusium *Epistle 1* 90; PG 78, 244. These words reflect the harsh attitude towards women by monks—the main ecclesiastic "ideologues" in Byzantium. It is probably the case that the common trend in Byzantium not to allow women's participation in choral singing can be explained by the influence of monasticism.

[52] Gregory the Theologian, *Oration 16* 13; PG 35, 952; John Chrysostom *Commentary on Matthew* 71,4; PG 58, 666; Basil the Great *Conversation During Time of Famine* 3; PG 31, 309 C; Aetheria *Pilgrimage* 24, 5.

[53] For more detail concerning this see Quasten, *Music*, 87–92.

[54] Even today the Bulgarian Orthodox Church has boy-readers who are tonsured by the bishop.

[55] Oliver Strunk, "Melody Construction in Byzantine Chant," *Actes du XIIe congrès international d'études byzantines*, Ochride, 10–16 septembre 1961, vol. 1 (Belgrade, 1961), 365–373.

[56] See, for example, G. Alekseeva, *Byzantine-Russian Musical Paleography* (St Petersburg, 2007), 99.

meaningless syllables could be inserted at the beginning or end of a song seemingly for the purpose of slowing down the movement of the text. These syllables were called *kratimata*/κρατήματα (from the word *krateo*, κρατέο—to hold, to suppress) or *echemata*/ἠχήματα (from the word *ichos*/ἦχος—"mode" or "voice"). Several variations of these unique vocal jubilations were given names that witness to their connection with particular ethnic (including foreign) traditions: *thettalikon*/θετταλικόν (Thessalonian), *persikon*/περσικόν (Persian), *frankikon*/φραγκικόν (Frankish), and others.[57] The most expressive *kratimata* were included in the *Kratimatarion*—a book which aided singers in mastering these "flight manoeuvres."

An exceptional master of kalophonic singing whose name went down in the history of Byzantine church singing next to the names of Saint Roman the Melodist and Saint John of Damascus was Saint John Kukuzelis (*c.* 1280–*c.* 1375). According to the account of his life, he was born in Durazzo (in the territory of present-day Albania). His mother was Bulgarian and the Greek language was not his native tongue. But while still a youth he mastered Greek with such perfection that he was able to compose verse in it. In his musical works Kukuzelis perfected kalophonic singing. He created new refrains, employed a wide range, and boldly utilized transitions from one mode to another. He permitted jumps to the major sixth and major seventh. The formation of late-Byzantine notation is associated with the name of Kukuzelis. This notation allowed for the recording of the most intricate melodic pieces that characterize kalophonic singing.

Byzantine singing principally bore a single-voice character throughout the entire span of its history. However, a low, supporting voice that moved little—the so-called *ison* (Gk. ἴσον—literally, "equal," "the same")—could be added to the major voice. The exact time of the ison's emergence in Byzantine singing is not known. Ison (or "drone") fulfills the function of accompaniment and creates a harmonic backdrop for the higher voice which leads the main melody.

Byzantine singing did not cease to develop after the fall of Constantinople in 1453 but in several regions it was subject to western influences and in other regions to Arabic-Turkish influences.[58] The traditional refrains were modified in regions of the former Byzantine Empire that were under Latin dominion for a long time. In particular, the Cretan School of singing appeared in this way and was transferred to the Ionian Islands in the second half of the seventeenth century, where Byzantine

---

[57] Gertsman, *Culture*, 532.
[58] Concerning the Turkish influence on post-Byzantine music, see, in particular, Şirli, "Sonorités turques dans la musique post-byzantine," *Byzantium and Eastern Europe. Liturgical and Musical Connections* (Moscow, 2003), 160–164.

singing was harmonized in the western spirit and performed in three voices. (On the island of Zakynthos this tradition has been preserved to the present day.)

During the seventeenth and eighteenth centuries numerous melodists and chanters perfected traditional Byzantine singing by composing music according to ancient models and editing ancient melodies. This activity was crowned by the reform of 1814 initiated by Chrysanthos of Madytos (*c.* 1770–1840) and approved by the Patriarchate of Constantinople. The reform was called "the New Method" and pertained both to notation, which was significantly shortened, and also to the melodies themselves, which underwent codification and editing. Chrysanthos especially gave new birth to the antique division of melodies into the diatonic, chromatic, and enharmonic types.[59] Byzantine singing edited by Chrysanthos is used in the Orthodox Churches of the Greek East up to the present day.

---

[59]Lingas, *Singing*, 358.

12

Russian Church Singing

Church Singing in Kievan and Muscovite Rus'. Znamenny Chant

Church singing appeared in Rus' at the time of the emergence of Christianity as the dominant religion during the reign of Prince Vladimir. The historical date of the baptism of Rus' is 988. One may consider this to be the official date of the beginning of Russian church singing, although individual churches and singers existed in Rus' even before that date.

In the opinion of a number of scholars,[1] Russian church singing derived from Greek singing by means of the simple transplantation of Greek melodies to Russian soil and the "hasty preparation" of Slavic translations of liturgical texts set to Greek church music. These scholars state that Byzantine neume notation arrived in Rus' together with Byzantine singing and that only later was it modified and transformed into the so-called *znamenny* or *kriuk* notation characteristic of Russian znamenny chant. The appearance in Rus' of Greek singers is also associated with the mission of Prince Vladimir. Archpriest Vasily Metallov states that "an entire clergy of Greek singers called the 'princess' choir'" accompanied Princess Anna to Kiev when she was brought by Vladimir from Byzantium.[2]

Other scholars contend that Old Russian church singing was the product of original creative works of the Russian people and arose on Russian soil independently, without outside influences.[3] This opinion was held by Stepan Smolensky: "By the eleventh century, that is to say, by the time of the baptism of Rus', we observe that the art of Russian singing was already excellent and fully systematized,

---

[1] See, Archpriest D. Razumovsky, *Church Singing* (Moscow, 1886), 57–58; Archpriest Vasily Metallov, *Essay on the History of Orthodox Church Singing in Russia* (Moscow, 1893), 52–53; N. Ouspensky, *The Art of Old Russian Singing* (Moscow, 1965), 20–25.
[2] Metallov, *Essay*, 52.
[3] *The History of Russian Music in Ten Volumes*, B 10, vol. 1, 80–81.

having developed a system of signs and possessing an impressive number of books and melodies so strong and folkloric that they have been preserved alive down to our own day."[4] Elsewhere Smolensky stated, "We really received the theoretical basis for our church singing by means of the Byzantines. . . . Perhaps, we also received a considerable number of melodies, but we developed them ourselves and perfected the melodic content of this singing and its written exposition exclusively by our own effort and fully independently of the Byzantines."[5]

There also exists the hypothesis of Johann Von Gardner concerning the Bulgarian roots of Russian church music. According to this hypothesis, "immediately after the baptism of Rus' and the establishment of ecclesial life in Prince Vladimir's realm, Bulgarian Orthodox church culture . . . became predominant." In this scholar's view, "the liturgical singing adopted by the Bulgarians from Byzantium at the end of the ninth century had already been adapted to the Slavonic language . . . and had incorporated the musical sensibilities of the Southern and the Eastern Slavs."[6] This version is based, in particular, on information from the Joachim Chronicle concerning the fact that Prince Vladimir, following his baptism, brought with him to Kiev "first Metropolitan Michael who was a Bulgarian and other bishops, priests, and singers."[7] If the first metropolitan was a Bulgarian, it is possible that the first singers were Bulgarians and not Greeks.

Direct evidence of the Greek origin of Russian church singing is lacking insofar as not a single manuscript is known to contain samples of such singing. On the other hand, a good deal of indirect evidence exists. Above all, chronicles speak of the activities of Greek singers in Rus'. The earliest testimony is contained in Novgorod's Sofia Chronicles (first quarter of the fifteenth century) in which in the year 6560 from the creation of the world (AD 1052) the following entry reads: "To Kiev came three singers: they came with their kinsmen."[8] This event is discussed in more detail in the *Book of Degrees* (*Stepennaia Kniga*) (1560–1563): "Three Greek singers, inspired by God, came with their families; it is from them that angel-like singing, wonderful singing in the Eight Tones (*osmoglasie*), as well as three-part

---

[4]S. Smolensky, "On Old Russian Singing Notation," in *Historical-paleographical Essay* (St Petersburg, 1901) 20.

[5]Idem, "On Russian Church Singing: A Reply to Mr. Missaelides, the Protopsaltis of Saint Photina Church in Smyrna," in A. Naumov and M. Rakhmaninov, ed., *Russian Religious Music in Documents and Materials*, vol. 3: *Church Singing of Reformed Russia as Understood by Contemporaries, 1861–1918*, 366.

[6]Gardner, *Church Singing*, vol. 2, 38.

[7]Martynov, *History*, 86.

[8]Cited in V. Adrianova-Peretts, ed., *Tale of Bygone Years*, vol. 2 (Moscow–Leningrad, 1950), 387.

sweet-singing, and the most-beautiful *demestvenny* singing to the praise and the glory of God originated in the Russian land."[9]

The fact that the chronicles make mention of Greek singers witnesses to the scale of their activity and doubtless their influence on the development of singing in Rus'. But exactly what type of singing did they bring to Rus'? How can we understand the terms *tripartite* and *demestvenny* when applied to church singing of the middle of the eleventh century? The author (or editor) of the *Book of Degrees* hardly could have in mind three-voice singing. It is also obvious that we are not talking about the so-called "demestvenny" singing which appeared in Rus' only in the fifteenth to sixteenth centuries. By all appearances, the author (or editor) of the *Book of Degrees* is referring to Eight-Mode singing brought by singers from Greece together with the tradition of kalophonic singing—the sweet-sounding, melismatic kalophonic singing—which he refers to as "demestvenny" in an extremely general manner, by way of analogy with "demestvenny singing" which was popular by the time of the definitive publication of the *Book of Degrees*—that is, by the middle of the sixteenth century.

Moreover, the term *tripartite* may possess a hidden theological meaning. According to the opinion of Bishop Porfirii (Ouspensky), "some mystery is concealed (in this term) known to our forefathers but today forgotten."[10] It is possible that the term *tripartite* (*trisostavnoe*) is called thus to identify the nature of church singing as consisting of three basic elements: the words, the music, and the spiritual content which actually makes it "of the church." These three elements combine and cooperate to form a synthesis called "angel-like singing." And while the words communicate the meaning to the melody, and the melody gives an emotional hue to the words, the spiritual content transforms both the melody and the words. In such a "transformed" singing the melody becomes that "sacred choir-leading" which, according to the above-cited expression of the Areopagite, establishes oneness of mind in relation to God.[11]

Yet another testimony to the Greek origin of Russian church singing is the presence of Greek words in Slavonic liturgical texts from the singers' manuscripts of Kievan Rus'. To cite an example, several Slavonic hymns contained in the *Blagoveshchenskii Kondakar'* (written no later than the middle of the twelfth century)

---

[9]Translated by Gardner in *Church Singing*, vol. 2, 30.
[10]Porfirii (Ouspensky), "Letter to Princess Vitgenshtein of Oct. 13, 1858," in Porfirii (Ouspensky), "Letters of the Right Reverend Porfirii (Ouspensky) to the Princess E. Vitgenshtein", *Bogoslovsky Vestnik* (1904, 1905).
[11]Dionysius the Areopagite *The Ecclesiastical Hierarchy* 3, 3, 5.

are sprinkled with Greek words and expressions ("*Tou ikumeni alelougia*," "*O theos mou alelougia*," etc.) and one hymn—the hypakoë on the feast of the Exaltation of the Cross—is written twice: once in Greek using Slavonic letters and once in Slavonic using Slavonic letters.[12]

It is evident that the Greek language was used together with Slavonic during divine services in Kievan Rus'. Even while the first Russian metropolitan was a Bulgarian, his successors were Greeks. (A sole exception was Metropolitan Hilarion in the middle of the eleventh century.) It is clear that there were Greek choirs and Greek singers during the period of Greek metropolitans. Divine services could be performed in both languages or in an alternating fashion in metropolitan cathedrals. One choir sang in Greek and the other in Slavonic. In Kievan Rus' both *Gospodi, pomilui* ("Lord, have mercy" in Slavonic) and the Greek *Kyrie eleison* were sung in the litanies. The Greek expressions: *Eis polla eti despota, Ton despotin kai archierea ēmon, Axios*, and others remain from this period in the contemporary hierarchical divine services of the Russian Orthodox Church.[13]

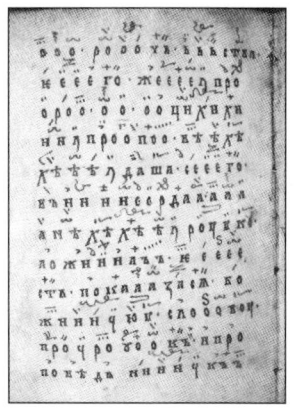

Troitskii Kondakar'.
Beginning of the 13th c.

The details of the origins of church singing in Rus', whether it was brought directly from Byzantium or through Bulgaria, may be debated, but the Byzantine roots of Russian church singing are indisputable. And the fact is obvious that the basic organizational principles of Byzantine singing were incorporated in Rus'. These include: (1) the eight-mode system; (2) strict unison character of singing; (3) tetrachord scale structure; (4) *popevochnii* technique; (5) neume notation.

Old Russian *kriuk* notation, known in manuscripts beginning in the twelfth century, is genetically linked with paleobyzantine neume notation, although it has substantial differences from it. But, as one scholar notes, "the graphic identity of formulae is not the same thing as its melodic identity." While the direct transplantation of Greek melodies to Russian soil occurred, once in Rus' the expressive and emotional Greek music "acquired a smoother and calmer character, the melodic line became more even, the sharpness of outlines was smoothed out, and this led in its turn to the appearance

---

[12]Archpriest Vasily Metallov, *Russian Semiography from the Field of Church Singing Archeology and Paleography* (Moscow, 1912), 15.

[13]Martynov, *History*, 88.

of specifically Russian original formulae called *popevki*.[14] Another scholar contends that "in the eleventh and twelfth centuries only Byzantine signs were incorporated, the rewritten neume inscriptions, and an original Russian type of music composed using these signs gradually appeared. Put differently, 'only the Old Byzantine "alphabet" was borrowed . . . but not the complete "lexicon" of a foreign musical "language"'."[15]

Manuscripts of the twelfth century contain two types of notation: *znamenny* (or *stolp* and the so-called *kondakarian* notation, which received its name from the Kondakaria (collections of kontakia).[16] In znamenny notation of this period the principle is strictly observed: one syllable—one sign. In kondakarian notation, the opposite holds true: for one syllable often several signs are needed. Songs of a melismatic character, similar to Greek kalophonic singing in their structure (but evidently not in their melodies), were recorded using this type of notation. Kondakarian singing existed only up to the fourteenth century; it disappeared when kondakarian singing disappeared. Znamenny singing and znamenny notation, on the contrary, appeared at the dawn of Christendom in Rus' and they were preserved in Russian liturgical singing right up to the eighteenth or nineteenth century. They continue to be used by the Old Ritualists up to the present day.

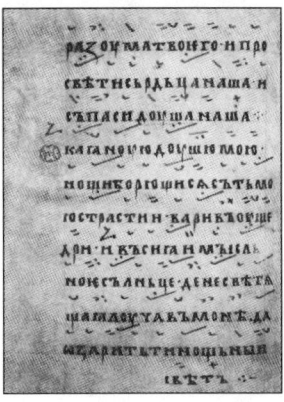

Irmologion with Notation. Beginning of the 13th c.

Znamenny chant is the basic, most ancient, and most stable form of Old Russian liturgical singing. It received its name from the word *znamya* (sign) which indicates the method of recording this chant. Signs, or *kriuki* (hooks), were neumes which indicated a particular sound or a musical phrase comprised of several sounds. As with Byzantine neumes, Russian kriuki were intended for recording voice movements: one kriuk could denote the movement of an upward second (D–E) while another could denote the falling movement of three sounds (F–E–D), and so forth. The duration of the sounds comprising one sign could also vary. Each *kriuk* had its own name: *kryzh* (cross), *slozhit'ia* (fold), *kliuch* (key), *pauk* (spider), *rog* (horn), *dva*

---

[14]Ibid., 90.
[15]V. Kholopova, *Russian Musical Rhythmics* (Moscow, 1983), 74.
[16]Of the five Kondakaria well known to researchers of this period, four (*Blagoveshchenskii, Lavrskii, Uspenskii, and Synodalnii*) are written exclusively in kontakion notation, and in the *Typographical Manual* some chants are presented in one notation while others in two.

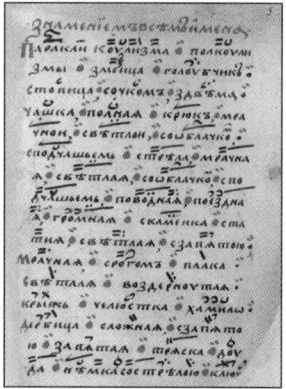

Beginning of Russian Kriuk Primer. Manuscript. 1506–1514.

v chelnu (two-in-a-boat), *kriuk prostoi* (simple hook), *strela mrachnaia* (somber arrow), *chashka polnaia* (full cup), *podchashie svetloe* (bright saucer), *golubchik borzoi* (bold little dove), *palka vosdernutaia* (upturned stick), and others. The overall number of kriuki contained in one of the primers of kriuki from the fifteenth century is forty-two.[17] Monk Christopher's *Key to Znamenny Chant* (1604) includes sixty-four signs including different versions of one and the same sign as well as several combinations of kriuki.[18]

Early forms of znamenny chant do not allow for a precise reading. For this reason, we can say nothing about the chant's melodic organization during the period of Kievan Rus'. A theoretical understanding of znamenny chant began no earlier than the fifteenth century and a precise determination of pitch for znamenny melodies became possible only at the turn of the seventeenth century when the so-called "cinnabar marks" were invented.[19] (We will discuss this matter later.) Manuscripts with kriuki without cinnabar markings, from the twelfth through sixteenth centuries, are deciphered only hypothetically. This is done on the basis of the retrospective interpolation of a precise outline of pitch, known from later manuscripts, onto older musical samples.

Besides inventories of songs marked with kriuk notation, various "primers" and "keys" were created in order to make the singers' work easier. These works contained descriptions of kriuki and *popevki* (melodic formulae). However, these descriptions bore such an approximate character that they could be of great help only in the case when a singer learned all the melodic models by heart. (Deprived of a living oral tradition, instruction provided by the authors of the *Primers* would lose all meaning:)

> A *simple kriuk* is sung in intermediate accordance in one voice, *somber kriuk* a little bit higher, *bright kriuk* even higher, *thrice-bright kriuk* even higher than that . . . *bold little dove* in two voices rapidly . . . *quiet little dove*: rise up two steps quietly . . . *two-in-a-boat*: swing vocally . . . *derbitsa*: boldly in four rising

---

[17] Gardner, *Liturgical Singing of the Russian Orthodox Church*, vol. 1, (Jordanville, 1977; reprinted Moscow, 2004), 376.
[18] Monk Christopher, *Key*, 72–73.
[19] T. Vladyshevskaya, *Musical Culture of Ancient Rus'* (Moscow, 2006), 48–49.

Russian Church Singing

steps ... *hornpipe* and *mute* are sung differently in three and five and eight steps ... *great kulizma* and *medium kulizma, shake, little sword,* and *spiders* in all voices are sung with various melodic formulae inconsistently ...[20]

As is well known in the manuscripts with cinnabar markings, the scale of znamenny chant includes twelve sounds, divided into four accordances: simple, somber, bright, and thrice-bright. Sounds of a single accordance are found at a distance of one tone spaced one from the other and the distance between accordances comprises a semitone:

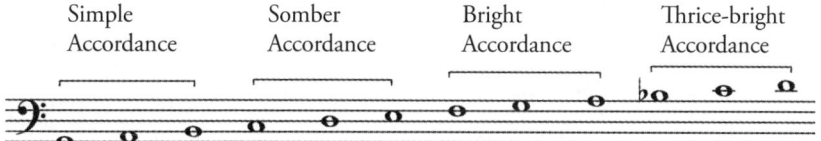

The resemblance of this scale to the "Lesser Perfect System" of antique music (diatonic inclination) is obvious. In both of these the tetrachordal thinking is fundamental, and the perfect fourths are melodically identical but not the perfect octaves. (When transcribed to lined notation "B natural" is found at the bottom of the scale and "B flat" is found at the top of the scale for this very reason.) The range of the znamenny scale encompasses the volume of sounds accessible to a bass singer. This is due to the fact that only men were singers in Rus' and men's high voices (tenors) were not popular. But as in the antique scales, the znamenny scale does not establish an absolute pitch; therefore, the scale's pitch could vary in choral singing depending on the available voices.

The full range of the znamenny scale is only employed in the most festive songs, for which lengthy melismatic insertions are characteristic. Usually znamenny singing uses a narrower scale and is characterized by "stepping in place" on several neighboring pitches in the framework of one or two accordances (often in the framework of a single tetrachord).[21]

---

[20]*Znamenny Key* (18th-century manuscript in the author's library), folios 24ᵛ–28.

[21]The notation for this chant, "Holy God," was deciphered by B. Kutuzov in the book *Znamenny Chant Liturgy*, 17.

Znamenny chant is distinguished by its unique rhythm, which to a considerable degree is related to the rhythm of the liturgical texts themselves. While the rhythm of the ancient Greek sticheron was constructed on the alternation of long and short syllables, the essential indicator of the peculiarity of the rhythm of znamenny chant is the musical accenting that reproduces the percussive and non-percussive syllables of the text. Together with accents of duration, accents of pitch and loudness, which determine the basic relief of melodic line, also exist in znamenny chant.[22] This is easily seen in the example of the hymn "Only Begotten Son" in znamenny chant:

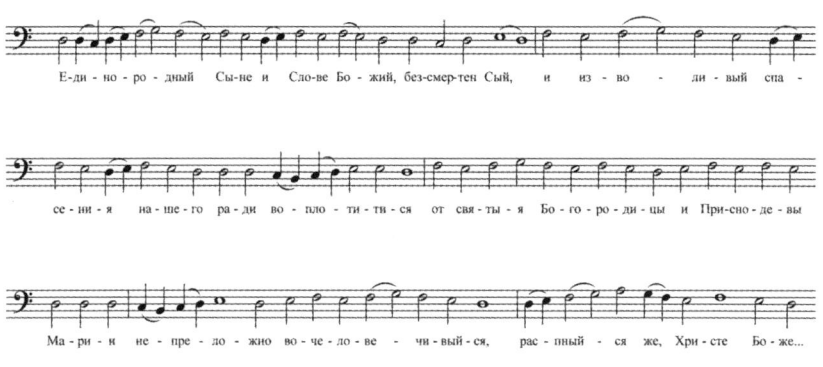

Separate graphic signs existed for percussive and non-percussive sounds. In particular, the kriuk was associated with percussive syllables while the "little step" was connected with non-percussive syllables. "Kriuki are written on strengths, that is to say, over the syllables which must be stressed. . . . *Little step* indicates a lesser fullness of sound than *kriuk*."[23]

Znamenny singing is extremely complex to study. In order to approach an understanding of the Eight-mode System, it is necessary not only to be able to read kriuk manuscripts and to understand well the musical material of the chant; it is necessary to correctly choose the initial positions and to determine the main criterion of analysis. Even such leading scholar-musicians of the nineteenth century as Archpriest Dimitri Razumovsky, Archpriest I. Voznesenskiy, Y. Arnold, and Stepan Smolensky did not succeed in accomplishing this. After studying numerous kriuk manuscripts from various periods and making the most valuable observations about many key questions of znamenny chant, they departed from incorrect

---

[22]Kholopova, *Rhythmics*, 26–27.
[23]L. Kalashnikov, *Primer of Liturgical Znamenny Singing* (Kiev, 1908), 4–5.

premises in their interpretation of the essence of the Russian Eight-mode System. These researchers strove to describe the Russian Eight-mode System on the basis of the ancient Greek melodic system. In their opinion, each tone of znamenny chant was characterized by its employment of a particular melody based on the unity of two tetrachords and had its own strong and dominant sounds. This speculative conception[24] was formed under the influence of Greek and partly western theories of music. With this approach to the Eight-mode System, an analysis of concrete models of znamenny chant could not be unbiased.

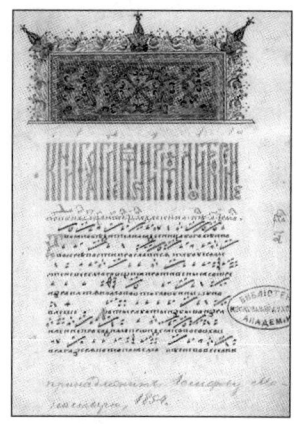

Irmologion. 16th c.

Archpriest Vasily Metallov (1862–1926) deserves credit for overcoming this view. Speaking about the supposed dependence of znamenny chant on the ancient Greek system of melodies and scales, he noted that "everyone studying ancient Orthodox singing is practically in the right to ask, what exactly is this dependence and where is it seen? . . . Where are these theoretical or practical data by which the earlier Russian singer and later the contemporary singer could determine the tones of Russian liturgical singing based on the ancient Greek musical system, using the method of technical arrangement of the Greek eight tones?"[25]

On the basis of numerous kriuk manuscripts that he researched, Metallov came to the conclusion that the musical material of znamenny chant consists of a particular quantity of ready-made melodic formulae, or *popevki*. Using the principle of a tone's character, various combinations of these melodic formulae comprise the basis of the Russian Eight-mode System. Put differently, each tone of znamenny chant is characterized not by scales or melodies, but by the sum of the melodic formulae—intonations characteristic of a single given tone.

The system of tonal melodic formulae (popevki) was definitively formed in the fifteenth and first half of the sixteenth centuries. It is difficult to say how it emerged. Apparently it was the result of the constant selection of the most characteristic intonations and their being established in the practice of singing. Metallov deems that the manner of using particular melodic phrases to express the tune of each tone could have been created by singers and clergy due to their not knowing the Greek

---

[24] In the twentieth century N. Ouspensky also developed this in his book *Old Russian Art of Singing* (Moscow, 1965).

[25] Archpriest Vasily Metallov, *Eight-tone Znamenny Chant* (Moscow, 1899), 1–2.

theory of the Eight-tone System. After first mastering ready-made Greek singing, Russian singers had no possibility of making a particular text "their own"—that is, without performing it according to known Greek models. Metallov considers the popevochnaia system of znamenny chant to be a purely Russian invention with no parallels in Byzantine church music or in other musical cultures.

But as we now know, the popevochnaia technique was known both to Byzantine music and Gregorian choral music. On the other hand, the hypothesis concerning the transplantation of ready-made melodic material from Byzantium to Rus', as stated previously, is not confirmed by the tradition of the manuscripts. Therefore the popevochnaia system of znamenny chant may be considered a fully original product of native musical culture and the fruit of maturation spanning many centuries, to which many generations of singer-composers contributed. While originally some connections existed between melodic formulae characteristic of Byzantine singing and of Russian znamenny singing, over the centuries these connections have completely disappeared.

Practically any hymn of znamenny chant is a collection of melodic formulae (popevki). Each melodic formula (popevka) has its own name and its own characteristic peculiarities. Old Russian music theory equipped each popevka with a certain name to enable better mastery of the singing material by pupils. The names of melodic formulae originated both from Slavic roots (*dolinka* [little valley], *kobila* [mare], *podkladets, zmiitsa* [little snake], *stezka* [little path], *nametka menshaia, skachok bol'shoi* [big leap], *perevertka menshaia, pereskok* [leap over]) and also Greek roots: (*khamilo, kulizma, kheleimeosa, eukhiteos*).[26] The name of melodic formulae in many cases had a descriptive character and reflected the content that singers put into a particular melodic phrase (*pereskok* [leap over], *nedoskok , skochok, pod'iom* [rise, lift], *pervoloka*).

Popevki in a znamenny hymn's composition were not lifeless formulae devoid of variety. On the contrary, it was possible in the framework of the popevochnaia technique to achieve great melodic diversity and variation. Speaking about the popevochnaia technique, the well known musicologist Yuri Keldysh wrote:

> Popevki were not definitively crystallized in a rigid stereotype; rather, they were a living organism subject to all possible variations of transfiguration. They could be freely stretched out or contracted. They could enter into diverse connections with other popevki or be broken into pieces. From the union of two

[26] See, for example, Monk Christopher, *Key to Znamenny Chant*, 75–77.

and sometimes more popevki could appear an altogether new popevka which received its own name. . . . Popevki were characterized primarily according to their concluding portion, which comprised its nucleus. The nucleus was the brightest melodic phrase (*oborot*) of a given popevka and was distinguished by its relative consistency. Its predecessor was the *dostupka*—the introductory portion—more changeable and melodically less clearly outlined. But the nucleus did not remain completely unchangeable. Depending on the context . . . it took on various forms, preserving only its basic melodic skeleton. A similar elasticity of the popevki made it possible to sing texts that varied in duration and grammatical construction using the same formula and to achieve a smooth and unbroken development of the melodic line formed by the joining of the popevki.[27]

Popevki were subdivided into two types: those characteristic of several tones and those peculiar only to a single tone. There were also popevki used only at the beginning of a hymn or only at the end. Each tone included a collection of several tens of popevki, and the overall inventory of popevki for znamenny chant consisted of several hundred. The operation of such quantity of musical material required great ability, love of labor, and mastery from singer-composers (*raspevschiki*).

An experienced singer-cleric should have not only known but also had the ability to freely utilize the entire arsenal of melodic formulae available for use in singing. For this it was necessary to possess more than an outstanding musical memory. In our time, when mnemonic methods of instruction have long since departed, we cannot even imagine the level of musical development and freedom of operation of the most intricate intonational complexities which were achieved by ordinary singers. They needed to train their musical memory regularly and to mentally make use of a huge quantity of intonational material.[28]

Besides popevki, there also existed in znamenny chant certain melismatic phrases (*oboroty*) which received the names *litso* and *fita*. These phrases, which are inserted into the basic fabric of the chant, were recorded using a special selection of kriuki, and the same kriuki were used as in regular *put'* chant, but within a *fita* or *litso* they acquired a new meaning. This principle was given the name *tainozamknennost'*

---

[27] Y. Keldysh, *History of Russian Music in Ten Volumes*, vol. 1: *Ancient Rus', 11th–17th Centuries* (Moscow, 1983), 204.

[28] G. Nikishov, *Monk Christopher of Saint Cyril-White Lake Monastery and His "Key to Znamenny Chant" (1604)* (Moscow, 1983), 216.

(mysteries being locked-up): a new content seemed to be ciphered (locked up) under the usual neumes. In primers of znamenny chant *litsa* and *fity* were also called "wise lines," "knots," or "the hidden sign."[29] More than twenty or thirty *litsa* and *fity* were widely used: Monk Christopher's *Key to Znamenny Chant* contains a catalog of twenty-three *fity*.[30] The general catalog of *litsa* and *fity* compiled by Maksim Brazhnikov (1902–1973) on the basis of all manuscripts known to him includes more than five hundred samples and together with their variants numbers around four thousand (!). Basically *fity* were widened variants of usual znamenny popevki and often included these popevki.

Popevochnaia technique lies at the basis of all types of znamenny singing including the small znamenny and *stolp* melodies. These two types were formed by the fifteenth century although even earlier znamenny chant was not uniform but included several varieties.

The syllabic principle—one sound corresponds to one syllable—lies at the basis of small znamenny chant and its related singing known as *na podoben* (to the podoben) of old znamenny chant, preserved almost unchanged since the eleventh century. Texts were sung and performed at daily worship services using this method.[31] This type of singing has its origins in "prosody"—the chanting of sacred texts using just one or a few notes. In this case the melodic line is fully submissive to the text.

Stolp chant was used for singing during divine services on Sundays and feast days. This chant owes its name to the Eight-mode System: a full circle of eight modes of the Oktoechos was called a *stolp* (pillar) and was repeated every eight weeks.[32] On the basis of stolp chant lies the neumatic principle: one sign (kriuk) corresponds to one syllable which can include one, two, three, or four sounds. The popevochnaia technique—characteristic for the whole culture of znamenny singing—is most completely revealed with the use of stolp chant.

So-called *anenaiki* and *khabuvy* emerged in znamenny hymns in the sixteenth and seventeenth centuries. These were meaningless syllables inserted into sung liturgical texts for the purpose of increasing the length of the melody. (We recall that a similar phenomenon had a place in Byzantine kalophonic singing.) These syllables (*na, ne, ni, kha, bu, va,* etc.) sometimes distorted the entire text of hymns to the point of rendering them unintelligible and depriving them of their

[29] M. Brazhnikov, *Litsa and Fity of Znamenny Chant* (Leningrad, 1984), 18.
[30] Monk Christopher, *Key*, 73–74.
[31] Vladyshevskaia, *Musical Culture of Ancient Rus'*, 50.
[32] Ibid., 48.

meaning.³³ The appearance of *ananaiki* and *khabuvy* is connected with the general tendency towards the development of melismatic singing in this period.

The melismatic type of singing plays an important role in the creative work of exceptional Russian singer-composers of the second half of the sixteenth and seventeenth centuries. These include Varlaam Rogov who became the metropolitan of Rostov in 1589 and founded an entire school of composers. Sources speak of him as "a pious and wise man, very skilled, [who was] a singer-composer (*rospevshchik*) and a creator (*tvorets*) of znamenny and troestrochny and demestvenny singing."³⁴ Among other famous singers are Markell Bezborody, Ivan Shaidurov, Feodor Khristianin (Krestianin), Ivan Nos, Stefan Golysh, Ivan Lukoshko, and Faddei Nikitin.³⁵

Ivan the Terrible is considered to be the author of several stichera. He was a protector of liturgical singing and retained a large staff of singer-composers. Included below is a fragment written by him of a sticheron containing extensive melismatic insertions for the Feast of the Vladimir icon of the Mother of God. (The authorship of not only the music, but the text as well, is attributed to Ivan the Terrible.)³⁶

The melismatic type of singing predominates in several types of chant which were developed in the sixteenth century: *putevoi (put')*, *demestvenny*, and *great znamenny*. These chants came to replace more ancient forms of melismatic singing such as the kondakarian singing that was mentioned earlier.³⁷

---

³³Gardner, *Liturgical Singing of the Russian Orthodox Church* (Jordanville-Moscow), 429.

³⁴V. Undolsky, *Notes for History of Church Singing in Russia* (Moscow, 1846), 22. (See also Gardner, *Russian Church Singing*, 261.)

³⁵Gardner, *Church Singing*, 261–262.

³⁶The stikheron is cited as it was deciphered by Nikolai Uspenskii.

³⁷For a discussion of the connection between kondakarian singing and the 16th-century chants, see G. Pozhidaeva, "Historical-liturgical Premises of Prolix Singing in Muscovite Rus'," in E. Lozovaya, ed., *Church Singing in Historical-liturgical Context: East–Rus'–West* (Moscow, 2003), 118–121.

Put' chant is a variety of znamenny chant but it possesses its own set of melodic formulae and is recorded using a special collection of kriuki. This collection includes both usual znamenny kriuki as well as those peculiar to put' chant alone; the latter were called *put' notation*. Hymns sung in the *put'* manner have melodies that are broad and drawn-out.[38]

Put' chant was used only in performing especially festive hymns. "Put' popevka," notes one scholar, "is a complicated intonational-rhythmic variation of znamenny chant. . . . It was characteristic in put' chant to combine syncopation of tiny durations with lengthy and drawn-out notes, which created the impression of exceptional zeal and exalted festivity."[39]

In the opinion of Archpriest Dimitri Razumovsky, put' chant owes its name to the "piety of its ancestors" who did not dare to use the usual znamenny chant while they were travelling on journeys (*puteshestvia*), since (this chant) belonged exclusively to the temple, so they created a version of it for use while on the road."[40] Gardner considers this explanation artificial and strained because the hymns of put' chant are considerably more extended than the usual znamenny hymns and "services performed while travelling are usually simplified in some fashion."[41] The word *put'* in the Slavonic language had

Demestvennik. 18th c.

---

[38] The hymn "As Many as Have Been Baptized into Christ" is cited as it was deciphered by N. Uspenskii from the manuscript in the National Library of Russia in St Petersburg, Solovki Collection, No. 644/618, l. 2 ob.
[39] Martynov, *History*, 37.
[40] Razumovsky, *Singing*, 37.
[41] Cf. Gardner, *Church Singing*, vol. 1, 108.

various meanings including "custom," "means," "rule," and "motion." Most likely the name *putevoi* had as its goal merely to indicate the special means of performing a particular hymn.

Demestvenny chant, or *demestvo* was yet another version of znamenny chant and had its own kriuk notation. The terms *demestvo* and *demestvenny* came from the Greek word "domestikos" (δομεστικός), from which in Rus' the word *domestic* signified the church choir director. On this basis several scholars suppose that demestvenny singing came to Rus' in the sixteenth century from Greece, but this supposition has no foundation. The popevochnaia structure is preserved in demestvenny chant but the inventory of popevki differs essentially from that of znamenny chant. Moreover, the boundaries between popevki became much more vacillating and moveable than in znamenny chant.[42] Demestvenny chant does not submit to the Eight-mode System and therefore is readily used by singer-composers for hymns outside the particular Octoechos tones. These include the majority of hymns sung during the Divine Liturgy, including "Only-begotten Son," which in its demestvenny version sounds like this:[43]

Great znamenny chant is a late variety of znamenny chant. It did not appear until the sixteenth century. It possessed its own inventory of popevki but was notated using usual kruiki. This chant too was used only for the most celebratory festal hymns. *Litsa* and *fity* played a large role in the formulation of this chant. Although at first they were melismatic additions to znamenny melodies, they became an integral part of the melody in the new chant.

The first models of Russian polyphony, known by the general designation *demestvenny strochny singing,* date to the sixteenth century. On the basis of this

---

[42] *History of Russian Music in Ten Volumes* vol. 1, 149.
[43] Deciphered by N. Ouspensky.

type of singing lays the "principle of '*lentochny*' polyphony in which voices sing the melody preserving its contour of pitch and rhythm almost precisely, and the principle of 'countervoice' polyphony in which counterpoint voices (*podgoloski* / "under-voices") are formed around the melody's sustained notes."[44] The unison melody of the basic voice is fused with two other voices. At times this creates a greatly whimsical dissonant chord (including, for example, parallel seconds). Dissonant chords predominate over consonant chords and comprise the basis of a vertical harmony.[45] The basic voice in strochny (linear) singing is the middle one called the *put'* (way). To this is added the *niz* (bottom) and *verkh* (top). (In some cases the top voice is called *demestvo*.) A vertical harmony is created by virtue of the modification of the basic melody in the two extreme voices:

> Starting with the unison of all voices, it is as though the linear fabric is pulled apart, (split, divided) into some kind of multi-layered chords. The bottom (*niz*) generally goes either to a unison or to a perfect fourth with the main *put'* voice.... The top (*verkh*) goes either to a major second with the main voice ... or to a perfect fourth with it.... A special fullness of overtones of this vertical arrangement is reminiscent of the tolling of bells and endows it with this unique character which sharply distinguishes Russian polyphonic thinking from all the other existing conceptions of polyphony.[46]

Demestvenny strochny polyphony, insofar as it is possible to judge, did not exist for long. The reason for its rather quick disappearance was primarily its own unusual and sharply dissonant character. On the other hand, its flourishing coincided with the time of intense penetration into Rus', through Poland and Ukraine, of samples of *partesny* singing ("part song") constructed on completely different—western—aesthetical models with their characteristic accords of thirds. The western influence on Russian liturgical music became so powerful that it resulted in demestvenny polyphony being completely driven out of usage. Monophony (single-voiced singing) was enriched with new chants that greatly differed from the traditional znamenny singing in Rus'.

The new chants of the seventeenth century include Kievan, Greek, and Bulgarian chants. Judging by their names we may assume corresponding Ukrainian, Greek, and Bulgarian origins. In the case of Kievan chant, evidence exists to sup-

[44] N. Ouspensky, *Old Russian Art of Singing*, 232–233.
[45] A. Konotop, "Strochny Polyphony and Folklore," in I. Lozovaya, ed., *Church Singing in a Historical-liturgical Context: East–Rus'–West* (Moscow, 2003), 248.
[46] Martynov, *History*, 150–151.

port this assumption. The possible Bulgarian roots of Russian "Bulgarian chant" will be discussed later. As for Greek chant, it supposedly emerged in Moscow and was connected with the general involvement of Greece during the time of Patriarch Nikon. There are no clear traces of the influence of Greek liturgical singing of the seventeenth century on Russian "Greek chant."

The znamenny chant scale was used in creating hymns of all three chants. But the scale was fully reconceived and no longer perceived as consisting of four "accordances." In fact we have in hymns of Kievan, Bulgarian, and Greek chant examples of "octave thinking." Melodies were sharply colored in major or minor tones. A new structure, strophic and characteristic of folk-singing, replaced the popevochny one. Symmetrical rhythm characterizes all three chants, which can be seen in this example of the Greek chant hymn "All Creation Rejoices in thee, O Full of Grace":

The cultural-aesthetical model of Greek, Kievan, and Bulgarian chants is outside of the tradition of znamenny singing and represents the product of Western musical thinking, although these chants maintain znamenny's unison character. It is no coincidence that we observe that once the systematic harmonization of Russian liturgical singing to Western ideas in the nineteenth century had begun, these very chants were the most adaptable to harmonization and suffered the least from being joined to unison melody of homophono-harmonic accompaniment.

Changes arose in znamenny chant itself in the seventeenth century. These changes were caused by the presence of foreign chants and the necessity, on the one hand, of "bottling up" the chant in order to preserve it from corruptive influences, and, on the other hand, of adapting to new standards that required more precision in specifying pitch. These two goals helped in bringing about the invention in the first half of the century of cinnabar markings—letters, written in cinnabar (red ink) to the left of the kriuki. This invention is connected with the name of the Novgorod singer-composer Ivan Shaidurov, although much evidence exists to suppose that

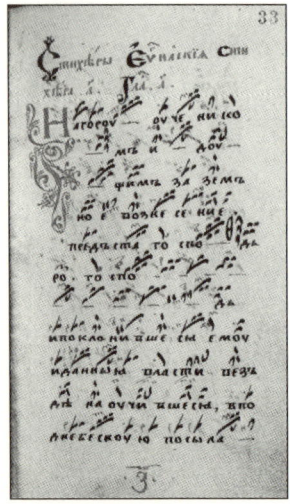

Song Anthology from the Collection of Dimitri Razumovsky.

it was the fruit of the collective creative work of many singers-composers.[47] Cinnabar markings indicated the absolute pitch (marks of degree) or made more precise the duration (indicator marks). There were six marks of degree: *gn* (Sl. *gorazdo nizko*, very low), *n* (*nizko*, low), *c* (*srednym glasom*, middle voice), *m* (*mrachno*, somber), *p* (*povyshe*, rather high), *v* (*vysoko*, very high). Marks were associated with the sounds of a hexachord: *do, re, mi, fa, so, la*. These notes corresponded to the basic core of the znamenny scale.

The appearance of cinnabar markings was a huge accomplishment, because from that time onward all notation written with kriuki became legible irrespective of the presence or absence of oral tradition. (Thanks to cinnabar markings, znamenny manuscripts may be read by contemporary performers.) At the same time, the introduction of cinnabar markings contradicted the very content of znamenny singing and, essentially, was a harbinger of its decline:

> Cinnabar markings—by limiting the specific freedom of intoning in the znamenny culture of singing, improvisation being the principal unique feature of znamenny singing and its metro-rhythmic freedom—ended up gradually destroying the znamenny culture of singing by introducing uncharacteristic elements into it. In this way, the instruction of cinnabar markings as the necessary attribute of znamenny notation radically changed the essential unique aspects of znamenny writing and was a reflection of the crisis which had begun in the culture of singing. . . . A violation (took place) of the balance of content . . . and of the content's form of expression reflected in the system of musical notation.[48]

The introduction of cinnabar markings was an artificial symbiosis between znamenny chant and the West-European musical conception of the New Era in which each sound should be clearly tied to a particular pitch. The introduction of cinnabar markings was followed by the translation of the entire body of hymns of znamenny and other ancient chants into western line notation. This process began

---

[47] M. Brazhnikov, *Old Russian Music Theory: Materials from Manuscripts of the 15th–18th Centuries* (Leningrad, 1972), 311.

[48] Nikishov, *Christopher*, 207.

in the eighteenth century and continued throughout all of the nineteenth century. With the blessing of the Holy Synod, the entire cycle of unison hymns of ancient chants was published in line notation in the nineteenth century. On the one hand, this decisively wiped out kriuk signs and kriuk notation while, on the other hand, it made this type of singing accessible to contemporary singers and listeners.

In discussing Russian liturgical singing of the pre-Petrine period, we cannot fail to note several features of the culture of performance connected with znamenny chant. Both in Byzantium and in Rus' there existed solo singing, responsorial singing, and antiphonal singing. Only men's choirs existed and they were overwhelmingly in the range of the bass voice. Women were not permitted to sing in the choir except in women's monasteries.

Information concerning the participation in choral singing performed by young boys is rather scant but there are numerous testimonies of singing schools where boys were instructed in kriuki, popevki, litsa, fity, and other aspects of znamenny chant. For training boys in singing the modes there existed so-called *poglasitsy*—tutorial hymns in which each line corresponded to one of the eight modes. The following is an example of a *poglasitsa*:[49]

>A monk goes out from the monastery. (Tone 1)
>Coming toward him is another monk. (Tone 2)
>"From where are you coming, brother?" (Tone 3)
>"I come from Constantinople." (Tone 4)
>"Let us sit, brother, and talk a while." (Tone 5)
>"Is my mother still living, brother?" (Tone 6)
>"Your mother died long ago." (Tone 7)
>"Woe, woe is me! My mother!" (Tone 8)

Of the singing groups that existed in Rus', the Choir of State Singing Clerics (Diaki), formed in 1479 during the reign of Tsar Ivan III was of special significance. Following the establishment of the Patriarchate in 1589, a patriarchal court was established, modeled after the tsar's royal court. The Ensemble of Patriarchal Singing Clerics and Sub-Clerics was formed under the aegis of the patriarchal court. Both the tsar's singing clerks and those of the patriarch were divided into several stations (groups) which alternated in singing on the kliros. (During one service usually two stations participated.)[50] A comparable ensemble of singers existed in

---

[49]See Gardner, *Russian Church Singing*, vol. 2, 358—Ed.
[50]Gardner, *Liturgical Singing of the Russian Orthodox Church* (Jordanville-Moscow), 412–415.

hierarchical courts in various dioceses. As a rule, the singing clerics of the tsar, of the patriarch, and of the hierarch were the main "legislators of fashion" in Old Russian singing. The most famous singer-composers (*razpevschiki*) labored in these choirs. The most intricate and newest chants took root there and the voices of the most famous singers were heard there.

The tradition of znamenny singing was preserved in the Russian Orthodox Church up to the middle of the nineteenth century and in some cathedrals (the Kremlin's Dormition Cathedral) and monasteries (Solovetsky, Valaam, and others) right up to the time of their closure in the Soviet period.[51] But the process of intensively driving znamenny chant out of use and replacing it with partesny singing in four voices was already underway in the majority of parishes of the Russian Church in the eighteenth century. Znamenny singing ceased to be a living tradition in the Russian Church after the closure of the last monasteries in the 1920s and 1930s and was preserved only in communities of Old Ritualists.

In discussing the significance of znamenny chant, we must not fail to mention the effect it has on the souls of those praying in churches. This effect is spoken of in Saint Ignatius Brianchaninov's story "Visit to Valaam Monastery" found in the first volume of *Ascetic Experiences*. The saint discusses the effect that the singing of the Valaam monks had on him when he visited Valaam while still an archimandrite:

> The znamenny melody is used—the so-called stolp melody—which is primordially Russian. The tones of this melody are majestic, drawn-out, and plaintive; the groans of the penitent's soul are depicted. . . . These tones are stretched out dolefully, mournfully, as a desert wind which gradually disappears as an echo amongst the cliffs and ravines which suddenly resound. Now with quiet remorse they lodge a complaint against sinfulness. . . . Now as if by unbearable heaviness they begin to wail and call for the succor of heaven.[52]

Why did the singing of the Valaam brethren produce such an unmatched impression on Archimandrite Ignatius, the then-rector of Saint Petersburg's St Sergius Monastery? In the middle of the nineteenth century, when the cited lines were written, znamenny chant had in fact already ceased to be used and was preserved only in certain monasteries where the piety was especially strict and the life of the brethren particularly severe. Moreover it was the singing which had existed in Rus' for many centuries and in all ages was considered to be canonically proper and

---

[51] B. Kutuzov, *Znamenny Chant: Theology in Song* (Moscow, 2001), 21.
[52] Ignatius (Brianchaninov), "Visit to Valaam Monastery," in *Collection of Works in Six Volumes* (Moscow, 2004), vol. 2, 235.

truly pertaining to the Church. For that reason it was considered to be singularly permitted in divine services. And although the nineteenth century was a period of almost complete oblivion and demise for znamenny singing, it retained then that inexpressible and unique beauty which a spiritually sensitive person such as Saint Ignatius could not fail to appreciate.

Znamenny singing is a part of the great culture of church singing that was formed over the span of centuries in diverse parts of the Orthodox world. The singing of the first Christian prayer congregations, the psalmodic melos of Egyptian and Sinai ascetics of the fourth and fifth centuries, Byzantine liturgical musical culture, and Russian znamenny singing—all these are revelations of a single spiritual order. Notwithstanding the differences between them caused by national particularities and the uniqueness of historical development, they all possess that which is common to all and which comprises the essence of Orthodox liturgical singing—the primacy of the tradition of song dating back, as Saint Ignatius noted, to Christ himself and to his apostles.[53]

Znamenny chant, in the form in which it came to exist in the sixteenth century (i.e., before the later "stratification" caused by foreign influences), was "theology in song."[54] Znamenny chant's main virtue lies firmly in the theological richness of znamenny singing and its inseparable link with the experience of prayer. Znamenny chant is built on the knowledge of the correspondence between the specific singing intonations and the specific conditions of the spirit of the person who is praying. We have already cited the words of Saint Augustine: "The several affections of our spirit, by a sweet variety, have their own proper measures in the voice and singing, by some hidden correspondence wherewith they are stirred up."[55] All of ancient liturgical singing is based on the knowledge of this "hidden correspondence."

The melodic formulae (*popevki*) of znamenny chant are not only musical intonations but also carriers of a particular spiritual state. In the popevki themselves the principle of "tripartedness" is fully revealed—that which pertains to music, the word, and the spirit.

This very principle is preserved in melismatic singing, which in Rus' was considered especially majestic, "beautiful," and which produced an exceptional impression on its audiences. As if violating the normal course of the divine services, it

---

[53]Idem, "Homily Concerning Prayer with the Lips and the Voice," in *Collection of Works in Six Volumes* (Moscow, 2004), vol. 1, 547–548.
[54]Kutuzov, *Znamenny Chant*, 1.
[55]Augustine *Confessions* 10, 33. <http://www.ccel.org/ccel/augustine/confess.xi.xxxiii.html> March 11, 2014.

compelled those at prayer to detach themselves from the usual language of words and to raise their reflection on high. Melismatic singing reflects the state of the soul of one at prayer as when the feeling of piety and tenderness overflows in the person praying to the point that he is no longer able to express it in words. Again it is fitting here to recall Saint Augustine who wrote, "While singing, words are suddenly forced out by a boundless rejoicing for which the language of words is insufficient to express. Then they (Christians) praise in jubilation since their voices express the state of their souls; with words it is impossible to convey that which excites the heart."[56]

In the words of Saint Augustine the idea is not so much about the emotional condition as of the spiritual, mystical experience. Ancient liturgical singing, in contrast to secular music, did not have as its goal to elicit in its audience particular emotions. One can speak about the fact that znamenny chant, as with Byzantine liturgical singing, is principally emotionless music, devoid of all sentimentality whatsoever. To one and the same melody texts are sung that have very different emotional contents: "The very same eight modes express the sorrow and suffering of Holy Week and the joy of Pascha and Pentecost."[57]

In the words of B. Kutuzov, znamenny singing is "our own lost Atlantis" and had the same tragic fate as the Russian icon—"first repudiated and forgotten for several centuries, but not long ago discovered and rehabilitated."[58] To compare znamenny singing with icons is only partly correct. The true rehabilitation of znamenny chant has not yet come, irrespective of the fact that its value was acknowledged by Russia's leading musicologists even during the Soviet times. The rehabilitation of znamenny chant will come only when it returns to the everyday practice of the Church. This process has already begun to take place and in several monasteries (particularly at Valaam) where once again znamenny singing is actively incorporated into the repertoire. But until that time, while aesthetic standards formed in the age of the "Italian captivity" (i.e., the eighteenth and nineteenth centuries) continue to dominate in church choirs, any discussion of the rehabilitation of znamenny singing would be premature.

---

[56]Idem, *Commentary on Psalm 32*.
[57]Archimandrite Vasileios, *Hymn* (Theotokos-St Sergius Monastery, 2007), 140.
[58]Kutuzov, *Znamenny Chant*, 20.

PARTESNY SINGING.
RUSSIAN LITURGICAL SINGING IN THE POST-PETRINE PERIOD

To a certain degree, the aforementioned processes that took place in znamenny singing in the sixteenth and seventeenth centuries—including the invention of cinnabar markings and the introduction of polyphony, as well as the appearance of new chants based on major and minor scales—served to set the stage for the appearance of *partesny* singing in the practice of Russian singing. This type of liturgical singing took shape in the seventeenth century in Ukraine under the influence of Catholic music and soon acquired popularity. By the 1650s it had already penetrated into Muscovite Rus' and, with the active support of Patriarch Nikon and Tsar Alexis Mikhailovich, came to be inculcated in liturgical usage despite the numerous protests of those zealous for the olden times.[59]

Patriarch Nikon. Miniature. Tsar's Tituliarnik. 1672.

Partesny singing (according to parts, voices) has no genetic link with the previous development of liturgical music in Rus'. Its introduction into the everyday singing practice of the Russian Church signified a true "cultural revolution" in liturgical singing. A cultural break occurred that went undetected by a significant part of church society. The Old Ritualists categorically rejected the new singing, rightly seeing in it a radical break with the many-centuries-long tradition of Russian liturgical music. Those zealous for the olden times upbraided Patriarch Nikon because:

> ... according to his own initiative and not the traditions of the saints, he brought Kievan "partesny" singing into the churches, on a par with worldly voice-breaking singing, and introduced Latin and Roman "partesny" screeching, condemned by the holy fathers. . . . This new type of Kievan "partesny" singing—a great deterioration executed with the movement of the whole body, the nodding of the head, and the waving of hands—has now been brought to Russia. . . . With body parts drooping and doing that which is indecent, it is an excessively flamboyant singing, fractured and dissimilar—appropriate for adversaries and entertainers, not for the Church of God.[60]

---

[59]Gardner, *Liturgical Singing of the Russian Orthodox Church*, vol. 2 (Jordanville-Moscow), 52–54.
[60]Cited in Gardner, *Liturgical Singing*, vol. 2, 57–58.

Partesny singing is one of the varieties of western European polyphony whose basic principles were shaped during the age of the Renaissance. In the western Church for an extended period the basic form of church music was Gregorian chant based on the same principles as Byzantine and Russian church singing. But during the first half of the second millennium there arose in Western church music various genres of polyphonic singing of both the polyphonic and responsorial-harmonic type. During the Renaissance musical standards—in which folk and secular music dominated—began to be actively inculcated in the daily practice of the Church. This resulted in a radical modification of the entire style and structure of church singing in the West. At the same time, the connection with Gregorian chant was preserved in the works of early masters of polyphony (Guillaume de Machaut, Johannes Ockeghem, Jacob Obrecht, Josquin des Prez, Orlande de Lassus, Giovanni Pierluigi da Palestrina). In later samples of Roman Catholic music this connection disappeared. In the Lutheran tradition homophonia with a simple folk-like melody and a clear harmonic vertical became the main type of singing.

The principle of using octave scales, of which the most basic are the natural major and natural or harmonic minor, is based on western European music stemming from the age of the Renaissance. The basic consonant chords within the bounds of a single octave were not only perfect fourths and perfect fifths but also thirds (major and minor) and sixths (major and minor). The role of dissonances is played by seconds and sevenths (major and minor). Triadic chords became the main harmonic thinking, and the empty fourths and fifths began to be perceived as dissonance and in need of being completed with chords containing thirds. Radical changes took place also in the field of rhythm. Music having definite two-beat, three-beat, and four-beat measures took the place of the unmeasured Gregorian music, in which the melody is subordinate to the word.

This type of music required its own notation capable of recording precise pitch as well as duration. Linear notation was invented by the beginning of the eleventh century by the monk Guido of Arezzo who set musical signs on four lines. Originally this type of notation was used to record Gregorian hymns. Over time it was significantly perfected and came to have five lines while the musical notes were changed from squares to circles. The chief merit of linear notation was that it made it possible to record new, earlier unknown, musical material. In the words of Vladimir Martynov, linear notation radically changed the understanding and nature of the very act of making music: "If earlier the goal of music making had been to reproduce something that had already been heard, on the basis of following similarities, now the goal was to produce something that had not previously been heard, on the basis of a succession of likenesses and distinctions."[61] The appearance of linear notation in the West signified a transition from the age of impersonal, collective, and "universal" music to an individual music, created by a composer.

Partesny singing, which penetrated into Rus' in the twelfth century, was one of the varieties of Western composer music. It was created by composers "by one's own composing." That is, it was not composed using prepared material of melodic formulae (popevki), but was the fruit of the free creative imagination of an author. Masters of partesny singing soon acquired fame and popularity despite the continued resistance to their activity on the part of the singer-composers who worked according to the ancient models.

One of the first famous masters of partesny songs was the Kievan Nikolay Diletsky (c. 1630–1670). He received his musical education in Warsaw and Vilna and the works of Polish Catholic authors were his models. In the third quarter of the seventeenth century Diletsky settled in Moscow where he founded a school for singers. "Pan Diletsky," as he was known by his contemporaries, was not only a composer and author of complicated polyphonic sheet music but also the author of the first "Musical Grammar" in which western terminology was widely used (*kliavishi, dispositsia, inventsia, dural'naya musika*[62], etc.) and the fundamentals of harmonic music were expounded. Diletsky considered it possible to use ancient chants for harmonization, but insofar as they did not have a particular measure, he supposed it necessary to detach from them those sounds which could not be written into the measure.[63] Diletsky wrote that, "the notes and singing of *herimoi*, which have no perfect measure, can be assigned to a perfect measure."[64] Thus the foundations were laid for the musical thinking and the method of harmonizing ancient chants which became characteristic of church composers in the eighteenth and nineteenth centuries.

A large quantity of partesny works in four, six, eight, twelve, and more voices were written by pupils and followers of Diletsky. (Two manuscript of choral concerts for forty-eight voices have even been preserved.)[65] Four voices are the main ones in partesny singing. Each voice can be divided into two or several parts: descant, alto, tenor, bass. Both homophono-harmonic and polyphonic methods

---

[61] V. Martynov, *Zona opus posthumous, or the Birth of a New Reality* (Moscow, 2008), 171.
[62] That is, major music (from the German "dur" meaning "major").
[63] Gardner, *Liturgical Singing of the Russian Orthodox Church*, vol. 2 (Jordanville-Moscow), 65–67.
[64] Cited in Metallov, *Essay*, 111.
[65] Vladyshevkaya, *Culture*, 196–201.

of execution were used in composing choral concerts by composers of the second half of the seventeenth and eighteenth centuries.

On the basis of partesny singing lies the principle of emotional expressiveness which Nikolay Diletsky formulated in this way: "*Musika* is that which stirs human hearts to pleasure or to pity."[66] Joy is associated with major keys and energetic tempos while sorrow is associated with minor keys or slower tempos. Sometimes music acquires a vividly expressed illustrated character. (For example, the agitation of the sea in the words "the sea saw and fled" is conveyed using complicated fugue music with gradually increasing volume.) While in znamenny singing the movement of the melody reflected the movements of the mind of the one praying and music in no way illustrated the text, in partesny singing "prayerfulness" and spirituality played no role whatsoever. This type of music relies on an external, emotional effect and is not connected with the experience of prayer. In all its basic qualities such music has a purely secular character. Only the liturgical text guarantees a connection with the spiritual tradition and this music is connected to the text only in a formal sense.

The creation of polyphonic partesny sheet music using a wide range of voices called for a fundamental widening of the choir's abilities. Boys with high voices were actively sought out for singing in the choir. (As before, singing in church was considered impermissible for women.) Schools for singing were created in Rus' in the second half of the second century in which children were trained according to the new fashion.

The reforms of Peter the Great struck across all of Russian culture, and liturgical singing was no exception. The transformation of two main choral groups—the Tsar's and Patriarch's Singing Clerks—were well known events in Peter's time. The Tsar's Singing Clerks were renamed in 1701 as the "Court Choir" and several years later moved, together with the entire court, to Saint Petersburg. The College of Patriarchal Singing Clerks was considerably reduced after the abolition of the patriarchate by PeterI in 1721, but several of its members remained in Moscow under the name "Synodal Singers." Both choirs were gradually reoriented towards partesny singing.

Peter the Great.
Paul Delaroche. 1838.

The chief legislator of musical fashion in the post-Petrine period became the Imperial Court Capella. The

---

[66]N. Diletsky, *The Idea of Musical Grammar* (St Petersburg: S. Smolensky Publications, 1910), 60.

partesny style of singing in the "Polish" manner, as it was practiced by Diletsky and other masters of his school, began to decline in use by the middle of the eighteenth century. It was replaced by the "Italian" style, no less distant from the traditional znamenny chant of Rus' which began to undergo even more decline in the eighteenth century. The Imperial Court Capella became the main guardian of Italian influence. Among its leaders were the Italians Francesco Araja (from 1735 through 1759), Baldassare Galuppi (from 1764 through 1768), and Giuseppe Sarti (from 1784 through 1801). These composers combined their management of spiritual music with vigorous activity in the field of secular music and the composition of operas for the theater. Other Italian maestros worked in Russia in the second half of the eighteenth century, mostly in the area of operas. These included Giovanni Battista Locatelli, Tommaso Traetta, Vincenzo Manfredini, Giovanni Paisiello, and Domenico Cimarosa.

As a rule, Italians who came to Russia did not burden themselves with the study of the Russian language. If they composed spiritual concerts, the music was written first and only later was a text in Slavonic chosen for the prepared music. (In this way, the text fulfilled an exclusively applied function and was connected to the music only in a completely formal sense.) The dubious honor of introducing into the everyday practice of the Russian Orthodox Church the so called "spiritual concerts"—performed during the communion of the clergy—belongs completely to the meisters of the Italian Court Cappella. Concerts of Italian composers were distinguished by their well known professionalism, sometimes even mastery and melodic vividness, but the spirit of these was absolutely foreign to the theology of the Orthodox Church. It was secular music which did not differ in style from opera music written by the very same composers. Some standards of Italian instrumental concerts, in particular the necessary use of alternating fast and slow parts, as well as the contrast between forte and piano, were automatically transferred to "spiritual concerts" intended for use in Orthodox churches.

Besides concerts, Italians composed actual liturgical music, especially Cherubic Hymns. (Some of their works, for example Sarti's Cherubic Hymn, are heard up to the present day in the choirs of Orthodox churches.) But the main characteristics of instrumental concerts were also transferred to authentic liturgical music. In particular, Italians introduced the custom of performing the first half of the Cherubic Hymn slowly and quietly while the second part—beginning with the words "that we may receive the King of All who comes invisibly upborne by the Angelic Hosts"—quickly and loudly. This does not correspond with the text of the

Cherubic Hymn or with the inner logic of the Great Entrance which is conducted during the singing of the Cherubic Hymn. This flawed tradition owing to the Italians and their disciples (especially Bortniansky) is so solidly entrenched in the everyday practice of the Russian Church that today the singing of the final line in a slow tempo requires a special explanation.

The composers Maxim Berezovsky, Artemiy Vedel, and Dmitri Bortniansky were disciples of the Italians beginning in the nineteenth century.

Maxim Berezovsky (1745–1777) did not leave a considerable trace on Russian church music. After receiving a degree as an academic in Bologna he returned to Russia, but his life in Russia was unsuccessful and he died before reaching the age of thirty-two years. According to some information, Berezovsky committed suicide while suffering from delirium tremens.[67] Berezovsky was the author of a number of spiritual concerts of which the most famous is a concert for the words "Cast Me Not Off in the Time of Old Age." Other works by Berezovsky are performed today extremely rarely.

The professional fate of the composer Artemiy Vedel (1770–1806) also proved unsuccessful. For a while he led choirs in Moscow and Kiev and later became a novice in the Kiev Monastery of the Caves where he began to manifest signs of a spiritual disorder. He died, according to some witnesses, in a lunatic asylum while others contend he died in his father's home after a serious illness.[68] The style of Italian concerts had a decisive influence on the creative work of Vedel but information concerning his studies in Italy or with Italian professors does not exist. The best known of his works is the spiritual concert setting of "Open to Me the Doors of Repentance." In this work we find echoes of several genres of secular music that were well known in that time: the typical *kant* manner of execution at the beginning of the hymn, the rhythm of a march at the words "my spirit rises early," the melody of a city romance at the words "by in thy compassion purify me" and finally, the intonation of the operatic *bel canto* at the words "have mercy upon me according to thy great mercy." The simplicity, even banality of melodic phrases, the poverty of harmonic language, the illustrative bent of the music, and its openly secular character did not hinder this "Hymn of Repentance" from occupying a solid position in the church choir and from keeping this position until the present day.

The most prominent of the Russian disciples of the Italian masters was Dmitri Bortniansky (1752–1825). He was born in Ukraine, and at seventeen years of age he

---

[67] See E. Levashev, A. Polekhin, *M.S. Berezovsky: History of Russian Music in Ten Volumes*, vol. 3 (Moscow, 1985), 160.

[68] I. Sonevitsky, *Artem Vedel i yogo muzichna spadpschina* (New York, 1966), 108–109.

was accepted into a choral capella. While still a boy he began to perform in women's parts in the Italian opera. After finishing school Bortniansky was sent to Italy where he studied with Galuppi. Returning to Russia, Bortniansky became the director of the Court Capella. Indeed his activity as a church composer is connected with the capella. Bortniansky was the author of numerous secular works but all of them were forgotten after his death. The spiritual music of Bortniansky received universal recognition during his lifetime and continues to be recognized to the present day.

Dmitry Bortiansky.

More than fifty-nine choral concerts were written by Bortniansky's hand and many of them are performed in churches up to the present day. Like the majority of Italian instrumental concerts, these concerts are comprised of three parts: a fast section is followed by a slow section and then the opposite takes place. The concluding part of the concert often has the character of a fugue. Bortniansky also wrote compositions for everyday use. In the words of one scholar, "elements of secularity are characteristic of these no less than they are characteristic of his concerts."[69] In particular, one can find traits of opera, *kant* melodies, folk-song phrases, and the rhythms of ball dances in Bortniansky's spiritual music. "All of these components form a special intonational fusion which has little in common with ancient church singing tradition."[70]

Among Bortniansky's compositions are nine Cherubic Hymns including seven written for four voices and two written for eight voices. The most famous is Cherubic Hymn No. 7. It became a true "hit" of church music. The custom of performing it on the most festive occasions (Pascha, Nativity, and other great feasts) is kept up to the present day.[71]

In Bortniansky's Cherubic Hymns the practice was firmly secured of performing the second part of the hymn (". . . that we may receive the King of all . . .") in a vigorous, march-like rhythm. As Gardner notes, "due to that arrangement, the meaning of the text is torn asunder because the logical subject is found in the first part of the Cherubic Hymn ('[We] who represent the Cherubim')—before the entrance and normally performed in a slow tempo—while the logical predicate is

---

[69] Y. Keldysh, *D.S. Bortniansky: History of Russian Music in Ten Volumes*, vol. 3: *18th Century, Part 2* (Moscow, 1985), 190.

[70] Ibid., 187.

[71] Cited in the edition of P.I. Tchaikovsky.

found in the second part ('that we may receive the King of All')—after the entrance and composed in a completely different movement and arrangement." In the words of the scholar, "in these works there is nothing Russian and nothing according to rules, nor can there be from a disciple of the Italians who studied for ten years in Italy during the years of his maturation, immersed in Italian music and called to practice it upon returning to his homeland."[72]

Bortniansky's significance is not limited to writing spiritual music of a secular character. He was interested in the harmonization of old chants and preferred Kievan and Greek chants whose melodies have a tonal basis. When he used melodies of znamenny chant, he used them very freely, preserving only the general base sounds.[73] Bortniansky also valued ancient znamenny singing and fought so "that those absurd and self-willed crossings of liturgical singing might cease which distort both its melody and course of measures." The composer proposed printing a complete cycle of znamenny hymns in kriuk notation, emphasizing the importance and necessity of using this very method of recording. "Ancient singing," he said, "being an inexhaustible source for the most novel singing being formed, would give birth to a native genius oppressed by thorns, whose own musical world would spring forth from the rebirth."[74] Bortniansky's project, however, was not implemented.

A younger contemporary of Bortniansky, the archpriest Peter Turchaninov (1779–1856) was engaged in the harmonization of znamenny chant melodies.

[72]Gardner, *Liturgical Singing of the Russian Orthodox Church* (Jordanville-Moscow), 226–227.
[73]Keldysh, *Bortniansky*, 190.
[74]Metallov, *Essay*, 163.

Numerous transpositions of ancient chants in four voices are his work. Like other figures of the "Italian period," Turchaninov used *obikhod* melodies and sped them up to a particular rhythm but he did this with greater delicacy than Bortniansky. In 1828 the metropolitan of Moscow Philaret upbraided Turchaninov for developing obikhod melodies "artificially, in a way difficult for singers" and "so imprecisely when compared to the antique models that it is not at all possible to recognize the ancient liturgical tune." The saint proposed submitting Turchaninov's transpositions to "examination of informed people under the observation of the Holy Synod and . . . to correct them such that this singing would resemble the ancient models precisely."[75]

Archpriest Peter Turchaninov.

Despite the Moscow saint's unfavorable commentary, the compositions of Archpriest Turchaninov were published, albeit with considerable delay, and soon entered into the everyday usage of church choirs. In 1893 Metallov witnessed the wide distribution of Turchaninov's works and gave them an appraisal exactly opposite to the one given by Metropolitan Philaret several decades earlier: "Turchaninov's adaptations are used everywhere with special respect for their closeness to the original obikhod melodies and for their artistic and both simple and generally understood harmonic interpretation."[76] Many of Turchaninov's compositions are used to the present day in churches of the Russian Orthodox Church.

Yet another religious figure who devoted himself to the task of harmonizing ancient chants was Archimandrite Feofan (Aleksandrov, 1786/7–1852).[77] Rector of Moscow's Donskoy Stavropegic Monastery and dean (*blagochinny*) of all the stavropegic monasteries, Feofan was famous in Moscow as a preacher. During his life he was considerably less well known as a liturgical composer. Nonetheless his compositional inheritance is extremely voluminous. During his life he did not publish his musical works and church choir directors often edited them according to their own discretion when copying them. Several of his works are widely famous in several versions. Many of Feofan's hymns were printed and reprinted without any indication of authorship. Some of them were marked with the words "Feofanov," "Kievan Chant," "Don" (which indicated the chant of Donskoy Monastery), while

---

[75] Philaret (Drozdov) *Collection of Opinions and Comments of Philaret, Metropolitan of Moscow and Kolomna* (Moscow, 1886), vol. 2, 245–246.
[76] Metallov, *Essay*, 130–131.
[77] For more about him see our article "G.A. Archimandrite Feofan (Aleksandrov)."

others were marked with the name "Feofan" and others even with the surname Grigoriev—which he never used.

In analyzing the hymns of Archimandrite Feofan one must consider that his theoretical training was lacking and in terms of composers' mastery he cannot be compared with Bortniansky or Turchaninov. The style of his musical writings is not distinguished by a wealth of harmonic methods and a certain monotony is characteristic of his work. Feofan's music is strictly diatonic and most often it employs a major scale juxtaposed with a parallel minor. In his music, modulations and deviations even in the closest tonalities are extremely rare. But the strength of Feofan's works lies firmly in their simplicity and "churchliness" which makes them sufficiently expressive in and of themselves. Feofan's irmoi for the Feast of the Nativity are sung to the present day in many churches, especially in Moscow, and often by the entire congregation.

Probably Feofan's most famous work and the one which is most beloved by the faithful is his setting of the Anaphora. (It is performed in practically in every village church.) The harmonic basis of this composition is a juxtaposition of the minor key and its dominant with the key and dominant of the parallel major:

Archimandrite Feofan's church music had at a certain stage a rather large significance: "By his own works he forced out from liturgical use the Catholic music of Sarti, Galuppi, and their innumerable imitators—many of whom were more gifted and stronger than he."[78]

[78] L. Pariysky, "The Church Composer Archimandrite Feofan," *Journal of the Moscow Patriarchate* 10 (1952), 41.

An important role in the development of Russian church music was played by Aleksei Lvov (1798–1870). After inheriting the responsibility of director of the Court Capella from his father F.P. Lvov, he headed the Capella between 1837 and 1861. During this period he "became, in the full meaning of the word, the legislator of church singing in the Russian Church."[79] During the junior Lvov's time, German influence replaced Italian influence in Russian music. Lvov used principles characteristic of German Lutheran chorale in harmonizing obikhod melodies and melodies of his own composing. At the same time Lvov was the first to understand the necessity of using asymmetrical rhythm for the harmonization of ancient chants.

Aleksei Lvov.

Lvov benefitted from the patronage and personal friendship of Emperor Nicholas I who bestowed upon him the rank of major general. His relationship with Metropolitan Philaret was not nearly as serene. In particular, Philaret blocked the approval of Lvov's transpositions in the Holy Synod. The metropolitan created a special committee to study these transpositions, to which the committee gave a negative assessment. Metropolitan Philaret reported to the Synod concerning his own participation in the work of this committee and his confrontations with Lvov: "When I suggested that for a particular irmos or dogmatikon the four-voiced transposition lacks resemblance to the melody of the church book, or—said differently—in four-voiced singing the church melody is not clearly heard but rather eclipsed by the harmony . . . I was opposed and told that the harmony was composed according to the rules and cannot be any other way."[80] In his personal correspondence Philaret was more critical in regards to Lvov and his harmonization:

> God sends us humility in that a general wishes to reteach singing to the Church in his own manner. If the singing is good at the Lavra, if it is founded on the basis of Greek singing, then for what purpose ought we tear up this foundation and propose four-voiced singing? If you provide to them a musical score, they will suggest to you a harmony in which you cannot recognize either your music or your melody. And when you say that it does not resemble what you

---

[79] Gardner, *Liturgical Singing of the Russian Orthodox Church* (Jordanville-Moscow), 277–278.
[80] Philaret (Drozdov), *Collection of Opinions and Comments*, vol. 3, 449.

Saint Philaret, Metropolitan of Moscow.

first had, you will be told that the harmony is correct and recognized by all of Europe.[81]

Without waiting for the approval of the Synod, Lvov instructed the Court Capella to publish his compositions. Due to this edition, Lvov's compositions entered into the repertoire of many church choirs even during his own lifetime. They continue to be performed in churches up to the present day.

The dissatisfaction of the Moscow saint was directed not only towards Lvov but also towards the state of church singing in general, which had been in the hands of secular figures for many years. This pertained especially to Saint Petersburg. Fighting for the preservation of the traditions of Old Russian singing, Philaret wrote: "Can Saint Petersburg, which is a newcomer to ecclesial life, offer many individuals with knowledge, experience, and good taste for the more ancient church music? Is it not possible to have more hope in seeking such people in the more ancient dioceses in which an attachment to that which pertains to the ancient Church has been preserved, in which the new taste has not been so decisively assimilated?"[82]

The saint deemed that the development of church singing should fall under the control of the diocese, which should guard it from a penetrating secular spirit:

> The first Church and Greek Church of subsequent centuries produced church singing by its labor. The Russian Church received it from the Greek Church and added several melodies to it by its own labor. The Church has recorded the ancient singing for its preservation by means of musical notation, first using kriuki and later clearer line notation, and the Church teaches the people how to use and preserve this style of singing. Is anything more needed to recognize the ownership right to this singing? If this right is taken away and church singing is given away for the completely arbitrary use of the people . . . a secular taste in singing could easily intrude into the church, take hold of the people, and introduce melodies unfitting for the holy place. We already see this in the Western Church where theatrical music is used in churches during

---

[81] Idem, "*Letter to Archimandrite Anthony,*" Part 3 (Moscow, 1883), 17–18. These words witness to the fact that antique unison singing was still preserved in the Holy Trinity-St Sergius Lavra during the time of Philaret.

[82] Philaret (Drozdov), *Collection of Opinions and Comments*, vol. 5, 828.

divine services as if those in charge assumed the responsibility of tempting the people—that the thoughts of those who came to pray might be drawn out of the church and into the theatre.[83]

Under the Holy Synod and Metropolitan Philaret, Church authorities continued to struggle to preserve the ecclesial character of Russian singing in the middle of the nineteenth century. In 1850 the Synod issued a decree concerning the prohibition of singing "spiritual concerts" during the communion of the clergy. But court composers paid little attention to the instructions issued from the upper ecclesial authority and continued to compose music in the Italian or German manner. On the other hand, the Synod's position cannot be considered to be completely consistent. While fighting for the preservation of ancient traditions, the Synod simultaneously gave official approval to the use of works written in the Italian and German styles.

Several notable hierarchs who were not members of the Holy Synod also fought for the purity of Russian church singing and its return to its "first image"—znamenny chant. Among them was Saint Ignatius (Brianchaninov), whose pronouncements concerning the singing at Valaam Monastery were cited earlier. In his article "Understanding Heresy and Schism," the saint devoted several paragraphs to church singing. He was highly critical of "Italian singing" and considered that "it is incompatible with Orthodox services" because "it came sweeping over to us from the West." In particular, "the communal verse has been replaced with a concert reminiscent of an opera." In Bishop Ignatius' opinion, true Russian church singing is znamenny chant:

Saint Ignatius (Brianchaninov).

> The holy Fathers rightly refer to our spiritual sensations as "joy and sorrow." This feeling is completely expressed by the znamenny melody which has been preserved in several monasteries and which is used in the "yedinovercheskye" churches. The znamenny melody may be compared to an ancient icon. By attentively listening to it, the same feeling conquers the heart as when one gazes at an ancient icon written by a certain holy man. The feeling of profound piety which penetrates the melody carries the soul to piety and tenderness. . . . Upon hearing a znamenny melody, the Christian who passes his life in sufferings,

[83]Ibid., vol. 3, 476.

who struggles continually with various difficulties of life, immediately finds in it a harmony with his own spiritual state. He will not find this harmony in the present singing of the Orthodox Church. The court singing . . . that has now entered into universal use in Orthodox churches, unusually cold and lifeless, is frivolous and hurried! The compositions of the latest composers express the mood of their spirit, a western mood, earthy, emotional, passionate, or cold—alien to spiritual sensibility.[84]

As the saint justly notes further, znamenny chant needs no harmonization:

Recognizing that a western element of singing can in no way coincide with the spirit of the Orthodox Church and rightly admitting the famous compositions of Bortniansky to be sweet-passionate and romantic, certain people wanted to help the matter. They transposed the znamenny melody into four voices while preserving all the rules of counterpoint. Was the labor satisfactory to the requirements of the Church and the requirements of her spirit? We are obliged to reply in the negative. A znamenny melody is written in such a way that a single note is sung (in unison) and not in beginnings (partheses). No matter how many singers sing the note, the singing stems from one singer. The melody should remain untouched and its transposition undoubtedly results in a distortion . . .[85]

These comments demonstrate that Saint Ignatius, though not a professional musician, nonetheless subtly and keenly perceived the uniqueness of Russian church music and recognized that it was not fit for harmonic arrangements. The saint justly criticized ecclesiastical composers of his day for the lack of competence with which they approached the harmonization of ancient tunes:

It is not right to put new paint on an old icon while leaving the icon's drawing untouched: that would result in the icon's distortion. No reasonable person who knows foreign languages perfectly well would undertake the translation of a book on mathematics if he did not know mathematics. Why cannot these experts of music, who do not understand the graceful spirit of the Church given by God for a profoundly pious life, be consistent with this good reason regarding church singing?[86]

---

[84]Ignatius (Brianchaninov), "Understanding Heresy and Schism," in *Theological Works* (Moscow, 1996), 295–296.
[85]Ibid., 296.
[86]Ibid., 296.

Gavriil Lomakin (1812–1885) was a contemporary of Lvov and his companion-in-arms in the matter of harmonizing ancient melodies. By his works he was one of the composers who defined the main trends in the development of Russian church singing for several decades to come.[87] Lomakin acknowledged that "much Italianism has crept into our church singing,"[88] it "has retreated from its origins, lost its prayerful character."[89] He considered it necessary to "resurrect primordial antiquity"[90] in giving new birth to a prayerful spirit of ancient church singing. Lomakin's work in the harmonization of ancient melodies had the character of intuitive searching: "He began to try out harmonies, searching for their origins . . . he attentively examined Palestrina and other classical authors, sat down at the piano, and searched for harmonies, remembered, divined. . . . Each new discovery he put into use."[91]

Gavriil Lomakin.

For many years Lomakin worked under the direction of Lvov: "When Alexander Fedorovich was writing his commentaries, they sometimes had meetings, argued, agreed and sometimes . . . (Lvov) listened without speaking, sitting at the piano, giving his approval with a sign or dozing under the monotonous sounds of the Octoechos. Lomakin wrote more than two thousand pages; near the end he wrote somewhat mechanically and perhaps carelessly, which was reflected in the flaws which ended up in the publication."[92] But over time there appeared serious differences between Lomakin and Lvov in their views on the harmonization of ancient melodies and this made their collaboration all the more difficult. Lomakin began to understand more and more distinctly that the harmonization of Russian church melodies in the spirit of German classical music corresponded as little to the spirit of ancient Obikhod singing as did their harmonization in the Italian style.

In the middle of the nineteenth century, Mikhail Glinka (1804–1857) was interested in the harmonization of ancient melodies. He considered Old Russian church

---

[87] Hilarion (Alfeyev), "To Resurrect Primordial Antiquity," *Journal of the Moscow Patriarchate* 4 (1988), 26.
[88] G. Lomakin, "Autobiographical Notes with Commentary by V. Stasov," in *Russian Antiquities* (1886), 660.
[89] Ibid., 664.
[90] Ibid., 662.
[91] Ibid., 660.
[92] Ibid., 651.

Mikhail Glinka.

singing to be connected with the church melodies of the Western Church. In 1856 he went to Berlin to study these melodies with Siegfried Dehn (1799–1858), the famous music theorist and specialist in the field of strict counterpoint.[93] "Dehn visits me daily," Glinka reported in one of his letters to his friends. "We are working vigorously: the main thing being church tones and then the Mass of John Chrysostom in three voices, not for a choir but for the lower clergy, as well as all possible canons." In another letter Glinka wrote, "I am almost convinced that it is possible to unite Western fugue and the conditions of our music within the bonds of legal marriage."[94]

Glinka's work was cut short by his premature death. The famous music theorist Prince Vladimir Odoevsky (1804–1869) recalled: "I saw Glinka for the last time when I was travelling from Berlin in 1857. . . . Glinka told me about his counterpoint works with Dehn and how he had completely immersed himself in church music."[95] Inspired by Glinka's example, Odoevsky began to propagate the idea of harmonization of Old Russian melodies in the "strict style" of Western church music, drawn to the idea given by Lomakin and another proponent of "homeland olden days," Nikolai Potulov (1810–1873). A club of common-thinking people headed by Odoevsky was formed. They met constantly and exchanged experiences and shared their discoveries with one another. They all shared a negative view of Bortniansky's music and those models of "Obikhod singing" which were published by the Court Capella. Odoevsky wrote:

> It is possible to identify in the operas of Galuppi entire passages incorporated by his disciple Bortniansky into our church music. But that is not all. The Paschal Matins Canon . . . found in the Obikhod. . . . Over time this tune took on the melody of a gay waltz tune whose words of old were "Ah, Don, You are our Don," while the latest words are "Grand Lady, Grand Lady." It was transferred in this form to the so-called Cycle of Simple Church Singing, used for many years at the Most High Court. It was published in 1837 and has now been transferred to the four-voiced arrangement published by the Capella.[96]

---

[93]E. Meshcherina, *The Musical Culture of Rus' in the Middle Ages,* 2nd Edition (Moscow, 2008), 15.
[94]Cited in I. Soloviev, "Glinka and His Religious-Musical Activity," in *Russian Church Composers and their Music* (Minsk, 2008), 236.
[95]V. Odoevsky, *Musical-literary Inheritance* (Moscow, 1956), 371.
[96]Opinion of Odoevsky, *Inheritance*, 71.

Russian Church Singing

But what were Odoevsky and his followers able to propose in response to Bortniansky and "Grand Lady"? It is necessary to admit that they did not manage to "resurrect primordial antiquity" and liberate Russian church music from Western captivity ("Italianism"). The major mistake of all the church composers of this period remained this: Desiring to find a harmonic attire appropriate for ancient melodies, they employed Western models. In this sense there is no radical difference between the harmonizations of Bortniansky and Turchaninov, on the one hand, and those of Lomakin and Potulov, on the other. The difference lies merely in that Bortniansky searched for a stylistic basis in Italian classicism while Lomakin studied the masses of Palestrina (while Glinka mastered the mysteries of church harmony with Dehn in Berlin).

The spontaneous process of simplifying these same melodies was taking place in parallel to the harmonization of ancient tunes to western melodies. Examples appeared such as the one mentioned by Odoevsky—the melody of the Paschal Canon. We will note that in many churches of the Russian Orthodox Church, the Paschal Canon is performed to this day on the motif of the folk song "Barynia, Barynia" (Grand Lady, Grand Lady):

Pyotr Tchaikovsky (1840–1893) was much interested in church music. As a secular composer he perceived church music overwhelmingly from the perspective of aesthetics. The state of affairs in Russian church singing did not satisfy Tchaikovsky: "I acknowledge several merits in Bortniansky, Berezovsky, and others," he wrote to the Baroness Von Meck, "but their music harmonizes so little with the Byzantine style of architecture and icons, and with the entire arrangement of the Orthodox services."[97] In another letter Tchaikovsky commented on Bortniansky and other composers of the Italian school even more critically:

> You have touched on a sore subject for me with your question concerning Russian church music. . . . Bortniansky's technique is child-like and routine;

---

[97] P. Tchaikovsky and N. Von Meck, *Tchaikovsky and Nadezhda Filaretovna Von Meck: Correspondence*, Book 1 (Moscow, 2004), 357.

Pyotr Tchaikovsky.

nonetheless he is the only one of the spiritual composers who had a technique. All of these Vedels and Dekhterevs and so forth loved music in their own way but they were ignorant and caused so much evil for Russia by their works that a hundred years is not enough to destroy it all. From the capital to the villages . . . Bortniansky's saccharine style is heard and—alas!—the public likes it. A messiah is needed who with one blow would destroy all the old and would take a new path consisting in returning to the days of old and communicating the ancient melodies in the proper harmonies.[98]

Tchaikovsky did not manage to become such a messiah himself although a number of original compositions for the church kliros as well as reworkings of Obikhod melodies belong to him. In 1878 Tchaikovsky wrote "Liturgy" and in 1882 "All-Night Vigil." The first of these compositions represents essentially "secular music attached to divine service texts" and stands very far apart from prescribed singing."[99] In the second composition the composer turns to the melodies of Kievan and Greek chant which he harmonized in the "strict style" of Western music. In the preface to the edition of "The All-Night Vigil" Tchaikovsky wrote:

> I did not wish to try to recreate the ancient harmonization of church melodies or to invent some type of harmonization totally my own. My pretensions are extremely humble. I know that to remake history is impossible; I know that to resurrect authentic ancient Russian church singing is also impossible just as any decisive return to the past is impossible. This is an indisputable fact and to fight against its obviousness would be pointless quixotism. But I hope that the attempt to sow Russian seeds on this foreign soil—which is forced upon us—will not be put to me as a reproach.[100]

Taking the path which he himself called "eclectic,"[101] striving to intuitively feel for the proper method of working out the church melodies, Tchaikovsky, like

---

[98] Cited in Metallov, *Essay*, 155.
[99] Gardner, *Liturgical Singing of the Russian Orthodox Church*, vol. 2 (Jordanville-Moscow), 377–378.
[100] P. Tchaikovsky, "Preface to First Edition of 'The All Night Vigil'," in A. Naumov and M. Rachmaninov, ed., *Russian Religious Music in Documents and Materials*. Volume 3: *Church Singing of Reformed Russia as Understood by Contemporaries* (Moscow, 2002), 187.
[101] See Metallov, *Essay*, 156.

Russian Church Singing

the majority of his contemporaries, did not understand the very essence of these melodies or the principle on which they had been created. He was certain that the uniqueness of ancient melodies was based on the special ranges (scales) on which they were constructed and that indeed these ranges were the reason for the difficulties confronting the harmonizers of melodies.

> I am now dragging out a drab life, without inspiration, without joys. . . . Now I am transposing from the Obikhod the fundamental singing of the all-night service for a full choir. The work is rather interesting and difficult. I want to preserve the ancient church melodies in their untouched state. The trouble is, as they are constructed in the ranges of totally special characteristics, they lend themselves poorly to the newest harmonization. But if I do manage to emerge victorious after all these difficulties, I will be proud that the first of the contemporary Russian musicians labored for the return of the original character and structure of our church music.[102]

Tchaikovsky's hopes of succeeding in becoming a reformer of church singing were not realized. Ultimately he came to the conclusion that it is not at all possible to reform church singing because the true knowledge of ancient melodies has been lost forever:

> I have already done a thing or two, but all by groping. I do not know very well either the history of church music or the services, or the correlation of all that is in the Obikhod to what is sung in churches. . . . Alongside all this a great chaos reigns. Many desire now to transfigure church singing and return it to its original purity and originality as much as possible. Alas! I am convinced that it is impossible. In the last century Europe-ism encroached into our church in the form of various indecencies as, for example, dominant-accord and so forth, and has established its roots so deeply that even in the remote areas, in the villages, certain diaki (chanters) who studied in city seminaries sing something incalculably removed from the authentic melodies recorded in the Obikhod's notation.[103]

Tchaikovsky was a believer and regularly attended church services. It would seem that his religiosity combined with a musical genius that won him fame as

---

[102] Tchaikovsky and N.F. Von Meck, *Correspondence*, Book 2, 1212.
[103] "Letter to his Brother Modest, May 24, 1881," in Tchaikovsky, *Letters to his Family: A Selection* (Moscow, 1955), 270.

the greatest Russian composer could have guaranteed him a respectable place in the ranks of church composers. But this was not to be. Tchaikovsky's knowledge in the field of church music turned out to be too superficial (which, by the way, he acknowledged himself) and he did not succeed in penetrating the essence of Old Russian melodies. Tchaikovsky's spiritual compositions are rarely performed in churches with perhaps the exception of the hymn "Holy God" based on the triple-chord melodic formula in the simplest harmonization including key-note, dominant and subdominant:

Among other secular composers who made a contribution to church music, Mily Balakirev (1837–1910) and Nikolai Rimsky-Korsakov (1844–1909) should be mentioned. Balakirev replaced Nikolai Bakhmetev (1807–1891) in 1883 as the head of the Court Capella and Rimsky-Korsakov became Balakirev's deputy. While during Bakhmetev's tenure the traditions set by his predecessor Alexei Lvov were strictly preserved in the Capella, during Balakirev's and Rimsky-Korsakov's tenure an attempt was made to bring the Capella back on the course of the Russian national tradition. In 1888 the Capella published *The All-Night Vigil in Ancient Melodies*, in which ancient znamenny melodies were harmonized "in the spirit of the national creative work,"[104] as it was understood by those who compiled it under Rimsky-Korsakov's direction. But this book was not widely distributed. Balakirev

---

[104]Metallov, *Essay*, 150.

and Rimsky-Korsakov also wrote their own compositions for the church kliros but the majority of them did not take root in churches. An exception is the "Our Father" of Rimsky-Korsakov which attained immense popularity in circles of the Russian emigration of the twentieth century.

The activity of the composer and director Alexander Archangelsky (1846–1924) came at the last quarter of the nineteenth and beginning of the twentieth century. He was the author of numerous compositions (more than eighty) distinguished by their high professionalism of choral writing, dominance of sorrowful moods, and corresponding minor tonalities. In Archangelsky's harmonizations a comparatively small range is used for each voice which makes many of his compositions manageable even for humble village choirs.[105] An important innovation is connected with Archangelsky's name, which essentially changed the subsequent history of choral singing in Russia: children's voices were replaced with women's voices in the choir he created in 1880. The introduction of women into church choirs had a great practical significance: it liberated the choir from the necessity of constantly replacing boy singers with new boys when their voices began to break. As one scholar notes, women sang earlier in several church choirs, "but at that time singers were placed in choirs where they were not seen by the people. It also was the case that girls were given hair-cuts and dressed in men's clothing as if they were boys. Now, at a time when there were no longer any serfs, the appearance of women among men in the choir no longer shocked anybody."[106]

Nikolai Rimsky-Korsakov.

Alexander Archangelsky.

A new period in the history of Russian church singing began in the last quarter of the nineteenth century and is in many ways connected with the activity of the Moscow Synodal Choir whose choir director, Vasily Orlov (1857–1907), was appointed in 1886. The director of the choir was the distinguished church

---

[105] V. Bakumenko, "Aleksei Andreevich Archangelsky," in *Russian Church Composers and their Music* (Minsk, 2008), 257.

[106] Gardner, *Russian Church Singing*, vol. 2, 395.

Alexander Kastalsky

choir director and musicologist, as well as professor of Moscow Conservatory, Stepan Smolensky (1848–1909). The choir director's assistant was Alexander Kastalsky (1856–1926). Under the direction of this triumvirate the Synodal Choir was transformed into one of Russia's best church choirs. Running parallel to the choir was the activity of the Synodal school which provided an eight-year musical education. In 1899 the Synodal Choir went to Vienna for the consecration of the newly-built Saint Nicholas Cathedral and performed a concert in the Hall of the Vienna Musikverein, which included many of Kastalsky's compositions. This concert represented a veritable triumph of Russian church music. Interest in Kastalsky's works abroad attracted even greater attention to his works in Russia.[107]

Kastalsky worked in the Synodal Choir for forty years, first as an assistant to the director and later, beginning in 1910, as a director of the Synodal College. Kastalsky went down in the history of Russian church music as a fruitful composer and author of more than two hundred compositions and transpositions. Smolensky and Kastalsky became founders of a movement known as the "New Direction" in church singing,[108] based on the striving to liberate church singing from "Europe-ism" by drawing it closer to models of popular Russian musical works. It is true that at this time Russian popular song was already being reworked in the European spirit and harmonized to a western tune and therefore it is rather complicated to give an exact definition of "popular music" as it relates to the end of the nineteenth century. At any rate, Kastalsky was focused on the same aesthetic standards by which secular musical arts of Russia existed beginning with Glinka and which found their highest incarnation in the work of the composers of the "Mighty Handful," especially Rimsky-Korsakov and Mussorgsky. Kastalsky's role in church singing is comparable to the role of Glinka in secular music.

The essence of the new direction worked out by Smolensky and Kastalsky is expressed by the latter in these words:

---

[107] Pariyskiy, "Recollections of the Church Composer A. D. Kastalsky," in *Russian Church Composers and their Music* (Minsk, 2008), 291.

[108] Hierodeacon Andrei (Danilov), "Stepan Vasilievich Smolensky: Founder of a New Movement," in *Russian Church Composers and their Music* (Minsk, 2008), 269–271.

> I too can only surmise what our future church singing will be like, but I have a feeling for what its true task ought to be. I am convinced that the task should be the idealization of authentic church melodies and the conversion of them into something musically exalted and powerful in its expressiveness and close to the Russian heart in its typical nationality. Perhaps our church music will express itself in successions of simple harmonies, unusual for the contemporary ear, with a suspension of continuous quartets. There may be unisons and solos but not the kind that amateurs delight in. The inspired improvisations of the ancient *psalty* (singers) are the ideal for the church solo. I would like to have a kind of music which can be heard in no place except the church, a music as different from secular music as liturgical clothing is different from secular suits.[109]

Kastalsky considered it necessary to focus on church singing in Old Russian melodies, using—albeit carefully—several elements of popular music:

> . . . We have a boundless source of distinctive church melodies; it is not possible to apply to them the usual banal formulae and just any harmonic sequences at all. It would not hurt also to forget about the "tenderness" of the saccharine minor, which in those days was considered necessary even for "Praise the Name of the Lord," apparently expressing the brokenness of those praying over their sins, but actually making them depressed. In our most ecclesial melodies a national element is to be found, but popular song phrases should be applied to them with extreme discretion, since a church is a church, and not a concert hall and not the street. The national coloring of Russian secular music was born from song, and church music should be created and developed on the basis of our Obikhod melodies.[110]

Pavel Chesnokov (1877–1944) made use of popular tunes including intonations of Russian city romances of the nineteenth century in his work. Chesnokov was a distinguished church choir director and composer, the author of more than five hundred choral works, including original compositions and transcriptions for church choirs. Characteristic features of Chesnokov's music are lyricism, often transitioning to sentimentality, harmonic diversity, and modulations in distant

---

[109] A. Kastalsky, "Concerning My Musical Career and My Thoughts about Church Music," in N. Zverev, A. Naumov and M. Rakhmaninov, ed., *Russian Religious Music in Documents and Materials, Volume I: Synodal Choir and College of Church Singing, Recollections, Diaries, Letters* (Moscow, 1998), 240.

[110] Ibid., 240–241.

Pavel Chesnokov.

tonalities. Chesnokov often used a solo voice with the accompaniment of a choir and he liked the sounding of homogenous choirs (men's and women's) for which he made transpositions of his own compositions.

The religious works of Sergei Rachmaninov (1873–1943) were an extraordinary and singular phenomenon in the culture of Russian church music culture of the beginning of the twentieth century. In 1910 Rachmaninov created his "Divine Liturgy" and in 1915 the "All-Night Vigil." While the "Liturgy" represents a work of the author's own creation, the majority of the compositions in the "All-Night Vigil" were based on Obikhod melodies. It is interesting that the idea of writing the "All-Night Vigil" came to Rachmaninov after listening to his own "Liturgy," which—in his own words—he "did not at all like since it did not fulfill the requirements of Russian church music."[111]

Rachmaninov's "All-Night Vigil" was dedicated to the memory of Stepan Smolensky. Indeed Smolensky was one of those who aroused in Rachmaninov the interest of studying ancient church singing. Another person who exerted a favorable influence on the composer was Kastalsky. Rachmaninov recollected:

> I composed the "All-Night Vigil" very quickly: it was completed in less than two weeks . . . Still in my childhood I was captivated by the majestic melodies of Obikhod. I always felt that I would be able to accomplish this in the "All-Night Vigil." I will not begin to deny that the first performance of the "All-Night Vigil" by the Moscow Synodal Choir gave me a happy hour of satisfaction. . . . At that time the Synodal College was directed by Kastalsky, the composer and author of religious music. . . . His works and conversations taught me quite a lot.[112]

The majority of the numbers for "All-Night Vigil"[113] were based on Obikhod melodies which Rachmaninov harmonized with unprecedented mastery and originality. No Russian church composer before or after Rachmaninov has succeeded in accomplishing such a natural combination of ancient melodies with harmony,

---

[111] S. Rachmaninov, *Recollections Recorded by Oscar von Riesmann* (Moscow, 2008), 147.

[112] Ibid., 147–148.

[113] In 1895 Rachmaninov wrote his First Symphony based on Obikhod themes. Performance of the symphony in Saint Petersburg ended in a complete failure and brought Rachmaninov to the condition of a profound depression. See Rachmaninov, *Recollections*, 76–78.

based on consonance of thirds. In effect, Rachmaninov accomplished in his "All-Night Vigil" the task on which Lomakin, Tchaikovsky, and Rimsky-Korsakov worked unsuccessfully: the task of liberating Russian religious music from "Europe-ism" and conferring on it a truly national sound. It stands to reason that Rachmaninov's music, both religious and secular, belongs to the European tradition, and in the "All-Night Vigil" all the basic elements of Western European musical thinking are present: the homophono-harmonic type, metrical melody, major-minor melodic structure, and the octave scale. But Rachmaninov succeeded in accomplishing such a harmonious synthesis of the Russian singing tradition and western musical thinking that his composition became the pinnacle of all the creative work of Russian church composers and harmonizers.

Sergei Rachmaninov.

The composer fully utilized the possibilities of the choir in "All-NightVigil" in moving the range of choral parties to the extreme. In "Bless the Lord, O My Soul," for example, the basses are lowered to "C" of large octave while in "The Prayer of Saint Simeon"—to the "B-flat" of the counter-octave:

Rachmaninov especially loved this part of the "All-Night Vigil." "I would like for them to perform it at my funeral," he wrote. When he played this passage for the choir director of the Synodal Choir, Nikolai Danilin (1878–1945), the latter, shaking his head, said, "Where on earth will you find such basses? They are encountered as rarely as asparagus at Christmas." "Nonetheless, he managed to find them," wrote Rachmaninov. "I knew the voices of my peasants and was completely certain that I could require anything of Russian basses! The public always listened with bated breath as the choir 'descended.'"[114]

The technical complexity of Rachmaninov's religious works became a reason for their being performed in churches extremely rarely. They are heard more often performed in concert halls. On the other hand, the 1917 Revolution hindered the introduction of these works into singing practice. The performance of Rachmaninov's religious works was a most rare occurrence in the Soviet Union because they had attained widespread fame and recognition in the West. Many Western music lovers know about Russian church singing thanks exclusively to Rachmaninov's "All-Night Vigil" which—like Rublev's "Trinity"—became a kind of international symbol of Russian Orthodoxy.

Alexander Grechaninov (1864–1956) was a great church composer at the end of the nineteenth century and first half of the twentieth century. A considerable number of his religious works were written in Russia before the Revolution but he continued to compose religious music while in the emigration. Four complete "Liturgies" are the work of Grechaninov. The first two, written in 1897 and 1902, were performed with great success at religious concerts. In 1917 Grechaninov wrote his third liturgy and called it "Demestvenny" although it had nothing in common with ancient demestvenny chant. A particularity of this composition is that it is written for soloists, a choir, stringed orchestra, organ, and harp. The possibility of introducing musical instruments into divine services was discussed in the period leading up to the Moscow Council of 1917 and, obviously, Grechaninov wanted to facilitate with his composition a positive decision to this question. Instruments, however, were not introduced into divine services (that is not surprising, considering the many-centuries-long negative attitude towards instruments in the Eastern Church) and his "Demestvenny Liturgy" remained purely a work for concerts and was performed extremely rarely. The most famous number of this composition is "Litany of Fervent Supplication," which Fedor Shaliapin performed and recorded more than once. This litany is sometimes executed in Orthodox churches—of course, performed by an *a capella* choir.

[114] Rachmaninov, *Recollections*, 148.

Russian Church Singing

The Russian Revolution of 1917 brought the development of church singing in the Russian Church to a halt for several decades. Music of nineteenth century composers was performed for the most part in those churches which survived and continued to function. Many church choir directors including Kastalsky and Chesnokov were required to abandon directing choirs in churches and take up secular work. In subsequent years, when persecutions of the Church somewhat lessened, a certain rise in church singing is observed as new works began to be created for the kliros. Among church composers of the Soviet period it is worthwhile to note the deacon Sergei Trubachev (1919–1995) whose reworkings of ancient melodies are marked by a high level of professionalism. It is impossible to go without mentioning the multifaceted activity of Archimandrite Matfei (Mormyl, 1938–2009). A composer and church choir director, he is the author of numerous transcriptions for men's and mixed choirs. His activity began back in the 1960s in the period of Khruschev's persecutions and continues up to the present day.

In the final two decades of the twentieth century several secular composers turned to the genre of liturgical music. Among them is the prominent master of choral writing Georgy Sviridov (1915–1998). Sviridov's compositions on religious texts were published posthumously in a collection under the general name "Hymns and Prayers," but they were performed during his lifetime. It is a collection of twenty-six hymns included in five suites: "Ineffable Wonder," "Three Stikhera (Monastic) for Men's Choir," "Having Beheld a Wondrous Nativity," "From the Old Testament," and "Other Songs." The collection contains much bright music in which the possibilities of the *a capella* choir are used with virtuosity. The very names of the suites and their contents, however, are enough to show that the hymns are not intended for divine services but rather to be performed in concerts. The musical style of the works testifies to this as well as the fact that Sviridov used divine service texts extremely freely: he substituted them for the sake of achieving symmetrical rhythm and shortened or added to individual words. Sviridov often made mistakes in stress. Sometimes it appears that he does not understand the meaning of the Slavonic text and reworks it to his own liking.[115]

Georgy Sviridov.

---

[115] For example, at the basis of the hymn "Judas' Betrayal" from the cycle of "Other Songs" lays the following text "Behold, O lover of money, him that for the sake thereof did hang himself; flee from that

Sviridov was a believer but even in the late years of his life was not a "practicing" Christian, and the verses of true churchliness were foreign to him. Even the very church service texts themselves remained foreign to the composer. He admitted this fact to his disciple Anton Viskov: "I don't know how to write music for these texts; (the poet) Yesenin, for example, is something altogether different."[116] Considering the strengths of all the mentioned qualities, Sviridov's religious music—which in itself is extremely original and expressive—belongs in the category of "para-liturgical works." It is hardly likely that this type of music will ever enter into the regular usage of the Church.

Yet another example of para-liturgical works is the "Liturgy of Saint John Chrysostom" written in 1988 by Nikolai Sidelnikov and dedicated to the millennium of the baptism of Rus'. This composition, under the heading "Liturgical Concert," was submitted to the Acquisitions Commission of the Ministry of Culture,[117] accompanied by the following statement:

> Notwithstanding the fact that these texts are taken from the Obikhod canon of the church's service, an enormous moral strength is contained in them. . . . I knowingly refrained from using ancient znamenny melodies in the concert in order to eliminate, as much as possible, the ritual limitations of the central idea and to bring it closer to today's life and to make it accessible to all people irrespective of their confession of faith and other principles of life. . . . My task was in turning this form not in the direction of ritual estrangement as it is supposed in the divine service but rather in the direction of open emotionality turned directly to the person and to his conscience—the world of his moral understanding.[118]

Of course, in reading this statement it is important to recall that it was addressed to the Ministry of Culture of a state that at that moment had not yet renounced official atheism. Nonetheless, it is obvious that the intention of the author was

insatiable soul that dared such things against the Master." Sviridov's text was modified so that it reads, "And . . . lover of money, for the sake thereof did hang himself. Flee, o insatiable souls, who dared such things against the Master.")

[116] A. Viskov, "The Apostle John's Successor," in *Georgy Svidirov Remembered by His Contempories* (Moscow, 2006), 575.

[117] The Acquisitions Commission was engaged in appraising and purchasing compositions of Soviet composers; after the purchase, the compositions became the property of the Ministry of Culture.

[118] N. Sidelnikov, "Statement to the Acquisitions Commission of the Ministry of Culture of the USSR," cited in A. Tevosian, "Temple Activity and European Concert in Historical-Liturgical Context of the 20th Century," in I. Lozovaya, ed., *Church Singing in Historical-Liturgical Context: East–Rus'–West* (Moscow, 2003).

to maximally distance himself from the Orthodox divine service and endow his composition with a "generally humanistic," supra-confessional, or even generally a-religious sound. In terms of style, harmony, and rhythm the composition stood very far apart from the ancient melodies and also from liturgical music of the later period. Sidelnikov merely used the liturgical texts but expelled them from their normal dwelling place—that is, the Orthodox divine services.

Contemporary State of Liturgical Singing in the Russian Church

The rebirth of the Russian Orthodox Church in the last decade of the twentieth and beginning of the twenty-first century was accompanied by a rebirth of church singing in all the post-Soviet territories. A number of new choirs, both professional and amateur, were created. The Choir of the State Tretyakov Gallery, created by A.A. Puzakov in the beginning of the 1990s, is distinguished by a high level of professionalism and profound churchliness. Among newly formed men's choir groups it is worthwhile to mention the choir of Moscow's Sretensky Monastery, whose director, prior to his episcopal consecration, was Hieromonk Ambrose (Yermakov). Several new choirs appeared in Kiev at the initiative of Deacon Dmitry Bolgarsky. These choirs combine a full liturgical life with an active schedule of concerts.

A.A. Puzakov.

Church choir directing courses are conducted in many dioceses, and also in religious academies and seminaries. These courses prepare leaders of church choirs and professional singers. A Seminary for Church Choir Directing and Singing exists in Moscow. Sheet music for church choirs, compact discs with recordings of liturgical music, study aids for choir directing, and periodic publications addressed to choir directors and singers are all published. Vast libraries containing sheet music have been created on the internet.

Over the past twenty years an interest in znamenny chant and other types of Old Russian unison singing has experienced a rebirth. Famous Russian experts in medieval studies, including A.V. Konotop and Boris Kutuzov, have been laboring to decipher famous manuscripts. Choir ensembles exist that specialize in the performance of ancient chants. One such group is the Choir of the Moscow Patriarchate under the direction of Anatoly Gridenko. (This choir was created at end of the 1980s with the participation of the composer Vladimir Martynov.) Ancient chants have been reborn in several monasteries, especially in Valaam Monastery where znamenny chant is the main type of singing (executed in the Greek manner with use of *ison*).

Archbishop Jonathan (Yeletskikh).

Many new works of church music were created in this period. Several of them are already being used, while others are gradually entering into regular use in church choirs. Archbishop Jonathan (Yeletskikh), a hierarch of the Russian Church who serves in Ukraine, is the author of original religious compositions and numerous harmonizations of Obikhod melodies. The church choir director and composer Gennadi Lapaev labors in Tver; Igumen Silouan (Tumanov) labors in Saransk; Bishop Jonathan (Tsvetkov) labors in Abakan. Owing to the activities of these and other contemporary church composers, the repertoires of church choirs—practically unchanged over the span of more than a hundred years—have been gradually renewed. Professional composers whose main sphere of activity is secular music have also become the authors of religious works. These include B.V. Dovgan, A.I. Mikita, A.O. Viskov. The Estonian Orthodox composer Arvo Pärt,[119] of whom we have spoken in volume one of this book, has created a large number of works based on religious texts including those clearly intended for liturgical use.

Besides the many positive phenomena in the field of church music, we cannot fail to note also the negative side which was inherited from the Church in pre-Revolutionary times. Primarily this discussion concerns the repertoires of church choirs whose renewal is taking place at an extremely slow pace. As before, the works of Bortniansky, Turchaninov, and Lvov continue to dominate the repertoires of the majority of church choirs. "Religious concerts"—whose performance was forbidden by the Holy Synod back in the middle of the nineteenth century—can be heard in many churches during the time of the clergy communion. Church choir directors preferred back then to ignore the prohibition, as they do today as well.

---

[119]See our *Orthodox Christianity*, vol. 1 (Yonkers, NY: St Vladimir's Seminary Press, 2011), p. 322.

In some choirs people become directors who are not well-churched and do not understand the essence of liturgical singing or how it differs from secular music. Many hymns are performed by choirs either too loudly—as a result, the serving clergy must shout louder than the choir— or too quickly—such that the clergy not have insufficient time to read the required prayers. (This especially concerns the singing of "Holy, Holy, Holy" during the eucharistic canon.) At other times the opposite holds true and the divine service is artificially prolonged because the singing is too slow.

The sanctuary and kliros often live their own separate lives during the divine services. One sacred activity takes place in the sanctuary while something altogether different takes place in the kliros—something resembling more a concert than a divine service. For the performance of a single church service the director usually selects hymns written by different authors from different epochs and different styles. This creates dissonance between the inner arrangement of the liturgy as a unified whole and those pieces which do not have between them any inner connection and are offered to the audience as musical accompaniment.

The lack of correspondence between the musical arrangement and inner content of the divine services is characteristic of the very musical works which have entered into the repertoires of church choirs. Many church composers of the nineteenth century, not being members of the clergy, could not penetrate the spirit of Orthodox divine services "from inside the sanctuary," and therefore their music sometimes did not correspond to the words of the liturgy or the liturgical actions being performed. The liturgy was perceived by composers as a series of concert numbers in which quick tempos alternated with slow tempos, forte alternated with piano. In this way a diversity, required by the traditions of secular music, was created, but the perception of the divine service as a unified mystery that unfolds in an uninterrupted manner was completely lost.

Ancient unison singing could be executed not only by professionals but by the entire society of the Church. At the present time, congregational singing exists only in several regions, such as Transcarpathia, where as a rule the whole congregation sings during divine services, led by the psalm reader. In the majority of churches the people participate only in the performance of several hymns: the Creed and the Our Father during the Divine Liturgy, and Having Beheld the Resurrection of Christ during the all-night vigil. Moreover, the tradition of congregational singing is deserving of more support from the church leadership and parish priests, since it allows the faithful to experience and understand the texts of the divine services more profoundly and to feel themselves to be participants in the divine services—not only as witnesses and audiences.

13

Church Singing in Other Local Orthodox Churches

IN CONTEMPORARY LOCAL ORTHODOX CHURCHES choir singing exists in three types: (1) one-voiced or one-voiced with ison-drone (Byzantine); (2) four-voiced homophono-harmonic ("part singing"); (3) three-voiced (Georgian). In the ancient eastern patriarchates—Constantinople, Alexandria, and Antioch—the dominant type is one-voiced singing with ison based on the New Method of Byzantine church singing devised by Chrysanthos of Madytos.[1] This type of singing is practiced in the Cypriot and Hellenic Churches. The homophono-harmonic type of music dominates in the church singing of the Russian and Serbian Orthodox Churches. In the Bulgarian and Romanian Churches two traditions exist: Byzantine (one-voiced) and western (four-voiced). In the Orthodox Churches of Poland, the Czech Lands and Slovakia, America, Finland, and Japan, music in the traditions of nineteenth century Russian church singing is used overwhelmingly. Three-part singing, which has no parallels in other singing traditions, is used in the Georgian Orthodox Church.

This situation is the result of many centuries of historical development. Since it is not possible to comment on all the national traditions of Orthodox church singing, we will focus on three: Georgian, Serbian, and Bulgarian.

Georgian church singing is a unique and original tradition. Information from the early period of development of church singing in Georgia is scant and is based not on musical sources but on liturgical and hymnographical sources. Eight tones were formed in the first millennium in Georgian church music: four basic and four plagal, as in Byzantine singing. Hymns were notated with the help of neumes which graphically differed from those of Byzantine notation. (The earliest Georgian neume manuscripts date to the first half of the tenth century.)

It is evident that the original Georgian singing was of the unison type. The first mention of three-voiced singing, however, can be traced to the eleventh century in

---

[1] This was discussed earlier, on page 282.

the commentaries of a Georgian philosopher, the monk Ioane Petritsi, concerning the compositions of Proclus Lycaeus. According to Ioane, three voices which flow together create a harmonic euphony.[2]

In the first half of the second millennium the large centers of development of Georgian church singing were Gelati Monastery in Georgia and Iveron Monastery on Mount Athos. In the thirteenth through sixteenth centuries, because of constant invasions and wars, Georgian church singing went into decline, but a rebirth came during the reign of King Irakli at the end of the thirteenth century. A new blow to Georgian singing tradition was dealt by the transformation of the autocephalous Georgian Catholicate in 1811 into the Georgian exarchate of the Russian Church. In many churches the Georgian language was replaced with Church Slavonic and ancient singing was replaced by partesny four-part singing. But neither the forced Russification in the nineteenth century nor the persecutions of the Church in the twentieth century resulted in the total disappearance of the national tradition of church singing. Even in Soviet times it continued to glimmer in individual churches, and beginning in the 1980s, with the personal support of Catholicos-Patriarch Ilia II, its planned rebirth began. Today singing in three voices—customary in the Georgian church singing tradition—is practiced in the majority of the churches of the Georgian Church.

A characteristic feature of this three-voiced singing is the relative independence of each voice. The main voice is the upper one. Consonant accordances in thirds appear in the movement of voices, but they do not comprise an indispensable base of the harmonic vertical arrangement. Often "empty" perfect fourths or perfect fifths arise, as well as seconds which are not perceived as a dissonance. The cadence phrase of the three accords is characteristic. In the first accord the voices are lined in two thirds; in the second accord they grow narrow to one third and in the third accord they turn into a unison accord.

The history of *Serbian* church singing[3] encompasses nearly eleven centuries. In many ways the development of church music in Serbia was similar to its development in Rus'. Ancient Serbian music, whose sources can be found in Byzantine church singing, bore an exclusively unison character. A system of eight modes was inherited from Byzantium but the melodies used were their own. Neume notation existed for recording church music. Manuscripts preserved from the end of the

---

[2]M. Andriadze, "Church Singing," in *Orthodox Encyclopedia*, vol. 8 (Moscow, 2006), 316.
[3]See N. Salaj, *Srpska duxovna muzika* (unpublished article).

fourteenth and beginning of the fifteenth century contain the works of the singer-composers Stefan Srbin, Isaija Srbin, and Nikola Srbin.

In the seventeenth and eighteenth centuries Serbian church singing was subject to various influences. On the one hand, singers from Constantinople and Mount Athos advocated Greek (post-Byzantine) church music. Byzantine singing was widespread in some regions inhabited by Serbs at the beginning of the eighteenth century. It was planted by Greeks who had settled in Serbia and Hungary and also by Greek teachers in singing colleges at monasteries. On the other hand, Russian singing experts were working in Serbia. Finally, Serbian musical culture could not avoid the influence of Western multi-part music in those places inhabited by Serbs in large numbers, such as Vienna, Buda, and Pest.[4]

A new direction in church singing, the so-called "Serbian Folklore-based Church Singing," was formed in the second half of the eighteenth century under the influence of Russian and Greek church music. Developed overwhelmingly in the Metropolia of Karlovac, it also was called "Karlovac Singing." Over the span of an entire century this singing existed in the oral tradition, but in the middle of the nineteenth century it was transposed to European staff notation by the first Serbian professional musician, Kornelije Stanković (1831–1865). Being a scholar of the Viennese professor Simon Sechter (1788–1867), Stanković did not limit himself to recording popular church melodies, but harmonized them in the traditions of European music using the same principles used by Russian composers of the same period (Lvov, Potulov, Archpriest Peter Turchaninov). Stanković published three collections of sheet music for four-voiced choirs under the name "Orthodox Singing of Serbian People" in Vienna with the support of the rector of the Russian embassy church, Archpriest Michael Raevsky.[5]

The collections of Stanković were widely circulated and entered into the regular usage of Serbian Orthodox choirs soon after their publication. The matter of collecting and harmonizing Serbian melodies was continued by several followers of Stanković including members of the clergy, a professor of theology, and students in the large centers of Serbian church education including Sremski Karlovci, Novi Sad, Sarajevo, and others.

A special contribution to the development of Serbian church singing was made by the eminent Serbian composer Stevan Mokranjac (1856–1914). After receiving a

[4]V. Peno, "The Communion Hymn in Serbian Unison Singing of the New Period," in I. Lozovaya, ed., *Church Singing in Historical-Liturgical Context: East–Rus'–West* (Moscow, 2003), 200–201.

[5]Meanwhile the first original liturgy for the needs of Serbian people was created in 1840, not by a Serb but an Italian, Francesco Sinico (1810–1855), a composer from Trieste.

professional musical education in Munich, Rome, and Leipzig, he devoted many years to the study of Serbian musical folklore. Popular melodies lay at the basis of fifteen choral rhapsodies by Mokranjac—the main result of his creative work as a composer. Mokranjac was a fruitful composer. (The full collection of his compositions, published in Belgrade in 1992, contains ten volumes.) Among his compositions are a full liturgy and other works for church choir which entered into the classical repertoire of Serbian church choirs.

Among other Serbian church composers one must mention Petar Krstić (1877–1957), whose liturgy was published in 1896 in Moscow, I. Baić (1878–1915), Josif Marinković (1851–1931), M. Miloević (1884–1946), Stevan Hristić (1885–1958), and Krstan Manojlović, the Orthodox disciple of Mokranjac. The repertoire of contemporary Serbian church choirs consists overwhelmingly of works of these composers. An essential place in this repertoire is occupied by the compositions of Russian authors including Bortiansky, Archangelsky, and Chesnokov.

The history of *Bulgarian* church singing[6] spans many centuries dating back to the ninth and tenth centuries. The main principles of Orthodox church music, including the system of eight modes, came to Bulgaria from Byzantium, but there remains an inexplicable degree of dependence of Old Bulgarian melodic material on the Byzantine material. In the period between the eleventh and fourteenth centuries various types of neume notation were used in Bulgaria to help to record original Bulgarian hymns.

In the fourteenth century Patriarch Evfimii II enacted a church reform which resulted in the introduction of the Mount Athos version of the Jerusalem Decree whereby the church singing tradition underwent intensive Hellenization: Greek melodies were adapted to Slavonic texts and original Bulgarian melodies were reworked in the spirit of late Byzantine neume notation and were also adapted to Slavonic texts.

In the same period in Greece and Serbia hymns began to appear, written with the word βουλγάρα (Boulgara) or βουλγαρικόν (Boulgarikon), which witnesses to the intensive church singing "exchange" between the Greek East and the Balkans. Considerably later, at the end of the sixteenth century and in the seventeenth century, hymns designated as "Bulgarian chant" came to Ukraine, whence they penetrated into Muscovite Rus'. To what degree did Bulgarian chant and its Russian version correspond to Bulgarian church singing of the sixteenth and seven-

---

[6]See E. Toncheva, "Bulgaria: Church Music," in *Orthodox Encyclopedia*, vol. 5 (Moscow, 2002), 612–614.

teenth centuries? This question has not been answered conclusively in musicology. The eminent Bulgarian musicologist and composer Dobri Khristov (1875–1941) considered that "Bulgarian chant" in the form in which it appeared in Western Rus' in the seventeenth and eighteenth centuries was true Bulgarian church singing.[7] Several musicologists consider Bulgarian chant to be linked with the singing tradition of the epoch of the second Bulgarian kingdom, while others completely reject its Bulgarian origin.[8]

In the period of Turkish dominion Bulgarian church singing preserved its original unison character. In the beginning of the nineteenth century a club of church singing was created, with the participation of Constantinopolitan *melurgoi*, whose intonation was similar to Greek intonation. The work of putting into good order church singing Obikhod in the first half of the nineteenth century took place in Rila Monastery where a full circle of hymns of the liturgical year in the Church Slavonic language was created. Both works of Greek masters transposed into the Slavonic language and original compositions of Bulgarian singer-composers were included.

At the turn of the twentieth century the music of Russian composers including Bortiansky, Turchaninov, and many others became widespread in Bulgaria. Their works soon entered into the regular use of church choirs and created a style of singing which began to develop parallel to the traditional Bulgarian monophonic singing.

Russian church music of the nineteenth century exerted an essential influence on the liturgical creative work of Bulgarian composers, including Atanas Badev (1860–1908), Emanuil Manolov (1860–1902), Dobri Khristov, and Petar Dinev (1889–1980). A combination of European musical styles with the use of traditional Bulgarian melodies is characteristic of their works. Several works of these composers attained fame beyond the borders of Bulgaria and entered into the singing practice of the Russian Church (in particular, "It is Truly Meet" and other hymns of Petar Dinev).

---

[7]D. Hristov, "Musical-Theoretical and Publicistic Inheritance," vol. 1 (Sophia, 1970), 293. Hristov based his conclusion on three heirmologia originating in Manyavsky Monastery in the Carpathians containing hymns called "Ancient Bulgarian Chant."

[8]Martynov, *History*, 155.

Section Two: Bells and Bell-Ringing

Our survey of Orthodox church music would be incomplete if we were to limit our discussion to choral singing and say nothing about bell-ringing. This is the only form of instrumental music which not only is permitted by the Orthodox Church but is an important component of Orthodox divine services.

14

Bells and Bell-Ringing

Bells and "Bila" in Byzantium

THE TYPIKON SEVERAL TIMES MENTIONS summoning to the divine services using bells. The ninth chapter of the Typikon is entitled "On How it is Meet to Call to Prayer during the Whole Day." It says, "A little before evening, the lamplighter, having received a blessing from the abbot, sounds on the kampan."[1] The exposition of the order of Small Vespers in the first chapter of the Typikon begins with the words: "Before the setting of the sun on Saturday, the paraecclesiarch, that is, the lamplighter, comes to the presiding priest and makes a bow before him . . ."[2] The description of the Nativity service is accompanied by the following indications: "At the seventh hour of the day he strikes the great kampan and all the heavy bells"; "at the tenth hour of the night a blagovest is sounded followed by a trezvon using all the bells."[3] According to the Typikon, on Theophany the parecclesiarch, "strikes the great bell and all the heavy bells;"[4] and at Pascha he "goes out and strikes the great bell and rings vigorously,"[5] following which they "strike all the bells and the large bells and ring vigorously."[6]

The term *kampan* is of Latin origin and strictly speaking denotes "bell." The terms *great* and *heavy* relate to another musical instrument called *klepal* in Slavonic (from the verb *klepati* which means "to knock," "to indicate," "to call") or *bila* (from the verb *biti* meaning to strike). This term was used to denote a percussive, signal instrument made from metal, stone, or wood, used for summoning the faithful to the divine service.

---

[1] *Typikon* (2002 Edition), Ch. 9 (44).
[2] Ibid., Ch. 1 (13).
[3] Ibid., 376, 379.
[4] Ibid., 411.
[5] Ibid., 955.
[6] Ibid., 956.

The practice of summoning people to the divine service using the *bila* (Gk. *semantron*, σήμαντρον, from *semaino*, σημαίνω—to give a sign) existed in the Christian East back in the fourth century. It is mentioned in the Rule of Saint Pachomius the Great, in the writings of Saint John Cassian the Roman, in the *Lausiac History* of Palladius of Galatia, and in a number of other sources. Up to the present time the wooden bila is used in Greek monasteries (especially on Mount Athos) for summoning the monks to the divine service. Differences are discerned in the types of striking: the great striking on a wooden bila (a squared beam measuring from two to four meters in length [6.56 feet to 13.12 feet] and a width of ten to ninety centimeters [3.9 inches to 35.4 inches] and a thickness of between four and seven centimeters [1.5 inch and 2.8 inches]), the small striking of a wooden bila (a smaller beam), and the copper or iron striking (for which a metal beam called *iron* is used.)[7]

The wooden bila in the East was often signified by the word *ksilon* (ξύλον—wood) and in the West by the term *lignum sacrum* (literally, "sacred wood"). In the West bells appeared, together with the bila, no later than the seventh century and gradually replaced the bila. Bells appeared in Byzantium somewhat later but for a long time they were perceived either as a pagan attribute or as a purely Latin custom. In the twelfth century Patriarch Theodore Balsamon wrote: "The Latins, after maliciously separating themselves from us and hardening their hearts under the influence of Satan . . . have another custom of summoning the people to the churches. Since they use one sign—I understand it is called kampan, from the word '*kampos*'."[8] In later centuries bells ceased to be considered a Latin custom in Byzantium, yet they did not enter into universal usage. Striking the wooden and iron bilas remained the most common means of summoning people to the divine services.

In Slavic countries, on the contrary, bells appeared rather early. Already by the middle of the tenth century the Arabic writer Al-Masudi pointed out a difference between the Greeks, who were under Arabic dominion, and the Slavs, in that the Slavs made use of musical instruments to summon the faithful to the divine services. "There are many nations among the Slavs; some of them are Christians. . . . They have many cities and also churches where they hang bells which they strike with mallets similar to the way our Christians strike boards with wooden clappers."[9]

---

[7]M. Yesipova, "Bila," in *Orthodox Encyclopedia*, vol. 5 (Moscow, 2002), 212–213.

[8]Theodore Balsamon, *Reflections*, PG 138, 1076C. The Latin "*campus*" signifies "field." Balsamon reproduces the traditional etymology of the word *campana*.

[9]Cited in A. Garkavi, *Legends of Muslim Writers on Slavs and Russians* (St Petersburg, 1870), 125.

Bell-Ringing in Rus'

The first references to bells in Rus' are encountered in manuscripts beginning in the eleventh century. In the words of a contemporary scholar, "the custom of ringing bells came to Rus' from the West where bells were used in worship, the art of bell casting was considered a sacred profession, bells were 'baptized,' and people gave bells personal names."[10] In the fourteenth and fifteenth centuries small bells came to Rus' from the West by way of Novgorod and Pskov. Italian and German master bell founders came to Rus' to fulfill orders for the manufacturing of larger bells. Later, Russians established their own production of bells and by the sixteenth century Rus' had already surpassed all other states in terms of the number and weight of the bells made.[11]

As in the West, bells were humanized in Rus', people gave names to them (for example, the famous bell called "Sysoi" in Uglich). A bell could be punished for a fault: it could be beaten with a birch, sent into exile, or its tongue (clapper) could ripped out. (Indeed, this is what happened to the bell in Uglich after it heralded the death of Tsarevitch Dmitry in 1593.)[12]

At the same time church bells were perceived as sacred objects that were regarded with reverential piety. Wonder-working power was attributed to bells. People considered that bells were capable, by their peal, of warding off natural disasters and driving away the enemy's power from people. "The Order for the Blessing of a Bell," contained in the Great Book of Needs, includes the deacon's petition: "That he will grant it the grace that all who hear its sound, whether by day or by night, shall be roused to the glorification of his holy name"; "That by the voice of its ringing all destructive winds, storms, thunder and lightning, and all harmful weather and destructive things of the air may be appeased, calmed and cease to be"; "That it may drive away every power, craft and slander of invisible enemies from all his own faithful people who shall have heard the voice of its ringing, and arouse them to the observance of his commandments." In the prayers following this litany, the priest pronounces:

> And now, O Most-holy Master ... with thy heavenly blessing and the grace of thine all-consecrating Spirit, do Thou bless (this bell) and consecrate it, and

---

[10] Vladyshevskaya, *Culture*, 208. An oblique (and rather late) confirmation of Western origin of bell-ringing in Rus' is the expression "raspberry peal" which indicates the Belgian town Malin (Mekhelen), the largest center of bell casting in the Middle Ages.

[11] "History of Bell Making in Russia: Bell Ringing in Russia" (CD), (Moscow, 2007), 2.

[12] Vladyshevskaya, *Culture*, 209.

draw down upon it the power of thy grace, that thy faithful servants, having heard the voice of its ring, may be strengthened in piety and faith, and with courage, may oppose all the slanders of the devil. . . . May storms, hail, whirlwinds, fearful thunder and lightning, evil and destructive winds befalling them be appeased, calmed, and made to cease at its ringing.[13]

Besides mentioning the trumpets of Jericho (see Josh 6. 1–19), the "Order of Blessing a Bell" contains a reading from the Book of Numbers with the following divine command: "And the priests the sons of Aaron shall sound with the trumpets; and it shall be a perpetual ordinance for you throughout your generations. . . . And in the days of your gladness, and in your feasts, and your new moons, ye shall sound with the trumpets at your whole burnt-offerings, and at the sacrifices of your peace-offerings; and there shall be a memorial for you before your God" (Num 10.8, 10). In this way, the bell is perceived as the successor to the Old Testament trumpets which served signal and other functions connected both with military actions and the practice of divine services.

The art of bell-ringing in Rus' reached its greatest flourishing in the sixteenth and seventeenth centuries. By this time the most commonly used bells were *yazykovoi* bells which emitted peals by the striking of a *yazyk* (tongue or clapper) along the body of the bell which remained immobile (or nearly immobile) during the ringing. These bells gradually forced out more ancient *ochepnoi* bells—from which the sound was emitted by means of swinging of the bell itself which struck on a stationary hanging clapper—adopted from the West. Groups of *yazykovoi* bells ranging in various sizes comprised a crucial attribute of belfries and bell towers which were added to large churches and cathedrals. Bells, with ropes attached to their clappers, were controlled either directly from the bell tower (or belfry) or from the ground. The bell-ringer used the fingers of both his hands and also his right foot to produce sounds from a large number of bells. (As a rule, the foot controlled the motion of the clapper of the most powerful and heaviest bell.) Several bell-ringers were often enlisted to control a large number of bells.

Foreigners who came to Russia in the sixteenth and seventeenth centuries were delighted by the power and size of Russian bells. The Polish military leader Samuel Maskevich who fought on the side of the False Dmitriy, described the Ivan the Great Bell Tower in his memoirs:

---

[13]*Great Book of Needs*, vol. 2, 185–186.

Bells and Bell-Ringing 349

There are up to twenty such churches in the Kremlin; of them the Church of Saint John, located amidst a castle, is remarkable for its high stone bell tower from which one can see for a great distance in all directions of the capital city. The bell tower contains twenty-two large bells; many of them are not inferior to the grandeur of our Sigismund Bell in Krakow; they hang in three rows, some over the others; there are more than thirty smaller bells. It is not known how the tower can hold such a weight, but it is helped by the fact that the bell-ringers do not swing the bells, as they do in our country; rather, they strike the bells with clappers; but eight or ten men are needed in order to get another clapper swinging. Not far from this church there is a bell cast of pure vanity: it hangs on a wooden tower two sazhens in width for it to be better seen and its clapper requires twenty-four men to swing.[14]

The manufacturing of bells in Russia reached a huge scale in the eighteenth and nineteenth centuries. Nearly twenty bell casting foundries were operating in Russia at the turn of the twentieth century and it seems that the overall number of bells of Russian churches and monasteries was in the hundreds of thousands:

> By the beginning of the twentieth century the Russian state became truly a state leader in bells, having surpassed both the Buddhist East and the Christian West in terms of number, weight, and harmony of its bell collections. Over the span of many centuries, the bells of Russia grew from primitive and euphonious devices used for signaling into complex and perfected instruments of often extremely significant proportions.[15]

Rostov bell ringing was famous all over Russia. Cast in the seventeenth century, the bells of Rostov's Dormition Cathedral have been preserved to the present day. The bells were cast according to a particular plan so that they would create a harmonious ensemble when rung together. The complete belfry included the following bells: *Sysoi* (weighing two thousand poods/thirty-six tons, cast in 1689), *Polieleiny* (one thousand poods/eighteen tons, cast in 1683), *Lebed'* (500 poods/nine tons, cast in 1682), *Baran* (eighty poods/1.44 tons, cast in 1654), *Krasny* (thirty poods/0.54 tons), *Kozel* (twenty poods/0.36 tons), as well as four nameless bells and two *zazvonnye* smaller bells. A bell named *Golodar'* was cast considerably later (1856). It weighed one hundred seventy-one poods and five pounds (3.08 tons) and

---

[14] N. Ustrialov, *Stories of Contemporaries Concerning Dmitry the Self-Proclaimed*, Part 2 (St Petersburg, 1859), 125.
[15] *History of the Bell Making in Russia*, 4.

was rung during the Great Fast.[16] At the end of the nineteenth century, Aristarkh Izrailev, a bell expert and archpriest from Rostov, recorded in notation the festive trezvon of Dormintion Cathedral:

This recording is extremely approximate because each bell, apart from the main tone, has numerous overtones that do not stack up in the usual sequence of the tempered scale. Indeed, this is the secret of that special effect which the bells' sound has on a person's hearing:

> We can speak of a bell's main tone by which its pitch is determined. A rich and characteristic collection of additional pure tones, lower and higher, is added to this main tone.... From this is produced a wealth of hues, a diversity of timbres which make it possible to distinguish the voices of the bells, even those which have the same pitch as the main tone, and a wealth of epithets by which we characterize their sounding: *zvonkoe* (clear), *glukhoe* (hollow), *rezkoe* (sharp), *miagkoe* (soft)...[17]

Each bell has its own unique overtone series which is not repeated in another bell and does not conform with the overtone series of tempered instruments including octave, twelfth, double octave, double décima, etc. Moreover, "bells cannot be

---

[16]Vladyshevskaya, *Culture*, 231–232.
[17]Y. Punkhnachev, *Mysteries of Sounding Metal* (Moscow, 1974), 22.

Bells and Bell-Ringing

simply categorized as instruments having a particular pitch of the main tone and harmonic overtones. Nor can they be categorized in the group of instruments which lack these. A dominant and strongest tone exists in the bell's spectrum but it is significantly veiled-over by the discordant overtones."[18]

These conclusions are based on the investigations of the eminent expert on bells Konstantin Saradzhev (1900–1942) whose activity took place in the 1920s and 1930s when churches were being demolished all over Russia and bells were being cast down from bell towers and barbarously destroyed. Saradzhev undertook the heroic labor of cataloguing Moscow's bells in the attempt to save them from death. Moreover, he constructed a belfry for demonstrations which allowed him to give "bell concerts" and he petitioned *Narkompros* (People's Commisariat for Education) for permission to open a belfry in *Park Kultury i Otdykha* (Park of Culture and Rest). Saradzhev's art was colorfully described by Anastasia Tsvetaeva, the sister of the great poetess Marina Tsvetaeva, in the narrative "Tale of a Moscow Bell Ringer":

Konstantin Saradzhev.

> The large courtyard of a church situated on one of the alleys of Zamoskvorechye District was slowly filling up with people.... The freezing temperatures nipped. Knocking their boots together to warm their toes, people were growing tired of waiting when, suddenly and without warning, their waiting was over. It was as if the sky above burst open! A thunder-clap! Boom! And another thunder-clap! In measured, regular steps, one after another, the musical thunder sounded and let fly a great boom. Suddenly a stream of bird's chirping sounded—the flowing singing of certain unknown large birds in a festal jubilation of bells! A shouting of sounds, bright and shining against the background of the rumbling and booming! Alternating melodies, vying and yielding voices. A flood which gushed forth in streams and inundated the neighborhood.... Deafening, unexpected combinations, inconceivable, in the hands of a single man! An orchestra of bells! ... Raising their heads, those standing in the courtyard looked and beheld the man above, playing: his

---

[18] L. Blagoveschenskaya, "Sound Spectra of Moscow Bells," in *Monuments of Culture; New Discoveries; Written Language, Art, Archeology* (Moscow, 1977), 35.

head thrown back, it looked as though he would fly away if not for the ropes attached to the clappers of the bells which he held in a self-oblivious manner, as if with his outstretched arms he were embracing the entire bell tower on which a great number of bells were hanging. The bells were like giant birds emitting brass, rumbling peals, golden and silver cries. They strike against the dark blue silver of swallows' voices, filling the night with an unusual bonfire of melodies. Tearing away from the thick of the sounds, they burst aflame with their own harmonies and flew up like flocks of birds: these sounds reached higher and higher into the sky and filled it.[19]

Saradzhev created a unique work entitled "Inventory of the Unique Characteristics of Large Bells of all Moscow's Bell Towers." This work was not published during his lifetime but was preserved in the form of a manuscript in the archives of the Institute of Russian Literature (Pushkin House) and was finally published in 1977. Possessing a super-tonic sense of hearing, Saradzhev could distinguish between six and twenty-six overtones in Moscow's bells. (As a rule, the larger the bell, the more overtones it has). All in all, Saradzhev investigated two hundred and ninety-five bell towers and recorded the scales of three hundred and seventeen bells. Many of these bells were destroyed during Saradzhev's life and others after his death. In this way, the recordings of Saradzhev are similar to inscriptions on tombstones. They remained as the sole remembrance of the existence of these martyred bells which shared the fate of the entire Church and hundreds of thousands of its members in the epoch of most brutal persecution of the Faith.

Saradzhev's manuscript allows for compiling a certain understanding not only of the sound spectrum of the bells but also of the selection of bells for a single bell tower. (In some cases Saradzhev gives information for more than one bell in a collection). The most interesting is the choice of bells for the Bell Tower of Ivan the Great in Moscow's Kremlin where the largest bell embraces twenty-six overtones besides the main tone.

In this specific case the main tones of several bells line up in a chromatic scale (using the convention of transferring the sounds of bells to a staff). In other words, in selecting bells of a given bell tower, they tried to guarantee the maximum diversity of tones and even the distance to the minor second was not perceived as

[19] A. Tsvetaeva, *N. Saradzhev: Master of Magical Bell Ringing* (Moscow, 1988), 13–14. In 1975, preparing her narrative for publication, Anastasia Tsvetaeva sent one of her copies to Dmitri Shostokovich. The great composer answered with the restraint which was characteristic of him: "I read your story with great interest. All that concerns music is written completely convincingly and did not arouse any objections in me." (Cited in Tsvetaeva, *Saradzhev: Master of Magical Bell Ringing*, 8.)

Bells and Bell-Ringing 353

dissonance. It is curious that old masters of bell ringing acutely sensed which bells were appropriate for others and which ones were not; that is, there existed a precise understanding of "the consonance of bells." But evidently it is not at all possible to formulate rules of such a consonance as it is "extremely dissonant in the classical understanding of the term."[20]

Bell-ringing is divided into several types or genres. Equal-measured strikes made on one and the same bell is called *blagovest*. (Blagovest is performed before the beginning of every divine service, but on feast days the blagovest becomes *zvon*, while on ordinary days it does not change.) *Perezvon* is the alternating striking of different bells: from the lowest to the very highest. *Perebor* is the alternating ringing of all the bells in a descending order, after which all the bells are struck together. *Trezvon* is the name given to the most festal ringing of several (five, ten, twelve, and more) bells, used on feast days. Regarding the term *zvon*, it applies to many ways of striking different rhythms with several bells. In accordance with its designation, types of ringing may have names such as *krasny* ("red" or "beautiful," Paschal, festive, especially beautiful), *vstrechny* ("greeting," used for greeting the hierarch), *vodosvyatny* ("blessing of waters," used during the prayer service for blessing water), *pogrebalny* ("burial"), *molebny* ("prayer service"), and others. Several

[20]Blagoveschenskaya, *Sound Spectra*, 35.

The Return of the Bells of the Historic Bell Tower of Danilov Monastery, 2007.

types of Rostov ringing are connected with the names of metropolitans and famous bell ringers: *Ionafansky* (Jonathan), *Akimovsky* (Akimov), *Yegorevsky* (Yegorev), and *Ioninsky* (Jonah).

The character of bell ringing is significantly determined by the pitch and power of the bells used. But no less important are other factors of the ringing—its rhythm and tempo. The Paschal ringing, for example, is characterized by a moving tempo, the use of high pitched bells, and small measures. The opposite holds true for bell-ringing during a burial: the use of a slow tempo with large measures and low timbres is characteristic. Owing to the wealth and diversity of timbres, rhythms, and tempos, masters of bell ringing have managed to convey the most varied states ranging from anxiety (sounding the alarm) and sorrow (the funeral peal) to festive gladness and rejoicing (the festal and Paschal trezvon).

The rhythm of bell ringing is based on the combination of measures divisible by the main measure. For example, the example of Akimov ringing cited above contains eighth-notes (the smallest measure), quarter-notes, half-notes, and whole notes (the largest measure). For one strike of *Krasny Bell* it is necessary to strike *Lebed' Bell, Polieleiny Bell, Sysoi Bell,* and *Golodar Bell* twice, any of the *Nameless* bells six times, and the *Zazvonny* bells eight times. As a rule, small measures are assigned to the highest pitched and clearest bells, while the largest measures are given to the lowest and most powerful bells (although the bell with the central timbre has the largest measure in Akimov ringing.)

Bell ringing is used not only before the divine services but also during the services to proclaim their most important moments. In particular, during the Divine Liturgy the bells are rung at the time of the eucharistic canon. During the All-Night Vigil ringing is called for at the beginning of Matins. The festal trezvon is called for at the time of the singing of the Polielei. The combination of the trezvon, performed outside the church, with singing inside the church creates a unique acoustic effect and endows the corresponding moments of the service with a character of festivity and rejoicing.

Abbreviations

CCL = Corpus Christianorum, Series Latina. Turnhout.
CSEL = Corpus Scriptorum Ecclesiasticorum Latinorum.
GCS = Die Griechischen Christlichen Schriftsteller der ersten drei Jahrhunderte. Leipzig, Berlin.
PG = Patrologia graeca. Edited by J.-P. Migne. 162 vols. Paris, 1857–1886.
PL = Patrologia latina. Edited by J.-P. Migne. 217 vols. Paris, 1844–1864.
PTS = Patristische Texte und Studien.
SC = Sources Chrétiennes.

Select Bibliography

Abramishvili, G. "Ateni Sioni." *Orthodox Encyclopedia,* vol.3, 675–677. Moscow: 2001.[Russian].

Acheimastou-Potamianou, Myrtali. Βυζαντίνες Τοιχογαφίες [Byzantine frescoes]. Athens: 1996.

Acts of the Seventh Ecumenical Council. In *Acts of the Ecumenical Councils,* vol. IV. St Petersburg, 1996. [Russian].

Adler, Alan. "The Shroud Fabric and the Body Image: Chemical and Physical Characteristics." In S. Scannerini and P. Savarino, eds. *The Turin Shroud. Past, Present and Future. International Scientific Symposium.* Torino, March 2–5, 2000. Turin: 2000.

Adrianova-Peretts, V., ed. *Tale of Bygone Years.* Vol. 2. Moscow–Leningrad: 1950. [Russian].

Aetheria. *Pilgrimage.* CSEL 39, 71.

Afanas'ev, K.N. *Construction of Architectural Forms by Old Russian Architects.* Moscow: 1961. [Russian].

Ainalov, D. "Byzantine Monuments of Mount Athos." *Vizantiiski Vremennik* 6 (1899): 57–96. [Russian].

Alekseeva, G. *Byzantine-Russian Musical Paleography.* St Petersburg: 2007. [Russian].

(Alfeev), Hilarion. "To Resurrect Primordial Antiquity." *Journal of the Moscow Patriarchate* 4 (1988): 26–29. [Russian].

Ambrose of Milan. *Commentary on Psalm Twelve Psalms of David* [Ennarationes in XII psalmos Davidicos]. PL 14, 921–1180.

Antiquities of the Russian State. Part 1. Moscow, 1849.

Apostolic Constitutions. Constitutions apostoliques. SC 320, 329, 336. English at *http://www.ccel.org/ccel/schaff/anf07.ix.html.* July 25, 2013.

Aristotle. *Politics* VIII 7, 1341b–1342c.

Arnobius. *Against the Heathen* [Disputationum adversus gentes libri septem]. PL 5, 713–1288.

Arvanitis, I. "Byzantine Notation." In *Orthodox Encyclopedia,* vol. 8. Moscow: 2004. [Russian].

Athanasius of Alexandria. *Apology to Constantine the Emperor* [Apologia ad Constantinum imperatorem]. PG 25, 595–642. (Russian translation in *Works*. vol. 2,. Holy Trinity-St Sergius Lavra: 1902–1903. Reprint Moscow: 1994).

Augustine. *Confessions* [Confessiones]. PL 32, 659–868; CSEL33/1.

———. *Commentary on the Psalms* [Ennarationes in psalmos]. PL 36–37; CCL 38–40.

Averintsev, S. *Poetics of Early Byzantine Literature*. Moscow: 1997. [Russian].

Bakumenko, V. "Aleksei Andreevich Archangelsky." In *Russian Church Composers and their Music* 254–266. Minsk: 2008. [Russian].

Barker, Margaret. *Hagia Sophia in Constantinople as the Temple* (forthcoming).

Belting, Hans. *Likeness and Presence: The History of the Image Before the Era of Art*. Moscow: 2002. [Russian].

Basil the Great. *Commentary on Isaiah* [Commentarium in Isaiam prophetam]. PG 30, 117–665.

———. *Homily on Psalm1* [Homilia in psalmum primum]. PG 29, 209A–228B.

———. *Homily During Time of Famine* [Homilia dicta tempore famis et siccitatis]. PG 31, 304–328.

———. *On the Holy* Spirit [De Spiritu Sancto]. PG 32, 37–217. English translation: Basil the Great. *On the Holy Spirit*. Stephen Hildebrand, trans. Popular Patristics Series, No. 42. Yonkers, NY: St Vladimir's Seminary Press, 2011.

Bishop's Service Book. See *Chinovnik*.

Blagoveschenskaya, L. "Sound Spectra of Moscow Bells." In *Monuments of Culture; New Discoveries; Written Language, Art, Archeology*. Moscow: 1977. [Russian].

Brazhnikov, M. *Litsa and Fity of Znamenny Chant*. Leningrad: 1984. [Russian].

———. *Old Russian Music Theory: Materials from Manuscripts of the 15th–18th Centuries*. Leningrad: 1972. [Russian].

Briusova, V. *Andrei Rublev*. Moscow: 1995. [Russian].

(Bunge), Gabriel. *Another Comforter: Saint Andrei Rublev's Icon of the Most Holy Trinity*. Riga: 2003. [Russian].

———. *Earthen Vessels: The Practice of Personal Prayer According to the Patristic Tradition*. Michael J. Miller, trans. San Francisco: Ignatius Press, 2002.

Buseva-Davydova, Irina."Russian Church Art: 10th–20th Centuries." In *Orthodox Encyclopedia* under *"Russian Orthodox Church,"* 518–580. Moscow: 1997. [Russian].

Canons of the Orthodox Church with a Commentary by Nikodim, Bishop of Dalmatia and Istria. Two volumes. Translated from Serbian. Moscow: 2001.

Chernogubov, N. "The Icon of Boris and Gleb in Kiev's Museum of Old Russian Arts." In *Old Russian Art of the 15th–16th Centuries*, 285–290. Moscow: 1963. [Russian].

Chinovnik [The bishop's service book] vol. 2. Moscow, 1983. [Slavonic].

Choisy, Auguste. *L'art de bâtir chez les byzantins.* Paris: 1968.
Christopher, Monk of St . Cyril-White Lake Monastery. *Key to Znamenny Chant.* M. Brazhnikov, G. Nikishov, eds and trans. Moscow: 1983. [Russian].
Clement of Alexandria. *Pedagogue.* Clemens Alexandrinus. Band I. *Protrepticus* und *Paedagogus.* O. Stählin, ed. GCS 12. Leipzig: 1905
Cyril of Alexandria. *Epistle 1, to the Monks of Egypt.* PG 77, 9–40.
———. *Commentariy on John.* PG 73, 604BD. Sancti pataris nostri Cyrilli archieposcopi Alexandrini. *In divini Ioannis Evangelium.* Vols. I–III. Ph. E. Pusey, ed. Oxford: 1872.
Cyril of Jerusalem. *Catechetical Lecture* 1–18. 14 PG 33, 369–1060.
(Danilov,) Andrei. "Stepan Vasilievich Smolensky: Founder of a New Movement." In *Russian Church Composers and their Music,* 286–287. Minsk: 2008. [Russian].
Danilova, E. "Praise to the Theotokos Who Makes Exhortation toThose in Abiding in Darkness." In *Akathist to the Most Holy Theotokos—Dionysius the Iconographer: Photographs of Yuri Holdin,* 158–159. Moscow: 2007.
De Clari, Robert. *The Conquest of Constantinople.* In Charles Hopf. *Chroniques greco-romaines inédites ou peu connues.* Paris: 1873.
Desk Manual for Clergy. Moscow: 2001.
Diletsky, Nikolay. *The Idea of Musical Grammar.* St Petersburg: S. Smolensky Publications, 1910. [Russian].
Dionysius the Aeropagite. *Ecclesiastical Hierarchy.* Corpus Dionysiacum II: Pseudo-Dionysius Areopagita. *De coelesti hierarchia; De ecclesiastica hierarchia; De mystica theologia; Epistulae.* G. Heil and A.M. Ritter, eds. PTS 33. Berlin: 1990.
———. *Concerning the Divine Names.* Corpus Dionysiacum I: Pseudo-Dionysius Areopagita. *De divinis nominibus.* B.R. Suchla, ed. PTS 36. Berlin: 1991.
Dmitrievsky, Aleksei. *Mitre. Historical-Archaeological Essay: Directions for Rural Pastors,* No. 11. Kiev: 1903. (Reprinted in *"Moscow Diocesan News,"* No. 4–5, 2003.) [Russian].
(Drozdov) Philaret. *Collection of Opinions and Comments of Philaret, Metropolitan of Moscow and Kolomna,* vol. 4. Moscow: 1886. [Russian].
———. *Letters of Metropolitan Philaret to Archimandrite Anthony,* Part 3. Moscow: 1883.[Russian].
Dubarle, André-Marie. "L'homélie de Grégoire le Référendaire pour la reception de l'image d'Edesse." *Revue des Études Byzantines* 55 (1997): 5–51. Translation by Mark Guscin available on line at <http://www.shroud.com/pdfs/guscin3.pdf>, September 9, 2013.
Džurova, A. *La miniatura bizantina: I manuscritti miniati e la loro diffusione.* Milano: 2001.

Elizbarashvili, I. "Georgian Orthodox Church: Church Arts/Architecture." In *Orthodox Encyclopedia*, vol.13, 283–291. Moscow: 2003. [Russian].

Eusebius of Caesarea. *Letter to Empress Constantia*. PG 20, 1545 AB–1550A.

———. *The Proof of the Gospel* (Demonstratio Evangelica). GCS 23, 366.

Evgarius Scholasticus *Ecclesiastical History*. St Petersburg, 2006. [Russian]

Evdokimov, Paul. *The Art of Icons: Theology of Beauty.* Klin: 2005. [Russian].

Evseeva, L.M., I.A. Kochetkov, and V.N. Sergeev. *The Painting of Ancient Tver.* Moscow: 1983, 8–9. [Russian].

Florensky, Pavel. "Theological Notes." *Bogoslovskie Trudy* 17 (1977): 85–248.

Florovsky, Georges. "Origen, Eusebius and the Iconoclastic Controversy." *Church History* 19 (1950): 77–96.

Galavaris, G. Ζωγραφική βυζαντινῶν χειρογράφων [Painting of Byzantine manuscripts]. Athens: 1996.

Garkavi, A. *Legends of Muslim Writers on Slavs and Russians.* St Petersburg: 1870. [Russian].

Germanus of Constantinople. *Church History* [Historia ecclesiastica, et mystica contemplatio]. PG 98, 383–453.

Gero, Stephen. "The True Image of Christ: Eusebius' Letter to Constantia Reconsidered." *Journal of Theological Studies* 32 (1981): 460–470.

Gertsman, Evgeny. *Development of Musical Culture. Culture of Byzantium. VIII–1st Half of XV Centuries.* Moscow: 1991. [Russian].

———. *Ancient Musical Thought.* Moscow: 1986. [Russian].

———. *Mysteries from the History of Ancient Music.* St Petersburg: 2006. [Russian].

Ghiberti, Giuseppe. "The Gospels and the Shroud." *The Turin Shroud, Past, Present and Future: International Scientific Symposium, Torino, 2–5 March, 2000.* Torino: 2000.

Golubtsov, A.P. from *Readings on Church Archeology and Liturgics.* St Petersburg: 2006. [Russian].

Grabar, I. *On Old Russian Art.* Moscow: 1966. [Russian].

Grabar, André. *L'âge d'or de Justinien. De la mort de Théodose à l'Islam.* Paris: 1966.

Gregory the Great, Pope of Rome (Gregory Dialogus). S. Gregorii Magni. *Opera: Registrum epistularum. Libri I–VII.* D. Norberg, ed. CCL 140. Louvain: 1982.

Gregory of Nyssa. *Concerning the Inscriptions of Psalms* [In Psalmorum inscriptiones]. PG 44, 431–608.

———. *On the Making of Man* [De hominis opificio]. PG 44, 123–256.

Gregory the Theologian (Gregory Nazianzus). *Orationes.* PG 35, 387–1252. Also Grégoire de Nazianze. *Discours 4–5.* J. Bernardi, ed. SC 309. Paris:1983.

———. *Orationes XIII–XIX.* PG 35, 852–1064.

Grishtennko, A. The Russian Icon as Pictorial Art. Vol. 3. Moscow: 1917. [Russian]. Cited in Ouspensky, *Theology.*

Select Bibliography   361

Grozdanov, C. *Kurbinovo and Other Studies on Prespa Frescoes*. Skopje: 2006.
Gruber, R. *General History of Music*, 1. 2nd edition. Moscow: 1960. [Russian].
Hatzidaki, N. Βυζαντινά ψηφιδωτά [Byzantine mosaics]. Athens, 1996
History of Bell Making in Russia: Bell Ringing in Russia. Compact disc. Moscow: 2007.
Holdin, Yuri. *Frescoes of Russia: Dionysius, the Golden Age of Iconography, 14th–15th Centuries*. Moscow: 2006. [Russian].
Hollemann, A.W.J. "Oxyrhynchus Papyrus 1786 and the Relationship between Ancient Greek and Early Christian Music." *Vigiliae Christianae* 26 (1972): 1–17.
Hristov, D. *Musical-Theoretical and Publicistic Inheritance*. Vol. 1. Sophia: 1970.
Ignatius the God-bearer *Epistle to the Ephesians*. In P-Th. Camelot, ed. *Ignace d'Antioche; Polycarpe de Smyrne*. Lettres; Martyre de Polycarpe. SC 10 (1969).
Ignatius (Brianchaninov). "Visit to Valaam Monastery." In *Collection of Works in Six Volumes*, vol. 4. *Moscow*: 2004. [Russian].
———. "Homily Concerning Oral and Vocal Prayer." In *Collection of Works in Six Volumes*, vol. 1. Moscow, 2004. [Russian].
———. "Understanding Heresy and Schism." In *Theological Works*. Moscow: 1996. [Russian].
Isaac the Syrian. *Isaac of Nineveh (Isaac the Syrian): The Second Part*, chapters IV-XLI. Sebastian Brock, ed. CSCO 554: Scriptores syri 224. Louvain, 1995
Isidore of Pelusium. *Epistolarum libri quinque*. PG 78, 177–1645.
Jacob, "Le chandelier à trois branches de l'évêque Pantoléon: A propos de l'inscription de Georges de Gallipoli." *Bolletino della Badia greca di GrottaferrataI* 53 (1999): 187–200.
Jerome. *Commentary on Ezekiel* [Commentariorum in Ezechielem prophetam libri quatuodecim]. PL 25, 15–490.
John Chrysostom. *Commentary on First Corinthians* PG 61, 11–382.
———. *Commentary on Matthew*. F. Field, ed. Sancti patris nostri Ioannis Chrysostomi, archiepiscopi Constantinopolitani. *Homiliae in Matthaeum*. 3 vols. Canturbury, 1839.
———. *Commentary on Psalms*. PG 55, 35–498. English translation: Robert Charles Hill, trans. *Commentary on the Psalms*. 2 vols. Brookline, Massachusetts: Holy Cross Orthodox Press, 1998.
———. *Commentary on First Timothy*. PG 62, 576.
———. *Laudatory homily in Praise of Meletius* [Homilia encomiastica in s. patrem nostrum Meletium, archiepiscopum magnae Antiochiae]. PG 50, 515–520.
———. *On the Holy Priesthood*. PG 48, 363–371. English: St John Chrysostom. *Six Books on the Holy Priesthood*. Graham Neville, tr. Crestwood, NY: St Vladimir's Seminary Press, 1977.

John of Damascus. *An Exact Exposition of the Orthodox Faith*. B. Kotter, ed. *Die Schriften des Johannes von Damaskos II: Expositio fidei*. PTS 12. Berlin, 1973. English translation found at <http://www.bible.ca/archeology/bible-archeology-jerusalem-temple-mount-east-orientation-jewish-temples-altars.htm>, July 25, 2013.

———. *Three Treatises on the Divine Images*. Andrew Louth, trans. Crestwood, NY: St Vladimir's Seminary Press, 2003.

Johner, P.D. *Wort und Ton im Choral*. Leipzig: 1953.

Josephus (Titus Josephus Flavius). *The Jewish War*. English translation at <http://www.sacred-texts.com/jud/josephus/war-5.htm>, July 25, 2013.

Joseph of Volokolamsk. *Otveschanie liubozazornym* . . . . In *The Great Menaion Reader of Metropolitan Makarii*. September, 1–13. St Petersburg: 1868. [Russian].

Kalashnikov, L. *Primer of Liturgical Znamenny Singing*. Kiev: 1908. [Russian].

Karabinov, I. "The Holy Chalice in the Liturgy of the Presanctified Gifts." Христианское Чтение [Christian Reading] 6 (1915): 737–753; 7–8: 953–964. [Russian].

Kastalsky, A. "Concerning My Musical Career and My Thoughts about Church Music." In N. Zverev, A. Naumov, and M. Rachmaninov, eds. *Russian Religious Music in Documents and Materials, Volume 1: Synodal Choir and College of Church Singing, Recollections, Diaries, Letters*, 235–241. Moscow: 1998. [Russian].

Kazarian, A. "The Byzantine Empire/Architecture." In *Orthodox Encyclopedia*, vol. 8, 287–303. Moscow: 2007. [Russian].

Keldysh, Y. "D.S. Bortiansky." *History of Russian Music in Ten Volumes*. Vol. 3: *18th Century*, part 2., 161–193. Moscow: 1985. [Russian].

———. *History of Russian Music in Ten Volumes*. Vol. 1. *Ancient Rus', 11th–17th Centuries*. Moscow: 1983. [Russian].

Kholopova, V. *Russian Musical Rhythmics*. Moscow: 1983. [Russian].

Kolyada, Yelena. The author and David J. Clark, trans. *A Compendium of Musical Instruments and Instrumental Terminology in the Bible*. London and Oakville: Equinox Publishing, 2009.

Kominis, A. ed., *Patmos: Treasures of the Monastery*. Athens: 1988.

Konotop, A. "Strochny Polyphony and Folklore." In I. Lozovaya, ed., *Church Singing in a Historical-liturgical Context: East–Rus–West*, 247–253. Moscow: 2003. [Russian].

Kvlividze, N. "The Apostles: Iconography." In *Orthodox Encyclopedia*, vol.3, 110–112.

Kochetkov, I. "Does the Donskaya Icon of the Mother of God Represent a Monument of the Kulikovo Battle?" In *Old Russian Arts of the 15th–16th Centuries*, 36–45. Moscow: 1963. [Russian].

Kolpakova, G. *Art of Ancient Rus: Pre-Mongol Period*. St Petersburg: 2007. [Russian].

———. *Art of Byzantium: Early and Middle Periods*. St Petersburg: 2007. [Russian].

Komech, Alexei. "Architecture." In *Culture of Byzantium: Fourth through First Half of the Seventh Centuries*, 586–595. Moscow: 1984.

Kutuzov, B. *Znamenny Chant: Theology in Song*. Moscow: 2001. [Russian].
Lauenstein, Dieter. *The Eleusinian Mysteries*. Moscow: 1996. [Russian].
Lazarev, Victor. *Byzantine Painting*. Moscow: 1971. [Russian].
———. *Theophanes the Greek and His School*. Moscow: 1961. [Russian].
"The Legend of the Edessa Image." In E. Von Dobschütz. *Christusbilder: Untersuchungen zur christlichen Legende*, vol. 3 Leipzig: 1899.
Lenten Triodion. Mother Mary and Archimandrite Kallistos Ware, trans. South Canaan, PA: St Tikhon's Seminary Press, 2002.
Levashev, E., and A. Polekhin. "M.S. Berezovsky." *History of Russian Music in Ten Volumes*. Vol. 3, 132–160. Moscow: 1985. [Russian].
Lidov, Alexei. "The Canopy over the Holy Sepulchre: On the Origins of Onion-Shaped Domes." In *The Iconography of Architecture*, 37–58. Moscow: 1990. [Russian].
Likhacheva, V. "Fine Arts." In *The Culture of Byzantium, Second Half of the 7th–12th Centuries*, 470–495. Moscow: 1989. [Russian].
Lingas, Alexander. *Byzantine Empire: Church Singing*. Moscow: 2004. [Russian].
Livshitz, L. *Monumental Painting of Novgorod in the 16th–18th Centuries*. Moscow: 1987. [Russian].
Lomakin, G. "Autobiographical Notes with Commentary by V. Stasov." In *Russian Antiquity* 3, 5, 6, 8 (1886).
Losev, Aleksei. *History of Ancient Aesthetics: Early Hellenism*. Moscow: 2000. [Russian].
Lossky, Nikolai. *The World as the Realization of Beauty*. Moscow: 1998. [Russian].
Lozovaya, ed., *Church Singing in Historical-Liturgical Context: East–Rus–West*. Moscow: 2003. [Russian].
Lukyanov, Valery. *Service Notes, Attempt at Understanding the Practical Aspects of the Divine Services of the Orthodox Church*. Jordanville, NY: 2001. [Russian].
Lyubimov, Lev. *The Art of Ancient Rus'*. Moscow: 1981. [Russian].
Manaphes, Constantinos. Σινά. Οἱ θησαυροί τῆς Ι. Μονῆς Αγίας Αικατερίνης [Sinai: The treasures of the holy monastery of St Catherine]. Athens: 1990.
Martynov, Vladimir. *History of Liturgical Singing*. Moscow: 1994. [Russian].
———. *Zone opus posth., or the Birth of a New Reality*. Moscow: 2008. [Russian].
Maximus the Confessor *The Mystagogia*. In Dom Julian Stead, O.S.B., trans. *The Church, the Liturgy and the Soul of Man: The Mystagogia of St Maximus the Confessor*. Still River, MA: St. Bede's Publications, 1982.
Meshcherina, E. *The Musical Culture of Rus' in the Middle Ages*. 2nd edition. Moscow: 2008. [Russian].
Mescherskaya, M. *The Legend of Abgar: An Early Syrian Literary Monument*. Moscow: 1984. [Russian].
Metallov, Vasily. *Eight-tone Znamenny Chant*. Moscow: 1899. [Russian].

———. *Essay on the History of Orthodox Church Singing in Russia.* Moscow: 1893. [Russian].

———. "Music and Musical Instruments of the Ancient Hebrews." In *Readings of the Society of Lovers of Ancient Written Languages* 6 (1912) 390–403; 7–8: 451–486.

———. *Russian Semiography from the Field of Church Singing Archeology and Paleography.* Moscow: 1912. [Russian].

Murray, C. "Art and the Early Church." *Journal of Theological Studies* 28 (1977) 303–345.

National Library of Russia, St Petersburg. Solovki Collection. Manuscript No. 644/618, l. 2 ob.

Nicholas Cabasilas. "Concerning the Sacred Vestments." In S. Salaville, ed. *Explication de la divine liturgie.* SC 4–bis, 364–366. Paris, 1967.

Nicephorus of Constantinople. *Refutation against Constantine Copronymus* [Antirrhetici adversus Constantinum Copronymum]. PG 100, 205–533.

Nicolai, V.F., F. Bisconti, D. Mazzoleni. *Roms christliche Katakomben: Geschichte–Bilderwelt–Inschriften.* Regensburg: 2000.

Nikishov, G. *Monk Christopher of the Saint Cyril-White Lake Monastery and His "Key to Znamenny Chant" (1604).* Moscow: 1983. [Russian].

Nikodim, Bishop of Dalmatia-Istria. See *Canons of the Orthodox Church.*

Nilus the Ascetic. *S. P. N. Nili Ascetae, discipuli s. Joannis Chrysostomi, Epistolarum libri quatuor.* PG 79, 81–581.

Obolensky, D. *The Byzantine Commonwealth.* London: 1971.

Odoevsky, V. *Musical-literary Inheritance.* Moscow: 1956. [Russian].

Ostrogorsky, Georges. *Histoire de l'état Byzantin.* Paris: 1956.

Ouspensky, Leonid. *Theology of the Icon in the Orthodox Church.* Paris, 1989. In English: *Theology of the Icon.* Anthony Gythiel, trans. Crestwood, NY: St Vladimir's Seminary Press, 1992.

Ouspensky, N. *The Art of Old Russian Singing.* Moscow: 1965.[Russian].

(Ouspensky), Porfirii. "Letters of the Right Reverend Porfirii (Ouspensky) to the Princess E. Vitgenshtein." *Bogoslovsky Vestnik* (1904, 1905).

Pariysky, L. "The Church Composer Archimandrite Feofan." *Journal of the Moscow Patriarchate,* 10 (1952).

———. "Recollections of the Church Composer A. D. Kastalsky." In *Russian Church Composers and their Music* .Minsk: 2008. [Russian].

Paschalidis, Zacharias. *Byzantine Church Music: Brief Theory and Practice.* Moscow: 2004. [Russian].

Paul of Aleppo. *Travels of Patriarch Macarius to Moscow in the Middle of the 17th Century.* St Petersburg: 1898. [Russian].

Paul the Silentiary. *Description of the Church of Hagia Sophia* [Pauli Silentiarii Descriptio Ecclesiae Sanctae Sophiae]. PG 86, 2119–2158.

Peno, V. "The Communion Hymn in Serbian Unison Singing of the New Period." In I. Lozovaya, ed. *Church Singing in Historical-Liturgical Context: East–Rus–West*. Moscow: 2003. [Russian].

Plato. *The Republic*. III 400.

———. *Timaeus*. 31c–32a, translated by Benjamin Jowett.: <http://www.doc.ic.ac.uk/~rac101/concord/texts/timaeus/>, July 25, 2013.

Pokrovsky, N.V. *Essays on Monuments of Christian Art and Iconography*. St Petersburg: 1910. [Russian].

Popova, O. *Aspects of Byzantine Art: Mosaics, Frescoes, Icons*. Moscow: 2006. [Russian].

Pozhidaeva, G. "Historical-liturgical Premises of Prolix Singing in Muscovite Rus." In E. Lozovaya, ed., *Church Singing in Historical-liturgical Context: East–Rus–West*. Moscow: 2003. [Russian].

Procopius of Caesarea, *The Buildings of Justinian*, translated from Greek into Russian by S.P. Kkondrat'eva. In Procopius of Caesarea. *The Gothic War* and *The Buildings of Justinian*, 138–301. Moscow, 1996. English translation on line at <http://penelope.uchicago.edu/Thayer/E/Roman/Texts/Procopius/Buildings/1A*.html>, July 25, 2013.

Prokhorov, V. "The Catapetasma of Ivan the Terrible, Gifted to Hilandar Monastery on Mount Athos." In *Christian Antiquities and Archeology* Book 6, 1–4. St Petersburg: 1863. [Russian].

———. "Fans in Novgorod's Saint Sophia Cathedral." In *Christian Antiquities and Archeology*, Book 3, 12–18. St Petersburg: 1863. [Russian].

———. "Materials Related to the History of Clergy Clothing: Phelonion." In *Christian Antiquities and Archeology*, Book 2, 3–8; Book 3, 19–22; Book 10, 103–107. St Petersburg: 1863. [Russian].

———. "Tetramorph, or Gospel Symbols Depicted on the Walls of the Church of the Entry of the Most Holy Theotokos into the Temple in Hilandar Monastery on Mount Athos." In *Christian Antiquities and Archeology*, Book 4, 5–9. St Petersburg: 1863. [Russian].

"Proskynitarion of Arsenius Sukhanov." *Orthodox Palestinian Collection*, Edition No. 21, vol. 7, ed. 3. St Petersburg: 1889.

Pseudo-Aristotle. *Problems* XIX 26.

Pseudo-Justin. Answers to the Orthodox [S. Justini Responsiones ad orthodoxos *(spuria)*]. PG 6, 1249–1400.

Punkhnachev, Y. *Mysteries of Sounding Metal*. Moscow: 1974. [Russian].

Quasten, Johannes. *Music and Worship in Pagan and Christian Antiquity.* Washington: 1983.

Rakhmaninov, S. *Recollections Recorded by Okcar von Riesemann.* Moscow: 2008. [Russian].

Rappoport, P. *The Construction Industry of Ancient Rus (10th–13th Centuries).* St Petersburg: 1994.

Razumovsky, D. *Church Singing.* Moscow: 1886. [Russian].

Rinaldi, P. "Un documento probante sulla localizzazione in Atene della Santa Sindone dopo il sacheggio de Constantinopoli." In L. Coppini and F. Cavazzuti. *La Sindone, szienza e fede,* 109–113. Bologna: 1983.

Russian Antiquities and Monuments of Art published in the Writings of I. Tolstoy and N. Kondakov. No. 6: Monuments of Vladimir, Novgorod, and Pskov. St Petersburg: 1899. [Russian].

Rybakov, B.A. *From the History of the Culture of Ancient Rus.* Moscow: 1984. [Russian].

———. *"The Tale of Igor's Campaign" and its Contemporaries.* Moscow: 1971. [Russian].

(Sakharov), Sophrony. *Silouan the Athonite.* Essex: 1991.

Salaj, N. *Srpska duhovna muzika.* Unpublished article.

Salpistes, Demetrios, et al. *Manuel Panselinos: From the Holy Church of the Protaton.* Thessaloniki: 2003.

Saltykov, A. "The Iconography of Andrei Rublev's 'Trinity'." In *Old Russian Arts of the 14th–15th Centuries,* 77–85. Moscow: 1984. [Russian].

Savio, P. *Ricerche storiche sulla Santa Sindone.* Turin: 1957.

Schäferdiek, K. "Zur Verfassenfrage und Situation der *Epistula ad Constantiam ad imaginem Christi.*" *Zeitschrift für Kirchengeschichte* 91 (1980): 177–186.

Schilbach, E. *Byzantinische Metrologie.* Munich: 1970.

Sextus Empiricus. *Against the Musicians.* In A.F. Loseva, ed. *Essays,* vol. 2, 191–204. Moscow: 1976. [Russian].

Shenborn, K. *The Icon of Christ: Theological Foundations.* Milan–Moscow: 1999. [Russian].

Shevelev, I.S. *Concerning Shape Formation in Nature and Art; The Golden Ratio.* Moscow: 1990. [Russian].

———. *The Principle of Proportions.* Moscow: 1986. [Russian].

Society of Russian History and Antiquities. *Readings in the Society of Russian History and Antiquities.* Book 2, Part 2 (1846?): 166. [Russian].

Simeon of Thessalonica. *Concerning the Holy Church* [De sacro templo]. PG 155, 305–361.

———. *Concerning Holy Ordinations* [De sacris ordinationibus]. PG 155, 361–469.

Select Bibliography

———. *Concerning the Holy Temple* [Expositio de divino templo et de sacerdotibus ejus ac diconis episcopisque ac de sacris stilis]. PG 155, 697–749.

Şirli, A. "Sonorités turques dans la musique post-byzantine." *Byzantium and Eastern Europe. Liturgical and Musical Connections*, 159–167. Moscow: 2003. [Russian].

Smolensky, S. "On Old Russian Singing Notation." In *Historical-paleographical Essay*. St Petersburg: 1901. [Russian].

———. "On Russian Church Singing: A Reply to Mr. Missaelides, the Protopsalt of Saint Photina Church in Smirna." In A. Naumov and M. Rakhmaninov, eds., *Russian Religious Music in Documents and Materials*, vol. 3: *Church Singing of Reformed Russia as Understood by Contemporaries, 1861–1918*, 361–370. Moscow, 2002. [Russian].

Soloviev, I. "Glinka and His Religious-Musical Activity." In *Russian Church Composers and their Music*, 232–241. Minsk: 2008. [Russian].

Sonevitsky, I. *Artem Vedel i yogo muzichna spadschina*. New York: 1966.

Sreznevsky, Izmail. "The Ancient Byzantine Tabernacle." In *Christian Antiquities and Archeology* 8 (1863), 25–48.

———. "The Antimension of 1149." in *Christian Antiquities and Archeology*, 4 (1863) 1–4. [Russian].

Stephen the Deacon. *The Life of Stephen the* New [Vita sancti Stephani Junioris]. PG 100, 1069–1185.

Strunk, Oliver. "Melody Construction in Byzantine Chant." *Actes du XIIe congrès international d'études byzantines. Ochride, 10–16 septembre 1961*. Vol. 1, 365–373. Belgrade: 1961.

Swift, E.H. *Hagia Sophia*. New York: 1940.

Taft, Robert, F., S.J. *The Great Entrance. A History of the Transfer of Gifts and other Preanaphoral Rites (A History of the Liturgy of St John Chrysostom*, vol. 2*)*. Orientalia Christiana Analecta 200. Rome: 1978.

Tchaikovsky P. and N. Von Meck, *Tchaikovsky and Nadezhda Filaretovna Von Meck: Correspondence*, Books 1 and 2. Moscow: 2004. [Russian].

Tchaikovsky, P. "Preface to First Edition of the 'All Night Vigil'." In A. Naumov and M. Rakhmaninov, eds. *Russian Religious Music in Documents and Materials*. Volume 3: *Church Singing of Reformed Russia as Understood by Contemporaries*, 186–189. Moscow: 2002. [Russian].

Tchaikovsky, P. *Letters to His Family: Selections*. Moscow: 1955. [Russian].

(Teodor) Zinon. *Conversations with an Iconographer*. 3rd edition. St Petersburg: 2003.

Tertullian. *Apology* [Apologeticum]. PL 1, 257–536; CCL 1, 85–171.

———. *On the Resurrection of the Flesh* [De resurrectione carnis]. CSEL 47, 25–125.

Tevosian, A. "Temple Activity and European Concert in Historical-Liturgical Context of the 20th Century." In I. Lozovaya, ed., *Church Singing in Historical-Liturgical Context: East–Rus–West*, 380–392. Moscow: 2003. [Russian].

Theodore Balsamon. *Reflections* (Meditata sive responsa). PG 138, 1013–1076.

Theodore the Studite. *Against the Iconoclasts* (Adversus iconomachos capita septem). PG 99, 903–1670.

———. *Theodori Studitae Epistulae*. G. Fagouros, ed. 2 vols. Berlin and New York, 1992. Also PG 99, 903–1670.

———. *Refutations of the Iconoclasts* (Antirrhetici adversus iconomachos). PG 99, 327–436. English in Catherine P. Roth, trans. *On the Holy Icons*. Crestwood, NY: St Vladimir's Seminary Press, 2001.

Theodoret, Bishop of Cyprus. *Church History*. Russian translation: Moscow: 1993. [Russian].

Theophanes the Confessor. *Chronography*. Translated with commentary in Russian in I.S. Chichurov. *Byzantine Historical Essays*. Moscow: 1980. [Russian].

Trajkovska, D. *St Panteleimon at Nerezi: Fresco Painting*. Skopje: 2004.

Trubetskoi, Eugene. "Two Worlds in Old Russian Icon Paintings." in *Icons: Theology in Color*. Gertrude Vakar, trans. Crestwood, NY: St Vladimir's Seminary Press, 1973.

Tsvetaeva, A. *N. Saradzhev, Master of Magical Bell Ringing*. Moscow: 1988. [Russian].

Typikon. Moscow: 2002.

Ustrialov, N. *Stories of Contemporaries Concerning the False Dmitry*, Part 2. St Petersburg: 1859. [Russian].

Vaklinova, M. "Early Christian and Early Byzantine Art on the Territory of Bulgaria." In *Orthodox Encyclopedia*, vol. 5, 594–600. Moscow: 2002. [Russian].

Yakovleva, A. "The *Hermeneia* of Dionysius of Fourna and the Iconographic Technique of Theophanes the Greek." In O. Podobedov, ed. *Old Russian Art of the 14th–15th Centuries*, 7–25. Moscow: 1984. [Russian].

Toncheva, E. "Bulgaria: Church Music." In *Orthodox Encyclopedia*, vol. 5, 612–614. Moscow: 2002.

Undolsky, V. *Notes for a History of Church Singing in Russia*. Moscow: 1846. [Russian].

Vasiliev, A. "The Iconoclastic Edict of Caliph Yasid II. Ad 721." *Dumbarton Oaks Papers* 9–10 (1955): 23ff.

Vasileios of Stavronikita (Archimandrite). *Hymn of Entry: Liturgy and Life in the Orthodox Church*. Elizabeth Briere, trans. Crestwood, NY: St Vladimir's Seminary Press, 1984.

Vasnetsov, Viktor. "Concerning Russian Iconography." In *The Acts of the Sacred Council of the Orthodox Russian Church of 1917–1918*, vol. 5, 39–56. Moscow: 1996. [Russian].

Viskov, A. "The Apostle John's Successor." In *Georgy Svidirov Remembered by His Contempories*, 540–614. Moscow: 2006. [Russian].

Vladyshevskaya, T. *Byzantine Musical Aesthetics and Influence on the Culture of Song in Ancient Rus'. Byzantium and Rus'*, 145–159. Moscow: 1989. [Russian].

———. *Musical Culture of Ancient Rus'*. Moscow: 2006. [Russian].

Voronin, Nikolai. "Architectural Monument as a Historical Source (Notes to Statement of a Question)." In *Sovietskaya architektura* 19 (1954): 41–76. [Russian].

Vitruvius. *The Ten Books on Architecture*. Moscow: 1979. [Russian]. English translation at <http://www.gutenberg.org/files/20239/20239-h/29239-h.htm>, July 25, 2013.

Walker, Susan and Morris Bierbrier. *Fayum, Misteriosi volti dall'Egitto*. Catalog of the Exhibition at the Fondazione Memmo in Rome (22 October 1997 to 28 February 1998). Milan: Leonardo Arte: 1997.

Weitzmann, Kurt. *Studies in Classical and Byzantine Manuscript Illumination*. London, 1971.

Wellesz, Egon. *The Akathistos Hymn*. Copenhagen: 1957.

———. *A History of Byzantine Music and Hymnography*, 2nd edition. Oxford: 1961.

Wilson-Dickson, Andrew. *The Story of Christian Music*. Moscow: 2001. [Russian].

Yazykova, Irina. *"Behold I Make All Things New": Icons of the 20th Century*. Moscow: 2002. [Russian].

———. *Theology of the Icon*. Moscow: 1995. [Russian].

Yesipova, M. "Bila." In *Orthodox Encyclopedia*, vol. 5, 211–214. Moscow: 2002. [Russian].

Zheltov, M., and Sergei Pravdoliubov. "Divine Service of the Russian Church: 10th–20th Centuries." In *Orthodox Encyclopedia*, vol. 9, 485–517. Moscow: 2005. [Russian].

Zheltov, M., and I. Popov. "Antimension." In *Orthodox Encyclopedia*, vol. 2, 489–493. Moscow: 2001. [Russian].

Zheltov, M. *"Dikirion"* in *Orthodox Encyclopedia*, vol. 14, 693.

Znamenny Key. 18th century manuscript in the library of the author.

(Zyryanov), Jonah. "The First Russian Iconographer (On the 850th Anniversary of the Repose of Saint Alypius of the Caves)." In *Journal of the Moscow Patriarchate* 9 (1964): 61–66.